A KIM JONG-IL PRODUCTION

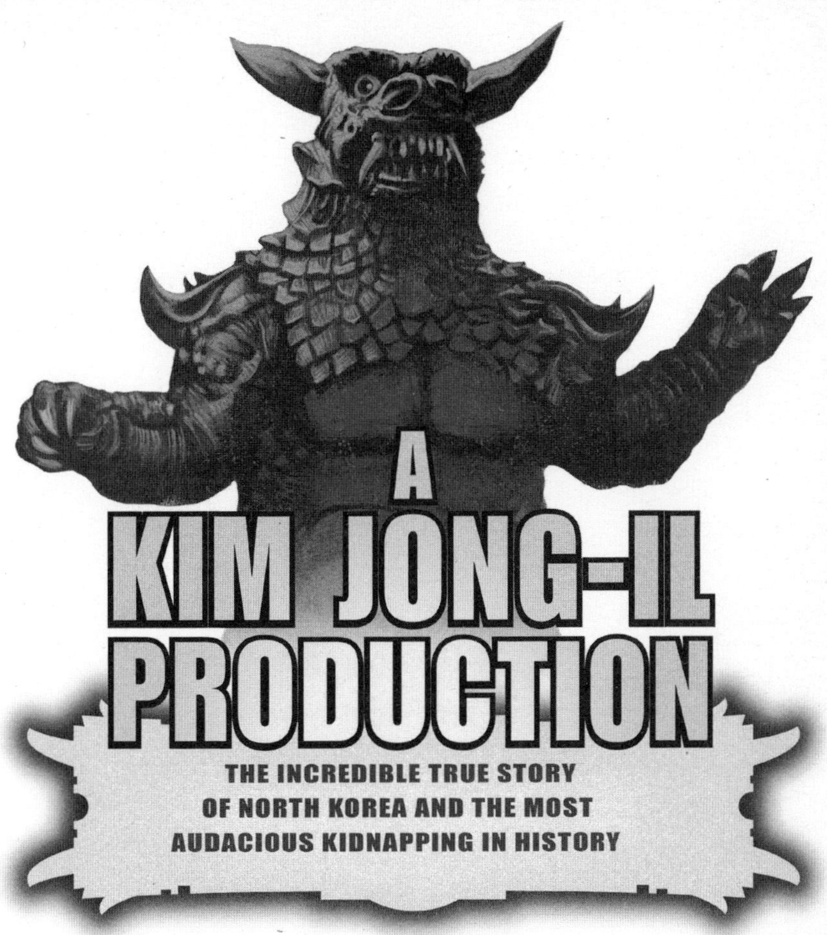

A KIM JONG-IL PRODUCTION

THE INCREDIBLE TRUE STORY OF NORTH KOREA AND THE MOST AUDACIOUS KIDNAPPING IN HISTORY

PAUL FISCHER

VIKING
an imprint of
PENGUIN BOOKS

VIKING

UK | USA | Canada | Ireland | Australia
India | New Zealand | South Africa

Penguin Books is part of the Penguin Random House group of companies whose addresses can be found at global.penguinrandomhouse.com.

First published in the United States of America by Flatiron Books 2015
Published in Great Britain by Viking 2015
001

Set in 11.28/15.43pt BemboBookMTStd
Typeset by Jouve (UK), Milton Keynes
Printed in Great Britain by Clays Ltd, St Ives plc

A CIP catalogue record for this book is available from the British Library

ISBN: 978–0–241–00430–2

www.greenpenguin.co.uk

For Mom, Dad, and Crosby

Contents

A Note on Sources, Method, and Names

The primary source for this book is the firsthand account of their time and experiences in North Korea by Shin Sang-Ok and Choi Eun-Hee. Shin and Choi have written several memoirs and articles about the years they spent working for Kim Jong-Il, which I have used as a starting point for the research and telling of this story, cross-checking dates and facts against other contemporary accounts, news archives, academic research, and original interviews. I have conducted nearly fifty original interviews with participants in the story as well as North Korean defectors, either involved in Shin and Choi's own story or who simply lived in North Korea in the 1970s and 1980s and informed my description of that time. And while North Korea largely remains a mystery to outsiders, there are tools today that can help confirm or disprove information, such as Google Earth, used by many studying North Korea to locate buildings and landmarks described by those North Koreans who have escaped. Wherever possible I have traveled to the locales of the action: to South Korea, Austria, Germany, Hungary, Hong Kong, and, of course, North Korea.

Most of the physical descriptions in the text are taken from contemporary photographs or footage. Dialogue is only in quotes if quoted in an original source, such as Shin and Choi's memoirs. On occasion, I have shortened dialogue, but I have made rigorous efforts not to excise elements that would alter the intended meaning or tone. Where dialogue was available from several different sources, I chose the translation that seems most accurate and natural in the context, or found the original source and commissioned a new translation from a professional native speaker. My own Korean is *extremely* rudimentary, so any errors of judgment are, of course, entirely my own.

It has become a truism about accounts of North Korea that, because of the DPRK's isolation and lack of transparency, each story must be taken at the teller's word. I have endeavored to corroborate facts wherever it was possible to do so. A more detailed discussion of the process employed to verify Mr. Shin and Madame Choi's personal version of the facts can be found at the end of this book.

Korean names are written with the surname first, followed by the personal name: for example, Kim is the family name, Jong-Il the first name. As there is no fixed style regarding spelling (Kim Jong-Il has sometimes been transliterated as Kim Chong-Il, and Choi Eun-Hee as Choe Un-Hui), I have chosen the most common spellings for all names involved. When there was any doubt, I tried to write the names in the most natural, readable way for a Western reader.

Until the early twentieth century, Koreans traditionally made no use of family names. It was the Japanese empire, when it colonized the peninsula, that legally required Koreans to do so. The vast majority of Koreans, seeing an opportunity to enhance the perceived prestige of their lineage, chose one of a handful of family names—Kim, Lee, Park, Pak, Shin—associated with the country's landed nobility, so that today only about 270 surnames are shared by over seventy-five million Koreans. Any people appearing here with the same surname are not related, unless specifically indicated.

Cast

KIM JONG-IL

The Great Leader's son, and head of the Propaganda Film Studios

SHIN SANG-OK

South Korean film mogul

CHOI EUN-HEE

South Korean film actress

KIM IL-SUNG

North Korea's Great Leader, founder of the DPRK

INTRODUCTION
August 1982

The last thing Shin Sang-Ok remembered was sitting in his cell, unable to feel his own heartbeat, too weak to move or stand. He had been held in a North Korean detention center for almost two years, crammed inside a solitary cell barely big enough to lie down in, with one tiny slit of a window high up on the wall and thick steel bars across it. Bugs teemed through cracks in the floor. Except for a thirty-minute lunch break, a ten-minute supper, and a thirty-minute "sunning" period in the prison yard, he was required to sit in the exact same position all day, head bowed and motionless, absolutely stock-still, or suffer even greater punishment.

He had been on a hunger strike for five days when he lost consciousness. Now, awakening in a prison infirmary, he struggled to breathe. The August air was hot and thick with humidity. A blinding headache blurred his thoughts. His mouth felt dry and metallic, and his stomach was seized with cramps. The simplest movement hurt.

"This guy is probably going to make it," a voice said. "He just moved his toes."

Shin blinked his eyes open. An investigator was standing by his bed, a high-ranking military officer at his side. A prison guard stood attentively behind them. The two men talked among themselves in agitated tones, never addressing Shin directly. After a short while, all three men left.

It was then that Shin became aware of another prisoner in the room. The convict pulled a chair up by Shin's bed and brought him a tray of food. Shin knew him. He was a trusty, an inmate given charge of basic tasks around the prison—sweeping, mopping, serving food, and delivering messages—in exchange for more freedom and time out of his cell. Often a trusty was also a snitch; it was the way he had obtained his position and the way he kept it.

"Eat," the trusty said.

Shin looked at the tray: rice soup, a bowl of stew, and an egg. By prison standards the food was luxurious. Shin turned it down anyway. When the trusty spooned some soup out of the bowl and tried to feed him, Shin pinched his mouth shut tight. "Take it," the trusty insisted. "It will do you good. You need to eat." The man persisted, and eventually Shin gave in. At first, the thought of food made him feel sick, but one taste and his hunger rushed back. He quickly devoured most of the meal but, in gratitude, left some of it for the trusty.

"What happened?" Shin asked.

"You missed roll call yesterday," the trusty said. "I went to check on you and found you unconscious on the floor. You should have seen their faces. They were so scared they'd let you die. They sent for the doctor and he checked your pulse and had you taken here. They'll be relieved to know you will live."

The trusty eyed him carefully. "Now I really know you're an important person. No one cares here if a prisoner dies. I went on hunger strike once. They told me that a man dies in ten days from hunger, a woman fifteen. It didn't take me long to give in and start begging for food. I've heard of important prisoners on hunger strike being held down and force-fed through a funnel—they wouldn't even do that for you. For the sake of your pride, they said. That's how important you are."

"Who was that officer?" Shin asked. "The stranger?"

It was the Minister of People's Security, the trusty explained, the head of all law enforcement in the country. "That's the first time I ever saw the Minister of People's Security come all the way out to the prison just because some prisoner was starving to death. He raised all kinds of hell."

"You must be joking."

The trusty shook his head, deep in thought. "You must be very favored for them to care what happens to you. Do you know someone? Who do you know?"

Shin closed his eyes. He thought of the prison around him: of the inmates tapping on each other's cell walls to communicate, of the ones suddenly and arbitrarily taken out to the yard to be executed, of their cruel and violent guards. For almost two years he had lived in brutal, meaningless captivity. Yet he didn't know a single person in the entire country.

Shin Sang-Ok was fifty-five years old, divorced, with four children. He was the most famous filmmaker in his native South Korea, where he had made blockbusters, won every possible award, and rubbed shoulders with presidents. Four years earlier his ex-wife, Choi Eun-Hee, the most famous actress in South Korea, had disappeared while in Hong Kong, and when he went to find her he had been tricked and kidnapped. Now, after an initial period of less stringent house arrest, he was trapped in Prison Number 6, two hours outside of Pyongyang, North Korea.

No, Shin did not know anyone, and he still did not know why he had been taken. But he did know one thing.

He knew who had ordered his abduction.

In Pyongyang, miles away from the reeking cells and corridors of Prison Number 6, Kim Jong-Il knocked back his Hennessy, put the glass down, and watched as a waiter silently poured him a refill.

The party in full flow around him was one of the weekly banquets that Kim held for top members of the Workers' Party Central Committee. The large, bright hall was decorated with an explosion of garish fake flowers and swiveling colored lights. At the tables laid out around the dancing area, party cadres and Central Committee officers were eating the finest food, both Western (lobster, steak, pastries) and Korean (including cold noodles, kimchi, *boshintang* or dog soup, shark-fin soup, *jokbal* or pig's feet in soy sauce and spices, bears' feet flown in from Russia). They drank cognac, champagne, soju (rice liquor), and other North Korean specialties such as ginseng wine, with the roots still twisting inside the bottle, and snake liquor, a thick, venomous asp infusing in each jar of grain alcohol. Beautiful young women, aged fifteen to twenty-two, moved across the hall, dancing, flattering, giggling. They wore revealing clothes and some of them gave massages; many would later perform sexual services for the guests. Known as the Gippeumjo, or Joy Brigade, the girls had been handpicked from schools across the country and trained, for up to six months, in manners, comportment, and sexual and massage techniques. While they served, they were banned from any contact with their families, who were rewarded handsomely for the privilege of having a daughter in such a favored position. It was said Kim Jong-Il selected all members of the Gippeumjo himself.

Musicians played a mix of North Korean and Russian folk songs as well as contemporary South Korean pop hits. Virtually all adult Korean males of the time smoked, and the air was thick with tobacco. After dinner the men would gamble—mah-jongg or blackjack—and dance the fox-trot, disco, or blues with the girls provided.

Kim sat at the head table. He had a plump, oval face, black eyes, a small mouth with full lips, and a wide, short nose. He wore square-shaped glasses, smaller than those for which he would later be famous, and favored gray or blue in his Mao-collared tunics, not the khaki he would adopt in the last decades of his life. He was five foot two but wore five-inch platform shoes and sported a tall, boyish bouffant hairstyle to disguise his small stature (the girls of the Joy Brigade were required to be five foot two or shorter, just in case). He was the son of Great Marshal Kim Il-Sung, military hero and founder and Supreme Leader of the Democratic People's Republic of Korea. Officially Jong-Il was the head of the Propaganda and Agitation Department and the director of its Movie and Arts Division, but while his father was still the country's official leader, by 1982 Jong-Il had effectively taken control. Schoolchildren around the country were told he was kind, sensitive, and caring; and were taught to call him Dear Leader. He was forty-one years old, and the North Korean public had never heard his voice.

Usually Jong-Il was the heart and soul of these gatherings, boasting and telling dirty jokes, instructing the band, and generally enjoying the fawning deference of lackeys who jumped to their feet whenever he called.

But tonight Kim was preoccupied. He was thinking about motion pictures.

After the party, in the early hours of the morning, a handful of people would follow Kim, an insomniac, to one of his projection rooms and watch one of the new movies produced by the state-run studios. Over the last decade he had found the work of his film crews increasingly repetitive and dispiriting. These films were unlikely to hold the attention of his people for much longer, let alone impress the world abroad, which was his lifelong ambition. They were simply not good enough. Not yet, anyway. Four years earlier he had put in action a plan to remedy this problem, but that plan had stalled. He had treated his guests, Shin Sang-Ok and Choi Eun-Hee, so well, but they seemed determined not to play along.

For now. Less than six months later, Shin would surrender to Kim's plans. And together, they would change the course of North Korean history.

REEL ONE

A SENSE OF DESTINY

"The course of our lives can be changed by such little things. So many passing by, each intent on his own problems. So many faces that one might easily have been lost. I know now—nothing happens by chance. Every moment is measured, every step is counted."

—Lisa (Joan Fontaine),
Letter from an Unknown Woman,
screenplay by Max Ophüls and
Howard E. Koch,
directed by Max Ophüls

1
A Photograph on the Blue House Lawn

Twenty Years Earlier

On May 16, 1962, Shin Sang-Ok was standing at the center of a party at the South Korean Presidential Residence. He was the talk of the evening—and, in that moment, of all of Seoul.

The reception was part of the closing ceremonies of the Seventh Asia-Pacific Film Festival, an annual competition to honor and give awards to Asia's best films. Thirty-five years old and standing tall in his white tuxedo jacket, crisp white dress shirt, and black slacks, Shin was the guest of honor and the subject of excited whispers among the guests. Five years earlier none of the people on the lawn had known his name. Now he was the country's hottest filmmaker, director of the biggest box-office hits of the previous two years. The critics loved him. His wife was the most beautiful and most famous actress in the nation. And tonight his new film, *The Houseguest and My Mother,* had won the Best Picture award at the festival, the first South Korean film to win the top prize in an international competition.

Shin shuffled his feet restlessly in the dry grass outside the Blue House. Once the royal garden of the Joseon dynasty, whose kings had ruled the peninsula for more than five hundred years, it was now the site of the presidential compound, a complex of traditional buildings with sloping blue-tiled roofs. The legendary tiles were individually baked in the sun in the old way and rumored to be strong enough to last for hundreds of years. The outskirts of the compound were, more pragmatically, protected by high walls and several checkpoints manned by units of national police and army guards. Very few outsiders were ever allowed inside the Blue House buildings. It was an honor just to stand on the grounds.

A few feet away from Shin, the photographer tinkered with his camera, getting the flash ready and the exposure levels right, as the other dignitaries arranged themselves in a line around Shin for the photo. There would be seven people in the photograph, but the real focus was on the three standing at the center: Shin; his wife of nine years, Choi Eun-Hee; and, between them, South Korea's new president, General Park Chung-Hee.

President Park was forty-four years old, short, with shrewd, hooded dark eyes and large jug ears. He had taken power in a military coup exactly a year earlier, on May 16, 1961. Prior to that he, too, had been largely unknown to the guests mingling on what was now his front lawn, a second-rank general with a commendable military record and no political experience. But he had great ambitions for the country that he loved and that he had watched descend, over the fifteen years since its partition, into poverty, corruption, and chaos. He had grown up in the countryside in the very south, surrounded by simple, patriotic folk who wanted a government as disciplined and hardworking as they were. Once in office, his first act had been to arrest dozens of corrupt officials and businessmen and parade them through the streets of Seoul, with sandwich boards slung around their necks that proclaimed I AM A CORRUPT PIG! The move had won him the immediate adoration of the masses, as had his announcement of a new constitution to be ratified later in 1962, followed by presidential elections in 1963. He had been making many appearances like this one, raising his public profile and introducing himself to the key industries, cinema among them, that he planned to use to change South Korea's image in the world. In most people's minds South Korea was a sad, aid-dependent third world country with little to offer the wider world, but today's award suggested much brighter possibilities. Accordingly, earlier that day, at the Seoul Civic Center, it had been Park who was onstage to hand the award for Best Picture to Shin and Choi.

The crowd had erupted into applause as Shin and Choi bounded up to the stage together. Shin had directed and produced the winning film, but Choi had starred in it, as in the majority of his other films. Shin was best known for his films about women (usually played by Choi) and made for women—the "rubber-shoed masses" living in Seoul and in the countryside provinces who made up South Korea's most fervent cinema audience. Husband and wife were inseparable in the mind of the public, a glamour couple whose joint company, South Korea's only film studio, Shin Film, and its logo of a flaming torch were immediately familiar to everyone.

Coming up to the stage Choi had walked ahead of her husband, a subtle indication of the modernity of this couple's relationship. As she neared President Park she stopped and bowed deeply, going so far as to drop to one knee, a wry grin on her face. The president and his First Lady burst out laughing at her cheeky mimicry of obsequiousness. Behind her Shin reluctantly nodded his head forward, as little a movement as he could get away with. Recognition he liked; rubbing elbows with the powerful likewise. Bowing down to them—that made him feel distinctly uncomfortable. Maybe it had something to do with his deep distrust of politicians. He had, after all, grown up in a Korea that had been swallowed up into the Japanese empire, given up, by *politicians,* to be colonized after thirteen hundred years of sovereignty. When he turned seventeen he had left Korea to study in Japan, only to find on his return that he couldn't go to his hometown anymore, because it was now, suddenly, in a completely different country, *North* Korea—all because of the maneuverings of politicians. Leftists, rightists, they were all the same to Shin, an ill to be borne and, if possible, taken advantage of.

Maybe it was that. Or maybe he just hated someone else being the center of attention.

On the lawn of the Blue House, Shin stretched his shoulders back and glanced over at Choi, talking with guests a few feet away. She was ravishing in a long dark dress, a cluster of ornamental jewelry drawing the eye to her breasts, as if the plunging neckline weren't mesmerizing enough. (The First Lady, in contrast, wore a traditional *hanbok* dress, long and baggy under the waist, hiding the shape of the hips and legs under endless folds, the collar closed at the neck.) Choi's thick dark hair was pulled back to accentuate her striking face. Glittering earrings dangled from her ears and carefully applied makeup highlighted those famous dark eyes and full lips.

Choi had been famous much longer than either director Shin or President Park; in fact, she had already started making a name for herself on the stage before the end of the Pacific War, when Korea was still one country. Since then she had been a fixture in movie fanzines and the gossip papers. During the traumatic Korean War, which lasted from 1950 to 1953, she had worked as a stage entertainer for *both* sides, and there were rumors that she had lived as an army camp prostitute, undressing in the soldiers' beds at night after she'd sung and danced for them on a stage earlier in the evening. Competing rumors said that she had spent most of the war as the mistress of an American general. After the armistice there had been further scandal when she'd left her first husband, an older, well-respected cameraman who suffered from tuberculosis and had been crippled in the war, for the young, attractive, struggling filmmaker Shin Sang-Ok. With Choi as his leading lady, Shin's fortune had suddenly skyrocketed—and with the success of their elegant, sophisticated movies, Choi had seen her status dramatically elevated from scandalous loose woman to national treasure.

The photographer waved at everyone to stand still and move closer together. A moment later, the camera's flash bulb popped, immortalizing these three people, who, each in their own way, were about to catapult South Korean cinema from obscurity into international recognition. The camera captured Shin with his hands behind his back and his shoulders arched, a proud, irreverent smirk on his face. The president stood next to him with the stiff bearing of an army man, his black suit melting into the darkness the flash wasn't powerful enough to illuminate around them, his face an enigmatic, faintly menacing mask.

As for Choi, she stood slightly turned to her right, captivated, her eyes glued to her husband.

2

Director Shin and Madame Choi

"I call my wife Madame Choi," Shin wrote many years later. "I call her this as a sign of my respect and affection for her."

They had met in Daegu, 150 miles south of Seoul, in the second half of 1953, just a few months after the end of the Korean War. Seoul had changed hands four times during the conflict, the retreating side blowing the bridges and tearing buildings to the ground each time; Pyongyang had been so badly bombed by American planes that only three major buildings were left standing by the time the armistice was signed. Daegu, however, had been held by the United Nations for the course of the conflict and escaped such widespread destruction, so that now, so soon after the fighting had ended, there were still parks to walk around, schools to study in, homes to live in, and—crucially for Shin and Choi—theaters to go to.

This particular evening Shin took his seat in one of the city's auditoriums, eagerly anticipating the show to come. He didn't especially care about the material: he had come to scout the play's star, Choi Eun-Hee, for his second film, a semidocumentary titled *Korea,* which he hoped would showcase the beauty of a country most famous now for war, poverty, and destruction. Choi Eun-Hee was already an established actress, but Shin knew precious little about her. The play was a swashbuckler, with much sword handling and acrobatic jumps. Midway through the evening, as Shin remembered it, Choi collapsed. A gasp rippled through the audience. "I shot up to the stage," Shin said, and kneeled by her side. He asked her if she was all right. When Choi didn't respond, Shin, in front of the stunned crowd, picked her up, popped her across his shoulder, and carried her, on his back, to the nearest hospital.

Choi had collapsed from exhaustion, and after a doctor examined her, she and Shin started talking. Shin was worried about Choi's current state. She looked fatigued and underfed. Her husband was unable to work because of a war injury. And she was poor, she told him—too poor to heat the house. Shin, who had always had his sights on fame and success, had never imagined that such a famous actress could be so poor. But she had persevered, pouring all her emotions into her work, something he respected and admired. Shin told her he was about to start work on *Korea,* and would she like to be in it? He was a young, unproven director and she was reluctant, so he promised her a good fee—as much as he could afford. Choi accepted the part.

"He had a beautiful smile," Choi later wrote of the dashing young film director she met that night. "He looked like he had no concerns or difficulties in life." Her scenes in *Korea* were filmed mostly in Seoul, and she and Shin spent a lot of time together, either on set or sitting in cafés: Choi smoking, watching passersby, and talking about acting and filmmaking, Shin rattling through his ambitions and ideas, how he dreamed of running an independent, integrated studio like those of the Hollywood Golden Age, making any films he wanted. When Choi returned to work on the stage, Shin waited outside the theater after every rehearsal and performance to walk her home, both of them taking their time ambling along the streets, sometimes caught outdoors past the official curfew and having to sneak home like teenagers, careful not to get caught.

Some people worked in show business out of a longing for glamour, others out of a need to be the center of attention. Shin and Choi were different: they both felt a deep passion for their work. It had been so their entire lives. Choi told Shin how she had seen a stage performance as a child in Pusan and fallen in love with it immediately; and how her conservative father had refused to acknowledge her interest, because in Korea actresses were traditionally viewed as little better than courtesans. Besides, a respectable girl's duty was to marry and raise children. So Choi, barely a teenager but already headstrong, had run away from home to pursue her dreams, and had made a success of herself. In return Shin told her about his childhood in Chongjin, in the north of the country, and how he had fallen in love with movies as a young boy, sitting in the traveling tent that came through town to show the moving pictures by foreigners with names such as Georges Méliès, Charlie Chaplin, D. W. Griffith, and Fritz Lang. It was such an elaborate, hypnotic process: the men busying themselves around the projector, one focusing the lens while others cranked the film through the machine by hand; the boys carrying the heavy reels back and forth while another child fanned the older men sweating in the hot tent. During the film the *byeonsa,* a male stage performer, narrated the silent black-and-white pictures that flickered to life on the screen like a magical window into an unknown world of hard men, beautiful women, and the odd comedy tramp, where men rode horses in vast deserts and criminals double-crossed each other in crowded cities of tall buildings and twisted light. Between showings water was poured on the screen to cool it off and prevent its catching fire.

Almost every day, Shin would tell her, "Any film I make, I want you to be in it." He described all the roles she could play, from the famous heroines of popular tales to barely defined ideas he was still sketching out in his mind. "This," Choi said, "was how he said he loved me." One day they were in a café when Choi ran out of cigarettes. She smoked Lucky Strikes, but the café didn't carry the brand, so Shin stood up, ran out, and returned with a pack of Luckys. Choi was touched. She opened the packet, slipped one between her lips, and offered him one.

"I don't smoke," Shin said.

"Why not?"

"I don't like smoking. My mother smoked."

"Then don't you dislike me smoking in front of you?" she asked.

He smiled. "Please, do as you wish. I don't mind." As he said this he leaned forward and lit Choi's cigarette for her. No one had ever behaved this way around her. He didn't smoke, he didn't drink, he didn't gamble; he was gentle and chivalrous. She liked his kindness. As for Shin, his feelings were undeniable. "It was my destiny," he later said, "to meet her."

Choi was twenty-seven when she met Shin, but already she had endured a life of pain and struggle. After running away from home at seventeen, her acting career began, unexpectedly, in an air-raid shelter during a drill, when she noticed an actress she liked, Moon Jung-Bok, huddled nearby. There were no class distinctions in the bomb shelters, so Choi gathered the courage to speak to the older woman, who invited her to come see her at her theater troupe's office in Seoul. She asked Choi if she had her parents' permission to leave home and start work. "Yes," Choi lied.

She started work in the troupe's costume department, mending dresses; within a month she was put onstage to play a bit part; and within a couple of years she had an acting career of her own. Offstage she was shy and quiet, but when she performed she came alive. In 1947, at age twenty-one, she was cast in her first film and shortly thereafter married the film's cameraman, Kim Hak-Sung, who was twenty years older than her. She soon regretted the decision. Kim had already been married, to a bar girl who had run away because of his physical violence. He beat Choi, too, and expected her to fulfill all of her duties as a wife (washing, cleaning, cooking, child rearing) as well as be the main breadwinner, since her career was on the rise while his had been slowing down.

When the Korean War broke out in 1950, Choi and her husband failed to make it out of Seoul in time to escape the North Korean army, and she was signed up by the newly established local Communist Party office as an entertainer for the troops and sent north. A year later Choi and some other performers took advantage of a few hours of panic during a retreat and broke off from their assigned platoon. They were taken in by the South Korean army and ordered to resume their work as army entertainers, only now for the opposite side. Being taken in by her own side should have been a relief for Choi, but instead her "rescue" was the beginning of two years of hell. Where the North Korean soldiers had been disciplined and focused on nothing but battle, the South Korean men eyed her like a piece of meat and wolf-whistled when she walked through the camp. One day a military police officer called her into his office, which had been set up in a deserted village near the front line. A pistol and an open bottle of soju rested on the table in front of him, and he stank of alcohol. He told her that her past work as an entertainer for the North Korean military was treason punishable by death. Luckily, he said, he had the power to erase her offense, and he felt in a lenient mood. He stood up out of his chair, walked over to her, and struck her, hard. He hit her several more times before pinning her to the ground and pressing the gun against her head. She felt him fumbling to open his trousers, his hot breath and the strong smell of the soju on her face. As he pushed himself inside her she heard screaming coming from the next room. On the other side of the wall, a singer who had performed with her since the beginning of the war was also being held to the ground while a policeman raped her. Choi desperately tried to fight the drunk man off, but he was big and heavy. There was no stopping him.

When the war was over Choi was sent back home, and her ordeal, in a society where rape traditionally went unreported and women were usually held responsible for the dishonor that came with it, remained a shameful secret. She found her husband in a hospital, badly injured from shrapnel to the legs. Kim would walk with a cane for the rest of his life. Husband and wife settled back into the new routine of daily life where they and everyone else were suddenly poor and living in ruins, unspoken anguish weighing them down. Soon rumors of Choi's alleged promiscuity during the war began swirling around town. Kim Hak-Sung grew morbidly jealous. He took to hitting his wife with his walking stick, beatings so bad they left her covered in blood and welts. One day, Kim held her down and violently raped her.

Choi didn't know how to run away. Korean women had no rights, only duties. A "wise mother, good wife"—the epitome of female perfection—was obedient to her husband, focused on raising the children, and loyal and respectful to her in-laws. It was her responsibility to preserve the family, whether her husband was a saint or whether he cheated on her or beat her. Only a few decades earlier, women still ate at a separate table from their husbands and were only allowed their leftovers. Women had few legal rights, and society looked unkindly on those who brought dishonor and gossip upon their husbands. Divorce was no option either: it may have been legal, but "one to the last," went the Korean saying—you married once, and you stayed married. The fate you made for yourself on that day was the fate you were stuck with for the rest of your life.

So Choi remained even when Kim forced himself upon her, even when the beatings left her with a scar on her face that never faded for the rest of her life. She had nowhere else to go.

It was Shin Sang-Ok who brought Choi's hopes and dreams back to life. He talked endlessly of wanting to "rebuild Korean cinema." He had the ambition she'd had, what felt like a lifetime ago, when she was seventeen and ran away from home, before the beatings, the violations, and the degradation. Spending time with him made her feel hopeful again.

Shin's life had been much easier. Born into an affluent family, his father a doctor of oriental medicine, Shin had gone to all the best schools and, having shown artistic promise from an early age, was eventually sent to study painting in Tokyo, the buzzing metropolis and capital of the all-powerful Japanese empire in which Korea was a colony. When the Second World War brought about the empire's fall, Shin returned to a Korea he struggled to recognize: the Allied powers had divided the country in half, creating two states. Shin settled to a life in Seoul, in the South, because his hometown of Chongjin was in the North, now off-limits to him. All the moderates were gone, too: suddenly everyone was either a Communist or a rightist, a patriot or a terrorist, an ex–freedom fighter or an ex-collaborator. There were student riots, brutally crushed by tanks and baton-wielding thugs in policemen's uniforms. There were American soldiers everywhere, broad shouldered and straight toothed, with pockets full of money and Korean girlfriends on their arms.

Nineteen, confident, tall, and dashingly good-looking, Shin found work painting propaganda posters for the American occupation forces and film posters for the handful of commercial cinemas that were still in business. He became an apprentice at the tiny, ramshackle, but independent Koryo Film Studio, its equipment antiquated and badly maintained, like a studio from old Hollywood's Poverty Row. When the Korean War broke out, Shin, now in his midtwenties, served in the government's Military Promotion Department, attached to the Air Force, making documentaries informing civilians about the course of the conflict and educating them in modern warfare. He used the opportunity—and the Mitchell 16mm cameras and free film stock the U.S. Army provided the South Korean propaganda departments, which Shin "borrowed" liberally during his time off—to make his first film as a director, *The Evil Night*. Rather than share a one-room "evacuation apartment" with several Seoul families whose homes had been bombed or destroyed, Shin had lately found cheap alternative accommodation sharing a room with a *yangbuin* girl—a "Western princess," the name for a prostitute who catered exclusively to American GIs. *The Evil Night* told the story of a *yangbuin* girl; its tiny budget was cobbled together with loans from Shin's father, his brother, and his new roommate. When the war ended the film was released to enthusiastic reviews and almost no business.

When they met the following year, Shin gave Choi a fresh belief in herself, while she gave him inspiration. They fell in love. Soon enough the talk made its way back to Kim Hak-Sung, who threatened to beat up both Choi and Shin if they didn't break off the affair. He leaked gossip to the papers, which ran headlines about Choi Eun-Hee, the infamous adulteress, who was now abandoning her crippled husband to run off with a younger man. Shin was accused of callously stealing an elder's wife, a shameful display in a country deeply steeped in Confucian values of respect for family, marriage, and one's elders. The young director found himself frozen out of the mostly conservative South Korean film industry.

But now Choi had finally had enough. The affair becoming public had almost been a relief. The guilt had tortured her, but now it was all in the open, and with Shin's unwavering affection, she was ready to stand up for herself. She sued for divorce and won. The moment she left the courtroom, she went straight to Shin. Chased by journalists, who had pitched camp at every friendly address at which they might turn up, the couple dashed into the first cheap motel they found and took a room. "Please remember today," Shin told her, as he pulled her to him. "March 7, 1954. Let today be our wedding day." He didn't believe in institutions, but they held to it as to any commitment made in a church. The next morning they woke up covered in bedbug bites, but with huge smiles on their faces. To Choi, the motel was the most beautiful honeymoon spot in the world, insect-ridden mattress, thin dirty walls, and all.

Shin and Choi's union would prove to be as professionally successful as it was personally fulfilling. They made four films together in the first three years of their marriage. The fourth, *A Flower in Hell,* starred Choi as a *yangbuin* girl and was shot in a neorealist style influenced by the Italian director Roberto Rossellini. It received rapturous critical praise, and critics still consider it the finest Korean film of the 1950s. The next year, 1959, he directed his wife again in the melodrama *A College Woman's Confession,* in which Choi played a poor, orphaned law student who is taken in by a local official's family and rises to become a judge. The film was a smash hit, running in cinemas for over a month. That same year Shin directed five more films, all of them melodramas starring Choi and all of them, in the span of just twelve months, box-office hits.

The film that clearly established Shin Sang-Ok and Choi Eun-Hee as the leading lights of the Korean film industry was the *The Tale of Chunhyang,* a big-budget adaptation of one of Korea's most beloved folk tales, which Shin decided to make in 1960 even though Hong Seong-Ki, the most bankable Korean film director of the day, was already making his own version of the story, starring his own wife, Kim Ji-Mi, the country's most popular actress. Hong owned the largest movie house in Seoul, and because of the market value of his and his wife's names, he had already been able to block-book his film in theaters across the country, guaranteeing that it would be given a major release on a vast number of screens.

None of this fazed Shin. He had decided he would be making his own *Chunhyang,* and not just that: he would be making it in Technicolor and CinemaScope, the first CinemaScope film in Korea. The process would cost nearly three times more than the biggest-budget film of the day, using expensive Kodak film stock that had to be sent to Japan to be processed. And he would let Hong release his film first, on Lunar New Year's Day, 1961, then release his own ten days later. It was an unprecedentedly bold decision, considering how high the stakes were: failure would bankrupt Shin Film.

The films shot almost simultaneously, and the industry whipped itself up into a competitive frenzy trying to predict who would come out of it triumphant. There were reports of sabotage between the two productions; just days before Shin's version was to be released his office was broken into and one of his staff members briefly kidnapped, in a failed bid to force Shin to delay the release of his film.

New Year's arrived. Hong's film was released. Its ticket sales were disappointing, and after fourteen days it was pulled from screens. Ten days after Hong's film was released Shin's *Chunhyang,* starring Choi, hit the screens—and broke every record. It played to sold-out crowds in Seoul's Myongbo cinema for seventy-four straight days. Nearly four hundred thousand people—more than ten times the audience of the average film, 15 percent of Seoul's *entire* population—came to see it in the capital alone, a record that stood for seven years. Later that year, two more Shin Film productions, including the melodrama *The Houseguest and My Mother,* sold upward of 150,000 tickets each. As one of Shin's associates put it, "We couldn't count how much money [we] earned. Every morning, several bags of cash were delivered. We could do whatever we wanted." The same year, Shin shot a huge-budget historical epic, *Prince Yeonsan,* in twenty-one days, because he wanted to release it on New Year's Day again, to repeat the previous year's success. It became 1962's highest-grossing film, and Shin became known as the New Year's Day Showman. Five months later *The Houseguest and My Mother* won the top prize at the Asia-Pacific Film Festival, Shin Sang-Ok met President Park Chung-Hee, and a decade of unprecedented dominance over the country's film industry by one man (Shin Sang-Ok) and one company (Shin Film) had begun.

3

Shrimp Among Whales

The South Korea of the 1960s was a deeply wounded nation. An independent, sovereign nation for over a millennium, Korea had the misfortune of being at the meeting place of three of the world's greatest nations—Russia, China, and Japan—all of which fought and competed over it for centuries. It was Japan, in the end, that successfully annexed the peninsula in 1910, to use it as a launchpad for the invasion of China. The Empire of the Rising Sun had a brutal way of assimilating new colonies. It turned Korea into a gigantic armed camp, deposing the Korean king and replacing him with a repressive military government, which immediately launched a series of mass executions and imprisonments as an example to the local people. Koreans were made to take Japanese names, to worship at Japanese shrines, and to learn Japanese at school. The Japanese army even drove metal spikes into the nation's sacred hilltops, to destroy what the Korean people saw as their land's spiritual energy. Heavy taxes—over 50 percent of every harvest—were levied on every farm to support the wars being waged throughout Asia and the Pacific. Men and women were drafted and shipped off to serve the war effort in the army and in factories, and Japanese soldiers stationed in Korea freely and forcefully helped themselves to any Korean girls they wanted for sexual services.

Japan's wars of expansion lasted until the summer of 1945, when the U.S. Air Force dropped Little Boy on Hiroshima and Fat Man on Nagasaki, finally bringing a war machine known for its war crimes and suicidal fanaticism to its knees. When Japan's emperor, Hirohito, surrendered over the radio on August 15, 1945, acquiescing to a treaty that formally required him to accept that he literally was no longer a god, many Japanese locked themselves in their homes, sobbing. Others committed ritual suicide, unable to cope with a world in which deities could be deposed by signed treaty. The people of Korea, for their part, ran cheering through the streets and threw spontaneous parades, waving both Soviet and American flags, unsure where their liberators had come from but sure of their gratitude. The first men of the U.S. Army to arrive in Seoul found a nineteenth-century city of single-story buildings, horse-drawn carts, and charcoal-motored vehicles, with not a single European face to be seen. The human excrement Koreans still used to fertilize the rice paddies gave the country a distinctive, thick stink in the clammy summer air.

Back in Washington, the realities of geopolitics took over. The Soviet army was already marching into Korea from the northern side, and President Harry Truman tasked his secretary of state, Edward Stettinius, with coming up with a plan to favorably determine Korea's fate. Stettinius, who had run General Motors and U.S. Steel and had participated in the creation of the United Nations, allegedly had to ask his staff where exactly Korea *was*. Stettinius's men came up with a plan to divide Korea in half, forming a temporary trusteeship—the Soviets looking after the North, the Americans after the South—until a further plan had been agreed. Looking on the map for the best place to partition the peninsula, the American administrative officers scratched a line across the thirty-eighth parallel.

Never in its history had Korea been divided in this way. That the Korean people, innocent bystanders of the war who yearned for freedom, were about to see their country carved up and occupied dumbfounded them. It also felt uncomfortably similar to the way the Japanese occupation had begun. The Japanese emperors, from Meiji to Hirohito, had seemed uninterested in Korea itself, viewing the proud nation as little more than a stepping-stone to China. Now Moscow and Washington faced off on Korean soil. It is one thing to undergo decades of horror and degradation as a conquered enemy. It is another to be an afterthought, of no real worth even to your oppressor.

The Koreans had an old saying: in a fight among whales, a shrimp's back always breaks. Korea had been a shrimp among whales for centuries. In May 1948 the United Nations oversaw elections in the South, which installed Syngman Rhee as the new Republic of Korea's first president. Rhee had lived in exile in the United States since 1904, had studied at George Washington University, Yale, and Princeton, and had married an Austrian woman. The elections took place against a backdrop of violence, instability, and corruption. In the North, Stalin installed as leader a baby-faced thirty-six-year-old Korean officer of his Red Army, Kim Il-Sung, who had joined the Soviet forces in the late 1930s when his own independent guerrilla efforts against the Japanese had ended in failure. Kim had no political experience and was no intellectual, but he was a self-disciplined and promising officer, with a reputation for reliability, bravery, and pragmatism. He spoke Korean, Chinese, and Russian, and was popular with the resistance fighters and Soviet-Koreans who would form the core of North Korea's first leading elite. A parallel government to Syngman Rhee's was created and called the Democratic People's Republic of Korea (DPRK), committed to the principles of Marxist socialism. Kim Il-Sung was declared its first premier.

Koreans might have expected that their suffering would end there and that now, even if divided, they would be allowed to rebuild. Not so. As early as June 1950, Kim Il-Sung made an armed attempt at reunifying the peninsula, sending his men, in Soviet tanks and with Soviet advisers by their side, rumbling across the thirty-eighth parallel and into South Korea. The South Koreans were taken completely by surprise, and within two days the DPRK army had occupied Seoul, unfurling huge banner portraits of Stalin and Kim Il-Sung on the government buildings. In the four months it took the United States to put together an army to fight back, the North Koreans committed mass murder, killing over twenty-six thousand South Korean civilians—an average of sixteen hundred men, women, and children a week. They threw open the doors of every prison they encountered, unleashing criminals, from political prisoners to murderers and rapists, onto the streets with authority to form People's Courts to try and condemn innocent civilians.

In October 1950, the combined forces of the United States, South

Korea, and a coalition of foreign nations, fighting for the first time under the United Nations flag, liberated Seoul and marched north, crossing the thirty-eighth parallel and taking Pyongyang. China, under its new leader, Mao Zedong, joined the fray on the side of the North Koreans, pushing the Allies back and retaking Seoul for the Communists. The UN forces, like a football team returning a punt, pushed back up the field again. In March 1951 they retook Seoul—the fourth time the city had changed hands in under a year. This was the way things would remain for the next two years, with the Communists holding Pyongyang and the Allies holding Seoul, their armies fighting back and forth across the thirty-eighth parallel. It was a brutal and traumatic time for the entire nation. In the countryside, villages and farms were burned to the ground lest they provide shelter for the enemy. Wandering across the razed fields were columns and columns of almost feral refugees, hundreds of thousands who had been left homeless and starving.

While negotiators worked out small points of argument, the North Koreans wasted time with ridiculous claims and absurd filibustering—one day, the North Koreans stared at their UN counterparts in silence for a full two hours and eleven minutes before standing up and walking out. The armistice, finally signed on July 27, 1953, essentially reinstated the pre-war status quo, except that five million people had died, more than half of them civilians, with many more millions left orphaned, widowed, and homeless. The border at the thirty-eighth parallel was fortified into a 160-mile-long, 2.5-mile-wide no-man's-land of barbed wire, surveillance turrets, and land mines known as the Demilitarized Zone (DMZ). And for the first time in a thousand years, the Korean people—who called themselves *danil minjok,* one people, priding themselves on their sense of unity—had fought to conquer and kill each other.

When Park Chung-Hee took power in 1961, eight years after the end of the Korean War, South Korea was the largest beneficiary of American aid in the third world and fast losing its race for legitimacy with the North, whose gross national product per capita was twice that of the South in spite of much more limited resources. Seoul was one gigantic slum. The country was in dire need of escapism, and there to provide it were Shin Sang-Ok and Choi Eun-Hee.

Within a few years of founding his company, Shin had become the industry's leading commercial director and its most influential producer. He ran Shin Film like a Hollywood studio, with directors and screenwriters under contract, working on his own back lot and soundstages, with his own distribution system and its own star system, Choi Eun-Hee its brightest light. He was the first Korean to make a film in Technicolor, the first to make a film in CinemaScope, the first to use a lens as wide as 13 millimeters and a zoom as long as 250 millimeters, the first to attempt a fully synchronized sound film. He made the biggest-budget films and paid Choi the largest fees ever paid to a Korean actress. He became involved in coproductions, most notably with the Shaw Brothers of Hong Kong, long before it was the norm. He allegedly even participated in the writing of President Park's Motion Picture Laws, which aimed to build up and standardize the practices of South Korea's film producers to enable them to compete with the giant corporations of Los Angeles and Tokyo, and which many filmmakers—including, eventually, Shin himself—found impossible to work under.

He made melodramas, thrillers, historical epics, martial arts films, even Manchurian westerns. Some of his films were big and lurid, filmed in bright colors and full of frantic zooms and moving cameras. Others he shot in restrained black and white, the camera still, the compositions painterly and deliberate. In the same year he might make a tame melodrama and follow it up with a film so erotic it threw censors into disarray: he found box-office success with both. He adapted Maupassant novels and then made ludicrous horror movies about vampiric cats, or about demon snakes transforming themselves into beautiful women in order to seduce Buddhist monks. He brought the spaghetti western to Korea, importing Sergio Leone's *For a Few Dollars More* and *The Good, the Bad, and the Ugly* and making them huge hits, along with Sam Peckinpah's *Straw Dogs* and Bruce Lee's *The Big Boss*. He held highly publicized talent searches through which he discovered new faces who quickly became the biggest stars in Korean films. He gave dozens of young film directors their start. At its peak in the mid-1960s, less than half a decade after opening for business, Shin Film employed more than three hundred people and turned out thirty films a year. In 1968 Shin bought the huge Anyang Film Studios south of Seoul, a twenty-acre facility that had been built a decade earlier but was unused since because of its scale, and put every stage and studio there back to work. He started a record company, a theater troupe, and an acting school, the latter of which was run by Choi Eun-Hee. In all of it Choi was an equal partner, inspiring the vast majority of Shin's stories and often investing her own money into the projects.

All this success was built on Shin and Choi's ability to deliver escapist fantasies to working people, so recently traumatized by occupation and war, who longed to escape the struggle and hard graft of their daily lives. They also delivered in their personal lives. Shin and Choi were South Korea's most glamorous couple. Shin was strikingly tall in his expensive suits, tailored in a style more French than American, his collar casually open at the neck and his hair in a Richard Burton–like splash over his forehead; Choi was always in the latest fashions, her hair cut in the trendiest styles.

The cinemas themselves were a popular place to be: air-conditioned and cool during Korea's hot, muggy summers, warm and cozy during the blisteringly cold winters. For a low admission price, especially in the provinces, families could escape their poorly insulated homes and spend the whole day in the cinema, watching the same film sometimes two or three times in a row.

Shin's films were the most popular in the country. And his loyalty was only to film, not to any politician or ideology. It's difficult to know what exactly Shin believed in, other than himself. He mocked peers who wanted to be auteurs while clearly craving the epithet himself. He made films that clearly called for women's liberation while publicly stating that to think his films did that was "just wrong," adding, "I personally admire Confucianism." He valued screenwriters, paying them huge sums of money and buying up all the best book and radio properties to adapt, but at the same time claimed that his films were mainly visual and that he wished he could screen them backward so as to negate their plots. "I really despise these pretensions of being an artist," Shin said during that period of success, "and pretending to have some sort of social conscience, that's just the worst. . . ."

Mostly, it seemed, he just *loved* making films. Everything else seemed small and unimportant. Choi Eun-Hee wrote later, with a mixture of disquiet and admiration, that Shin would have sold his own wife, "without hesitation," if doing so helped him to make a film. Shin's contemporary, film critic Kim Chong-Won wrote of Shin that "he would have jumped down to hell if he had to in order to make movies."

As for Choi, she was the embodiment of modern Korea at a time when the country was torn between the traditional and the modern. Still driven by its old Confucian values, post–Korean War South Korea was entering an era of flashiness and consumption, encouraged by President Park, who was aggressively encouraging Korea to emulate the capitalist West. Modern American appliances became such sought-after signs of status and wealth that the middle-class Korean homes of the day could look a touch surreal: refrigerators standing proudly like trophies in the home's front foyer, toasters displayed in the living room, empty packaging set out on mantelpieces silently boasting of the family's access to certain goods and products. President Park himself was known for his flashy aviator sunglasses and the way he smoked his cigarettes from long, thin holders. As so often, the battle between the preservation of traditional ways of life and the acceptance of modern culture was fought over what was and wasn't considered appropriate, or safe, for women to do. Time and time again in Shin's films, Choi Eun-Hee personified that struggle, whether she played a prostitute, a war widow, a chaste student, a queen, or a promiscuous barmaid.

Offscreen, Choi's public image was similarly pulled between these two forces. Male audiences couldn't help but sexualize her, and after watching any film she starred in men's conversation unfailingly drifted from the quality of the movie to Choi's body. The popular media, encouraged by Shin Film's publicists, portrayed Choi as a dutiful and devoted wife who worked hard, both on set and at home, for her husband, a woman who loved knitting and ironing her husband's shirts. "She is a great actress and a great wife at the same time," exclaimed the fanzines and newspapers.

But then there was the Choi Eun-Hee who campaigned for women's rights, who so publicly made her name outside of the family unit that some consider her the first fully professional woman in South Korean cinema.

She directed three of her own films in the 1960s, the third Korean woman ever to step behind the camera, and all three were critical and commercial successes. When one of Shin's more popular directors, Lee Jang-Ho, married, it was Choi who officiated at the wedding—a duty almost unheard-of for a woman to perform. She was more bankable than her husband and a canny networker, more at ease with the rich and powerful than Shin ever was. Duty, emancipation, sexuality: Choi carried and expressed them all at the same time, her work and her life both an embodiment of the limitations placed upon women and a prism through which to glimpse a world in which there were none.

Throughout it all, husband and wife were always mentioned together: Shin and Choi, Shin Film and its star Choi, the director Shin Sang-Ok and the female lead Choi Eun-Hee. In the public mind as in their own lives, they were inseparable—through the highs, and through the lows.

With the money from their films they bought a Western-style house in Seoul's Jangchung-Dong district, just around the corner from the National Theater, and settled into an idyllic domestic routine. They installed an editing bed and projector at home, editing their films together. Choi loved the house deeply. After they moved in she started buying expensive furniture for each room, but as the weeks passed she noticed that different pieces would temporarily disappear. It wasn't long before she figured out what was happening: any time Shin came home to a piece he liked, he took it away to dress a film set. At first the habit annoyed Choi, but soon she came to love even this about her husband, another sign of his infinite passion for making films.

It was a busy but blissful existence, and the only thing lacking, for Choi, was a child. Children mattered little to Shin—"Our films are like our children," he told her—but he didn't have any objections, so long as they could find the time to raise a family around their demanding work schedules. When they finally tried, however, Choi discovered she was unable to bear children. Whether the cause was genetic or due to damage from the sexual abuse she had undergone a decade earlier was impossible to confirm, but Choi was heartbroken just the same. In Korean culture it was a terrible shame for a woman to fail to produce a child for her husband; an almost weekly plot point in soap operas featured barren women crying and begging forgiveness from their families. Shin didn't seem to care—"I like you just the way you are," he told her time and again—but for Choi, who in 1970 was entering her forties and longed desperately for a family, the pain only grew worse. So they decided to adopt. In 1971 they brought a baby girl, Myung-Im, into the family, followed three years later by a boy, Jung-Kyun. The first time Myung-Im called her "Mum," Choi cried with joy.

As the 1960s drew to a close, South Korea was, against all expectations, becoming a regional power: peaceful, economically independent, its people's dignity restored. Homes were being fitted with running water and reliable electricity, and the first skyscrapers had begun to spear up into the Seoul skyline. The one storm cloud on the horizon was the country's shadowy neighbor: the Democratic People's Republic of Korea.

During the war, North Korean soldiers had demonstrated a fanatical devotion to the People's Republic, swarming down upon the enemy in suicidal human wave attacks, professing an ideological commitment that many South Koreans found bewildering in people whom they had, until very recently, called their neighbors and brothers. Nor had the war's end concluded the conflict. Within a few years Kim Il-Sung's army was again multiplying its attacks and provocations on the South. In 1958 Kim's men hijacked a Korean Air plane, releasing only some of the passengers and crew two months later (eight people remained in North Korea, their fates unknown). Then in 1965, North Korean jets had opened fire on an American reconnaissance plane over the Sea of Japan. At the same time the Pyongyang regime had hermetically sealed its borders, letting few foreigners in and virtually no information out, so that the outside world was only given sporadic, unsettling glimpses of what lay within.

As a result, South Korean schoolchildren were shown cartoons on the dangers of the satanic "Reds," and taught always to be vigilant and committed, if needed, to fighting them. Many were even taught that

Northerners were actually red-skinned, with hooves, horns, and spiky tails. On the news the government never referred to Northerners as Koreans, referring to them only as “the Reds” or “the Northern monsters.” There were rumors that even being “exposed to communism” for a few hours could turn you Red. Under the National Security Law, introduced in the late 1940s but reinforced under Park, it became a crime punishable by jail—and, on occasion, by the death penalty—to sympathize with or praise the North, to recognize it as a political entity, or to dispute the government’s stance on any issues related to North Korea. Soon people were jailed for reading socialist pamphlets, for listening to North Korean music, even for owning North Korean stamps. Any unsupervised contact with a North Korean citizen—even if that citizen was your own brother, sister, mother, or father, and had become a North Korean for no reason other than where on the peninsula they had stood in the second half of 1945—was a most serious breach of the law.

Moreover, ordinary South Koreans had never seen Kim Il-Sung’s face, for his likeness was banned in all forms, lest the simple sight of it foster feelings of dissent or, God forbid, latent Marxism. Nor did South Koreans know anything at all about his son, Kim Jong-Il.

4

A Double Rainbow over Mount Paekdu

No place holds more mystical power over the Korean people's consciousness than Mount Paekdu, densely forested and shrouded in mist, where the nation's great founder and first emperor, Tangun, descended from the skies more than five millennia ago. Tigers, leopards, bears, wolves, wild boar, and deer roam in the shadows of the birch and pine trees. It is here, according to Kim Jong-Il's official biography, in a humble log cabin tucked away under the snow-covered evergreen trees, that the Dear Leader was born on February 16, 1942.

Kim's father, Comrade Great Leader Kim Il-Sung, had conducted the resistance against the Japanese oppressor for years and had made Paekdu the secret headquarters camp for the Korean Revolutionary Liberation Army. Among the partisans was a small group of female fighters; the bravest of these women, Kim Jong-Suk, had become the Great Leader's bodyguard and then his wife. At the height of winter, at the very end of a stormy, freezing February night, Kim Jong-Suk had huddled in the cold cabin, with nothing but a small fire for warmth, and given birth to the Dear Leader. The very instant that the infant slipped out of his mother's womb the thunderstorm relented and the skies fell quiet. The dark clouds parted and a double rainbow—the most vibrant double rainbow man's eyes had ever seen—shone overhead, bright in the pale dawn sky. A new star appeared in the heavens at that exact moment, to mark the day forevermore.

The Dear Leader's birth had long been expected, foretold by a swallow, who had sung of how a prodigious general was coming who would rule all the world. When the newborn's first cry echoed throughout the base, the guerrilla fighters rushed out of their tents and huts. They hugged and celebrated and blessed the birth. They burst into joyful song, pledging to fight harder than ever for an early liberation of the fatherland. Some took out their knives and carved messages of hope in the trees while others painted messages in bloodred ink.

The newborn was the newest addition to an honored line of patriots: his father, Comrade Kim-Il Sung, was leading the resistance against the Japanese, his grandfather had been imprisoned for his own revolutionary activities, and his great-great-grandfather had planned and led the small group that had attacked and burned the armed American ship the *General Sherman* when it had forced its way up the Taedong River in 1866. There was no doubt in anyone's mind that the Leader's newborn son would add to this long list of achievements.

As his biography attests, Jong-Il did not disappoint. At just three weeks old he was walking around the camp. At eight weeks he was talking. As a three-year-old, shortly before the Korean Revolutionary Liberation Army successfully liberated the fatherland from the Japanese, he walked into a classroom containing a map of the Japanese islands. The child dipped several fingers into an inkpot, marched straight up to the map, and smeared it with black ink. As soon as he did so, the most violent typhoons and hurricanes lashed the real Japan, resulting in great destruction and many deaths.

A few years later, in the summer of 1952, the boy's father, Great Marshal Leader Kim Il-Sung, stood among the rocks in the mountains of Kangwon province. Since Jong-Il's birth he had defeated the Japanese and chased them out of Korea; now he was fighting the American imperialists who were trying to take over Korea from the south. Kim Jong-Il came walking up to his father. The boy, just ten years old, had volunteered to visit the front line, where his father was personally leading the fighting.

"Do you know what day today is?" Kim Il-Sung asked his son.

"It is the birthday of my late grandfather," Jong-Il answered.

Pleased with his son's answer, the Leader picked up a heavy packet wrapped in red cloth. "When I was fourteen years old," he told his son, "my mother gave me a very important gift, which had been left to me by my father. On his deathbed he gave this gift to my mother, with orders to give it to me when I was old enough to join the fight for independence. The gift was his two pistols, which he carried with him always. Before he died he told my brothers and me, 'I am leaving this world without realizing my dreams. I trust that you will realize them for me. Don't you ever forget that you are sons of Korea. You must recover Korea even if your bones are smashed and your body is cut to pieces.' It was the last thing Father told us." With this the Leader handed the packet to his son. Jong-Il unfolded the red fabric. Inside were the two old pistols.

"I give this to you today," the Leader said. "Take it as a baton in the relay race of our revolution. These guns keep the will of our family genealogy—you must take care of them all your life." He stepped closer to his son and repeated the words of wisdom that he had often heard his own father say: "Armed struggle is the supreme form of struggle for independence. When you fight an enemy who is armed, you need to be armed yourself to fight and win the duel. Remember this: a revolutionary must never part with his gun throughout his life. Guns are your closest friend."

Jong-Il had already seen enough to understand what his father meant. Even if North Korea's war for independence was finally won—as of course it would be—vigilance must never be abandoned. The guns would always be needed, and so would a leader.

And so it was decided, in the fog of the Fatherland Liberation War, that Kim Jong-Il would in time succeed his father as Leader, and continue defending the Korean people.

These accounts of Kim Jong-Il have been the undisputed truth for decades. North Koreans are taught these stories every day, by rote, from the moment they are old enough to walk, and no one is allowed to contest them.

None of them, of course, are true. It's not just the obvious things—the talking swallow, the double rainbow, the new star in the sky, the apparent use of magic to unleash natural disasters on Japan. Yes, there was in the 1930s a Korean revolutionary force and later a war, and yes, during the war a baby was born to revolutionaries Kim Il-Sung and Kim Jong-Suk—but Kim Jong-Il wasn't born in 1942, nor was he born in Korea, and he wasn't a prodigy. His ancestors hadn't orchestrated the burning of the *General Sherman* or any other U.S. ship, for that matter. And Kim Jong-Il never stood on the front line of the guerrilla battles of Kangwon Province, because there *were* no guerrilla battles of Kangwon Province, instead just a sad, drawn-out, futile trench war that lasted nearly three years. For the first two decades of his life, the boy wasn't even called Kim Jong-Il.

Nothing illustrates Kim's awareness of the power of a good story better than the official, state-approved story of his own birth, which is, in itself, a story about the creation of story. The myth of Kim Jong-Il's birth has echoes, like much of the Christian messianic canon, of an archetypal hero narrative. The exceptional, long-suffering mother; the absent father off fighting for a noble cause; the precocious wisdom and the proud lineage: Kim devised his story deliberately and ticked all the necessary boxes, mapping out classic patterns and paradigms. It took Kim a few years and several drafts to get it right; elements of the story started appearing in official propaganda in the 1970s, to be rewritten in the early 1980s, then stamped into history in Jong-Il's first official biography, published in 1984, then "updated" and reissued in 1995, this version introducing details like the log cabin and the exact name of the nearest village, Samjiyeon-Gun, which all citizens were now expected to visit regularly to "educate" themselves. Many marveled that the log cabin was still standing, fifty-three years and two wars after Kim's birth, but they shouldn't have; the army had only just built it. The paint on the "spontaneous" carved messages on the trees was still drying when the first visitors climbed off the bus.

If North Koreans were allowed to know what the rest of the world knows, they would know that Kim Jong-Il was in fact born on February 16, 1941, not 1942, in a Soviet army camp near Khabarovsk, a Russian town almost eight hundred kilometers north of Mount Paekdu. The date had been altered in order to align the son's birth more harmoniously with his father's, putting an exact thirty years between them. Traditionally, Koreans attach great importance to five-year anniversaries: 1942 reads more tidily than 1941, thirty years better than twenty-nine. (This detail of the story was introduced in the 1982 edition, with the real 1941 date approved by the government up until then; to reset the timeline the Central News Agency exhorted the Korean people to celebrate Kim's fortieth birthday two years in a row, as if nothing had happened.)

Kim Jong-Il's father, Kim Il-Sung, was born on April 15, 1912, in a hamlet on the southwest outskirts of Pyongyang. He was only seventeen when the Japanese first arrested him for starting a local Marxist-Leninist union that promoted anti-Japanese activities. They threw him in jail and broke his fingers. When they released him he joined a band of guerrillas in Jilin, in northeastern China, who were fighting for Korean independence. He was a charismatic, passionate man with a common touch, an easy leader of men. For some years, he led a disorganized band of Korean resisters (there was never any such thing as the "Korean Revolutionary Liberation Army"). A couple of Kim's raids into Japanese-controlled villages had made headlines, and the Japanese governor of Korea eventually put a not-inconsequential price on his head. In 1935, to evade capture and certain execution, Kim fled Korea and folded his troops into the Chinese army. In China, Kim was best known for his unusual recruitment methods, which involved kidnapping Korean boys of suitable age to fill the ranks, and for the Mafia-style protection racket he imposed on the local ginseng and opium farmers. But Kim never did any real damage to the Japanese, and by 1940 he had traded his coarse guerrilla camouflage garb for a fresh Red Army uniform, becoming a battalion leader in the Eighty-eighth Special Reconnaissance Brigade of the Soviet Twenty-fifth Army.

Kim Il-Sung's wife, Jong-Il's mother, was one of the women the Korean guerrillas kept to do their menial chores and housework. Kim Jong-Suk was, by all accounts, a woman who could handle herself. She was famous for once allegedly saving Kim Il-Sung's life in battle, shielding his body with her own and shooting down two Japanese when she and Kim were ambushed. She fought, the official documents say, "with fury." She was striking if not beautiful, small in build, with long eyelashes and tanned skin from spending days outdoors. Lee Min, one of the female comrades who shared her quarters, remembered her as quick and generous. Kim Il-Sung himself, in his memoirs, describes his wife as considerate, sacrificial, and devoted. Their relationship was built with traditional, hierarchal formality.

The baby born to the Kims in February 1941, like all the children born in the Soviet camp, was given a Russian name. Yura, as he came to be known—short for his full Russian name, Yurei Ilsenovitch Kim—was joined two years later by a younger brother, Shura, and in 1946 by a sister, Kyong-Hui. Of the three children only she was born in liberated Korea—liberated, that is, by the Americans and the Soviets, not by Kim. A Russian name for her was not needed.

Kim Il-Sung never fought the Japanese from Mount Paekdu, as the story of his son's birth claims, and far from leading the liberation of his homeland, he was assigned to a Russian army camp in Khabarovsk, in the far east of Russia, and sat the event out entirely. As for Kim Jong-Il, he wasn't given the keys (or rather, the guns) to the country when he was ten years old. He wasn't properly considered a potential successor to his father until he was well into his thirties. He was an overprivileged, aimless young man who did not serve in the military and demonstrated no excellence in any field of bureaucracy or economics. He never won an election and was no champion of the people of North Korea, who didn't hear his voice for the first time until a full decade and a half after he had taken the reins of the country. But what Yura Kim did have was a sense of narrative, of drama and of showmanship, of mythmaking and its power. All of which he learned not by studying politics, or religion, or history.

No, what Kim Jong-Il learned, and what he then built in North Korea, he learned from the movies.

5
Kim Jong-Il's First Loves

Jong-Il fell in love with cinema the very first time his parents took him, as a young child, to the DPRK's brand new Korea Film Studio in Pyongyang. In the early years following the division of Korea, the two states had become competitive about absolutely everything, including the cinema, and a race was on to make the first postwar "liberated" Korean film. The North Koreans lost that race when Choe Yong-Kyu's *Hurrah Freedom* was released in the South in 1946, but they were easily winning the battle for quality. While South Koreans made films independently, in a slapdash and often rudimentary manner, Kim Il-Sung insisted that all film projects in North Korea should be placed under state control, and should act as the state's shop window. "Of all the arts," Lenin had said, "cinema is for us the most important," a sentiment with which Kim Il-Sung agreed. Following the Soviet example, he decreed that film should form a core part of the "ideological guidance" of the people, entrusting it to the newly created Propaganda and Agitation Department of the Workers' Party, North Korea's central unit of government. Under Soviet tutelage, with Moscow providing both funding and technicians to teach filmmaking skills to North Koreans, Kim Il-Sung created the National Film Production Center and the North Korean Theater and Film Committee, which together formed the core of the film apparatus and answered to the Propaganda and Agitation Department. Their mission was to create a North Korean film industry; the first North Korean movie would be called *My Home Village*.

Little Yura loved going to the Korea Film Studio. He accompanied his mother and father on studio visits as often as he could. Maybe it was a child's simple fascination with what must have seemed like a gigantic toy set, or maybe it was, already, the lure of complete control over a world and the people inhabiting it. Maybe the isolated boy saw in the movies sudden access to an untold number of worlds other than his own, a form of freedom. Whatever it was, Yura loved it.

My Home Village is legendary in North Korean cultural history, not least because, as the official North Korean propaganda tells us, it reveals the first signs of Kim Jong-Il's cinematic genius. In the oft-repeated story, Yura attended a preview screening of the movie, aged only seven, and—like a young Jesus in the temple—started dispensing notes to the filmmakers present. "The film showed winter scenes of the falling snow," the official version recounts. "At this sight [Yura] shook his head dubiously and told an official of the film studio that he wondered why no snow was found on the heads and shoulders of the characters while it came down copiously [around them]. . . . The official blushed with shame in spite of himself. . . . [Yura] noticed that a bad job was made of trick shots." He even pointed out that the fake snow was clearly made of balls of cotton wool, "too crude" in his opinion. Thanks to the young prodigy, the scenes in question were reshot adequately before release. (It's worth noting that the Soviet filmmakers supervising the film had been making movies with weather effects for decades, and that as early as 1925 Chaplin had used salt and flour for snow in *The Gold Rush*, rather than cotton.)

The film, released in 1949, tells the story of the liberation of Korea—not by the Allies, not by the Red Army, but, single-handedly, by the Korean guerrilla fighters and their unseen leader: Kim Il-Sung. The film invented the "Korean Revolutionary Liberation Army" and set forward the myth that would become state doctrine. Not only did Kim Il-Sung chase the Japanese out of Korea, *My Home Village* says, but no one other than Kim Il-Sung could have. The film was much more technically advanced than anything being made in South Korea, thanks to the guidance of the Soviet filmmakers. All of it was put to the service of glorifying Kim Il-Sung as defeater of the Japanese oppressor and liberator of the Korean people.

The movie was a huge success with its audience, which it found mostly through a network of "mobile film groups," which traveled through the North Korean countryside with a print and a projector. Film was still an exciting novelty to many Korean peasants, and the people filled the screenings with barely contained anticipation. Many of them, especially in rural areas, had never experienced the marvel of moving images, let alone images telling *their* history, or more accurately a version of it they aspired to. The film tapped into what every Korean of that time longed for after decades of degradation and oppression. It ignored the reality, ignored the collaborators, ignored the grating humiliation of being liberated by the Soviets and Allies rather than by their own means, and presented instead the exact fantasy the people wanted to believe in. This fantasy is what Kim Il-Sung would build his dictatorship on for decades to come.

The film's very first shot—the very first motion picture image in North Korean history—is of Mount Paekdu, the holy volcanic mountain that is Korea's spiritual cradle, which the Kims would appropriate for themselves over the next half century. The film's makers couldn't travel to Paekdu, so *My Home Village* opens, fittingly, not on the real thing but on an unconvincing scale model.

Yura saw the final cut of *My Home Village* with his mother, at the film's very first public screening, one of his last and most powerful memories of her; she died just a few months later.

Her loss left an overwhelming absence. His mother had been the one steady presence in Yura's life and he loved her deeply. He was a shy and quiet boy who played alone at home. He liked to dress up in his custom-made child's military uniform and march around the pond in the backyard, barking orders and swinging his arms as stiffly as he could. In pictures taken at home, Yura always has a huge smile on his face, especially if his mother is near him; he looks happy and at ease. (He felt less of a bond with his father: the Supreme Leader was often away, busy building a new nation, and—unbeknownst to Yura but painfully clear to Jong-Suk—filling his free time with the many younger women he took a shine to.) Yura's younger brother,

Shura, had died two summers earlier, at four years old, drowning in the center of a pond while Yura watched helplessly, and his mother's death, so soon after his baby brother's, devastated Yura. When asked, decades later, who the most influential person in his life had been, Kim Jong-Il answered without hesitation, "My mother, may she rest in peace. My mother would never have imagined the way I turned out. I owe her a great deal."

His early memories of the movies became ineradicably tied to his memories of his mother, binding them to her in a way, attaching him even further to the silver screen—to those images that seemed to control and hold on to time, to halt its passing, even to defy death. The memories of his mother, of happiness and playacting, and of the cinema, became bound together in his future official biographies. (Though Kim Il-Sung remarried, Jong-Il hated his stepmother, and he would later erase her and his three half siblings out of official history). Not all the stories were factually accurate, but the adult Kim Jong-Il had a hand in their writing, and they carried a deep psychological truth. He painted the past in a way that intimately links together the cinema and wanting to please his mother, as if his love of cinema were also his love for his mother. A little like Laurence Olivier, who always felt he was acting for his beloved mother, who had died when he was twelve; or Ingrid Bergman, who linked wanting to be an actress with playacting as a child in the clothes of a mother who had died when she was a toddler and whom she didn't remember; Kim Jong-Il soon started making movies, in a way, as an attempt to recover the lost love of the woman who had given birth to him and loved him, but was torn from him much too soon.

His mother's early death was often given as an excuse for Yura's difficult behavior as a young man. Without a maternal guiding hand, the Premier's son became accustomed to the shrinking, bowing deference of all around him. He spoke back to teachers and resented all forms of authority. He was prone to bursts of anger and bad temper. He coasted on his status as the Supreme Leader's son. Yet he could be charming with his peers, and his hedonistic tendencies earned him popularity as an undergraduate student at

Kim Il-Sung University. At a time when a bicycle was a luxury attainable by only the best-connected North Koreans, the sight of Yura zooming in and out of campus on his imported motorcycle was legendary. He threw the best parties, sponsored the best movie screenings, dance performances, and music concerts. Being his friend meant having access to worlds of which other students could only dream. He was active in university extracurricular activities—especially in organizing anti-American demonstrations, which were rumored to be the best place for students to meet girls—and he was put in charge of his class's graduation party. He threw himself into every activity with energy and passion: that was his style. The elite at Kim Il-Sung's court used words like *playboy* and *dilettante* to describe him. At twenty years old, Yura was decades away from the iconic Kim Jong-Il who wore ridiculously big square glasses and had a closetful of identical khaki jumpsuits. Young Yura wore trendy black frames and a tunic, usually dark blue, sometimes black, with a narrow Mao collar. His shoes were black, polished to gleam. If he wore a coat it was a long, thick wool overcoat, urbane and smart, rather than the awkward parka of later years. He liked motorcycles, fast cars, expensive cognac, and sleeping with actresses.

Kim Il-Sung didn't know what to make of his son. He had tried to interest Yura in matters of state, even taking him to Moscow in 1959 on a state function, but Yura had stayed behind at the hotel during most of the meetings and official events. The early 1960s were a heady time in North Korea, which had established itself as the more secure and affluent of the two Koreas. In Pyongyang there were rumors that the Great Leader Kim Il-Sung was, already, turning his mind to the grooming and eventual appointment of a successor. After Stalin's death a decade earlier Kim Il-Sung had been openly critical of the Soviet Union's new leader, Nikita Khrushchev, whom he felt was disgracing the principles of communism, tearing down statues of Stalin and opening trade talks with the West. With all the nationalist talk coming out of the Workers' Party's official news agency, it became increasingly awkward for the Supreme Leader's own son to be walking around with a Russian name. Kim pressured Yura to choose a Korean name and to stick with it. So, one morning, Yura came into class and made an announcement.

"I am no longer Kim Yura," he told his classmates. "I have changed my name to Kim Jong-Il. Call me by that name from now on."

The future leader's very name was a calculated composition. In it Yura had combined his mother's and father's first names, *Jong*-Suk and *Il*-Sung becoming *Jong-Il*, thereby directly linking him to both the Great Leader and the Mother of the Nation. Although few noticed it then, this was far more than just a Korean stage name. It was legitimacy.

Still, the new Kim Jong-Il cared as little about his studies as the old Yurei Ilsenovitch Kim had. What he cared about was movies.

The Central Film Distribution Center, which housed the government-owned film collection, became Kim Jong-Il's regular haunt. He spent full days and nights there, watching movie after movie. Jong-Il had never traveled much outside of North Korea's borders—only to Russia, and Manchuria during the Korean War—nor would he for the rest of his life, with the exception of a summer stay in Malta in the early 1970s, to learn English, at which he did poorly. In his life he had very few glimpses of real people and their daily lives, at home or abroad. For the young man who would become leader one day, with power over armies, commandos, nuclear warheads, and the lives of millions of people, the movies were his portal to the outside world. All he knew of it—of the Americas, of Africa, of Europe—came either from a government report or from a movie.

Jong-Il quickly exhausted the Film Distribution Center's catalog. He craved Western movies, most of which weren't distributed on the eastern side of the Iron Curtain, let alone in distant North Korea. There was no way to legally rent, purchase, or import them. Jong-Il took it upon himself to acquire the films by any means necessary, launching what was both his first film operation and his first illegal activity: he created a network to bootleg and smuggle them.

In the typically over-the-top style of an obsessive movie buff, he gave his "distribution" setup the dramatic name of Resource Operation No. 100. Under the supervision of First Deputy Foreign Minister Yi Jong-Mok—who could not disobey the Leader's son, but must have wondered why his time was being wasted setting up a film piracy outfit—North Korean embassies around the world, from Vienna to Macao, were fitted with professional copying and dubbing equipment. Local embassy staff borrowed 35mm projection copies of the newest films, allegedly for private screenings at the embassy, and without watching them—they were not permitted to—made copies. Every acquirable new release was obtained, from Hollywood movies to Japanese gangster epics, comedies, and soft-core erotica, so many of them that the embassies were overwhelmed and dedicated print facilities had to be built in Prague, Macao, and Guagzhou to handle the volume of film reels coming from embassies everywhere. The reels were then put in diplomatic pouches and shipped to Pyongyang, where they were translated and dubbed into Korean, the dubbing performed by professional actors of the government's film studio, and each final, exclusive copy was then sent on to Jong-Il, either at the Film Distribution Center or at his residence in Pyongyang. In all, the Pyongyang movie library staff swelled to about 250 full-time employees: actors, translators, subtitle writers, dubbing experts, printers, and archivists.

Resource Operation No. 100 remained in operation throughout Kim Jong-Il's life, and these first films became the basis of his gigantic personal film collection. Jong-Il obsessively watched every single one of them. His cinephilia was a concern to his father and his father's entourage. It seemed unhealthy. But increasingly Jong-Il perceived, behind all the stories, exotic settings, and beautiful people, the riveting potency of the moving pictures. They created a rare heightened focus as one sat cut off from the outside world in that dark room. Every image, every cut, every camera angle, every sound, every focus rack—every one of the filmmaker's *choices*—was a suggestion, the whole film a series of subtle suggestions subconsciously manipulating the viewer to a specific thought, feeling, or experience. The power they had on him, Jong-Il saw, was a power they would have on others, too. It was a power he wanted to wield.

Suddenly the younger Kim became active in the student arm of the Workers' Party, focusing on ideological training and propaganda. He started attending his father's cabinet meetings and party conferences, even if only as an observer. Before he finished university he did his compulsory military service, completing it in two months instead of the ten years legally required of every other North Korean male. He didn't need so long, propaganda literature explained, because "in the span of eight weeks Comrade Kim Jong-Il mastered the entirety of military tactics and guided the other students in learning real-time battle tactics and leadership skills," and the training camp he attended has since been turned into a historical shrine. The military training was a mere formality, a box that needed ticking on his revolutionary CV. All he took from it was a lifelong fondness for guns. He loved shooting rifles and pistols as soon as he was introduced to them, and had a personal shooting range built for himself, which he visited regularly for the next four decades. His shooting instructor, Ri Ho-Jun, went on to win the gold medal in 50m rifle prone shooting at the 1972 Munich Olympics, North Korea's first-ever Olympic gold medal, and later became Jong-Il's closest personal bodyguard.

Another important person entered Jong-Il's life around this time: his uncle, Kim Yong-Ju. Uncle Yong-Ju was eight years younger than his brother Il-Sung. "In the official Kim family mythology," writes DPRK expert Bradley Martin, "Yong-Ju is described as having spent his childhood in terror, fleeing search parties. Kim Il-Sung wrote in his memoirs that, while he himself battled Japanese troops, the Japanese authorities hunted for Yong-Ju as part of their attempts to pressure rebels. They distributed photographs of the youngster, Kim Il-Sung said, so 'my brother had to roam aimlessly, under a false name and by concealing his identity, about cities and villages all over the three provinces of Manchuria and even in China proper.'" Ever since then he had been a survivor. Yong-Ju grew up to study economics and philosophy at Moscow University and became a devoted Marxist. He was a smarter, more profound man than his elder brother. A stern-looking man with a high forehead and downturned mouth, his eyes narrow behind thin wire-rimmed eyeglasses, Yong-Ju was not especially fond of the shrill nationalism and overbearing narcissism Kim Il-Sung was starting to use as tools in consolidating his power, but he was loyal, devoted to the cause of the Workers' Party, and had become the head of the Central Committee, the main organ of government policy making. He had his brother's ear, and whenever talks were to be held abroad it was Uncle Yong-Ju that the Great Leader sent to represent him. He was North Korea's number two and widely accepted as the Leader's most likely successor. Now, either following his own instincts or at the request of his brother, he became Kim Jong-Il's guardian angel, protecting him from any negative consequences of his indiscretions and failings but also keeping him disciplined and making sure he fulfilled the minimum duties required of him. No one had ever had the courage to reprimand the Supreme Leader's son before. Every now and then, just often enough, when Jong-Il returned to the army camp after fobbing off training to watch foreign movies, his supervisors were waiting to punish him with a physical beating. The order to do so always came from Uncle Yong-Ju.

In May 1964, Jong-Il graduated from college, and his career in the leadership ranks of the Party, the career that had always been expected of him, began. His first post was as a member of the secretarial staff of the Central Committee, under Uncle Yong-Ju, who took him under his wing and taught him everything he knew about the Party's inner workings—how personnel was hired, promoted, and demoted; how every department worked and how it reported back to the Leader. Uncle Yong-Ju had a large brood of his own children and was looking after their interests too, making sure they all reached positions of importance within the Party. After a year his uncle moved Jong-Il to the Executive Department to learn about housing allotment and food rationing. Jong-Il didn't take to what was, essentially, the life of a civil servant, and did the work without much dedication. "He wasn't taken seriously," former Central Committee member Kim Duk-Hong said. "He was regarded as the black sheep of the family." Jong-Il's half brother Pyong-Il (born to Kim Il-Sung and his second wife, Jong-Il's despised stepmother) was much more promising: he spoke very good English, had served in the military, and looked and carried himself like his father. Jong-Il, on the other hand, seemed erratic and undisciplined, with rich tastes and unreasonable appetites but lacking in charisma. He seemed destined to live a life of idle, useless leisure.

In truth, Jong-Il was happy to be underestimated. He knew what his strengths were and was waiting for a way to put them to good use. Luckily, an opportunity to distinguish himself was coming—and along with it the one job he wanted most in the entire Party.

Purges are a regular part of life in a dictatorship's elite, feared and expected in equal measure, coming a few times every generation, like a medieval surgeon bleeding a patient to balance his humors and keep him in health.

The Kapsan purge, when it came, was the bloodiest in North Korea's history. The People's Republic had had an impressive fifteen years since the end of the so-called Liberation War. Bankrolled by the Soviet Union and by China, the country had rebuilt rapidly after the war and taken huge economic strides, attracting headlines worldwide as a model socialist state, a shining example that *communism could work*. The regime claimed proudly that all of its citizens now had roofs over their heads, reliable and regular food rations, and jobs to give them purpose; that every village was wired for electricity; that there was no crime, homelessness, or unemployment. By and large the regime was telling the truth. The system was Spartan, but, for a time, it worked.

Now there were disagreements about the next step to take. Vice Premier Pak Kum-Chol suggested demilitarizing, decentralizing, and investing the funds currently being funneled into ideological campaigns into skills training and innovation to create a generation of scientists and engineers who could move the republic forward. His followers, known as the Kapsan faction after a county in Ryanggang Province, attempted the production of a motion picture celebrating their leader. This was their mistake. North Korea was Kim Il-Sung's country and his alone. He did not share the spotlight. In the spring of 1967 Pak and his followers were charged with treason, flunkyism, and factionalism, and removed from their posts. Many of them were "sent to the mountains"—the euphemism North Koreans were beginning to use for being condemned to a labor camp—or executed. The purge became an excuse for a far-reaching attack on "revisionists." Books, including the works of Karl Marx, were burned on bonfires; Soviet songs and "unsuitable" traditional Korean tunes were banned; dozens of painters, writers, and artists were sent to penal colonies for work suddenly deemed "too Western." When the dust had settled, no one was left in North Korea who disagreed with or undermined the genius and omnipotence of Kim Il-Sung.

But there was still the problem of the Korea Film Studio, which had taken part in the failed Kapsan film project. Several of its leaders, who thought they had merely been doing their jobs by developing a complimentary picture about the vice premier, a Party hero, were now being accused of "anti-Party activity." In September 1967, Kim Il-Sung convened a special Politburo meeting at the studio. His son, who never missed an opportunity to go to the studio, went along. After all the studio executives had stood up and meekly confessed how they had failed the Party, it was Kim Il-Sung's turn to speak. He launched into a long, vituperative sermon, jabbing at the men with endless accusations and rhetorical questions. "Does anyone here," he growled, "actually have the courage to volunteer to guide this studio back in the right direction, in accordance with the Party's policies?"

Jong-Il was standing in the back of the room, watching. His voice, thin and almost feminine, rose unexpectedly behind everyone. Heads turned to look at him. "I will take on the responsibility," he said. "I'll try it."

The Great Leader must have smiled. Jong-Il had worked in the Central Committee and was familiar with its functioning, he was blood, and he had been an obsessive fan of the movies since he was seven years old. As far as Kim could tell, the boy had as good a background as anyone for the job. On the spot, Kim Jong-Il was promoted to Cultural Arts Director of the Propaganda and Agitation Department, in charge of movies, plays, and publishing.

He was twenty-five years old.

As soon as he took over, Jong-Il called a special meeting, to which he invited a few of the key filmmakers and actors. "All of us are comrades and fighters for the Party," he told them, "who share life and death with each other. . . . Nobody is more precious than comrades to a revolutionary fighter.

I shall believe in you, and you will have to believe in me, and we will work together." One by one he handed each of them official photographs of themselves, which he had duplicated from the studio's personnel files. When they looked down they saw that each photograph bore a handwritten note—"Let's work together forever," or "To our eternal comradeship, let's advance forever along the same road"—with, below, the date and Jong-Il's signature. Just weeks before, these men had been convinced their fates were sealed and that they would join the other victims of the Kapsan purge. Now the Leader's son stood in front of them and promised to stand by them if they returned the favor.

After a few token "subversive elements" had been dismissed, Jong-Il bestowed Party membership on all remaining film workers, at a time when Party membership was a highly prized social honor reserved for the elite. He improved the crews' food and lodging; built a dedicated department store for the film workers, where they could buy goods unavailable through their weekly rations; and provided a bus service between their homes and the studio so they wouldn't have to cycle or walk to work. He also showered them with gifts—"clothes, food, watches, record players, and television sets," an insider said—some of the items so lavish that the average North Korean could spend a whole lifetime without ever setting eyes on one of them. When a film worker died, Jong-Il made sure the Party paid for the funeral and that surviving family members were looked after, and had the most distinguished actors, directors, and screenwriters approved for burial in the cemetery reserved for Patriotic Martyrs, on a hill overlooking Pyongyang. "Comrade Kim Jong-Il loves and treasures especially film artists," a studio handbook said of him. "When he gets something good, he shares it with the film artists. And he immortalizes them while in life and even after their death."

When the workers had been retrained ideologically, Kim set out to retrain them artistically. He pulled past Soviet and North Korean films from his private collection and screened them with the staff, critiquing them and asking for suggestions about how the work could be improved. The Korea Film Studio hadn't been renovated since the war, so he expanded it to a ten-million-square-foot lot (by comparison, the MGM lot in Culver City, California, the largest back lot of Hollywood's golden age, was a mere 7.6

million square feet). He got rid of the old Soviet equipment from the 1950s, flying in the latest available cameras, lights, editing beds, and shooting rigs from Moscow and East Germany. He watched rushes of every film and gave his notes on them, his feeling of where a story was falling short, contributing what he called his "innate sense of the minute flow" of a picture. The young son of the Leader, by virtue of his wide-ranging film education, had insight that none of his underlings could possibly have. His dedication impressed his subordinates. The Korea Film Studio had so far been run by Party politicians, never by someone who really loved the movies—or knew anything about how they were made. Jong-Il, on the other hand, virtually moved into the studio, spending long hours on the premises day after day.

Two things are to be expected of a great movie impresario, and Kim Jong-Il made sure to do both his very first year in charge of the studio. First, he made an epic, defining film, one that official histories would dub his first "Immortal Classic" and come to represent his filmmaking style. *Sea of Blood* was based on an operetta allegedly written by Kim Il-Sung during his guerrilla days, and tells the story of a 1930s Manchurian family standing up to Japanese oppression. It features all the elements that would become Jong-Il's trademarks: a popular theme song, a strong female lead (in this case, the family's mother, who joins the Communist resistance and starts smuggling explosives for them), stock foreign villains, an undercurrent of racial nationalism, and a curious mix of violence and schmaltz. North Korean films didn't have credits, fostering the illusion that they were entirely collective works, but *Sea of Blood* was produced by Kim and directed by Choe Ik-Gyu, the studio's previous head. Arguably the single North Korean most knowledgeable about film, other than Kim, Choe had studied in the Soviet Union in the early days of the North Korean film industry, had studied Russian language and literature at Pyongyang University, and by 1956 was running the Korea Film Studio, at the age of twenty-two. He was the one man in North Korea whose experience Jong-Il was keen to learn from. *Sea of Blood* was filmmaking on a grand, epic scale, the equivalent of a modern blockbuster tentpole production. North Korean audiences were surprised and delighted by it, and suddenly Kim Jong-Il, the Leader's son and artistic prodigy, was the talk of Pyongyang.

Next Jong-Il did the other thing all good old-fashioned film showmen did: he fell in love with one of his actresses.

Sung Hye-Rim was one of the most famous leading ladies in North Korea. She looked striking, with a wide face, thick eyebrows, and strong chin, her skin pale and bright. She was kind and introverted. She had studied at the Pyongyang Movie College in the fifties, dropping out at eighteen to have a daughter before reenrolling and graduating. She had married young to Lee Pyong, the son of the head of the Korean Writers' Association, and the marriage was not happy.

She was five years older than Jong-Il, and he was smitten from the instant he met her. On his regular visits to film sets he always made sure to see her. Hye-Rim's affection for the Leader's son was less immediate, but she was moved by his stories of his motherless childhood and felt a kinship with his love for the arts, and Jong-Il, unlike her husband, knew how to be charming and treat her well. Hye-Rim completed the movie she was filming, quit acting, and left her husband and child to move in with Kim.

Their relationship became, out of necessity, the best-kept secret in North Korea. Jong-Il knew from the start that he could never marry Hye-Rim, because she was already married with a child but also because she was older than him, a balance of ages that was still severely frowned upon in Korean society, especially for the Leader's son, who would be expected to embody Korean virtues. He had to keep the affair a secret from the public and from his father, who was sure to put an end to it. Still, the relationship managed to be romantic and exciting. Jong-Il had Hye-Rim accepted into the Party and bestowed on her the title of Distinguished Actress, reserved for performers whose work has especially served the revolution. He flew her to international film festivals, giving her an international platform no other North Korean actress had yet received, and when she returned he spent all his free time with her, picking her up from the studio in one of his cars (by now he owned a Mercedes 600, two Mercedes 450s, several Cadillacs, and a Rolls-Royce) and at least once flying her to a location by private helicopter. At night they stayed together in one of Kim Il-Sung's many empty villas. At first, Hye-Rim enjoyed being in a discreet relationship, away from gossip and social pressure. She didn't foresee that the relationship would remain hidden for its full term.

It was still dark and cool outside when Hye-Rim's sister, Hae-Rang, was woken by the stubborn honking of a car outside her bedroom window. The noise echoed between the walls. Only the wealthiest among the elite *owned* a car. Who could possibly be parked outside now, making a scene like this?

As the honking grew more insistent she jumped out of bed and ran to the door. A luxury Mercedes was parked outside, Kim Jong-Il standing beside it. He asked her to get in the back with him so they could talk privately. She climbed in, quietly shutting the door behind her. "My relationship with your sister," he began, "may have become more complicated." Hye-Rim was about to give birth to a son. Under no circumstances could Kim Il-Sung find out about it.

6

Fathers and Sons

Kim Jong-Il's son, Jong-Nam, was playing in his huge playroom. Choosing what toy to play with was always a bit of a challenge; the playroom was restocked every year with new toys flown in from overseas, so many it would take a whole day to just walk around the room touching every one of them, but Jong-Nam was rarely allowed to leave the house, so he had gotten used to it. His minders were sitting in the corner, keeping a distracted eye on him. As Jong-Nam unconsciously moved closer to them, he saw one of them rub his cheek and complain that he needed a filling, but that the state dentist didn't have enough gold to fit one, so he'd had to wait. To Jong-Nam, this sounded like a very peculiar problem to have. He put his toy down and ran to his personal safe, spun the dial to unlock it, and took out a solid gold bar. His babysitter had jumped up and followed him. Jong-Nam handed the bar to him, a smile on his face, and asked, "Maybe the dentist can make a filling out of this?"

The man peered inside the opened safe. He spotted several more such gold bars, stacks of banknotes in various foreign currencies, and, most disturbing of all, what looked like the boy's very own handgun.

Kim Jong-Nam was, his aunt tells us, "the biggest secret in North Korea." When Hye-Rim checked into the maternity ward in May 1971, Kim Jong-Il had to stay hidden, waiting outside the hospital in his car. After the baby was born, Hye-Rim got out of bed, walked over to the light switch, and indicated the birth of the child and its sex by flicking the room's light on and off in a prearranged sequence. Jong-Il communicated his understanding by flashing his car's lights. He waited until Hye-Rim turned the lights off and went to sleep and, still unable to see his newborn son, drove through the nighttime streets of Pyongyang, honking his horn and shouting to himself, "It's a boy! It's a boy!"

Jong-Il and Hye-Rim had just recently moved into a sprawling compound resort on the outskirts of Pyongyang, which made avoiding Kim Il-Sung's gaze much easier. Jong-Il was already relying on his own channels of power, networks of certain Party and embassy staff who, either out of fear or because they were from Jong-Il's generation and had grown up with him, were loyal to him rather than to his father. Protected by members of Jong-Il's new personal bodyguard corps, all handpicked by the younger Kim without the Leader's input or consultation, the new family lived in luxury. Jong-Il, in particular, doted on his son. The room had a thousand-square-foot playroom for Jong-Nam, and on his birthday embassy staff in Hong Kong, Tokyo, Berlin, and Geneva sent crates full of the latest toys to fill it. Jong-Nam couldn't attend school or go out with other children, lest he give away the secret of his illegitimacy and of his parents' relationship, so he was tutored at home and only occasionally allowed out into the city, in a chauffeur-driven Mercedes he was not allowed to exit. He pressed his nose against the glass and looked out, wondering what the lives *out there* were like.

His son's seclusion did mean that Jong-Il could spend a lot of time with him. When he worked late into the night, eating dinner at his desk, it became habitual for Jong-Nam to join him; Jong-Il would pick the boy up and sit him on the desktop next to his papers. He read Jong-Nam books before bed—his favorite was *Anne of Green Gables*—and if the boy couldn't sleep, Jong-Il would patiently walk up and down the hallways with him on his back, the rhythm gently lulling him to sleep.

Maybe Jong-Il didn't realize he was repeating the same dysfunctional family environment that had been applied to him growing up, or maybe he thought necessity made it unavoidable. In any case, Jong-Nam grew up cheerful and optimistic, but like his father, the isolation also made him moody and demanding. It didn't help that Jong-Il spoiled the child. When a very young Jong-Nam commented on how much he liked his father's Cadillac, Jong-Il bought him his own. When he told his father how exciting it was to watch him shoot guns, Jong-Il started giving the boy guns as presents, including a special pistol from Belgium that inspired a tantrum when it was delayed in transit. When Jong-Nam wished that he could see his favorite South Korean comedian perform live rather than on television, Jong-Il tried to have the comedian abducted; when that failed he sent his men on a nationwide search for a lookalike, trained him to mimic the comic, then had him perform for Jong-Nam instead. The boy immediately recognized the man as a fake and stormed out in a tantrum. The impostor, having seen too much for his own good, was shipped off to an unknown fate.

When Jong-Nam was five, Hye-Rim's sister, Hae-Rang, moved in with the Kims, at Jong-Il's request, to help look after the child. Ever since the boy's birth, Hye-Rim, locked away inside the residence compound, had suffered from insomnia and depression, nervous disorders that would cling to her for the rest of her life. A widow, Hae-Rang brought her two children, who were older than Jong-Nam, with her. The whole family lived in what she called a "luxury prison" for the next two decades. They were forbidden to speak of the family outside of the villa. One friend of Hye-Rim's, a dancer called Kim Young-Soon who had performed for the Great Leader, spoke of her friend's relationship with Kim Jong-Il publicly just once. She was arrested with no warning and, without a trial, was sent to the notorious Yoduk prison camp to do hard labor for nine years. When she was finally released, after ten years of imprisonment, her guard's parting words were "Sung Hye-Rim was never Kim Jong-Il's concubine. They never had a child. These are all fabrications, nothing but lies. Talk about it again and you will find no mercy." Kim Young-Soon's parents and two sons died in the camp alongside her.

Hae-Rang, in spite of herself, liked Kim Jong-Il. "He has a talent for making people feel at ease when he wants to," she said. He would crack jokes, often at his own expense. "He is a cultured man and respects knowledge. He enjoys beauty. I'd see his face relax comfortably when he saw something humble and unpretentious. On the other hand, if he saw something shabby and gaudy, he'd yell unmercifully." When displeased, he was volatile and violent. "When he is happy, he can treat you really, really, really well. But when he's angry he can make every window in the house shake." He had screaming and throwing fits when frustrated. Hae-Rang, like others, blamed his upbringing. "He grew up on his own in a place surrounded by unlimited power and luxury without interference from anyone, motherly love and care. . . . Unlimited power, lack of education, the absence of a mother, and that totalitarian society produced his personality. . . . Had he grown up in a poor home," she speculated, "he would have been an artist."

He was hard to live with. "The contradictions in his personality can be confusing and incomprehensible," Hae-Rang said. Words she used to describe him include "romantic" but also "extreme," "harsh" and "very dangerous."

"There are as many interpretations of [Kim Jong-Il's] personality as there are witnesses," agrees North Korea expert John Cha. "People who have come in close contact with him have completely different views of him." Jong-Il's longtime sushi chef, Kenji Fujimoto, described him as "a warm person with many hobbies, [who] always wears a smile," but "when something goes wrong, he yells and screams . . . like a madman." His bodyguard Lee Young-Kuk, at first in awe of Kim, eventually called him "extremely cruel," "impatient and sly. . . . Inside, he is always scheming, making secret plans. And he is very clever. . . . There are two sides to him, always." Jong-Il made snap decisions regarding the people who worked for him, hiring, dismissing, or punishing them on a whim. He utterly despised liars, in spite of being one himself. One Party member remembers the young Kim Jong-Il giving his staff a lecture praising Ernst Kaltenbrunner, head of the Gestapo and one of the heads of the SS during World War II, for his "simple and accurate" reports to Hitler. When disagreed with, he threw tantrums; Lee, the former bodyguard, says one of Jong-Il's mottos was "If the enemy gives you a problem, yell louder than him, and he will back down." He was quick-tempered, narrow-minded, jealous, insecure, and often cruel.

He was also very, very careful. It was around this time that he had decided he was going to be the one to succeed his father and take over the running of North Korea, and his private life was his weakness, his fragile corridor. The way to the leadership, Jong-Il had found, was simple: in a country where life depended on pleasing Kim Il-Sung, he would have to be the one to please Kim Il-Sung the most. Soon, he would accomplish this through his greatest passion, about to become his most effective weapon: film.

7
Inside the Pyongyang Picture Show

Kim Jong-Il's film world was, almost without a doubt, one of the world's most surreal and, on a national policy scale, influential.

Cinema's purpose in North Korea had always been to inculcate the right thinking into the people. Unlike Soviet cinema, which was seen as a tool to "enlighten" the masses, North Korean cinema did not seek to educate, inform, or lift the people's knowledge of historical class struggles or the importance of equality and collective ownership. The films, especially under Kim Jong-Il, existed to drill the regime's core principles into the populace: that the Supreme Leader Kim Il-Sung was the greatest man who had ever lived; that loyalty to him and to the national "family" was a greater virtue than any other; and that the Korean people were a purer race, more virtuous and valuable, than any other. Only a Korean could have been the Supreme Leader, the Sun of Humanity, and since the Supreme Leader was the most Korean of Koreans, anything less than blind obedience to him made you a traitor to your nation, your race, your very blood. Follow him, however, and the Workers' Paradise becomes reality.

In the first few years following the DPRK's founding in 1948, Korean society was rural and malleable. Ideology would reach the people not through books or debates in cafés, but on a projection screen. Film was cheap and easy to control, with the exact same print of the exact same film being shown everywhere during the same release window. It was popular, a novelty, entertainment as much as it was art or education. The people were enthusiastic about it and unlikely to notice they were being fed propaganda—or if they did, at least they were likely to enjoy the experience. Where books and newspapers were read privately, film viewing was a public, collective experience, perfect for a socialist society looking to inculcate a collective consciousness in its people. And where a book was written by one person, films were a collaborative endeavor, less likely to go off-message and, in North Korea at least, impossible to make and distribute without state approval. The complex logistics of making films meant they could be controlled by the state as no other art form could.

But when, following the end of the Korean War in 1953, Kim Il-Sung had rid himself of all rivals, he had also sent home all possible foreign influencers in government, including in culture and the arts. Left to its own devices, isolated from innovations elsewhere in the world, and limited by the needs of propaganda, North Korean film spent fifteen years churning out the same tedious stories of selfless factory workers and exemplary farm girls.

With Jong-Il in charge, technical quality increased dramatically. North Korean filmmakers knew nothing of the state of cinema outside their borders, but Jong-Il had seen every new release of the last decade. The year he took over at the North Korean studios, 1968, was the year of *2001: A Space Odyssey, Rosemary's Baby,* and *Once Upon a Time in the West;* the world's biggest stars were Clint Eastwood and Steve McQueen. The Dear Leader, as the Party had lately started encouraging the people to call the Premier's son, spared no expense in bringing his industry up to speed—flying in equipment, refurbishing the film studios, informing his crews of modern styles even if he wouldn't, or couldn't, let them watch foreign films for themselves.

But while Jong-Il had both unlimited money and wide-ranging knowledge as a film viewer, he had absolutely no practical experience of filmmaking itself. Choe Ik-Gyu, the studio's former head, did, and he became Jong-Il's right-hand man and closest collaborator. Seven years older than Kim and taller, Choe was a thin man with a high forehead, receding hairline, flat nose, and prominent Adam's apple. Big glasses, lightly tinted a smoky yellow, and a serious, doglike facial expression gave him the faint look of a Sean Connery–era Bond villain. He wouldn't have looked out of place carrying a briefcase full of stolen state secrets in *You Only Live Twice*. He became Kim's closest creative partner; he has even been described as Kim's "film tutor." Kim had grown up on a gluttonous and unrestricted diet of worldwide film. Choe had a formal arts education and had learned filmmaking under the rigorous Stalinist Soviet model. They complemented each other perfectly. Until Kim Jong-Il's death Choe could be seen in official pictures, standing close behind his leader, applauding him along with everyone else.

Kim and Choe's first collaborations—Jong-Il as producer and supervisor, Choe as director—were huge successes with audiences and became so important in North Korean cinema history that they are known in the country as the Immortal Classics, beginning with the epic *Sea of Blood* and culminating in the 1972 drama *The Flower Girl*. *The Flower Girl* was Jong-Il's baby: he helped write the script, cast the unknown teenage girl who played the film's lead, supervised its editing, and was on set almost every day supervising filming and deciding on shots and staging. The film, again based on a play allegedly written by Kim Il-Sung while a Japanese prisoner in 1930, tells the story of Cot-Bun, a girl from a rural village during the Japanese occupation who sells flowers to help support her family. Her father is dead, her mother ill and toiling day and night in the employ of a tyrannical landlord, her brother in a Japanese jail, her sister blind after having had boiling water thrown in her face by the landlord's wife. The "plot" is a succession of cruel turns of fate dealt to Cot-Bun and her family until, just as she is finally about to give up, she is rescued by her liberated brother and Kim Il-Sung's Korean Liberation Army. The Koreans are all exemplary, bound by solidarity and compassion, the Japanese and their collaborators sneering and sadistic. Over and over the characters long for "someone precious, like in the old tales," a messiah—Kim Il-Sung.

The importance of *The Flower Girl* in North Korean cultural history is almost impossible to exaggerate. The film was a gigantic popular success, both in North Korea and in China, the first time a North Korean film found a large audience abroad. It won a special prize at the Karlovy Vary International Film Festival in Czechoslovakia, the first international prize for a North Korean film (and, until the early 1980s, the only one). Its star, Hong Yong-Hee, was so iconic that her face was plastered on murals across

Pyongyang and on the North Korean one-won banknote. In 2009, when the Chinese premier Wen Jiabao visited Pyongyang, it was Hong Yong-Hee who greeted his plane. The celebrated Chinese author Tie Ning describes the experience of seeing *The Flower Girl* in her novel *How Long Is Forever?*: "A North Korean movie named *The Flower Girl* was playing at theaters in major cities across the country. This movie practically drowned everyone in tears. . . . Sitting in front of me was an adult crying so hard that he hit his spine painfully against the back of the seat. He became hysterical and made a lot of noise, but no one complained because everyone else was too busy crying."

The Flower Girl also cemented Choe Ik-Gyu's place as Jong-Il's most trusted creative collaborator. From now on Jong-Il entrusted Choe not just with films, but with the creation of the state's highest-profile public events, such as Kim Il-Sung's birthday celebrations and Day of Liberation marches. Choe would be instrumental in creating the awe-inspiring, huge-scale displays of synchronized unity that developed into the famous Mass Games. The modern North Korean state, which is a production, a display performance of its own, owes as much to Choe Ik-Gyu's taste and talents as it does to Kim Jong-Il.

A year after *The Flower Girl* was released Jong-Il published *On the Art of the Cinema*, a treatise based on speeches he had given his directors and screenwriters over the previous five years. ("Marx worked for four decades to complete *Capital*," the official Party news organ informed the People. "By contrast, it only took Comrade Kim Jong-Il two to three years to write *On the Art of the Cinema*.") The book summed up his filmmaking philosophy and producing policies. He dismissed the idea that, to be masterpieces, films had to be big epics "dealing with immense historical facts." Instead he instructed that "a masterwork should be monumental not in size but in content" and encouraged his writers and directors to favor character over plot, emphasizing "the different fates and psychology of persons . . . rather than the events themselves." He pushed for realism ("officials and creators should always remember that truth is the lifeblood of an artwork and that especially films, a visual art, should describe life truthfully in every detail") while also asking for emotions and events to be heightened to a histrionic, melodramatic pitch. He suggested films be based on everyday stories of the sterling members of the People, or even on popular songs (forty years after Arthur Freed had based *Singin' in the Rain* on a popular tune). More important than any of that, however, Kim's greatest contribution as a critical thinker—the one North Korean schoolchildren were taught to associate with how he advanced culture and the arts—was what he called the "seed." The seed was a film's "main nucleus and ideological kernel . . . as a farmer selects and sows a good seed and tends it well to reap good fruit, so the seed of a film should be chosen correctly and its depiction deepened on that basis to produce an excellent work." The seed was the propagandistic message the film was designed to promote and inculcate in the audience, and which every scene, line of dialogue, and aspect of performance should serve. Jong-Il used the term almost constantly, from conception to distribution. The Hollywood producer Samuel Goldwyn supposedly stated that his movies didn't have an agenda—"just write me a good comedy," he said; "if you want to send a message, use Western Union"—but Kim Jong-Il could not have felt more differently. His message, sent in every single film, was simple: Kim Il-Sung—the Great Leader, the Outstanding Marshal, the Sun of Korea—was the liberator and protector of the People; the People could not exist without him; there was no higher virtue than obeying and serving him like a father, and disagreeing with him made you, deeply and insidiously, un-Korean. Everything from the choice of behind-the-camera talent to the selection and writing of stories was determined by how it served the myth of Kim Il-Sung. Where, in the past, a character might have done his heroic deeds "for the Party," now the same character's dialogue was rewritten so that he had done it "for the Leader." Virtually all films were set between 1920 and 1953, so that they could repeatedly show a world blanketed in darkness and suffering—until Kim's men, like the cavalry in a western, rode in to the rescue. Emphasizing the collective good was paramount, and stories of individual fulfillment and heroics, so common in the West, were banned.

Jong-Il's duty as the head of the film studio, as he saw it, was not just to make better movies. His creative work was his way into his father's heart and his trust: he would operate, essentially, as if he were Kim Il-Sung's publicity guru. On the silver screen the People's Republic won the war over and over again. Kim Il-Sung, the films said, had saved the nation—was still saving the nation every single day.

Kim Il-Sung loved the films his son made for him. Their depiction of him as a saint and hero fed his ego. The partisans who had fought alongside him, and who now wielded serious influence inside the Workers' Party, ate them up as well.

The author Bradley Martin tells the story of how he once asked a North Korean official what the Party would do after the death of President Kim Il-Sung. The official replied, "*If* he dies—erm, I mean, when he dies—we'll find another leader."

What would happen after he died had actually been on Kim Il-Sung's mind for some time. He had watched as Khrushchev and Brezhnev had turned their backs on Stalin, how Deng Xiaoping and Hua Guofeng were minimizing Maoist principles and opening China to free-market dynamics. Stalinists were being removed from power in Poland; a popular revolution had taken Hungary by storm in 1956; Václav Havel was fostering dissent in Czechoslovakia. Kim Il-Sung was concerned with what would happen in North Korea after he had passed away. The only way to preserve the Workers' Paradise, he saw, was to appoint a successor and consolidate that person's power before his own death. He had to choose someone close and loyal—not just so that they would remain true to his aims and ambitions, but also so that they would not be tempted to hurry their own coronation by getting rid of him before his time.

A blood relative seemed safest. That left only three serious candidates: his younger brother, Kim Yong-Ju, and his own sons, Kim Jong-Il and Kim Pyong-Il. Uncle Yong-Ju was more experienced and better educated, had already been working at the top level of the Party for three decades, and had actually been a part of the fight against the Japanese. Pyong-Il was young, driven, and took after his father. It was Jong-Il, however, who understood his father best of the three. He saw that the very traits Uncle Yong-Ju deplored in Il-Sung—his ego, his narcissism, his desire to be seen as Korea's modern-day emperor and messiah—were the very things to feed to receive his father's favor. The Sun of Korea, as Kim liked to be known, had eliminated rivals and purged entire families and political factions to hold on to power. He had had novels and multiple-volume biographies written about himself to amend history in his favor. He didn't just want to be the leader of the nation: he wanted to *be* the nation. Jong-Il understood that his father would not choose as his successor the man who promised to be best for North Korea or for the people. His father would choose the man who promised to be best for Kim Il-Sung, even after Kim Il-Sung himself was dead. Like all shrewd politicians, what Kim Il-Sung cared about was the future as much as the present: he cared about legacy.

His son set out to ensure it for him. Along with cinematically idolizing and deifying his father, he would prove that no one else was more devoted to Il-Sung. In a country where Confucian values still held powerful sway and where filial loyalty was everything, this would become Jong-Il's public persona, his brand. The good son. The worshipful son. The humble son, who would set an example for the people by loving the father and never daring to question him. Though Jong-Il was ruthless in his quest for power, his most remarkable trick was that he managed to do it while retaining a reputation as someone who was not especially keen on power anyway. "He was jealous and cunning," Hwang Jang-Yop, one of Kim Il-Sung's close advisers, said. "I could see that he craved power. . . . He has always organized everything in secret and executed his plan in secret. That is his specialty." He stayed in the background, portraying himself as respectful, artistic, and devoted. When foreign dignitaries visited, Jong-Il always hung back, letting his father take center stage, only sending fruit baskets to the guests' rooms along with a note to express his best wishes. He never spoke in public. All the while, Hwang said, "he singled out people near Kim Il-Sung. Arguing that these people were not loyal and citing doubts about their ideology and competency, he would relentlessly attack and remove them," replacing them with close allies of his own.

Jong-Il's first recourse was rarely violence. He liked to plant recording devices in people's offices and homes, learn what they liked (a certain foreign car, a kind of brandy, maybe a preferred ethnicity of prostitute), and then try to buy them. If that didn't work, the same information could be used for blackmail. Only when pushed, or insulted, did Jong-Il resort to violence. In those early days, when he was still widely underestimated, it happened often. Vice Prime Minister Nam-Il was crushed to death by a passing truck in a country with virtually no cars, his death mentioned only briefly in the back pages of the official Party newspaper, *Rodong Sinmun,* in spite of his having been a national hero. Former Vice President Kim Tong-Kyu was snatched out of the blue and sent to a prison camp, without being told his crime, and died there. He was joined by several other men, mostly army generals and Party dignitaries, charged with "gross incompetence" and "factionalism." The guilty men all happened to have been part of Uncle Yong-Ju's inner circle.

In September 1973, the Party Central Committee had convened for an emergency meeting at the behest of Kim Il-Sung, and elected his son Kim Jong-Il to membership of the Politburo. In the same meeting Jong-Il was named the new Party secretary for organization and guidance, replacing the outgoing secretary, his uncle Kim Yong-Ju. Uncle Yong-Ju was made vice premier, an honorary post in a country where honorary posts are considered "the mark of a failed life." He spent the next twenty years under house arrest.

Around the same time Jong-Il introduced his father to two pretty young things from his performance troupe. He knew his father's taste. Jong-Il's aging, despised stepmother found herself isolated and out of influence, unsure what, exactly, had caused her fall from grace. Her son, Kim Pyong-Il, was sent into exile, in a series of postings to Yugoslavia, Bulgaria, and Finland. The whispers in Pyongyang were that Jong-Il's wiretaps in his half brother's office had turned up conversations in which Pyong-Il had openly been talking about replacing his father, and all Jong-Il had had to do was to deliver the recordings to the Great Leader. And just like that, in the race to become the new leader, Kim Jong-Il was the last man standing. Skeptical key officials still had to be won over, possible hidden opponents rooted out and eliminated. A very, very long game still had to be played, for twenty years would pass between now and his official assumption following Kim Il-Sung's death, twenty years during which, if he let his guard down, his own life would be on the line. "He's on a speeding train," Hye-Rin's sister, Hae-Rang, said. "Any move to stop it or get off, and it will crash."

The North Korean film industry, citizens were told, was fast becoming the most advanced in the world, with Jong-Il as its blazing torch, lighting a creative path never walked before. In fact, the Korea Film Studio was home to the most absurd, wasteful practices anywhere. Charles Jenkins, a former United States soldier who defected to North Korea in 1965 and lived there until 2004, was one of the people given a glimpse into Kim Jong-Il's surreal movie world. Jenkins, one of four U.S. defectors residing in North Korea in the 1970s, was shuffled from job to job by his Korean guards, who seemed unsure of how best to use their Western "guests." One of the U.S. defectors' jobs had been to transcribe random English-language audiotapes, word for word, which were then translated into Korean by a Pyongyang interpreter. There was no image, just sound, and the Americans received only a few minutes at a time, to hide from them exactly what they were listening to. But one day Jenkins recognized the dialogue from a Walt Disney movie and realized he and the others were part of the team creating subtitles of foreign movies. Jenkins transcribed several dozen movies which he occasionally identified—*Kramer vs. Kramer* and *Mary Poppins* were two that he knew—but most of which he never learned the titles of. The films were being prepared for Kim Jong-Il, most likely as part of Resource Operation No. 100, the film bootlegging operation he had begun when still a student.

In the late 1970s Jenkins and the other defectors were again enlisted to aid Jong-Il's cinematic endeavors, this time on camera. Until now, Westerners had been played by North Koreans in caked white makeup and wigs, speaking Korean with an odd, made-up accent that was meant to pass for American, British, or Continental European. Now Kim had at his disposal four actual Americans to play his pantomime villains and profiteers. One day Jenkins's live-in guard came to tell him that he had been "cast" in his first movie role, an epic multipart saga called *Unknown Heroes,* playing "the evil Dr. Kelton, a U.S. warmonger and capitalist based in South Korea whose goal in life was to keep the war going to benefit American arms manufacturers." Jenkins's head was shaved and his face covered in heavy makeup. He shot his part and was returned to his residence. Since no American names could appear on a DPRK motion picture, Jenkins was given the stage name Min Hyung-Chun.

Jenkins was called upon again numerous times throughout the years, until as late as 2000, to play different roles in North Korean movies and television shows. There was such a shortage of foreign faces that the families of diplomats and visiting businessmen were drafted when possible, too, a limited stock of ill-fitting uniforms, wigs, and detachable facial hair mixed and matched on them so that they could play as many villainous parts as possible. Jenkins was eventually given a medal for his creative work. "You had to appear in two installments of *Unknown Heroes* to get a medal," he recalled.

Even he, who had no previous film experience, could see the North Korean film industry was "a joke" when he first got involved in it. "They didn't bring any common sense to planning the filming. For example, they would often film the scenes in the order that they appeared in the script rather than in the order that made shooting more efficient. If, say, there was a scene at Claus's office, then a scene at my office, and then a third scene at Claus's office, they would film it in that order, breaking down Claus's office and rebuilding it after filming my scene rather than just filming both of Claus's scenes in a row and then filming mine. . . . I actually think that even the North Koreans couldn't have been that stupid. I suspect part of the reason they filmed it that way was because they were often writing the story as they went, all the way up to the day of shooting." Synchronized sound was still rudimentary in Pyongyang, fifty years after the first Hollywood talkie, so dialogue was often badly dubbed in postproduction. The most popular actors regularly disappeared from screens from one day to the next: declared guilty of some obscure offense, they were never seen publicly again; their faces were cut out of old films, rendering the films unintelligible.

The propaganda got in the way of good storytelling, too. Jong-Il had decreed a set of peculiar visual codes: South Korea and Japan, if shown, always had to be shown in rain, never sunshine, and preferably at night. It is, of course, always sunny in the Workers' Paradise. American characters were not allowed to look normal and must have one or several over-the-top physical features—a limp, perhaps, or muttonchop facial hair. The Supreme Leader—with the exception of a film biography of him, made in 1982—was never shown, only spoken of. The heroes were always young, plump, rosy-cheeked girls or young, strapping men. Because all films were shot on the Korea Film Studio back lot, which consisted of one stock South Korean street, one stock "colonial days" street, and one stock "Japanese city" street, every single scene set abroad or in a certain time period seems to take place on exactly the same street of the same city—whether, for instance, the film calls for Seoul in 1975 or a small South Korean village in 1949. And because Kim's crews had a limited stock of equipment to work with, the movies all had an identical film grammar: flat lighting, no zooms, specific shot sizes matching specific emotions, and specific story beats across every picture, regardless of genre.

North Korean audiences, who knew no better, ate the films up. Cinema going was compulsory. If there was no cinema in your town, the local factory or Party office would be turned into one for a new film's release, and every adult and child was required to attend a showing as well as a post-viewing "criticism session" afterward to ensure they had correctly absorbed the film's key message.

By the 1970s, Kim Il-Sung's regime was demonstrating aspirations to global importance. His diplomats were forging ties with left-wing governments and socialist parties in Europe, and consular "missionaries" were being sent to countries throughout Africa, the Middle East, and the Caribbean to preach the cult of Kim Il-Sung. In culture, too, efforts were being made to improve North Korea's international standing. Kim Il-Sung's works were translated into a dozen languages and leather-bound copies shipped abroad, and Pyongyang's circuses and opera troupes were touring China and Eastern Europe with their most impressive shows, the stage version of *Sea of Blood* among them.

These initiatives met with varying degrees of success. Embarrassingly for

Jong-Il and his acolyte Choe Ik-Gyu, however, the failings of North Korean film were never more evident than when the movies were sent abroad. At a time when the United States was giving us *The Godfather, Star Wars,* and *Jaws,* and Asian cinema was exporting stars like Bruce Lee and Amitabh Bachcan, North Korea was stuck in a time warp. Domestic audiences might have swallowed everything they saw on film as fact, but the few foreigners who saw local films laughed at their simplicity and cringed at their tediousness.

For Jong-Il, this was a serious and important failure. He had improved his nation's cinema, and he had made sure it contributed to the regime's control over the people. But south of the thirty-eighth parallel, Park Chung-Hee's government had turned South Korea into an export country. South Korean products, from textiles to electronics, were everywhere in Asia, and Seoul's prestige had grown accordingly. South Korean films and music, too, were beginning to receive international attention, scholarship, and respect. Kim Jong-Il, who was responsible for the entirety of North Korea's cultural output, all of it state controlled, was falling dangerously behind.

It was Akira Kurosawa who changed Shin Sang-Ok and Choi Eun-Hee's life—indirectly, unwittingly, and twenty-eight years before the fact.

After the humiliation and isolation of World War II, Japan had made it a policy goal to establish itself as a "leading cultural country," using the arts to improve its image and raise its prestige abroad. Cinema was selected as the best cultural shop window. One of the ways the Japanese government intended to establish its cinematic prowess was by winning awards—and, at the time, the major European film festival awards (Cannes, Berlin, Venice) were as prestigious as it got. But, half a decade after the end of the war, not only had Japan failed to win a prize, it was putting itself in embarrassing situations trying to do so. In 1951 the Cannes Film Festival sent an invitation for Japan to enter a feature in that year's competition, only for the Motion Picture Association of Japan to realize that the one production it felt suitable had ripped off a novel by French writer Romain Rolland, something French cinephiles on the Riviera were sure to notice and, with their adoration for auteurs, equally sure to get up in arms about. A short film was humiliatingly submitted instead. Some weeks later the Venice Film Festival came along with an invitation for a Japanese submission. This time the Motion Picture Association had no problem submitting the Rolland-based film—only to have to pull it again when it came to light that Toho, the film's producer, was so broke it couldn't afford to make a 35mm print with Italian subtitles. The Japanese were about to regretfully turn down their second opportunity in two weeks, likely ruining any chances of being invited again in the future, when, unexpectedly, a little-known Italian lady by the name of Giuliana Stramigioli, head of an Italian film company's operations in Japan, called in to suggest a small independent film she had recently seen, the "strangeness" of which she had liked. The film was *Rashomon,* directed by Akira Kurosawa.

Rashomon had almost not been made. It was considered so offbeat and weird that Kurosawa's usual employer, the Toyoko Company, bound to make any script the director brought to them while under contract, had fired the filmmaker rather than embarrass itself by paying for it. It took another producer, Masaichi Nagata, to get *Rashomon* made, almost by accident. Nagata, a businessman who was best known for his cheap, unoriginal, but wildly successful genre pictures, nonetheless had a fascination with prestigious artists and a longing to be associated with them. When Kurosawa became available Nagata offered him a distribution and production contract that allowed him to make any film he chose. Kurosawa chose *Rashomon*. When *Rashomon* was explained to Nagata he refused to make it and tried to break the contract, only giving in because of Kurosawa's stubborn insistence.

Now, with the film just completed, here came Signora Stramigioli, suggesting it should represent Japan in Venice. Nagata was horrified. He was sure the film would be a humiliating failure. But Stramigioli seemed sure, and in the 1950s a foreigner's opinion held quite a lot of weight, so *Rashomon* headed to Venice—and won the Grand Jury Prize. The win caused national jubilation and kicked off a string of Japanese victories at prestigious film festivals, including awards at Cannes, Venice, and Berlin in the following two years. In 1954, having learned his lesson, Nagata sent another one of his films, Teinosuke Kinugasa's *Gate of Hell,* to Cannes, where it won the Grand Jury Prize on its way to winning two Academy Awards, including

Best Foreign Language Film. The Japanese people started to take film festivals seriously, some critics even beginning to compare them to the Olympic Games and exhorting Japanese filmmakers to enter and win each and every one of them for the glory of the motherland. If a film was sent to Cannes or Venice and failed to win a prize, the filmmakers returned home to issue groveling public apologies and pen articles with titles like "What I Learned at Cannes About Producing Prizewinners."

Following *Rashomon*'s win, the world had taken notice of Japanese cinema. By the 1970s, when Kim Jong-Il was leading his country's studios, Akira Kurosawa was working for 20th Century–Fox, and up-and-coming American directors such as Steven Spielberg, George Lucas, and Martin Scorsese were name-checking him as an influence and one of their favorite filmmakers. In both Koreas, where filmmakers had always sought to emulate Japanese cinema and where the government, like Japan's, saw movies as a potentially vital cultural export, producers dreamed of ways to repeat Kurosawa's success and become national heroes themselves.

This was the kind of recognition Kim Jong-Il craved.

If he was to impress his father and to fulfill his own lifelong dream, Jong-Il needed to make a mark internationally. He had the ambition and the resources; what he lacked were the experience and filmmaking talent. But in a country known as the Hermit Kingdom, where no one on the inside was allowed out and no outsiders were allowed in, where could he find it?

It was then, in 1977, that Kim Jong-Il came up with his master plan.

All he needed was one thing—or, more precisely, one person—to pull it off.

8

A Three-Second Kiss

Shin Sang-Ok had it all. He was making films loved by millions, revered by the critics, showered with awards; his film company was the most successful in his country's history; he was rich and healthy; and he had two children with the most beautiful, outstanding woman in all of Korea, a woman he had loved and craved since their first conversation. Yes, Shin Sang-Ok had absolutely everything a man could want.

And he might have kept it, too. If only he hadn't kept wanting *more.*

The 1970s were a difficult decade for everyone in South Korean cinema. Millions of Korean households now had television, the economy slowed after the 1973 oil crisis, and the government's regulations had become so demanding and confusing that most filmmakers spent more time trying to beat the system than they did actually making films. The entire country, in fact, was adjusting to increased governmental oversight. President Park's administration was growing rigid and paranoid in panicked response to repeated North Korean attacks and provocations. In 1968, Kim Il-Sung's men captured the American warship USS *Pueblo,* killing one of the crew, and launched a failed commando raid to assassinate Park. Nine months later a hundred North Korean commandos landed on the east coast of South Korea and tried to spark a revolution, also in vain; in 1970 North Korean agents planted a bomb at the site of a scheduled speech of Park's, but they botched that as well. Four years later, a North Korean assassin killed the South Korean First Lady with a bullet he had intended for her husband, a tragedy that devastated Park Chung-Hee. That same year, South Korean forces discovered an underground infiltration tunnel dug under the DMZ by North Korean operatives. Two more tunnels were later discovered. All three were large enough to accommodate four columns of infantry soldiers, as well as any number of five-ton trucks and 155mm Howitzer guns. Unbeknownst to the public, around this time Kim Il-Sung had traveled to Beijing to request Zhou Enlai's support in a second Korean War. He was refused, but it seems Kim had planned on putting those tunnels to use sooner than anyone realized.

Kim Il-Sung managed to keep South Korea in a state of constant paranoia, and the South Korean government's response was to grow more tyrannical itself. Decreeing martial law, Park Chung-Hee introduced a new constitution giving himself dictatorial power for life. Troops and tanks occupied the streets of Seoul to discourage any protests. Many in South Korea were gnawed by confusion and insecurity. If North Korea was such a terrible dictatorship because people weren't allowed to do or say as they pleased, how was the South, as they were told, a democracy, since people there weren't free to do or say as they pleased either?

As a filmmaker, Shin was confronted with new motion picture laws that tightened the already stringent censorship code and introduced a rule whereby the right to freedom of speech could be suspended at any time if the state deemed it necessary. Censorship became so stringent that even a scene in which a character complained too strongly about the weather could be considered "antisocial" and ordered removed. One year the law insisted all production companies should make fifteen films, forcing them to grow; the next it would reverse, banning any single company from making more than five films, and producers, having just gone to great pains to expand so they could produce a wide slate of films, were now forbidden to do so. The system had descended into a farce of incompetence, corruption, and bullying.

Not that any of it was truly to blame for Shin's pushing Shin Film ever closer to the abyss. He was good at making money, but had little talent for holding on to it. Shin Film had always lurched from huge success to near financial ruin on a worryingly regular basis. One year the situation was so dire, the studio looked like it might have to downsize; eighteen months later the company was flush and expanding. A few months after that it was on the brink of bankruptcy again. So far Shin Film had withstood every storm. But this time Shin had overstretched his company's resources by buying the vast Anyang Film Studio near Seoul, the biggest physical studio in Asia, with three echoing soundstages, an audio recording studio, offices, an editing suite, a company canteen, a swimming pool, and a gym. Predictably he struggled to make efficient use of so much space, and soon had to resort to renting parcels of it out to fellow producers. And, after years of using creative (albeit unlawful) practices to successfully circumvent the government's regulations over import and export quotas, Shin finally got caught.

He had always been laid-back about rules and laws. He saw them as things that applied to other people, *ordinary* people, not to him, and he had no problem breaking them. His friendship with Park Chung-Hee had often come in handy in that sense. In 1965, when the Office of Public Ethics had wanted to ban one of Shin's films, all he'd had to do was call Park to have the order reversed. A year later the government took Shin to court, accusing him of embezzlement, fraud, and tax evasion for falsely claiming that his latest release, *Monkey Goes West,* had been a coproduction with Hong Kong company Shaw Brothers, when in fact it was a straight Shaw Brothers production. Needing a coproduction on the books to fulfill the government's import quotas, Shin had bought a print from Run Run Shaw, spliced in a few close-up shots of one of his Korean actors, slapped on his own credits, and dubbed Korean dialogue onto the print, releasing the film as one of his own. He was found guilty and fined 210 million won (USD $775,000) but, astonishingly, was still given permission to release the film. To Shin, that was all that mattered. Two months later he was arrested again, for the same offense on another film. Again he was found guilty, fined, and allowed to release the film anyway.

Many Korean filmmakers were inventive improvisers when it came to finding ways to bend the rules, but Shin was the canniest of them all. When the law banned companies from making more than five films each, he quietly reorganized Shin Film into what was technically four smaller companies, thereby allowing him to make twenty films. When the censorship board ordered him to cut an offensive scene from a certain film, Shin followed the order—and then spliced the provocative scene into the final cut of an entirely different picture, which had already screened in front of the board and received approval. When he needed an extra couple of movies to fulfill quotas, he put his name on Chinese films he hadn't actually directed and passed them off as his own.

Shin's self-confidence had turned into hubris. He was starting to feel invincible.

As he would soon discover, he was anything but.

IT TURNED OUT TO BE SHIN'S SON!

It was August 1974. Choi Eun-Hee woke up ready for a day like every other. She was forty-seven years old and acting less often, but had few regrets. She had performed for twenty-seven years and starred in over seventy-five films—a good run. She was enjoying being a mother. Four years earlier, at Shin's urging, she had opened a performance academy on the Anyang back lot, and had surprised herself by becoming all-consumed by the process of guiding and mentoring young actors. Shin Film was tiptoeing just the right side of bankruptcy, and Shin's films were a little less popular than they used to be: tastes had moved on and, just maybe, the sheer volume of films the law demanded had exhausted his inspiration a little, but she felt sure things would be all right.

And then today, there it was. The headline. Screaming at her from the front page of the film magazine, along with a picture of Oh Su-Mi, a young starlet who was starring in Shin's new picture, *Farewell,* about a man torn between his wife and a young employee of the Korean embassy in France, played by Su-Mi. Shin and the cast and crew had just returned from Paris, where they had filmed location shots for the movie. Choi had already heard rumors that Oh had been flirting with Shin, even that she and Shin had shared a hotel room during the shoot. Shin had had the occasional short fling before but Choi always turned a blind eye, because "I knew that he loved only me, so it didn't bother me much." He was in love with her and he was in love with making movies. The few women who came and went were only distractions. But "this time it felt different," Choi said. Oh was an actress, and much younger than her; it felt like her husband had brought his indiscretions into their business, *their* filmmaking.

The headline screamed, "IT TURNED OUT TO BE SHIN'S SON!" The words kicked the air out of her chest. Shin had been carrying on with the twenty-five-year-old Oh Su-Mi for a while now, the article said, and the young actress had recently given birth to a baby boy.

Shin's baby boy.

Choi struggled to take it in. *My husband's baby boy.*

When Shin came home from work that night, he was spooked by the anxiety and pallor on his wife's face. "What's wrong?" he asked. "Are you all right?" Choi didn't answer. It can't be true, she was thinking. We have been everything to each other. Something like this can't happen to us.

She felt too embarrassed to ask friends or colleagues to confirm the headline—she still held out the hope that this was sensationalist gossip. So, a few days later, she went to Oh's house. She stood across the street, hesitantly staring at the door. Night fell. She was about to give up and go home when, right before curfew, Oh's door opened, and Shin Sang-Ok snuck out, collar up to hide his face.

The argument was hideous. Shin promised Choi the fling was a mistake, that he was no longer with Oh Su-Mi.

"It's just a rumor. You can't believe a rumor like that," Shin shrugged.

"I saw everything with my own eyes! I went to her house! I saw everything," she repeated. "Is it true she gave birth to your son?"

Shin's face grew ashen.

"It's nothing," he finally said. "Give me some time . . . I'll sort it out . . ." She screamed at him to leave the house. She pushed him out of the room, slammed the door on him, locked it, and held it shut.

"Please just wait," she heard her husband say again and again on the other side. "I'll take care of it."

She could never forgive him.

She had so much to make sense of. Oh was now happily talking to the film magazines, enjoying the column inches. She told a journalist that she didn't want to marry Shin, nor did she expect him to get a divorce; "I just want to be near him." Desperate to confront her, to ask how she could be doing this to a family, Choi went to Oh's house. It wasn't uncommon, in those days, for a wife to show up at her husband's mistress's doorstep looking to pull some hair off her head and knock some teeth out of her pretty mouth. Choi just wanted to talk. She knocked. When the door opened, there stood Oh, looking young as a child—and carrying in her arms an infant boy. Choi's anger drained out of her, unbearable pain rushing in to replace it. "I almost forgot why I was there when I saw the baby," Choi wrote many years later. "I just wanted to hold him, because he was my husband's son."

Oh refused to say a single word to her. She just stood there with what Choi interpreted as defiance. "Her silence," Choi said, "felt like she was saying, 'I am the woman who gave birth to his child, when you couldn't.' "

At home that night, Choi cried more than she had ever thought she could. She didn't stop until it was nearly dawn.

Shin was taken to court again, this time for bribing a censorship official. He denied the accusation even though he admitted the entire censorship system had become "all about who one bribed and how much one paid." This time, while officials waited for a trial date, they briefly put Shin in jail—to teach him a lesson, maybe, and remind him what real power, not film producer power, was. With her husband sitting in a cell, nearly bankrupt, Choi's heart softened just a little. She hadn't seen Shin since the night she'd thrown him out of the house, but now she went to visit him in jail. She brought scissors and told him he needed a haircut. Shin was ecstatic to see her. She cut his hair in silence, wiped his neck clean, and left. She still couldn't speak to him. Then, a few days later, she learned that Oh was visiting him regularly, and that he wasn't turning her away.

Shin was released and moved out of their home. Choi was devastated and lonely. She had lost her husband, her best friend, and her closest creative partner. She couldn't sleep. She smoked too much. Every night she drank herself to bed. The ups and downs were heartrending. One day she found out that Shin wasn't living with Oh but in a temporary rental by himself, and was heartened; another day she learned that Shin was remaking *Chun-Hie,* a film in which she had starred sixteen years earlier, this time with Oh in the title role, and the pain was as fresh and blinding as before.

The judge acquitted Shin of the bribery charge. Rather than admit he had just narrowly avoided ruin, Shin took it as a sign that he would always come out on top. Yet the loss of Choi was, from a business perspective, a disastrous development. In traditional Korean society, wives were expected to find happiness and prosperity through their husbands, because they *provided.* When Choi—who had been famous first, who had always personally made more money, who in so many ways was wiser and more sensible—left Shin, it exacerbated his precarious situation. Until now his success had depended in great part on Choi's creative, strategic, and financial contributions.

Bankruptcy soon began to look unavoidable. Shin Film was bleeding money, and Shin's recent efforts at refilling its coffers by making erotic, sensationalist films—exploitation pictures with soft-core hints of lesbianism and titles like *Female Prisoner 407* and *Cruel Stories of Yi Dynasty Women*—had not only failed to pack theaters but had diminished Shin Film's aura of quality and sophistication. Shin Film had always been like a family business: two of Shin's brothers worked for him, as did Choi's younger brother, and everyone's personal funds were tied into the company's fortunes. When assets had to be sold, Shin and Choi lost their house, as did Choi's parents. One day Choi's younger brother stood in Shin's office and shouted in his face for several minutes, blaming him for mismanaging the company and spending too much money. It was the first time Shin had ever been scolded by someone younger than him.

Shin's friends and colleagues had never seen him this stressed. Censorship had become his bogeyman, and he railed constantly about "the system" and how politicians meddled with things they didn't understand. He did everything he could to taunt the government. He wanted to provoke it and to beat it, without realizing how isolated he had become. The older generation had never forgotten the young upstart who had stolen an older man's wife, and the more jealous and resentful of his peers felt it was only fair that, after profiting from what they had come to call "the bad film laws," those laws should bring Shin Sang-Ok back down to earth—and *hard*. The Oh Su-Mi scandal had put him at odds with the generally conservative morals of his country, and Choi's friends were deserting him, including President Park. It was *his* censorship system Shin was mocking—Park, after all, *was* the system—and on a deeper, more personal level, Park was a very conservative man. He had been devoted to his wife until the day she died, killed by the bullet intended for him, and since then he had slept with her picture, flowers, and a book of poetry dedicated to her by his bedside table. Shin and Choi had been friends of his and his wife's, they had visited the Blue House and had couples' dinners together. That Shin had treated Choi with such disrespect was unbecoming and disappointing to Park's sensibilities.

In 1974, Shin submitted his new film, a war picture called *A Thirteen-Year-Old Boy,* to the Berlin Film Festival without bothering to get a stamp of approval from the Ministry of Information. When the film festival accepted the movie, a formal invitation card was sent to the ministry, which turned down the request, apologizing that the film wasn't an approved Korean production. Shin considered appealing to Park, but he was dissuaded from it. The president, he was told, was "furious and betrayed" by the filmmaker's recent behavior. With that, Shin had lost his last political ally.

In the end—after all the controversies, the arrests, the affair, the scandal, and the bankruptcy—it was a three-second kiss that ended Shin Sang-Ok's career.

In November 1975, Shin screened a preview of his new coproduction with Shaw Brothers, *Rose and Wild Dog*, for an audience made up mostly of high school students. A shot of a couple kissing, the woman topless, had been ordered cut by the censorship board, but at this screening it had been left in, in what seemed to be, on Shin's part, either indifference or insolence. The students told their families about the kiss, and the story hit the newspapers. The penalty, according to the law, was for screenings of the film to be canceled until the offensive scene was removed. But the Office of Public Ethics had had enough of Shin Sang-Ok. Citing a violation of the public morals code, it stripped Shin Film of its production license, effective immediately.

It says something about Shin Sang-Ok that he was stunned. He had never imagined it would come to this. Stubbornly, he sued in court, refusing to accept the censorship decision. After he had filed the suit, Shin said, he received a visit from agents of the Korean Central Intelligence Agency. They took him to Namsan.

Namsan, the mountain in central Seoul, was the location of the KCIA headquarters. This is where activists, dissidents, suspects, and witnesses were dragged in for questioning, many of them tortured. Some never left. The KCIA was famous for its "Korean barbecue," in which a detainee was strung up by his wrists and ankles and hung over a bonfire until he confessed. None of this, luckily, befell Shin. He was seated in a dark room, refused food or sleep, and questioned at length. Pressure was brought to bear and it was made clear to him that his license would never be restored. By the time the agents let him go, Shin had withdrawn his lawsuit and accepted his punishment.

The Shin Film office in Myeongdong was shuttered, sending shock waves through the industry. An era was over. In truth, the studio was well past its former glory: in the 1960s, the company had had up to three hundred employees on the books; in 1975 it had fewer than ten.

With Shin Film out of business and the Anyang lot deserted, Choi's Academy of Cinematic Arts also fell into financial difficulties. The school had become Choi's baby, and her husband's selfish, headstrong foolishness threatened to take that away from her, too.

In 1976, Oh Su-Mi's second child by Shin, a girl, was born. Shin had kept insisting he was through with her. Choi, who had been hoping for a way to eventually repair their marriage, didn't even know the girl was pregnant. After twenty-two years of marriage, she asked for a divorce.

Choi was brokenhearted, disgraced, and humiliated. She felt a muffled hate for her husband, out there in Seoul, living a secret life after tearing hers down. And yet, "I missed him," she said.

Her mother died weeks after the divorce was granted, and out of respect, Shin attended the funeral. It was the first time Choi had seen him since the divorce. He looked wrecked, his "vibrant side," Choi said, completely gone. He was still coming to terms with a life in which he wasn't allowed to stand behind a camera and make movies. They spoke briefly. Shin told her he was going to the United States, in the hope he could go on making films there.

For the next two years, Choi would look after her children and try to keep the Academy—the last thing she had left—afloat. Shin traveled the world, applying for visas, looking for somewhere he could find legal status and money to start making movies again. They drifted apart. Those years, Shin said later, "represented the most difficult, frustrating, and unbearable period of my life." His career as a filmmaker was over.

9
Repulse Bay

Choi Eun-Hee stared into the rumbling ocean waters below and told herself to jump. The freighter groaned and vibrated under her feet as it plowed through the waves, spreading white foam on either side of the hull. Do it, Choi thought. Jump in and it will all be over.

Hesitating, she looked to the horizon. In the distance, Chinese fishing ships gently bobbed in the water, the smoke of their cooking fires rising thin and white against the blue sky. The freighter rushed past them and they were gone.

Nearby on the deck, the ship's crew were laying out several different national flags, ready, she had been told by the men, "for when we need them." Choi thought of her own family with anguish. She squeezed her fingers on the handrail, her knuckles turning white. She had to do it.

She pushed back on her heels and prepared to jump, but the guards spotted her. They ran to her, grabbed her arms, and pulled her back. She tried to fight them off, but it was no use.

As they dragged her back to her cabin, she silently cursed herself for not listening to Shin Sang-Ok.

The two years after Shin Film's closing were a sad, difficult time. Choi didn't act in another film. She spent most of her time trying to save the Anyang performing school from being sucked into the vortex of Shin

Film's bankruptcy. The school had seven hundred pupils and she felt responsible for every one of them. They had to be looked after.

In the fall of 1977, she was visited by a man calling himself Wang Dong-Il, who told her he ran a film studio in Hong Kong. Wang had a similar performing academy at home, and he wondered if Choi might want to form an affiliation, and perhaps also run the Hong Kong school? He invited her to the Hong Kong Film Festival later that year to discuss the project further. Choi was unable to travel to the festival, so regretfully turned down the invitation. Wang stayed in touch. One day he sent her a film script, asking her if she would direct it. The paycheck would be enough to save the Anyang school—for a while. Choi agreed to fly to Hong Kong and discuss the project.

Before she left she called Shin. They hadn't seen each other in weeks. He had been flying back and forth to the United States and to Hong Kong, trying to find a way to restart his filmmaking career, so far without success.

When she told him her news, he sounded uncertain. "Isn't it weird for someone from Hong Kong to come and ask *you* to be a director, when they have so many famous directors and staff members at their disposal?" he asked. He couldn't find work: Why had someone gone out of their way to hire Choi when she wasn't even a director? "And why do the Chinese want to be affiliated with an unestablished acting school such as Anyang?"

Shin "was always trying to look out for me," Choi later said, but she wondered if she heard some resentment and jealousy in his voice. She ignored him. She would prove to him that she could do fine without him. On January 11, 1978, she packed her bags and boarded a Cathay Pacific flight from Kimpo Airport, destination Kai Tak Airport, Hong Kong.

As the chauffeur-driven car sped smoothly through the brand-new underwater tunnel linking Kowloon to the island of Hong Kong, Choi apologized to Wang Dong-Il for being unable to accept his invitation sooner, and for only being able to stay a few days. The car emerged back into the orange evening light, and straight into a canyon of skyscrapers.

Hong Kong, then still under British rule, was experiencing dramatic changes as it reinvented itself, moving away from a manufacturing economy to become one of the world's leading financial centers. The skyline bristled with cranes as a result of the Ten-Year Housing Program started in 1972 to provide quality housing for nearly two million people. Supermarkets and corporations were replacing mom-and-pop stores and local businesses. Banks and brokerage houses blossomed, and nearly half a million Hong Kong citizens were becoming stock investors.

Wang dropped Choi off at the Parma Hotel, where a room had been reserved for her on the sixth floor, with a stunning view of Victoria Harbor. They would meet again the next morning, he told her, at 10 a.m. sharp.

For the next two days Wang showed her the city, wining and dining her at the best restaurants. For all the luxurious hospitality, Choi was frustrated by the lack of business talk—and made uneasy by two Chinese-looking men she noticed following her, taking pictures as she explored the city. On the third day Wang was nowhere to be found, so Choi went to the local Shin Film office, which was still open, waiting for Shin Sang-Ok's future to be decided. The Hong Kong company director, Lee Young-Seng, and the manager, Kim Kyu-Hwa, awaited her, along with a woman in her early fifties and a cute little girl of about twelve years of age. Kim introduced the woman as an old friend of his, and the girl as her daughter. "Hello, I am Lee Sang-Hee," her mother said, greeting Choi. That night at dinner, Mrs. Lee and Choi bonded, Mrs. Lee telling Choi that she was a huge fan and had seen all her movies. Mrs. Lee offered for her and her daughter to spend the next day with Choi while she waited for Wang—who, she had been told, was unexpectedly detained, but would be able to resume and conclude talks with her shortly—and Choi accepted.

The next day, January 14, Choi met with Mrs. Lee and her daughter. Mrs. Lee seemed overexcited. "She talked nonstop," Choi said. "She wanted to introduce me to her many acquaintances in Japan, especially an older man who was interested in culture and art. He would be useful in the management of my school, she thought." Halfway through lunch at a Japanese restaurant, Mrs. Lee excused herself to make a phone call, and when she returned told Choi she had just spoken to one of those influential acquaintances. Would she like to meet him today? Choi, who had no prior engagements, agreed. Her friend, Mrs. Lee told her, lived about an hour's drive away, in a house on Repulse Bay.

Repulse Bay, on the far southern side of Hong Kong, had been used in the nineteenth century as a base by pirates, who preyed on the British merchant ships on their way to trade with Japan. The pirates had long ago been repulsed—hence the bay's name—and the strip of land turned into tourist beaches.

Choi looked out the window as their taxi drove down the deserted road. It was 4 p.m. in winter, and the air coming off the sea was cool. She could see houses in the near distance, villas and vacation homes, the nearby beach empty of people. She had no idea where they were. Suddenly Mrs. Lee asked the taxi to stop beside a small strip of beach.

"We're getting out," she said.

"Should we ask the taxi to wait?" Choi asked.

"We can phone for one and it'll come right away."

Mrs. Lee got out of the car, Choi and the little girl following. The woman stood and looked around.

Choi asked what was going on but got no answer. Mrs. Lee seemed to be waiting for someone. After a minute, Choi and the young girl wandered toward the sea. It was late afternoon and their shadows were stretching across the sand.

Mrs. Lee's voice rang out, calling for them. Choi turned around and saw her standing by the waves about forty yards away, motioning Choi to come over. There was a group of long-haired men by her side. A small white motor skiff bobbed in the water, with more young men, all with long hair, sitting inside it, looking in her direction. Uneasily Choi walked over. Mrs. Lee explained that the man they were meeting had sent the men to take them to his secluded villa, ten minutes away across the bay. Choi hesitated. The little twelve-year-old girl seemed happy enough, surely a good sign, but Choi wasn't comfortable. She didn't know where she was. She had only met this woman the day before. A queasy uneasiness twisted her stomach. She had been in enough bad situations to recognize that this was another.

"I have a six o'clock dinner engagement . . ." she said.

"Don't worry, don't worry," Mrs. Lee said, in the same agitated tone she'd had all day. "It only takes ten minutes to get to the villa. You will have plenty of time to get to your engagement."

Choi was about to reply when the men in the motorboat nodded at one another, leaped out, and grabbed her. She tried to fight, but they overpowered her and threw her into the boat. Directed to follow, Mrs. Lee and her daughter climbed in as well. The skiff's motor rumbled to life. Choi was terrified. I am being robbed, she thought. The boat turned and headed away from the bay—toward the open sea. Choi turned to Mrs. Lee, but she looked serene. She put a cigarette between her lips and offered Choi one. "Everything is all right," she said.

One of the long-haired men called Choi's name. She turned to him. He was middle-aged, probably the oldest of the group.

"How do you know my name?" she asked.

"I'm Korean," he said, using the North Korean term *chosun* rather than the South Korean term *hanguk*.

Choi's heart sunk into her stomach. "Where is this boat going?" she asked in a weak voice.

"Madame Choi," he said solemnly, "we are now going to the bosom of General Kim Il-Sung."

"What? What did you say?"

The man took the long-haired wig off. "I said, we are going to the bosom of the Great Leader, Comrade General Kim Il-Sung."

Screaming, Choi jumped to her feet, and the boat rocked side to side. Hands reached up for her and pinned her back down onto her seat. Her vision blurred. Her body went limp, and she fainted.

She drifted in and out of darkness. She remembered feeling someone carrying her up a gangway, someone giving her an injection, then oblivion swallowing her back up. When she finally woke she was aboard a freighter, in the captain's cabin. A large ceremonial portrait of Kim Il-Sung smiled down at her.

She was on the ship for six days, a doctor and his wife looking after her and managing her shock, and two other men, including the middle-aged man from the boat, whom she later learned was Im Ho-Gun, Deputy Director of North Korea's covert operations department, keeping a twenty-four hour watch on her. Choi could hear Mrs. Lee sobbing in the next cabin, and gathered that she had agreed to help the men take Choi but had not foreseen they would force her to come along. Choi, too, cried. She couldn't eat but forced herself to drink the broth of the noodle soup they brought her. On the fourth day they took her up to the deck and she stared into the ocean, trying to gather the strength to throw herself in. On the fifth day a typhoon forced the boat to drop anchor, and she watched the storm pass. At 3 p.m. on the sixth day, January 22, 1978, the ship pulled into Nampo Harbor, North Korea. They unloaded Madame Choi onto another small white motorboat, which took her to a small quay a twenty-minute ride from the main port.

Her legs wobbled as she stepped onto the pier. She followed the guards with her head bowed, struggling to stay on her feet. "Someone important is coming," one of them whispered.

A short man in his midthirties was walking toward her. He wore a thick, fashionable wool coat over a dark Mao-collared uniform. A shiny Mercedes idled behind him, and a photographer stood by his side, camera ready. With a smile, the small man extended his hand to her.

"Thank you for coming, Madame Choi," he said. "You must be exhausted from the journey. Welcome. I am Kim Jong-Il."

REEL TWO

GUESTS OF THE DEAR LEADER

"Pay no attention to that man behind the curtain."
—The Wizard of Oz (Frank Morgan),
***The Wizard of Oz*, screenplay by Noel Langley,**
Florence Ryerson and Edgar Allan Woolf,
from the book by L. Frank Baum;
directed by Victor Fleming.

10
The Hermit Kingdom

Choi knew the name, but little more, of the man grinning in front of her. The South Korean newspapers had been full of headlines for the past year that Kim Jong-Il had been in a terrible car accident and that he was a human vegetable, strung up to medical equipment on a hospital bed in one of his father's villas. Some papers dismissed the car accident story and said he had survived a botched assassination. Yet here he stood in front of her, fully intact and disarmingly genial.

She stared at his outthrust hand and slowly, her own hand trembling, reached out to shake it. Immediately a flash popped—twice, three times—as the photographer took photos of the moment. Choi sunk her chin inside her coat collar.

"Don't take my picture!" she cried. Her voice sounded like someone else's, thin and hysterical. In a rush of thoughts it came to her that she didn't want a record of this moment, that besides, she was unkempt and would look terrible on film, and then that it was absurd to worry about *that*. Jong-Il gave a slight sign to the photographer, who put his camera down.

"You look very nice," he told Choi. "Those bell-bottom slacks suit you very well." She was wearing the same clothes she had put on the morning of her abduction. She didn't answer. Kim let go of her hand and suggested she take a walk around the pier to steady herself after the long journey. He signaled to two of his men, who gently each took one of Choi's arms and led her up and down the pier for ten minutes. Finally they walked her over to the long, imposing black Mercedes, Kim walking ahead of her. The driver, who wore an army uniform, jumped out of the front seat and opened the back door. Kim moved aside to let Choi climb in, then stepped inside himself, the bodyguards cramming in the front seat by the driver. Smoothly, the engine giving a quiet noise like a lion's yawn, the car turned and pulled away in the evening light. Behind it, two more Mercedes-Benzes turned their lights on and followed.

In spite of living most of her life in Seoul, just thirty-five miles south of the border, Choi knew next to nothing about North Korea. Her own government demonized the North Koreans at every turn, and since the end of the Korean War the North had kept itself reclusive and apart, releasing little information to the outside world. What little information North Korea shared suggested a quiet, peaceful prosperity within their borders, in direct contradiction to the Kims' clear, terrifying zeal for murder, kidnapping, and terrorism outside of them.

Choi thought of all of this as she stared out the car window at the landscape outside. Next to her Kim Jong-Il was making pleasant conversation, as if they were on a short taxi ride to dinner, asking her questions she didn't hear and didn't answer. It had been cold when she got off the ship and now she noticed snow across the fields and on the side of the road. "The road was unpaved," Choi wrote later. "There were no signs of people and the scenery had the desolation of a war zone." They drove through a small village. "Red and white posters were unfurled at every intersection. They bore slogans such as 'Long Live Kim Il-Sung,' 'Long Live the Korean Workers' Party,' 'Speed Battle, Annihilation Battle,' 'Absolutism and Unconditionality.' . . ." Two hours later the road had become lined with apartment buildings, none higher than ten stories. They were entering Pyongyang. Choi squinted but couldn't make much out. The city was pitch black—the street lights off, the windows in the homes and offices dark. As she would learn later, North Korea had defaulted on $2 billion worth of foreign loans in 1976 and had started to ration electricity.

"This is Potong Gate," Kim was saying next to her, pointing at the invisible sights out the window, "and that's Moran Peak . . ."

Forty-five minutes later, the car pulled off the main road and onto a winding, unpaved drive that led to a guardhouse. The soldier standing there saluted and the gate rose behind him. A few dozen yards down the road they came to another guardhouse, another saluting soldier. At the end of the drive, tucked in between tall pine trees, was a grand, single-story villa. The car stopped.

Inside, Kim gave Choi a tour of the ostentatious villa: the en-suite bedrooms, the living room and library, the home cinema. There was a tacky crystal chandelier or two in every room and Japanese gadgets on every surface, giving the house a gauche, unrefined energy—"a Las Vegas–meets–Vladivostok feeling," as Choi described later. They circled back to the front of the house, where a woman in her early forties stood waiting. She wore simple clothes and her expression was hard to read.

"This is Comrade Kim Hak-Sun," Jong-Il told Choi. He turned to Hak-Sun. "Take good care of our guest. Make her feel comfortable." Then, to Choi, in a gentler voice: "Please make yourself at home." He took a step back and nodded to one of his men, who immediately approached Choi.

"Madame Choi, you are carrying a South Korean passport on you. Please let me have it." There was no point resisting, so Choi took her passport out of her handbag and handed it to him. "You also have a South Korean identification card," he said. "Please hand it over." After she did the man walked over to Kim Jong-Il and handed him the documents. He pocketed them, nodded, and left.

Kim Hak-Sun indicated to Choi to follow her outside and to the dining hall, a separate building about 150 yards from the main house. Inside, the dining table was groaning under the weight of "fried shrimp, raw fish, beef ribs, and a smorgasbord of Korean, Japanese, and Chinese dishes," Choi said. Her throat tight, her stomach churning, all she could eat, no matter how much Hak-Sun encouraged her, was some soup.

Later that night Hak-Sun led Choi to the master bedroom, which had been prepared for her.

"Good night," the North Korean woman said before retiring to her room. Choi pushed the bedroom door shut. She noticed it didn't lock.

None of the doors in the house did.

The villa, Choi learned, was called Building Number 1. It was to be her home for the next nine months. Every day Kim Jong-Il sent her fresh flowers and a doctor who would check on her health and dispense nutritional supplements. Every night for the first several weeks, she called out the names of her children and cried herself to sleep.

The North Koreans spoke little, if at all. The doctor, Choi observed, was "refined and gentlemanly" but evasive. If she asked about his hometown, whether he had ever been to the South, or if he knew why she had been kidnapped, he suddenly went quiet or changed the subject. The guards and Kim Hak-Sun behaved the same way, although Hak-Sun, who spent every day and night in the house, eventually grew close with Choi. Hak-Sun's job, as Choi's "guidance officer," was to supervise her at all times, look after her every need, and tactfully introduce her to North Korean ways. In younger days she had been a singer in the Mansudae Art Troupe, which is how she had met Kim Jong-Il and, she told Choi, become his "confidante." Whether this was a euphemism Choi couldn't tell. But Kim Jong-Il trusted Kim Hak-Sun entirely, and as she grew too old for the Art Troupe—the Kims liked their entertainers no older than twenty-five—she had been posted as the attendant here, in Kim Jong-Il's compound. To pass the time Hak-Sun played the piano, softly singing tunes taken from *The Collection of 600 Songs* and *The Kim Jong-Il Songbook,* all of them hymns glorifying the Leaders Great and Dear. She and Choi also took walks in the gardens outside the house, during which Choi noticed there were four other buildings in the compound, which was surrounded first by a concrete wall and, on the outside perimeter, by a barbed-wire fence. Armed soldiers patrolled every side of the wall at all times of day and night.

Before Choi had moved in, the house had been stocked with every amenity and luxury she, or anyone else, could have dreamed of requesting. In addition, to mollify her, Kim Jong-Il sent her gifts almost every day: Estée

Lauder cosmetics, Japanese-made lingerie, and boxes full of dresses, both in the traditional style and in more modern cuts. The beauty products were the exact kind she used back in Seoul, and the clothes, from the underwear to the formal dresses, had been tailored to fit her perfectly. Every meal laid out for her was a banquet.

On the afternoon of the fifth day, Hak-Sun burst into Choi's room. "The Dear Leader Comrade Kim Jong-Il has invited you to a dinner party!" she announced breathlessly. "We must hurry up and get ready." A Mercedes took them into Pyongyang, down a side street and into another walled compound. Waiting on the front steps was Kim Jong-Il. He smiled as Choi and Hak-Sun walked up to him.

"Welcome, Madame Choi. Have you been able to rest up?"

Choi said nothing but, following Hak-Sun's lead, bowed at the waist—as slight a bow as she could manage.

"Let's go inside," Kim said. He led them down the entrance hall, talking every step of the way. "The South Koreans are blabbing around saying I'm brain dead, a human vegetable," he said, referring to the rumors of a car accident. He chuckled. "What do you think of that?" When Choi didn't answer, he stopped and struck a vain, dramatic pose. "Come on, Madame Choi, what do you think: How do I look? I'm small as a midget's turd, aren't I?"

Choi almost laughed. Unexpectedly, she felt her anxiety fade a little. Kim seemed pleased with his icebreaker. He showed her down another corridor and into a large room, ornately decorated, with fake flowers and bright lights everywhere. It looked, Choi thought, like a discotheque.

"How about it?" Kim asked proudly. "What's on the inside is always more important than what's on the outside. From the outside something doesn't look like much, but when you bother to come inside, it's generally like this." He walked her to a round table in the middle of the room where dinner was being served—Western and Korean delicacies, washed down with cognac, French white wine, ginseng wine, and soju. As Choi stood at her designated seat, she recognized the other guests: they were the men from the motor skiff in Repulse Bay, their long-haired wigs removed to reveal army crew cuts; the man who had looked after her during the sea journey to

Nampo; and the bodyguards who had ferried her off the boat. She realized she had been invited to have a polite, sociable dinner with the men who had ripped her from her home and children and imprisoned her in a foreign land.

Kim Jong-Il sat down and, as if released, the others did as well. A waiter poured the Dear Leader a full glass of Hennessy. Kim took a deep drink and looked at Choi. "Please, Madame Choi," he said. "You must have a drink."

It was the first of many of Kim Jong-Il's dinner parties that Choi attended during her years in North Korea, usually on a Wednesday or Friday, starting at 8 p.m. and lasting into the early hours of the next morning. The dinners always took place in the same building, which Party members referred to as the Fish House, named after the floor-to-ceiling, twenty-five-foot-long aquarium of large ocean fish in the second-floor ballroom. Sometimes, like that night, the gatherings were small affairs, dinner followed by a movie, but more often the guest list stretched to forty or fifty people, members of the People's Republic's tiny core elite.

Kim Jong-Il's weekly parties were notorious in Pyongyang's power circle for their influence on state policy. "Many key decisions are made there," Hwang Jang-Yop said, "personnel matters in particular." Kim invited important members of the Party and Politburo, influential generals, his favorite film and stage stars; the guest list was a reflection of the people who formed his inner circle—or who, through invitation to the party, were being auditioned to join. Kim's younger sister, whom he loved dearly, was almost always present. Guests were handed a single whiskey, brandy, or cognac at the entrance, to be knocked back in one gulp, the price of admission. A few weeks in, Hak-Sun taught Choi to always carry a handkerchief when coming to a party so she could discreetly spit the cognac out before heading inside.

Kim Jong-Il rarely came early, preferring to join the party once it was in full swing. When he arrived, guests stood and clapped until he had taken his seat. Once Kim had sat down—always at the head table, closest to the stage, with just a handful of special guests accompanying him—waiters would bring out the food. Kim liked to direct the band, interrupting it in midflow, requesting certain songs, often ordering a specific guest to stand up and sing a song of his own choice, sometimes because he liked their voice but equally often so he could belittle them. There was no refusing a request from Jong-Il. Whenever he spoke to another guest, Choi said, the guest "sprang to his feet with his mouth full of food and answered, 'Yes, sir!,'" standing to attention until Jong-Il had waved at him to sit back down.

After dinner there was mah-jongg and roulette to be played, and girls for the guests' entertainment. The girls of the Joy Brigade were one of the great draws of Jong-Il's parties. They were the most beautiful young women in Korea, hand-selected by Jong-Il himself, obedient and with exquisite manners. Officially part of the military, each girl was given the rank of "Lieutenant of the Bodyguard Division" and assigned to one of three "pleasure groups": the "dancing and singing group," which entertained guests, the "happiness group," which provided massage, and finally the "satisfaction group," which provided sexual services. Jong-Il himself never touched the girls at these functions; nor did he dance or sing. He preferred to sit, drink, smoke his Rothman Royals, and *direct*. He picked up his baton and conducted the band or encouraged guests to gamble with more panache. Occasionally he did gamble, briefly, always ending up playing a hand one-on-one with the dealer and going all in very quickly. ("I think I understood something of Kim Jong-Il's personality as I watched from behind," Choi says.) A Party staff member hovered near him throughout the evening, and anything the Dear Leader said that sounded remotely like an order was noted down, recorded, and disseminated throughout the Party, immediately becoming an official instruction—whether Jong-Il had said it in sober conversation at 8 p.m. or stinking drunk at three in the morning. In his drunken moods he promoted or fired guests on a whim. He was hard to keep up with in conversation, rambling, then changing subjects without warning, and delighting in saying things he shouldn't.

Occasionally, the party could veer into the absurd. Hwang Jang-Yop claimed to have witnessed several nights in which Jong-Il had staff hang six-foot-diameter balls filled with gifts—essentially gigantic piñatas—which he then shot at with a special gun, sending presents showering onto the guests, who shamelessly scrambled over each other to get to the best items. On at least one other occasion, according to Hwang, Kim instructed a handful of dancers to strip naked and start dancing, then ordered the members of the Politburo to dance with them, saying, "Dance, but don't touch. If you touch, you're thieves." The men shuffled over to the women and danced, careful to keep their hands visible. After a short while Jong-Il barked at all of them to immediately stop. "These parties were probably the means through which Kim Jong-Il formed his group of vassals," Hwang said. "By inviting his trusted subordinates to a party, he can observe their personalities at close range and imbue them with pride at being close attendants of the Great Leader. . . . At these drinking parties, those who get drunk only need to be respectful to Kim Jong-Il; they can say anything they like to anyone regardless of his title."

Jong-Il considered the party a sacred sanctum, and anyone who leaked what happened there was liable to be severely punished. He was adamant that the gatherings were none of his father's business and must be kept a secret, and enforced this dictum violently and ruthlessly. In one famous story Hwang confirms, "one of Kim Jong-Il's secretaries got drunk once and told his wife about Kim Jong-Il's life of debauchery. The good wife, a woman of high cultural and moral standards, was genuinely shocked, and after much thought, she decided to write a letter to Kim Il-Sung asking him to reprimand his son. Needless to say, the letter went to Kim Jong-Il, who threw a drinking party and had the woman arrested and brought before him. In front of all the guests at the party, he pronounced the woman a counterrevolutionary and had her shot on the spot. . . . The poor woman's husband actually begged Kim Jong-Il to let him do the shooting. Kim Jong-Il granted the secretary his wish, and gave him the weapon to shoot his wife."

Choi never saw any killings or piñatas in the ballroom. On one occasion she did witness a bizarre game, in which Jong-Il would suddenly, in the middle of dinner, shout out "Army uniforms!" and all the male guests had to reach for army uniforms tucked under their seats, put them on, and run around their table in circles until Jong-Il called for them to stop. Later he would call "Navy uniforms!" and it began again with a different costume. While the guests rushed around, a waiter helped Kim put on his own general or admiral jacket, gigantic stars and decorations clanging on his shoulders and chest. Once, after laughing at what the guests called disco dancing ("They just hopped around," Choi said), she was asked to give everyone—generals, covert operatives, and dancing girls alike—a disco-dancing lesson. Another week she came to the party in a pink traditional *hanbok* dress. Jong-Il complimented her—"the long skirt goes so well with short hair"—and then declared that all female members of all theater groups should wear their hair short and their dresses longer to emulate her.

Mostly Choi seemed to be there as a trophy, seated next to Jong-Il and proudly introduced to eminent guests. It was at these parties that Choi first realized it was not Kim Il-Sung who had ordered her abduction but his son. Jong-Il, despite his sociability, was an annoying host, demanding and boastful. "He thought he could do anything he wanted," Choi remembered. "He was always showing off." He talked about South Korean movies constantly, ridiculing them for the poor way their actors portrayed a North Korean accent (this coming from someone who had regularly used Koreans in whiteface makeup to play Caucasians), and he liked to make Choi sing for him. South Korean songs were his favorite, but everyone in the country except him was banned from listening to them (outside of his parties): finally he had someone who knew the lyrics to the tunes he was humming. Almost every week he asked Choi to join the band and sing a song or two for him, the more melancholy the better, like Patti Kim's "A Parting (Farewell)."

Sometimes I can't help but think of him, even though he is aloof,
About the promise of that night, something he may regret,
Over the mountains we are separated, far far away.

As Choi sang her voice would crack, her lip trembling. Tears rolled down her cheeks. Each time, thinking it a committed theatrical performance, the guests jumped to their feet and broke into deafening applause.

One night, about a month after her abduction, Choi was sitting in her room when the phone rang. She knew immediately it was Jong-Il: none of the phones in the house could make outgoing calls, and this line was reserved for the Leader's son. She picked up and was surprised to hear Jong-Il excited—and, she thought, a little tipsy.

"Are you doing anything?" he asked.

"No."

"Would you please come visit my home? It's my birthday."

Within moments, a Mercedes arrived and ferried her to Jong-Il's house. He was waiting at the door when the car pulled up the drive.

"Madame Choi! How is your health? I hear you are getting better." He led her inside and praised her outfit. She thanked him for the compliment.

"Are you uncomfortable with anything?" he asked as they walked. "If you are uncomfortable, please let me know."

"Oh no. I am indebted to you for your concern."

He laughed. "Now, now—do you really feel that way?"

They walked through the guest room, which had a movie projector set up in the corner. She was surprised by how modest the house was. "Dear Leader," Choi ventured, emboldened by being in his home, "I'm sorry to ask this, but would you please send me home to South Korea? I have work to do there. I have a family, teachers, hundreds of students to take care of. I can't sleep because I'm always thinking of them. Please."

Jong-Il made a show of thinking for a short while. "I understand your dilemma," he said, finally, "but please bear with me. I have some plans for us. . . . This problem will soon be resolved." He seemed about to say something else, Choi observed, but at that moment a chubby little boy came running into the room. The boy wore a dark blue military-style uniform. He had a round face and short hair, and looked like his father.

"You have a son!" Choi exclaimed.

"Yes, and a daughter—but she's not here now."

Choi bent down toward the child. "What a handsome boy you are," she said. "How old are you?"

"Seven," he replied.

"What's your name?" At this the boy looked unnerved. He looked at his father and spluttered, "Why is she asking me my name?"

Jong-Il chuckled and patted the boy's head. "When an adult asks you your name you should answer with good manners, by saying 'My name is . . .'"

"Oh." He turned back to Madame Choi. "My name is Kim Jong-Nam." The boy had never met someone who didn't already know what his name was. As Jong-Il showed Choi to the dining room, a minder, who appeared to be Jong-Nam's babysitter, appeared and led the boy away from the adults to another part of the house.

Six men sat around the dining room table. A woman stood off to the side by herself. Kim walked over to her.

"Teacher Choi, this is my wife," Jong-Il said, even though he and Hye-Rim had never formally married, "and those are my relatives who have come to celebrate my birthday."

Choi had expected a large, debauched birthday party, not a small family dinner. Hye-Rim said hello. Choi thought she was about five foot two, the same height as Kim, and glamorous, even though she was dressed in casual Western home wear. "I'm very happy to meet you," she told Choi in a very quiet voice, then, to Jong-Il: "You invited so many people at the last minute. What am I going to do?"

"Oh, don't worry. Madame Choi is a special guest."

Hye-Rim didn't say anything. The last few years she had fallen prey to anxiety attacks and episodes of depression as Jong-Il drifted away from her, having affairs with actresses, with old university classmates, and with the wives of his father's ambassadors. All his conquests, people noticed, looked strikingly like his late mother. In 1974 Kim Il-Sung, still unaware of his son's life with Hye-Rim, had instructed Jong-Il to finally take a wife, and Jong-Il had meekly obeyed, marrying Kim Young-Sook, a typist in Kim Il-Sung's office and the daughter of one of his generals. Young-Sook quickly bore him a daughter, but Jong-Il didn't care for his official wife. He didn't make her a member of the Party and she never meaningfully entered his life. "She had no more significance than the fact that she was the legal wife,"

Hye-Rim's sister later wrote of her. Around the same time Jong-Il started a third long-running relationship, with a Japanese-born dancer from the Joy Brigade named Ko Yong-Hui, who in the early 1980s would bear him two more sons. Hye-Rim threatened to run away with their son, even threatened to tell Kim Il-Sung about their secret relationship. Jong-Il had pleaded with her to have faith in him, to wait just a little bit longer—and then had ordered the staff at the resort to never let her out of the house, "for her own safety and privacy." In 1975, two years after he had gotten rid of Uncle Yong-Ju and all but secured his hold on the succession, Jong-Il finally told his father about his firstborn son with Hye-Rim. Kim Il-Sung, aides say, was briefly upset, then overcome with pride when he laid eyes on his male grandchild. Hye-Rim, however, remained locked inside the four walls of her own home, terrified of Jong-Il's fits of anger and megalomania. She had grown tired of the pain and loneliness. Anxiety chewed through her body like a disease.

For her Jong-Il's birthday dinner, Hye-Rim served live carp, still moving on the plate, followed by pear kimchi, the spicy fermented cabbage stuffed inside the sweet fruit. Everyone drank Hennessy, taking turns to toast Kim Jong-Il, fresh glasses brought out for each new toast. Choi, too, offered a toast to the Dear Leader's birthday. It seemed rude not to. Jong-Il was extremely cheerful.

"My wife doesn't know much," he told Choi. "She is a simple homemaker—isn't that what women should be? After all, the duty of a wife is to keep house and bring up the children. You know, you should go to the hot springs with her." He called out to Hye-Rim, who was bustling in and out of the kitchen. "Dear, take Madame Choi to the hot springs next time you go. She has trouble with a weak heart."

Choi didn't know how Jong-Il possibly knew this about her. She had mentioned nothing to the doctor who came to check up on her health. "Oh, do you?" Hye-Rim said. "I have the same condition. I'll definitely have to take you to the hot springs."

As the party wore on, Jong-Il, like many family men of the late 1970s, left the table and returned with his Super 8 camera to record the merriment. He zoomed in on faces, focusing on Choi for a long time. When the table had been cleared he led his guests to the living room, slipped the freshly processed film into the projector, and played the footage for everyone. The picture came out blurry, shaky, and pink. Everyone laughed about it, including him.

At around sunset the party subsided and Choi prepared to leave. As Kim and a guard escorted her out into the garden, she was startled by a series of loud explosions. The sky turned blindingly bright. Seeing her flinch with terror, Jong-Il laughed. "Our comrades are setting off fireworks for my birthday!"

The scene stuck in her mind as the Mercedes drove away. Just weeks before, she had been at home, divorced with two children, worrying that her small school might go out of business. Now she had just spent the day with Kim Jong-Il, son of a Communist dictator, as he filmed his own birthday party to the bursts of fireworks.

11
Accused

"I had hoped 1978 was going to be a good year for me," Shin Sang-Ok wrote later. He hadn't made a film in two years, but things seemed to be looking up at last. With the help of Kim Hyung-Wook, a friend and former KCIA chief who had also fallen out of President Park Chung-Hee's graces and now lived in exile in New Jersey, Shin was applying for a visa to emigrate to the United States. Hollywood was the home of his favorite filmmaker, Charlie Chaplin, and of the studio, Columbia Pictures, that Shin Film had emulated, and filmmaking there was free of political constraints and censorship. Shin hadn't quite broken off his relationship with Oh Su-Mi, but he wasn't especially keen on living out his life with her either. With the stringent travel controls the South Korean government placed on its citizens, Oh Su-Mi would likely not receive permission to follow him to the United States, and that would be that. Shin would come back to Seoul often enough, he was sure, to see his children, who for now lived with him but stayed with his brother's family while he traveled, and he and Oh could stay in touch. That his life plans might throw Oh's in complete disarray didn't seem to cross his mind for very long.

It was only Choi Eun-Hee that bothered him. Two weeks after she had left for Hong Kong she had yet to return to Seoul. Shin had a flight to Los Angeles booked for the next day and was growing concerned. He decided, before leaving, to call Lee Young-Seng, his Chinese representative in Hong

Kong. He was probably just being foolish, Shin thought, and Lee would quickly put his mind at ease.

"Have you seen Eun-Hee?" Shin asked, after exchanging some pleasantries with Lee.

There was a short silence on the line. "I can't discuss it on the phone," Lee finally said. "Come to Hong Kong."

"What do you mean? What's happened to her?"

"You have to come to Hong Kong. Just come. Please."

The next day Shin was met at the Hong Kong airport by Lee Young-Seng, who looked anxious and uncertain, and Kim Kyu-Hwa, the Shin Film manager who worked with Lee. At the hotel Kim filled Shin in on the facts: Choi had disappeared on January 14, leaving her luggage behind in the hotel. No one had heard from her since, and no one had been in or out of her room.

For a while, Shin sat bewildered.

"She hasn't used her room in more than ten days," he said.

"It looks that way," Kim answered.

"Could she have been robbed? She probably wasn't carrying much money." He knew his ex-wife.

"Probably wasn't a traffic accident, either," Kim suggested.

"If it had been, it would have been in the newspapers," Shin agreed.

"The hotel is quite upset. They've just left her bags in her room."

"There has to be some trace of her, some clue. Who did she meet with in Hong Kong?"

"Wang Dong-Il," Kim began, "and Lee Sang-Hee, and—"

"Lee Sang-Hee?" Shin remembered the woman. She was a friend of Kim's who frequently visited the Hong Kong office, that cute daughter of hers always in tow. Sang-Hee had always unsettled him a little, however. Every time she saw him she took endless pictures of him, calling them "souvenirs." She had run a café in the movie district of Seoul for years, if Shin remembered their conversations right, then considered running for the

National Assembly, and later traveled to innumerable trade fairs in Macao and Guangzhou. Her husband was a pro–North Korean businessman who had left South Korea for China and was engaged in trade with the North. Mrs. Lee said he often traveled to Pyongyang.

All this information crossed Shin's mind in a flash, but his thoughts snagged on one word, like a shirt sleeve caught on something sharp: *Pyongyang*. There had been rumors, the past couple of years, of people abducted by North Korean forces, and some presumed defectors had escaped from the North claiming they had never voluntarily gone there in the first place. The pianist Paik Kun-Woo and his wife, the actress Young Jung-Hee, alleged that North Korean agents had tried to kidnap them in Zagreb in July 1977, just six months earlier.

"How did they meet?" he asked.

"I introduced them and they seemed to hit it off pretty well," answered Kim.

"Where is that woman now?"

"I tried to call her several times, but no one answered the phone. I went to her house, but no one was there either."

"Then they might have both disappeared together!"

"It looks that way," Kim conceded.

"Do you think the North Koreans are behind this?" Shin let slip, off the cuff.

Kim knew Shin was thinking of Mrs. Lee's North Korean husband. "I wouldn't think so. Why would they do something like this?"

"Who actually invited Eun-Hee to Hong Kong? Who paid her expenses?" Shin asked.

"I don't know," Kim said. He looked embarrassed.

They were both quiet for a while. They had barely begun and they were at a dead end already.

Shin reported his ex-wife's disappearance to the police and to the South Korean embassy. He tried to track down Mrs. Lee's daughter and learned that she had not appeared in school for some time. And then, in a display either of his characteristic self-centeredness or merely of his desperation not to jeopardize his plans, he left for Los Angeles. In his memoir, he writes of his decision, "My plane reservation had been scheduled and it was hard to change the ticketing, especially with the big Chinese lunar New Year's celebration approaching." With that, he left the mystery of his ex-wife's disappearance unsolved and boarded the plane.

During the nearly three weeks he stayed in the United States, Shin met with his friend Kim Hyung-Wook, the former KCIA chief. He put an immigration lawyer on retainer—paying him a first fee of $2,000, a sizable chunk of the money he had left since the bankruptcy—and he filed an application for a temporary O classification visa, reserved for individuals "with extraordinary ability and internationally recognized record of extraordinary achievement in the arts." To secure it he needed a U.S. company to sponsor him, so he also visited Robert Wise, the director and producer of *West Side Story* and *The Sound of Music*. While filming the Steve McQueen picture *The Sand Pebbles* in China in 1966, Wise had fallen in love with the Far East; he had a great sense of community and was passionate about helping fellow filmmakers. Wise agreed to sponsor Shin. In his free time Shin sketched out ideas for a film of *Sleeping Beauty,* which he was considering as his first English-language project—the universality of the tale helping him over the language barrier—and he fell in love with a 1972 novel by David Morrell titled *First Blood,* about a Vietnam vet named John Rambo who brings the war back home to Madison, Kentucky. The book had been purchased by Columbia Pictures, who then sold it to Warner Bros., who then sold it to someone else, and so on for the previous six years. Shin thought he might be able to get in line to buy the film rights and get Akira Kurosawa's longtime collaborator, Ryuzo Kikushima, to write an English-language film adaptation. Shin knew very little English and Kikushima none; they planned to write in Japanese then have the screenplay translated.

While Shin was in California, the news of Choi's disappearance hit the Korean newspapers. The American correspondent of the *Hankook Ilbo* newspaper managed to track Shin down and flooded him with questions. Shin answered the best he could, but then the reporter said something that startled him.

"You know, many people suspect you might be somehow involved in Madame Choi's disappearance."

"That's nonsense," Shin replied. It almost made him laugh.

When he landed in Hong Kong on February 28, a dozen reporters were waiting for him at the arrivals gate. With them were police detectives of the Criminal Investigation Department of the Hong Kong Police Force.

12

Musicals, Movies, and Ideological Studies

"I want you to show Madame Choi some movies," Kim Jong-Il said. "The first one I want her to see is *The Forty-First*. You know the one I mean."

Kim Hak-Sun nodded. The three of them were sitting in the back of Jong-Il's car, parked outside the Korea Film Studio. It was two in the morning. Earlier that evening Choi and Jong-Il had attended a performance of the Mansudae Art Theater. Afterward, the conversation had drifted to movies.

"Are there film studios in North Korea?" Choi asked.

"Yes, of course we have a film studio!" Kim answered. "Would you like to see it?" Choi was about to say that yes, she would, maybe later in the week, but Kim had already jumped to his feet. He ordered the nearest guard to get his car ready.

They drove to the studio and, without getting out of the car, Kim gave Choi and Hak-Sun a guided tour, driving down the silent, deserted sets. There was a street made up to look like Korea in the colonial era, another dressed as Meiji-era Japan, a third that was a seedy version of a Seoul city block from the 1950s. The "European set" seemed to consist of nothing but a Tyrolean-looking chalet and an English country house facing each other on a hill. Down below them a fake vineyard and country church were reminiscent of the south of France. As the car drove around the buildings, Choi saw that each side of the houses had been made to look like a different stereotypical house from a certain European culture, as if the buildings were architectural Rubik's cubes. She had hoped Kim's decision to visit so late meant a night shoot might be under way, but there wasn't a soul other than them in the whole studio. What she saw of the place looked rather small and shabby, Choi thought.

Now they were outside the gate, idling in the car after the impromptu tour. "You know the film I mean," Jong-Il repeated.

Hak-Sun nodded, like a deep bow from the shoulders up. "I'll set it up first thing in the morning."

The Forty-First, oddly, was not a North Korean film but a Soviet one, made in 1956 by Grigori Chukhrai. It had been a Russian box-office hit and won the Special Jury Prize at the Cannes Film Festival, but Choi had never heard of it. The print wasn't subtitled, so Hak-Sun explained the narrative as it went on. Set during the Russian Civil War, the film told the story of an expert Red Army sniper, Maria, with forty White Army victims to her name. She fails to kill her forty-first target but takes him prisoner, finds out he knows sensitive information about his camp's strategy, and decides to escort him back to headquarters herself. The ship taking them across the Aral Sea is capsized and they are stranded on a small island, sole survivors. Over time the pair fall in love. Then, one day, a boat appears offshore, with the promise of rescue—but the boat belongs to the White Army. The male officer, ecstatic, rushes into the sea and starts swimming toward the ship. Maria calls out to him to stop, but he keeps swimming. She loads her rifle, places it against her shoulder, and aims. "Don't!" she pleads. He doesn't listen, so Maria, her eyes full of tears, shoots him. Overcome with grief, she drops the weapon and dives into the sea behind him, embracing his corpse and slowly drifting away.

Choi wasn't sure why Kim had chosen this film to show her first among all others. Maybe he had seen it when younger and always remembered it, or maybe it was the kind of film Jong-Il hoped to make—melodramatic, with big emotions against a dramatic historical backdrop, full of politically approved propaganda but still artful enough to win the second-highest prize at the world's most prestigious film festival. Choi was pondering this as she stood and Hak-Sun turned the lights back on.

"That movie was made just after Khrushchev took power in the Soviet Union," Hak-Sun said. "You understand the bottom line of the film, don't you? If you're a traitor, it doesn't matter if you're a lover, a friend, or what . . ."

She left the words hanging in the air.

A few weeks after her arrival in North Korea, Choi began to be allowed out of the compound. The excursions were always meticulously planned and tightly controlled. She would be informed at the last minute, and then she and Hak-Sun would climb into a Mercedes, two or three guards following in another car behind them. The convoy usually headed into Pyongyang.

Pyongyang, reduced to rubble by American bombs, had been redesigned from scratch as the state's most emblematic work of propaganda, full of imposing monuments, vast plazas, and wide boulevards, all of it made out of white concrete, completely free of pollution and traffic jams. This was, Kim Il-Sung had claimed, the perfect city, and the perfect capital for the perfect People's Paradise.

In fact, it was a show city accessible only to the elite, and the paradise, of course, was no such thing. Rather than a state of equal brotherhood and sisterhood, Kim had introduced an elaborate social order in which the eleven million ordinary North Korean citizens were classified according to their perceived political reliability. The *songbun* system, as it was known, ruthlessly reorganized the entire social system of North Korea into a communistic pseudofeudal system, with every individual put through eight separate background checks, their family history taken into account as far back as their grandparents and second cousins. Your final rating, or *songbun,* put you in one of fifty-one grades, divided into three broad categories, from top to bottom: the core class, the wavering class, and the hostile class. The hostile class included vast swathes of society, from the politically suspect ("people from families of wealthy farmers, merchants, industrialists, landowners; pro-Japan and pro-U.S. people; reactionary bureaucrats; defectors from the South; Buddhists, Catholics, expelled public officials") to *kiaesaeng* (the Korean equivalent of *geishas*) and *mudang* (rural shamans).

Although North Koreans weren't informed of their new classification, it quickly became clear to most people what class they had been assigned. North Koreans of the hostile class were banned from living in Pyongyang or in the most fertile areas of the countryside, and they were excluded from any good jobs. There was virtually no upward mobility—once hostile, forever hostile—but plenty downward. If you were found to be doing anything that was illegal or frowned upon by the regime, you and your family's *songbun* would suffer. Personal files were kept locked away in local offices, and were backed up in the offices of the Ministry for the Protection of State Security and in a blast-resistant vault in the mountains of Yanggang province. There was no way to tamper with your status, and no way to escape it. The most cunning part of it all was that Kim Il-Sung came up with a way for his subjects to enforce their own oppression by organizing the people into *inminban* ("people's groups"), cooperatives of twenty or so families per neighborhood whose duty it was to keep tabs on one another and to inform on any potentially criminal or subversive behavior. These were complemented by *kyuch'aldae,* mobile police units on constant lookout for infringers, who had the authority to burst into your home or office at any time of day or night. Offenses included using more than your allocated quota of electricity, wearing blue jeans, wearing clothes bearing Roman writing (a "capitalist indulgence") and allowing your hair to grow longer than the authorized length. Worse still, Kim decreed that any one person's guilt also made that person's family, three generations of it, guilty of the same crime. Opposing the regime meant risking your grandparents, your wife, your children—no matter how young—being imprisoned and tortured with you.

Historically, Koreans had been subject to a caste system similar to India's and equally as rigid. In the early years of the DPRK, the North Korean people felt this was just a modernized revitalization of that traditional social structure. By the time they realized something was awfully wrong, that a pyramid had been built, and that at the top of it, on the very narrow peak, sat Kim Il-Sung, alone, perched on the people's broken backs, on their murdered families and friends, on their destroyed lives—by the time they paused and dared to contemplate that their liberator, their savior, was betraying them—in fact, had *always* betrayed them—it was already much, much too late.

As a "guest" of Kim Jong-Il, Choi was often taken to the otherwise inaccessible Pyongyang, as well as to famous sites of the revolution, such as Kim Il-Sung's birthplace in Mangyongdae, a thatched-roof peasant hut and small barn just outside of the city center. Both buildings looked as if they had just been built, like a make-believe set in a theme park. Faking a peasant hut from the 1910s was nothing for the Kim regime: in later years they would create bogus ancient tombs to give their regime legitimacy, "proving" that the legendary Korean king Dongmyeong, whose dynasty ruled for seven centuries, had lived *north* of the thirty-eighth parallel. The tales said Dongmyeong was born from an egg impregnated by the sun and rode a unicorn into battle. In November 2012, the regime's Central News Agency announced the further news that the unicorn's grave had been discovered, conveniently right in the center of Pyongyang and under a rectangular rock marked UNICORN LAIR. The director of the DPRK's National Academy of Science declared, "This discovery proves that Pyongyang was a capital city of Ancient Korea as well as of the Koguryo Kingdom." That it also "proved" the existence of a mythical creature, remarkably, seemed secondary.

Disappointingly, Choi's outings involved no unicorns but a lot of looking at statues, including the gold-plated effigy of Kim Il-Sung himself, in front of which Choi was ordered to bow and of which she was proudly told that it was "a full three yards taller than the Egyptian sphinx." (Later in 1978, the Chinese premier Deng Xiaoping visited Pyongyang and, upon seeing the shining gold idol, expressed concern over how Beijing's money was being spent. The gold covering was stripped and replaced by an equally shiny copper.)

She was taken to museums, too. The Great Leader *loved* museums. He had so many built that North Korea even has a Museum of the Construction of the Museum of the Construction of the Metro. Most of them were in Pyongyang, like the Korean Art Museum, which consists exclusively of paintings of Kim Il-Sung and Kim Jong-Il, but at the time several were being built in other provinces, like the Sinchon Museum of American War Atrocities, full of "historically accurate" painted portrayals of the U.S. Army's brutality during the 1950–53 war: shooting children in the head, loosing wild dogs to feed on innocent peasants, skinning men alive, burning them on bonfires, scalping them with bone saws, nailing capitalist propaganda through their foreheads. The Americans are all depicted with pale skin, long noses, and demonic, wild-eyed glee. There are, of course, no photographs anywhere in the museum. Choi was taken to the Korean Revolution Museum, dedicated to Kim Il-Sung's forebears, and the Victorious Fatherland Liberation War Museum, where she was told the North Koreans had won what they called the Liberation War and shown pictures of U.S. Army vehicles surrendering, white flags held out their windows (these were, in fact, taken at the first armistice talks in Kaesong, when the UN command had been convinced by the North Koreans to arrive with the flags as a sign of peace). The museum downplayed North Korean casualties, exaggerated those of the enemy, and omitted the involvement of the Chinese and Soviets in the conflict. Later in the year Choi was taken to Kim Jong-Il's brand new International Friendship Exhibition Museum, which he had opened in August and which the Central News Agency boasted had been built in only three days. Made of nuclear-blast-resistant lead-lined concrete, the museum housed gifts presented to Kim Il-Sung by foreign dignitaries, "proof," the regime said, "of the world's endless love and respect toward the Great Leader." Highlights included a bulletproof limousine sent by Joseph Stalin, an armored train car from Mao, and a stuffed crocodile waiter, holding teacups on a tray, donated by Communists in Nicaragua. Soldiers with silver-plated machine guns searched guests at the door, and all visitors had to bow to the portrait of Kim Il-Sung at the entrance and then slip disposable shoe covers over their footwear so as not to tarnish the floors.

Choi's education, as it was called, continued with her attendant. Hak-Sun never stopped talking about the Great Leader and his achievements. Every day she urged Choi to join her at the piano and learn songs praising Kim

Il-Sung and Kim Jong-Il. Soon men came to ask her to make a propaganda radio broadcast stating she had come to the North voluntarily to "place [herself] under the care of the Great Leader," but she refused. They never pushed too hard, and their instructions seemed to be to win Choi over rather than bully her. One day, the man who had asked for Choi's passport and identity card when she first arrived returned and moved into the guesthouse. His name was Mr. Kang, from the Investigations Department of the State Security Department. He told her he had been assigned to her as her instructor. From that point on Kang managed Choi's everyday activity and oversaw her ideological reeducation. Choi was given a three-volume biography of Kim Il-Sung and asked to read it aloud. She found herself stumbling on the strange vocabulary and the long, sycophantic sentences.

"Try to read better," Kang said.

"Can't I just read it to myself?"

"No. Read it aloud."

For two hours a day, every day, she slogged through the book. Regularly Kang asked her to memorize passages and recite them back, word for word. Her progress was so slow and the books so thick and fulsome it took two months to get to the end of the third volume. "Every chapter idolized Kim Il-Sung and his ancestors," Choi remembered. His father was "courageous and patriotic," the book said, his mother "worked for the army fighting for national independence . . . [living] her life for her son and the national struggle," and Kim Il-Sung himself was like a benevolent sun, shining on all of Korea. Choi found the whole thing absurd. She didn't know yet that every child in North Korea read the same book at school, memorized even longer passages, and was told every word was undisputed fact.

In addition to history (the lives and exploits of Kim Il-Sung), economic theory (the economic policies of Kim Il-Sung), and culture (great songs and tales of Kim Il-Sung, produced by Kim Jong-Il), Choi was also instructed in the Great Leader's "groundbreaking" philosophy, known as *juche*. *Juche,* which can be translated as "self-reliance," took basic Marxist ideas about the conflict between wealthy landlord and working proletariat and added a strong element of nationalism. According to *juche,* after the People had taken control of the modes of production, they were in charge of their own fate, and their power in determining that fate lay in subsuming their individual needs to the will of the collective. The collective was led and represented by an absolute, supreme Great Leader, who must not be questioned, and had been sent to lead the Korean people because they were a special, chosen people, purer blooded and more virtuous than any other, a further reason why they must go forth into enlightenment without the help of other, lesser races.

Or something like that. *Juche* was a famously confusing, contradictory doctrine, one that North Korea watchers and analysts have tried to make sense of for forty years without being able to agree on what, exactly, it means. Choi Eun-Hee couldn't find any logic in it either. Often she found herself arguing with Kang. "The Communists insist that in this nation everyone is equal and lives happily," she told him one day. "But in my opinion the class system is even stricter here. What do you think?"

"This is the transitional period," Kang replied, in a loud, self-aware voice, as if he were reciting a memo. "Before one can reach the ideal Communist society, one must pass through this transition."

"Then what is the difference between capitalism and present-day socialism?" Choi asked innocently.

Kang looked flustered. "What are you trying to say? How can you possibly compare socialism to capitalism, where the rich get richer and the poor get poorer—a system based completely on the survival of the fittest?"

"But the welfare of society is also a capitalistic goal."

"Nonsense. There is a difference, an essential difference."

"What is the difference? Can you explain the difference more clearly?"

"If I say it's different, it's different!" Kang shouted. "Why do you ask so many questions?"

Every conversation went like this: brought to a premature end by the evasive promise that if she only stopped thinking for herself and simply embraced the revolution, all would be well. Every now and then the instructor would suddenly ask, "Madame Choi, you have many acquaintances in high places in South Korea, don't you? They say you were very close to the head of the KCIA, Kim Jong-Pil. Is it possible that Kim Jong-Pil could be the next president?" or "What does President Park think of so-and-so?" Choi knew they were trying to extract information from her, so she told Kang he overestimated her. "I've been stuck out in the country running my school in Anyang," she said. The man just laughed and, on another day, started asking again.

Choi had a question of her own: Why had she been kidnapped? "When we carry out the revolution in South Korea under the leadership of the Great Leader," Kang answered, "on that day you will have an important role to play. The South Koreans think of us as monsters and savages. So after liberating South Korea, no matter how we try to explain our ideology to them, do you think they will accept it? But if *you* stand in the forefront and tell the South Korean people—and just say a single word—it will be more persuasive than a hundred words from us." The idea seemed absurd to her, but over the weeks Kang kept bringing it up.

"I can't stand the idea that my family may be suffering and thinking I'm dead," Choi told him one day. "Without me they may starve to death."

"Starve?" He shrugged. "No matter how bad things get, people find a way to survive." Besides, he said, if she was so worried she just had to agree to the broadcast and they would know she was alive.

"What, tell the world I'm happily living here under the care of the Great Leader and all that crap?"

"Calm down. You must bear some pain for the good of the revolution."

"What the hell *is* this revolution?" she snapped.

Kang held her glare. "You need to study in a more revolutionary manner in order to understand it. We need to have a revolution in order to reunify the country. Only after reunification can you be reunited with your family and relatives. Please try to endure it until then."

On another occasion Choi received a lesson in which she was told Park Chung-Hee and his wife were American spies, that the First Lady had been hated in the South and her killing celebrated by the people. "I knew the First Lady," Choi interrupted angrily. "She was a wonderful, generous person. What proof do you have for this nonsense?" She insisted on proof until the instructor shouted at her and left. Every time she challenged Kang she was disinvited, like a grounded child, from the next weekly party.

She watched movies, too, of course, starting with *Sea of Blood*. Kim

Jong-Il watched it with her, and when it was finished he asked her for a critique. She told him the story was exciting and the performances genuine. He grinned happily when she told him the film was on a scale impossible to replicate at that time in South Korea. He seemed less happy when she suggested that North Korean works seemed to her repetitive, as they were all about duty, commitment, and self-sacrifice.

"It seems to me," she added, "that in the final analysis, revolution aims to enable the people to live well, doesn't it? There are a lot of other themes that can make people feel happiness."

Jong-Il blinked dubiously. "Such as?"

"Well, love, for example. The love shared by a man and a woman." Jong-Il still looked unconvinced. Surely, Choi suggested, *The Forty-First* was such a powerful film not just because of the political message, but because the characters at the heart of the story were in love? Isn't every story better with a love interest?

Jong-Il thought about that for a while, then gave a little shrug.

"When Director Shin gets here, we can figure it out."

Choi went numb. It was the very last thing she had expected to hear.

"What? What do you mean? What for? How?"

"He visited just a few days ago," Jong-Il said.

Surely that couldn't be true, Choi thought, it was nonsense—but then, could anyone lie that well? Seeing her hesitate, Kim turned to his bodyguards. "Comrades, didn't Director Shin promise to return after his last visit?" That was a bet too far—the men looked confused and embarrassed. "Yes," they mumbled after a second.

"See?" Jong-Il said to her before changing the subject. "You know, when we have a North–South Korean press conference, you must participate . . ."

Much to Choi's surprise—and to the surprise of his entourage—Kim had decided to make her his cultural adviser of sorts. He took her to the theater to see musicals he had commissioned, to the opera, the circus, and to his movie theater. For a man whose national philosophy was based on self-reliance and on the North Korean race's alleged superiority, Jong-Il seemed desperate for his guest's approval; in fact, everyone in North Korea, Choi noticed, seemed desperate for an outsider's approval. They boasted endlessly of everything's size and scope. "How about this theater!" Jong-Il asked Choi the first time she entered Pyongyang's main stage, the Mansudae Art Theater. "In terms of size and facilities, it's really world class, isn't it? And it was built in just one year." When he took her to the circus, he welcomed her by saying, "This is a special show for your benefit. Our troupe always wins prizes at international contests in Eastern Europe."

Choi became the only person to whom Kim Jong-Il would genuinely listen and whose opinions he sought, the only person allowed to criticize the Immortal Classics he was conceiving. She didn't hold back. They developed an odd bond, the younger man alternatively looking up to and talking down to her, she growing to like and even enjoy his company even as she cursed and loathed him for abducting her from her children and life. He took to occasionally calling her Teacher Choi, in the traditional formal Korean manner, especially when asking for her advice. He seemed at ease with her and could speak more openly than he allowed himself with his compatriots, but Choi was also keenly aware that she had never once been alone with him, that there were always bodyguards and underlings quietly standing by, waiting in the shadows.

13
Taken

After interviewing him, the Hong Kong police officers took Shin Sang-Ok to the Hilton Hotel, where he had booked a room. Earlier in the day a young British officer had listened patiently as Shin told him his theory of how his ex-wife had been taken by DPRK agents somehow connected to Mrs. Lee's North Korean husband. When North Korean Vice Premier Pak Song-Chol had visited Seoul during rare talks between North and South in 1972, he had requested a copy of *The Houseguest and My Mother* to bring back to Kim Il-Sung; Shin said he thought that might have something to do with all this. When he was done the officer thanked him, told him he would be in touch, and asked him to remain in Hong Kong until the investigation was concluded.

Shin sat in his hotel room, picked up the phone, and called his brother back home in Seoul. His brother told him the whole family was in "chaos." Shin's house had been searched, and the police and the press were suggesting he might have done harm to Choi, either out of desperate revenge for her leaving him or, somehow, given his ongoing financial difficulties, for monetary gain. Feeling cornered, Shin called a press conference that evening in his hotel room and repeated his theory about North Korean involvement to the dozen journalists who showed up. He had always mistrusted Mrs. Lee, he said, and added that he thought he might be at the center of a political conspiracy. The reporters had plenty of questions, but almost all of them were about his own alleged involvement in Choi's disappearance. He was getting nowhere.

After an uneasy night's sleep he headed to the Korean consulate and met with an intelligence officer and two policemen, to whom he repeated his story. The intelligence officer asked to see Shin's passport and authorization to travel, after which he recommended Shin return to Seoul and cooperate with the South Korean police's investigation. Shin told him he gladly would, on the condition that he be granted an exit visa in advance. He was unable to work at home, he explained, and needed the guarantee that he would still be able to travel and seek a new place of work. The intelligence officer answered he could guarantee no such thing. When Shin left the consulate, he noticed that the two police officials were following him. That evening, the Hong Kong police ordered him not to leave his hotel room. Officers took shifts guarding his door overnight.

It wasn't unusual for South Koreans of the day to mistrust their own authorities, an attitude borne from decades of civil injustice and exacerbated by recent political repression. Shin, from personal experience, felt this suspicion even more keenly than most. When the middle-aged Englishman knocked at his hotel room door and introduced himself as a detective of the Criminal Investigations Department, Shin knew immediately the direction in which his morning was heading.

"You're here to formally interrogate me as a suspect, aren't you?" he asked the Englishman.

"I am."

Shin let him in and they sat. "You are behind the disappearance of Choi Eun-Hee, aren't you?" the Englishman asked. He spoke in enunciated, concise single sentences, as if used to interlocutors who didn't understand much English.

"No," replied Shin.

"You have hidden Choi Eun-Hee and Lee Sang-Hee somewhere, haven't you? We searched Lee Sang-Hee's apartment in North Point and found the script for your movie *Hell Ship*. You planned everything with her, did you not?"

"No, it's not true."

"Then what was your script doing in her apartment?" the detective asked.

"I don't know," Shin said. "She was always dropping in to our office. Maybe my manager, Kim Kyu-Hwa, lent it to her. Let me speak with Kim Kyu-Hwa and we'll get to the bottom of this whole thing."

This policeman seemed determined to actually get some answers, Shin observed with relief. He had Kim, along with a Japanese interpreter, brought to Shin's room by a police officer. "We don't have Korean-speaking staff on hand, so you," the detective told Shin, "speak through him"—he pointed to the interpreter—"in Japanese. Mr. Kim will also answer in Japanese, and the answer will be translated into English for us. I don't want either of you saying anything to the other in Korean. Understood?"

Shin nodded. He looked at his manager, Kim. "How are you involved in this?" he asked bluntly. The more he thought about it, the more he felt Kim was holding something back. When Kim didn't answer, Shin asked, "Who invited Eun-Hee to Hong Kong?"

"The Kum Chang Corporation," Kim answered in Japanese.

"I've never heard of a company by that name."

"It's a small company." Each of them stopped in turn so the interpreter could repeat every sentence in English.

"How much did they pay you to make the introduction?" Shin continued when the interpreter had finished.

"Not much," Kim said in his native tongue, looking away.

"No Korean," the interpreter jumped in.

"How much?" Shin repeated.

"I received a few thousand dollars," Kim answered in Japanese.

Son of a bitch, Shin thought. "Who wanted you to send an invitation to Eun-Hee?"

"As a matter of fact," Kim answered, "it was Mrs. Lee."

Shin grew furious and shouted at Kim. The conversation descended into chaos as the two men raised their voices, yelling back and forth in a quick fire of question and answer, the interpreter struggling to keep up, the policemen unable to stop them.

"Where have they taken her?" Shin snapped. Kim didn't answer. Shin stepped toward him. "She was kidnapped to North Korea, wasn't she!"

"I never thought it would come to that—" Kim stammered.

"Don't you have any conscience?"

"I didn't know that would happen. I was taken in by that woman."

"I have nothing else to say to you. Get out of here."

"I didn't intend to do anything wrong. I was just a middleman—"

"Get him out of here."

The Hong Kong police arrested Kim, had his work visa revoked, and sent him back to Seoul, where he would eventually be convicted of breaching the National Security Law by consorting with North Korean citizens and given a fifteen-year prison sentence. Though everything was making more sense to Shin now, it offered him no comfort. Using Mrs. Lee, the North Koreans had paid off both Kim and the Chinese Wang Dong-Il to get Choi to Hong Kong, and from there had taken matters into their own hands. But there the trail ended. Shin had no idea what had happened next or how to go about finding out. Wang had since disappeared back to the mainland, and no one had been with Choi but Mrs. Lee—who was gone too. The North Koreans must have wanted Choi for a reason to go to so much trouble, Shin reasoned, which meant she was likely alive—but she had a bad heart, and what if the stress . . . ?

To make matters worse, Shin couldn't afford to stay in Hong Kong. It was late March already. South Korean passports were restrictive and issued only for one-, five-, or ten-year terms linked to the bearer's travel needs, and Shin's would expire in the summer, just a few months away. Once that happened his future travels would be at the mercy of the same authorities who had unjustly revoked his filmmaking license. He couldn't let that happen.

For the next four months, Shin traveled as far and as widely as he could afford to. All he needed was one film to be green-lit somewhere—anywhere that would offer him a resident visa—and his life would be back on track. He went to Japan looking for films to distribute and met the screenwriter Ryuzo Kikushima to discuss *First Blood*. Someone told him it was easier to get U.S. visas when applying from France, because South Koreans could enter the country visa-free, so he tried that, but with no luck. He stopped in West Germany to apply for political asylum, but the legal procedure was too expensive for his dwindling savings. A distributor in Singapore expressed interest in distributing some of Shin Film's existing films, which would at least refill the coffers, but was slow to confirm the agreement.

Events, unexpectedly, led back to Hong Kong. Shin had a bank account there, and the last remaining subsidiary of Shin Film was also based in Hong Kong. From there he could decide which of his remaining realistic options to choose: return to Seoul, or go to West Germany and spend what money he had left on an uncertain asylum application.

It was mid-July. His passport expired on August 9.

Shin hung up the phone. He was sitting in the Shin Film office and had just finished speaking to his brother in Seoul. Reluctantly, he had promised to give up on West Germany and return to Seoul. The government had relaxed its Motion Picture Law, his brother had said; maybe they could get a new license and start a new company. Shin had agreed to come home only to placate his brother and put an end to the conversation. In truth, he had no idea what he would do.

He slumped in his chair, exhausted. He had worked his whole life to build a film empire and here he was, nearly fifty-two years old, broke, divorced, out of a job, and at a loss to locate anyone, anywhere in the world, who wanted to give him one. He still thought of Choi every day, but it was starting to sink in that he would probably never see her again or find out what had happened to her. He thought sadly of his children and their anguish that their mother wasn't with them and never would be.

Lee Young-Seng, the director of the Hong Kong office, was watching him in silence. Finally he said, "Director Shin, I think I might have a solution. Will you tell me what you think?"

"A solution?" Shin answered.

"Yes, a way to resolve the problem with your passport." Gingerly, Lee told Shin he knew someone who could get him a genuine passport from a Central American country for $10,000. Shin was skeptical, but it wasn't unheard of. Eichmann and other Nazis had escaped to Argentina in 1945 under fake travel and identity papers. And in Southeast Asia, a crossroads for trafficking—drugs, wildlife, people—there was rumored to be a thriving black market for stolen and forged passports. Lee's idea sounded risky but also irresistible—what if it worked? It wouldn't solve all of Shin's problems, but it was a start: he wouldn't be forced to return to South Korea and would be able to travel, explore his options and, he hoped, find somewhere new to make films—and money.

Ten thousand dollars was a third of what Shin had left. He looked up at Lee.

"Can I trust this guy?"

"Of course."

"Okay," Shin said, nodding. "I'll do it."

Neon shopping signs flickered to life in the fading evening light as the car drove into Repulse Bay. Shin gazed out the window at the few villas dotted along the hill. The bright lights in the windows came on as the sun sank behind the horizon. The people living in those houses with their families must be happy, he reflected. Somehow the thought made him feel depressed.

Shin and Lee had taken the ferry from Kowloon, where the office was located, to Hong Kong Island. The white Mercedes and chauffeur had been waiting for them on the other end, sent by Lee's contact. They'd driven through the main tourist area, past the villas and resorts, and now they were leaving even the more remote homes in their rearview mirror.

Suddenly the car screeched to a halt. Four long-haired men were blocking the road. They walked up to the car, yanked open the passenger door, and pulled Shin out. One of them put a flick knife to his throat.

"Give me money!" he hissed in broken English.

"Please—don't—just take my money," Shin stammered. He reached for his pocket, but suddenly another one of the men slipped a nylon bag over his head and unfurled it all the way down to his feet, covering his whole body. A rope was tied around his ankles. Shin panicked, starting to run out of air, but then he heard the sound of fabric ripping and felt the knife's blade slicing just an inch away from his nose. Fresh air rushed in, cool against his face. As he opened his mouth to take a deep breath, one of the men pressed a bottle to the jagged opening and sprayed a liquid in Shin's face. The smell of it burned his nostrils. Within a few seconds he had passed out.

When he blinked back to blurry consciousness, he felt himself being carried. He could hear waves hitting the shore just under him. That's it, he thought. They had robbed him and they were going to kill him. He was going to end his life at the bottom of the ocean inside a nylon bag.

The men carrying him stopped. Shin thought he heard a motorboat in the distance, growing closer.

"I wonder if the comrade doctor is on the boat," one of the men said, his voice close to Shin's ear, startling him.

Shin felt his body flood with relief. He wasn't going to die after all.

His relief was short-lived. The man's accent was North Korean.

Shin's journey was much the same as Choi's. He woke on the same freighter, in the same cabin, with the same smiling, Santa Claus–like face of Kim Il-Sung beaming down at him. He, too, was told he was being delivered to the People's Republic "to answer the call of the Great Leader."

When Shin asked one of the omnipresent guards where the Chinese man who was traveling with him had gone, the guard laughed. "You think Lee Young-Seng is Chinese? He's one of us!" The man thought it hilarious that Shin had been duped for years. Shin asked another crew member whether Choi Eun-Hee was all right. Was she in Pyongyang? The man shrugged. He didn't know, but he'd heard the South Korean intelligence service had kidnapped and executed her for cooperating with the North's army during the Korean War. Utter nonsense, Shin thought. Or was it?

After three days the freighter weighed anchor near Nampo and Shin was transferred to a small motorboat and taken to shore. There was no personal welcome from Kim Jong-Il for him, just two men in Mao-collared tunics standing by a Mercedes-Benz.

"Welcome to the Socialist Fatherland," one of them said.

It was still afternoon when they drove him through Pyongyang, and Shin—who was born in the North but hadn't been able to set foot there since the division in 1945—found himself entering a city he hadn't seen in over thirty years. Only Pyongyang looked nothing like it used to. The wide boulevards corresponded to none of the previous streets. All the buildings were new and made of concrete, many of them covered in tiles, "look[ing] exactly like the inside of a public bathhouse," Shin wrote. As a city it was, simply, otherworldly. The monuments looked fake, the statues hollow. There were no shops, no restaurants, no billboards, no signs for businesses, no outdoor seating, no kiosks, no delis, no cafés, no bars, no street vendors. The entire city was empty of commerce, empty of vehicles, empty of old people and animals, empty of any cheer, noise, or joy. There were no street names, no signs on official buildings. Kim Il-Sung's face, though, was everywhere: from statues to posters to the giant propaganda hoardings and placards on the rooftops. "No one was out in the streets," Shin noticed. "[The city] was as silent as a grave." Revolutionary songs and propaganda drifted, faintly, from concealed loudspeakers everywhere.

Shin was driven to a villa about an hour outside of Pyongyang, in an area he was told was called the Chestnut Valley. The villa's screening room was ready and staffed for him. The cosmetics he used at home were lined up in the bathroom and the wardrobe was fully stocked with suits, shirts, ties, cuff links, underwear, socks, and casual wear. The shirts fit Shin exactly, down to his large 16½-inch collar and his short thirty-two-inch sleeves. When he sat down for dinner, a steel dish of cold broth full of noodles was placed in front of him.

"I understand," his guard said casually, "that your favorite dish is cold noodles."

For the next two months Shin lived inside that house. He never met or spoke to Kim Jong-Il, although he was told more than once that "everything is being done on special instructions from the Dear Leader Comrade

Kim Jong-Il." A man everyone called Comrade Deputy Director came every day to look after his reeducation, acquainting him with Kim Il-Sung's glorious life and career, and occasionally took him on sightseeing day trips. If Shin asked after Choi, the deputy director flew into a rage and scolded him.

Shin glimpsed Kim Jong-Il once, in the front row of a performance at the Mansudae Art Theater, recognizing him by the way everyone stood and applauded when Kim did, someone shouting out "Long live the Comrade Dear Leader!"

"When we left the theater," Shin recalled, "it was dark. The fountain out in front of the theater was spewing water high in the air, bathed in a sea of multicolored lights. It was time for the changing of the guard at the building, and a column of goose-stepping soldiers marched past. For the first time I really felt I was in North Korea."

He would feel that same disquieting recognition once more just a few weeks later. September 9 was Independence Day, the anniversary of the founding of the Democratic People's Republic of Korea, and the end of the Arirang Festival, a monthlong series of festivities. On that morning the deputy director brought Shin a badge in the shape of a red flag with Kim Il-Sung's smiling face pasted on it, and showed Shin how to pin it on "with the proper reverence." Then he drove Shin to the Pyongyang People's Gymnasium, where they took their reserved seats in the VIP section. Twenty thousand screaming people packed the rows of seats all around the indoor stadium. The roar was deafening.

The Arirang Festival was named after a folk story representing the division of Korea, in which a young couple is torn apart by an evil landlord. It has since become known as the Mass Games, famous for its goose-stepping army parades, highly choreographed gymnastic demonstrations, and huge mosaic pictures created by tens of thousands of trained audience members holding colored cards up in the air at the right time. All of the performances are by ordinary citizens, who can be chosen as early as their fifth birthday, and for the rest of their lives much of their time, every single year, is spent training and preparing for the event. Kim Jong-Il had invented the Mass Games in 1972, for his father's sixtieth birthday, and it was one of the ways he hoped to demonstrate his virtues as an heir. The games were at the center of what came to be known as "succession art," write historians Heonik Kwon and Byung-Ho Chung, "considering that the central objective of the era's artistic production was to sublimate Kim Il-Sung's authority in preparation for transforming his personal charisma into a historical, hereditary charisma" that could be passed on to Kim Jong-Il.

Shin stood at his seat and looked down. He could see Kim Il-Sung at the front of the VIP section, the Chinese premier Deng Xiaoping and other foreign dignitaries filling the seats by his side. Kim Il-Sung looked fatter than in his official portraits, which were all paintings, and what looked like a large tumor swelled on the back of his neck. After a while Kim Il-Sung stood at the main platform and gave a ceremonial speech. Every few sentences he was interrupted by the loud, rapturous applause of the crowd. Across from him students held up colored placards to create a mosaic of the North Korean flag. Then, with the greatest of ease, they formed Kim Il-Sung's face among undulating waves and floating clouds. Shin had never before seen such a large, well-coordinated crowd—nor had he ever felt so completely alone.

Choi Eun-Hee sat in a different section of the stadium that day, maybe even—if either of them had happened to look carefully—within view of her ex-husband. This was the first time in her nine months in the country that she had seen a North Korean celebration that involved ordinary citizens. Everyone around her was applauding endlessly, clapping so hard and for so long that her hands hurt trying to keep up. It was clear to her that everyone in the arena adored Kim Il-Sung as "the absolute being," she wrote later. Will I someday applaud with as much fervor as them? she asked herself. As she watched the cards flip and change, she thought of the young people holding them—how long it took them to prepare, how they were treated, whether they had time to do anything else or have any fun. She looked down at the field full of children, waiting in their colorful uniforms for their turn to perform, and noticed that some of the children, who were not allowed out of the ranks in case they disturbed the flow of events, were wetting themselves where they stood.

The show lasted for several hours. Neither Shin nor Choi knew the other was in the same building that day.

14
The Others

Choi knew nothing of her ex-husband's arrival, yet it was around that time that Kim Jong-Il stopped inviting her to his parties.

No official reason was given, but Jong-Il had become more and more preoccupied with affairs of state lately. He was playing an increasingly central role. In September 1978 he made a rare, highly visible appearance, meeting foreign guests arriving to celebrate the Arirang Festival and the thirtieth anniversary of the founding of the DPRK. In December he introduced a new national slogan, "Let's live our own way," an indicator that North Korean policy was moving away from socialism, and from now on would be about nationalism.

Choi kept requesting to see the Dear Leader, hoping to plead again for her return to South Korea, but no answers were forthcoming. He did send Choi gifts almost daily: boxes of bespoke clothes for every season, textiles, fur coats, cosmetics. He also sent copies of every single picture taken of her by his photographers, from her arrival at Nampo Harbor through the parties and sightseeing visits. As time passed, Choi sank into a depression. Having Hak-Sun's company made the days bearable, but "when she went to her quarters at night," Choi says, "I was overcome with nostalgia and anxiety and terror. I would go into the bathroom and turn on the water full force and just sit there and cry." She found that after midnight, when the military scrambling had been turned off, the two radios by her bed picked up a South Korean frequency. She listened to it every night, the blankets pulled over her and the radio to muffle the sound. "It was my only pleasure, my only consolation."

And then Kim Hak-Sun was removed, too. There was no good-bye. One morning she was just gone from the house. "She returned to Pyongyang for good," Choi was told by the other attendants. This new, additional loss confirmed to Choi that, in all likelihood, she would spend the rest of her life without purpose in this surreal prison just a couple of hundred miles from her homeland. Once a famous actress with friends, family, and a career, she now found herself in an alternate universe where people spoke her language but where she was unable to relate to anything. She couldn't eat, she couldn't sleep. When she did drift off she was haunted by nightmares of her children, whom she was sure she would never see again. She thought of suicide, but the pain it would cause her loved ones was too high a price to pay. "It was an awful time," she says.

As the weather got warmer her instructors, fulfilling a promise made earlier by Kim Jong-Il, took her to a lakeside villa for a fishing weekend. On the first day, as she was headed down to the water, she passed "a large house surrounded by a concrete wall and a barbed-wire fence" by the side of the path. As she walked by the wall a sharp voice behind it anxiously cried out, "Who are you?" Choi's attendant asked her to wait and went to the house's gate, just a few feet away. When he returned he hurried her back up the path. "We should go back," he muttered. "This area is off-limits."

A couple of days later Choi was in a fishing boat with Mr. Kang and an attendant when she saw the same house in the distance. A woman stood in its front courtyard, walking in and out of the lake. She wore a light green gown, the hem of it drifting over the surface of the water, her hair carelessly tied and gently fluttering in the breeze. She looked sad and refined.

Staring at her with fascination, Choi couldn't help notice that keeping a watchful eye on the woman was a pair of attendants just like her own.

Around the time of the Arirang Festival, Choi was made to change residences. In the middle of the night Kang came into her room and told her to pack a suitcase. An army jeep was waiting outside. Kim Jong-Il preferred to move people under cover of darkness, so that they were more difficult to follow—and so that they would have a harder time keeping track of where, exactly, they were being taken.

They drove up mountain roads for two hours before arriving at a two-story building in Tongbuk-Ri. It was hidden in the woods, Choi recalls, "like a haunted house in the darkness." Choi was introduced to her new private attendant, a middle-aged woman who looked like Kim Hak-Sun; this woman's name, Choi was told, was *Ho* Hak-Sun.

The Tongbuk-Ri house was much more modest than the previous one. Choi's room was a traditional room with tatami mats on the floor, with only a bed, a wardrobe, and a table for furniture. There was no radio. Choi felt discarded. She spent her time knitting and taking strolls in the mornings, and watching films in the afternoon. Her children's birthdays came and went. She celebrated them in sad silence, full of pain. She hoped her son would grow up "a good, honest man" and that her daughter would "go on with [her] life . . . and marry a wonderful man." She wondered where their father was and if he was taking care of them.

She remembered a day when she was a child and her mother had suddenly returned from running errands, hugged her daughter, and told her, "I just had to come home earlier because I was thinking of you." At the time, Choi had giggled and shrugged it off. Now she understood the longing. She was desperate to see Seoul again, too. She missed the sight of "young women promenading in front of the stone wall of Toksu Palace, arm in arm; young men climbing up Paegundae and shouting 'Yahoo!' to hear the echo; the whole family sitting gathered around the television set after finishing supper and watching some drama and crying; people having little spats about some trivial thing and people rejoicing in sharing small pleasures with one another. Oh, how I wanted to see them once again!"

Mr. Kang introduced new elements to her ideological training. For 9/9 Day she was asked to write a "congratulatory message" to Kim Il-Sung, using an official book collection of congratulatory messages as a guide. The examples in the volume were "very lengthy and tedious," Choi said. "The endless adjectives of praise and respect made the sentences meaningless." She tried her best, jotting down a few sentences in the euphoric, sycophantic style expected of her. Kang read over her letter, nodded, and put it in an envelope. Then he handed her a form headed "Autobiography for Party Cadres."

"Now you must write down the history of your life and submit it to the Party," Kang said. "You must write only the truth. You must try hard to examine and judge yourself and your actions. Then write down your conclusions."

"I've never written an autobiography," Choi protested. She found the exercise not just absurd but upsetting. The last thing she wanted to do was revisit, in depth, the life she had been forced to give up. "How can I just sit down and write one?"

"This is the solicitude of the Dear Leader Comrade Kim Jong-Il."

"Solicitude?"

Kang gestured at the form. "Now write it quickly."

Choi picked up a pen. *I was born on November 9, 1930,* she began. *I am the third daughter of my father Choi Young-Hwan. . . .* As she wrote, Kang read her drafts and requested more detail here, or the specific inclusion of an uncle or a cousin there. Choi didn't understand the logic of it, but she understood that it was some kind of test, an initiation. To what, she had no clue.

When she wasn't working on her autobiography, Madame Choi filled her days the best she could. Along with reading and knitting, she took to walking through the nearby woods. She noticed that large parts of the compound's grounds were blocked off by signs announcing they were off-limits. After a couple of weeks she was joined by a stray dog, and she started taking food from the table to feed him. She also made friends with one of the gardeners, and whenever she could she would be outside with him, on her knees, ripping up weeds and planting flowers. She liked manual work. "Working with my hands netted results—tangible results. Knitting (or gardening) seemed honest and down-to-earth in my life, where everything else was in chaos." She kept a diary, too, and that helped keep her sane and her perspective steady.

Her new attendant, Ho Hak-Sun, was a warm and reassuring presence.

She brought Choi ginseng liquor when she was anxious. "Drink a little of this," she would urge. "You'll feel less tense." Often she would squeeze Choi's hand and try to soothe her. "Please calm down, Madame. It's bad for your health. Be strong and learn to bear it. Better days will come."

"When I first met her," Choi recalled, "she was in her midfifties. She was not beautiful, but she wasn't ugly either. She seemed kind and loyal. Though she had little education, she was very intelligent. I praised her, saying, 'If you had received a formal education, you would most definitely have been a great success in life.' She was born to a poor family of slash-and-burn farmers in the mountains of Onsong, North Hamgyong Province. She was married when she was eighteen, in the same ordinary clothes she wore every day." Shortly after the wedding she had had a child, and shortly after that her husband had gone to fight in the Korean War. There he died, along with every other adult male member of the family. Like all war widows, Hak-Sun was made a member of the Workers' Party, in remembrance of her family's sacrifice, and thanks to this she was able to improve her station. She started work in a small Party-run store, taught herself to read, write, and count, and rose to managing the store. By 1964, eleven years after the end of the war, she was transferred to Pyongyang to work for the Central Committee, where, she told Choi, she "was involved in sensitive, secret work." She worshipped Kim Il-Sung. She kept two savings books in her home, both of them always of the same amount: 4 won, 15 chon in the first (representing Kim Il-Sung's birthday, April 15), 2 won and 16 chon in the other (Kim Jong-Il's birthday, February 16). Her greatest ambition in life was to distinguish herself enough to receive a Kim Il-Sung watch, engraved with the Great Leader's name. "The name watch," Ho Hak-Sun told Choi, "represents the glory of the Communist Party and confers privileges on the wearer." Choi found her a remarkable woman and took to calling her auntie, or sister.

As 1978 drew to an end the weather turned bitingly cold. Hak-Sun brought Choi a People's Army winter uniform, a drab, mustard-colored, quilted cotton jacket, pants, and padded cotton shoes, and asked her to wear it on her walks. They were the warmest clothes she could find. Choi hadn't seen a North Korean army uniform since 1952. Looking in the mirror, she thought she looked ridiculous.

She walked twice every day, once in the morning and once in the afternoon. As the weather dropped below zero, sometimes as far down as minus twenty degrees Celsius (minus four Fahrenheit), she saw people climbing trees to get over the compound walls, collecting firewood to bring home. Choi learned later that families in the local area were given small rations of coal dust, which they were supposed to turn into briquettes to use for cooking and heating, a process that no one had the time for, busy as they were with six-day workweeks, daily compulsory ideology training sessions, and "volunteering." One man, when he saw Choi, froze and started to tremble. "He kept bowing to me," Choi remembered. "He looked over seventy years old. He had icicles on the end of his mustache and his cheeks were sunken." She stepped forward to help him, but the old man panicked, apologized, and scuttled into the woods in terror. When the guards caught people such as him, they shot them or sent them to prison camps for theft. Sometimes Choi heard human beings wailing in pain in the distance, in rhythm, as though they were being flogged or beaten.

Most of all her curiosity was piqued by the other houses. Tucked away in the far corners of the compound, the small houses were all spread out from one another, but every now and then she would see a jeep or a Mercedes drive to one of them. Someone else must live here, Choi thought.

The Arab woman was the first one she met.

It was during one of her afternoon strolls that Choi ran into her. The woman was walking the other way and Choi abruptly stopped in surprise. It was the first non-Korean face Choi had seen in the country. "She had a high, shapely nose," Choi describes, "and a beautiful complexion." The Arab woman looked as curious about Choi as Choi was about her. Choi used the little English she knew and asked, "Where are you from?"

"I'm from Jordan," the woman answered. She seemed relieved to talk.

"Jordan? You're a long way from home."

"Yes. Where are you from?"

"I'm from Japan," Choi lied. She wasn't sure why, but she didn't want to say she was from South Korea.

"Where did you buy that hat?"

Choi was wearing one of the knitted hats she made to pass the time. "I made it myself."

"Really? It's really nice."

Choi smiled. Neither of them spoke much English, and the conversation reached an impasse.

"Good-bye," Choi said. She walked past the woman, but a few steps later she heard, "Are you happy?"

Choi stopped. She turned around. "Oh . . ." she mumbled and shrugged.

"It's so frustrating," the Jordanian woman said. "I cannot even write to my family."

"Oh. I'm sorry." There was a pause. "See you again."

When Choi told Hak-Sun about the encounter, the attendant frowned and suggested she avoid her—and anyone else—in the future. Choi ignored her. She knitted the woman a hat, and in return the Jordanian woman gave her one of her scarves for Christmas. A couple of months later she left, and Choi never saw her again.

Throughout December Mr. Kang was in the house more frequently than ever, pushing Choi to write New Year's greetings to Kim Il-Sung and Kim Jong-Il, "written with lofty words and . . . four to five pages in length. It had to be the best writing possible. Even the paper it was written on had to be the best available." If Choi made a mistake, or if a single character wasn't "neat and clear," she was required to restart that page from scratch. Kang read every draft. He criticized her for being repetitious or for using the same compliment to both men. "The right titles are missing here," he said, pointing at a specific line. "Comrade Choi! Why do you still use this spelling? That erroneous spelling is only used in the South." On Christmas Day, Kang finally approved drafts of both letters and brought her expensive paper to write the final missives. Not a single letter could be crooked, he reminded her, and every character was to be evenly spaced, or she would have to start over. "It took me two full days to write the two letters," Choi says. "I wrote them so many times I still remember them almost verbatim. The letter I sent to Kim Il-Sung went: *As the New Year approaches, I would like to send my regards to you, our sun, our father, our leader. Undefeated in hundreds of battles, man of steel and our esteemed leader who led the defense of our country against Japan and refused to kneel before the U.S. imperialists. . . .*" The letter to his son began: *Light of our people, our teacher, our dear Comrade Kim Jong-Il, I would like to express my deepest gratitude and thanks. I would also like to wish you good health for the next year. I thank you for taking me into your confidence and helping me to see the new light. . . .*

Kang was pleased. Not everyone was privileged enough to send letters to these great men, he told Choi, and even among those letters, only a few, such as hers, would be personally read by them. Choi shook her head. The man genuinely believed she should feel blessed to write letters of gratitude to the men who had kidnapped her.

It was another six months before Choi met the beauty from Macao. She was on her usual stroll when she glimpsed the woman coming toward her. She was tall, with stylishly short, straight hair. Choi knew immediately she wasn't North Korean. They both stopped in the path, facing each other for a moment. They exchanged greetings. The woman's Korean was imperfect but good enough.

"Where are you residing?" Choi asked, stiffly and politely.

"There," the woman pointed. "In Building Number Four." It was the same house the Jordanian woman had lived in.

"You're not from here, are you?" Choi asked.

"No, I'm Chinese, from Macao," the woman answered.

Choi looked around. No one seemed to be watching them. She gestured at the woman to follow her to a more remote part of the woods.

"You speak Korean well," she said when they stopped. "Where did you learn?"

"I learned it after coming here. I've been here for nearly a year."

"What is your name?"

"My name is Hong. My English name is Catherine." She didn't ask for Choi's name.

"What are you doing nowadays?" Choi asked.

"I'm studying Kim Il-Sung's writings." She stopped for a moment, then blurted out: "I know who you are, sister. You're the famous actress, Choi Eun-Hee."

"How do you know me?" Choi asked, surprised.

"In Macao I saw your picture in the newspapers quite often. I recognized you right away."

Choi took a deep breath. Her whole body charged with curiosity, her voice trembling, she asked Catherine the question she had wanted to ask since the second she had first laid eyes on her.

"How did you get here?"

Catherine Hong was one in a long list of people abducted by North Korean operatives during the 1970s. Late at night on May 29, 1970, Lee Jhe-Gun and twenty-seven fellow fishermen were sailing their ship, the *Bongsan,* when several ships suddenly smashed into the side. Commandos swarmed aboard the fishing vessel, pointing their assault rifles at the fishermen and shouting, "Do you want to die? Get out! Get out!" The fishermen were lined up, and the *Bongsan* was tethered to one of the other ships and towed into North Korean waters.

In June 1974 two ethnic Korean Japanese children, aged three and seven, were taken by North Korean spies from their home in Saitama, Japan. They were brought to Tokyo, where they were kept for six months, before being put on a North Korean ship bound for the homeland. Their father, a leader of the network of North Koreans in Japan known as the Chosen Soren, had recently fallen out of favor with Pyongyang.

The next year, South Korean Go Myung-Seob and thirty-two fellow fishermen were sailing off the coast of Korea when the boat unknowingly drifted too far north. Suddenly the thirty-three men found themselves in North Korean custody, being forcefully sailed to the North. When they arrived, they were put to work doing hard labor. It was twenty-nine years before Go managed to escape back to South Korea. By then he had been forced to marry a North Korean, had fathered two children, and the majority of his crewmates had died. When he escaped, he felt certain his wife and two children would be killed as punishment.

In November 1977, thirteen-year-old schoolgirl Yokota Megumi had just finished badminton practice in her hometown of Niigata, a harbor city on the west coast of Japan. She waved good-bye to her teammates and friends and headed on the short walk home, her racquet stuffed in her white bag over one shoulder, her black school bag in her hand. She paused at a traffic light. Suddenly, strange men grabbed her off the sidewalk, trussed her, and stuffed her into a Soviet military cargo bag. She woke up on a rusty fishing trawler headed for North Korea. For the next sixteen years she underwent isolation and reeducation in Pyongyang, was forced to teach Japanese at Kim Jong-Il Military University, and then was made to marry another abductee, this one from South Korea. She reportedly committed suicide following a nervous breakdown in 1993.

In June 1978, the family of Yaeko Tagushi, a twenty-two-year-old bar hostess in Tokyo, received a phone call from the nursery where her two young children were enrolled. Yaeko had not turned up to pick up the children; was something wrong? She had gone out to buy herself a new blouse and was never seen again. Thirteen years later, her family learned that she had been taken, against her will, to North Korea.

That same summer, five South Korean high school students disappeared from island beaches and were presumed drowned. Two decades later the teenagers, now middle-aged adults, were discovered in North Korea, working as instructors at Kim Jong-Il's spy school, teaching North Korean would-be operatives about the culture and lifestyle of South Korea.

Yasushi Chimura and his fiancée, Fukie Hamamoto, were twenty-three years old on July 7, 1978. They were taking a walk after a date on the rocky beach of Wakasa Bay, near Obama, Japan, when they were attacked by North Korean men and forced onto a nearby boat. They were presumed missing for more than twenty-five years before the North Korean government admitted to their abduction. They were returned to Japan in October 2002, leaving behind the three children they had while in the DPRK, who are considered full North Korean citizens by the Pyongyang regime.

Later that month, twenty-year-old Kaoru Hasuike and his girlfriend Yukiko were on a secluded corner of the beach near Kashiwazaki City, trying to get away from the summer crowds. A man walked up to Kaoru with a cigarette and asked if he had a light. Before Kaoru could answer, the man struck him in the face and other strangers ran over. Within seconds, the stunned couple had been gagged, pinned down, and shoved into two large body bags. The young couple was left on the ground for a short while. They could hear the men standing around them, probably waiting for any potential witnesses to clear off. Then the men loaded the two onto an inflatable dinghy, which took them to a larger ship farther out at sea. When Kaoru and Yukiko were let out of the bags they were drugged. As the cool evening air stroked their faces, they watched the lights of their home city fade into nothingness over the horizon. Two days later they were in Chongjin, North Korea.

Thirteen days after Hasuike and his girlfriend vanished from the beach, nineteen-year-old Hitomi Soga and her mother, Miyoshi, were buying ice cream on Sado Island, forty-three miles across the water from Kashiwazaki, when three men ran up to them and beat them to the ground. They gagged them, stuffed them into black body bags, and carried them to the nearby river, where a small motor-powered skiff awaited. The boat took them to a larger ship off the coast. Hitomi was locked in the hold until the next morning, by which point land was nowhere to be seen on the horizon. She didn't know where her mother had been taken.

The same evening she and her mother were abducted, just a few hours later, Suichi Ichikawa, twenty-three, and Rumiko Matsumoto, twenty-four, both disappeared from Kagoshima Prefecture, 870 miles away on the southern tip of Japan; they were married in North Korea the following year.

A month later, two Japanese men called an escort company in Singapore and requested that five beautiful ladies be sent to their yacht for a "floating party." Twenty-four-year-old Diana Ng Kum Yim, twenty-two-year-olds Yeng Yoke Fun and Yap Me Leng, and nineteen-year-olds Seetoh Tai Thim and Margaret Ong Guat Choo were sent to the yacht to spend the evening with the men. All of them—men, yacht, and young escorts—disappeared that night and were never seen again, except for Yeng Yoke Fun, who in 1980 resurfaced working in a Pyongyang amusement park.

In June 1979, South Korean Ko Sang-Moon got into a taxi in Oslo, Norway, and asked to be taken to the South Korean embassy. The driver—by accident or by design—took him to the wrong Korean embassy. The next time anyone heard of Ko, he was in North Korea, and Pyongyang claimed he had defected of his own free will. That same year four Lebanese women were told by an employment broker that there were four secretarial jobs paying $1,000 a month in Japan. They all eagerly signed up and got on a plane they thought was bound for Tokyo, but its actual destination was Pyongyang. As soon as they landed, their passports were confiscated and they were sent, one of them said, "to an institution where we were trained in spy activities including judo, tae kwon do, karate, and eavesdropping, as well as being given indoctrination lectures to believe the teachings of Kim Il-Sung. There were twenty-eight young women in the institute, including three French, three Italians, and two Dutch ladies, among other Western European and Middle Eastern women. They were equally powerless in rebelling against their captors."

Some people were luckier and managed to evade capture. In 1977 the actress Young Jung-Hee and her partner, the pianist Paik Kun-Woo, narrowly escaped an attempted abduction by North Koreans in Zagreb, Yugoslavia. They had been told that a wealthy Yugoslavian wanted Paik to perform for him live at his home. Zagreb's police chief had been paid $30,000 to cooperate with North Korean operatives hiding inside the residence, ready to pounce on the couple as soon as they arrived. But Young and Paik had grown apprehensive, and as soon as they arrived in Zagreb they took a taxi to the U.S. embassy. The embassy was closed, but the vice consul was in his first weeks in the post and working late. He took the couple to the Palace Hotel, where he was staying while he found a residence, and booked them a room on the same floor as his. At 6 a.m. there was a knock on their door. Paik called the vice consul, who looked out his own door. "There are three North Koreans outside your room," he told Paik. American personnel was called to the hotel and helped the South

Korean couple escape to the lobby via the service lift, then took them straight to the airport.

On August 15, 1978, a Japanese man and his fiancée in Takaoka City were attacked by six suspicious men after returning to their car from an afternoon swimming in the ocean. They were saved by a dog barking nearby, which startled their attackers as they tried to bind them and stuff them into body bags. The woman ran to a nearby house, which happened to be inhabited by a retired policeman. The man, with the bag still tied around his head, managed to run to another house a couple of hundred yards away. When local police investigated the crime scene later that day, they recovered a handmade rubber gag, with a hole cut through it so the victim could breathe, rubber ear covers to prevent the victim from hearing, as well as large green nylon bags, a rope, and several towels.

Throughout the 1970s, North Korean operatives kidnapped foreigners from the South China Sea and the Sea of Japan; from London, Copenhagen, Oslo, Hong Kong, Macao, Zagreb, Beirut, and several cities in South Korea, China, and Japan. The head of North Korea's special forces and covert operations division during those years, the man who would have given or approved every single order, was Kim Jong-Il.

Catherine Hong's story of her abduction was much the same as the others. She had been working as a tour guide in Macao in 1978 when two men in their thirties hired her. "I took them around town for a few days," Catherine told Choi. "They paid me well and spent a lot of money. They said they were from Southeast Asia and seemed to be sons from rich families. They spoke English very well. One day they asked me to take them to the coast." When they arrived at the beach a Thai woman was waiting there. "She said she worked in a nightclub. She was about ten years older than me—I was twenty then. The four of us got in a boat and circled the coast for a while. Then we got farther out into the sea." The motor skiff took them to a bigger ship, which seemed to be waiting for them. Catherine and the Thai woman were forced aboard. They were brought to Pyongyang first, Catherine said. But she had tried to escape, without luck, and then tried to commit suicide several times. After that the North Koreans took her to a small cottage, took away everything in her room—*"everything,"* she repeated—so that she couldn't harm herself, and punished her by limiting her food to a small bowl of rice and one vegetable a day. "I was famished," Catherine told Choi. "It was then I decided to change. I concentrated on learning Korean. They took it favorably, because a month later I ended up here and have been receiving better treatment."

Catherine was lucky. The majority of abductees who resisted or didn't prove useful were sent to concentration camps. Most of the kidnappings were random, the victims picked more out of convenience than any sort of grand plan—although on the rare occasion, as with Shin and Choi or the pianist Paik Kun-Woo and his wife, they were specifically targeted for what their name would bring to the regime. As early as the Korean War the Kim regime had used kidnapping as a political tool. When the war started Kim Il-Sung had issued a memorandum, entitled "On Transporting Intellectuals from South Korea," giving North Korean soldiers permission to go into private homes and "repatriate" specific individual targets—for the most part intellectuals, journalists, students, and public officials—to work in the farms, factories, and offices of the new People's Republic. In this way anywhere between seven thousand and eighty-three thousand South Koreans were forcibly relocated to North Korea between 1950 and 1953. The North Koreans even kidnapped fifty-five foreigners, mostly diplomats and journalists, during the war, only to be made to release them afterward, claiming that they had only been trying to "protect" them. When the Korean War ended the North Koreans "failed to repatriate" somewhere between forty thousand and sixty thousand South Korean prisoners of war. Historian Sheila Miyoshi Jager writes that those thousands and thousands of prisoners "were forced to remain in North Korea as virtual slaves. Many of the ROK prisoners were unaware that an armistice had even been signed." The process slowed down but didn't stop after the armistice: the Korean Institute for National Unification in Seoul believes a further four thousand South Korean citizens were abducted to the North between 1953 and 2005, "partly because North Korea may have found their knowledge and manpower useful."

There were less dramatic abductions, too, ones that never involved covert ops, war, or physical assault. There were the South Korean fishermen who ventured a little too close to the Northern Limit Line, the maritime border between the two Koreas, and found themselves "rescued" by the North Korean navy and then paraded on newsreel propaganda broadcasts, celebrated through the streets of Pyongyang like repatriated People's heroes, before being sent to detainment camps once they had served their publicity purposes, the Workers' Party claiming they "have chosen to remain in the Workers' Paradise and not return to the living hell of the capitalist South." There were the ninety-three thousand ethnic Koreans lured back from Japan with promises of riches and preferential treatment, only to have Kim's functionaries meet them off the boat, assign them a manual worker's job and a state-owned house, and send them off to toil for the republic, never again allowing them to return home.

The late 1970s were undoubtedly the Golden Age of North Korea's practice of kidnapping. The reason was simple: Kim Jong-Il. The Dear Leader had never had any military training, never studied espionage, never worked in an intelligence agency, never left his country; *but* he had seen and loved every James Bond film. (He later hinted to Shin Sang-Ok that he believed such Western films were virtually docudramas.) Information gathering, strategic planning, and other tedious espionage practices meant little to Kim Jong-Il. But kidnapping, which his men did throughout the 1970s; assassination, as when his men, after he had taken control of foreign operations in 1974, targeted Park Chung-Hee and carried out the deadly Rangoon bombing of 1983; infiltration, which his men attempted throughout the 1970s and 1980s in South Korea via the coast and the tunnels dug under the DMZ; and terrorism, as demonstrated in the bombing of Kimpo Airport in 1986, which killed five, and the hijacking and bombing of a Korean Air flight in 1987, killing all on board . . . *that* was the kind of cloak-and-dagger work Kim seemed to believe a man with his power and ambition must use to further his aims. "Kim Jong-Il *loved* covert operations," Hwang Jang-Yop testifies.

"Abduction . . . was vehemently pursued from the mid-1970s," adds former North Korean special operations agent Ahn Myong-Jin. "On being designated as successor to Kim Il-Sung in 1974, Kim Jong-Il immediately embarked on taking charge of the Party bureau responsible for South Korean infiltration. . . . Kim Jong-Il then ordered the bureau to ensure that agents could impersonate the local population to perfection and to bring locals to North Korea as teachers for the agents. Under this order, Japanese, Korean, Arab, Chinese, and European citizens were abducted in an organized manner. I was taught this as an example of Kim Jong-Il's success in improving infiltration activities while I was at Kim Jong-Il Military University." Jong-Il had some of the Japanese citizens abducted to become language and "culture" teachers in his spy schools, teaching future covert operatives how to act like genuine Japanese citizens once they had reached enemy territory; others were taken simply so that North Korean spies could use their identities. There were women abducted for their looks and married off to North Korea–based Japanese terrorists as a reward for their work. Those left behind—the families and friends—were also victims. People they loved had suddenly disappeared, never to be seen again, their fates likely never to be known.

The Japanese Association of the Families of Victims Kidnapped by North Korea alleges that citizens of at least twelve countries have been abducted to, and possibly still remain in, North Korea, including nationals from France, Italy, the Netherlands, and Jordan. Between 1978 and 1982 Choi Eun-Hee saw many of them: Catherine Hong and the Jordanian woman but also, later, a female professor from France, who told her she felt sure her government would campaign to get her rescued and repatriated. The hairdresser Kim Jong-Il sent to her house told her many similar tales, of European women seduced by North Korean agents posing as wealthy Chinese and lured to Pyongyang; the hairdresser said he had met the women in houses nearby, where they were now living under guard, "undergoing brainwashing."

All those people—sleeping, eating, taking walks, coming in and out of the villas on the compound—were like ghosts; and Choi realized that she, too, was becoming a sort of ghost. Was anyone even looking for her? To the outside world, did she even still exist? Or had she simply disappeared forever?

15
Escape from the Chestnut Valley

"Deputy Director," Shin Sang-Ok asked his instructor as they sat in the projection room watching a movie, "why did you kidnap me? To show me all these films for free?"

The Deputy Director shrugged. "You used to make films, so they probably want you to make movies."

You used *to make films*. It surprised Shin how it could still make him flinch. "My movies are expensive to produce," he answered churlishly.

"Don't worry about such nonsense—just concentrate on your studies. The Dear Leader Comrade Kim Jong-Il has *gold mines*. He takes the money from them and uses some of it for movies, plays, music, and other artistic endeavors. I wouldn't worry about *money*."

As they spoke, Shin discreetly stuffed his pockets with the small cakes and nuts that were always laid out for the movie screenings. Later that afternoon he would take his daily ramble around the grounds, timing his pace and assessing his endurance. It didn't matter why Kim Jong-Il had had him kidnapped, or whether he could afford to pay to resurrect his career. Shin wasn't planning on staying in North Korea long enough to find out.

His routine had been the same since he had arrived in the Chestnut Valley: two hours of ideological study in the morning, lunch, a nap, then two, sometimes three films chosen specifically by Kim Jong-Il, broken up with a walk around the valley, then dinner and bed. The compound was surrounded by a high concrete wall topped with barbed wire and patrolled by armed guards. Attendants slept in the house with Shin. Even so, "my determination to escape became stronger every day," Shin later wrote. No one would tell him where Madame Choi was or even if she was alive. He felt sure she must be dead and felt no desire, as he said, "to leave my fate to their tender mercies."

His early plans hadn't come to much. First he thought that if he could persuade them to take him to Kaesong—his instructor kept talking of "sightseeing trips"—and smuggled the small scissors from the manicure kit in the bathroom along with him, he might be able to slash one of the car tires and force them to stay in Kaesong for a few hours, maybe even overnight. He'd noticed the car had no spare tire. Then all he had to do was get away from his minders somehow, "make my way to the Imjin River, then jump into the river and try to swim away." The Imjin had become known as the River of the Dead, named after the hundreds of bodies that washed down it from the North, especially following famines or purges. The river flowed right through the DMZ, and Shin would have to avoid land mines, barbed wire, and being shot at by soldiers of both sides to make it across. "Looking back, it was an absurd plan," he said, "but desperation was already beginning to get the better of my common sense." The only thing that kept him from attempting it was his instructor's refusal to take him to Kaesong. "It's still too soon," the Deputy Director told him whenever Shin prodded. "Just study. Sightseeing will come later."

Then he thought he could dig a tunnel under the perimeter wall. He found a shovel in a fishing shed by a nearby lake and hid it, but never had the opportunity to sneak out and even start digging. After that he asked for a bicycle—"for exercise," he said—and was surprised when the request was granted. He planned to slip out in the middle of the night, retrieve the food he had stashed in the cabinet of the radio in his room, ride to the railroad line, and hop a train headed for the Chinese border. That plan had to be abandoned almost as soon as it was conceived, when he discovered that his attendants locked the bike away after sunset. When a color TV was delivered to the villa he snatched some of the plastic shipping materials to make a life preserver, in case his escape eventually involved crossing a wide, rough river; that night he stole to the nearby lake to test his makeshift flotation device and nearly drowned.

He even considered sneaking off during the hustle and bustle of the 9/9 Day festivities. Climbing out a window of the Pyongyang apartment he and his instructor were staying in overnight after the Mass Games, he barely made it outside before one of his attendants flung the front door open. "Where are you going?" she shouted.

"I—I'm going to watch the fireworks," he stammered, his heart pounding, sweat dripping down his face. She immediately brought him back inside.

"There was no way to escape," Shin finally had to concede. "There just wasn't any way."

Watching movies should have made the days easier for such a film fanatic as Shin, but if anything they made time seem to go even slower. The North Korean pictures were all so awful, he thought, and they all had the same exact theme, repeated over and over. After every showing the Deputy Director asked him to write a critique, which Shin did from a filmmaker's point of view. Inevitably he was asked to rewrite it "from a proletarian point of view." The screening room, which Shin had expected to be a haven, came to annoy and frustrate him as much as every other room in the house.

As the temperatures dropped he was, paradoxically, spending more and more of his time outdoors. The attendants had provided him with a winter suit, fur-lined hat, and winter boots, and he wanted to test how they withstood long hours in the wind and cold. But he had also become mesmerized by the car that was parked out front.

There was a chauffeur who sat all day in a Mercedes-Benz outside the guesthouse. Every night after dinner, the man went indoors to play cards with the cook and the off-duty attendants, usually from eight until eleven o'clock or so. He never came outside to check on the vehicle. Shin could hear the noises of the card game, laughter mixed with cursing and the clinking of glasses, from where he sat in the dining room. The car was parked slightly to the side of the guesthouse, its nose pointing down the hill toward one of the compound gates, located near the lake Shin walked to and from every day. Every single night the chauffeur parked the car, turned the engine off, and went in for dinner and his game of cards.

And, crucially, he always left the key in the ignition.

As the ownership of private property was against the law in North Korea, only members of the regime—and the people the regime gave cars to as gifts and signs of privilege and influence—were allowed to own automobiles. Accordingly, most people had never seen the inside of a car and very few people knew how to drive one. To become a driver, a socially exalted profession in the DPRK, one must have a neutral or positive *songbun* and be selected for a one-year course covering theoretical and applied driving practice, basic structure of the vehicle, and basic maintenance, at the end of which a diploma, rather than a license, was awarded. Upon graduation most new drivers were assigned to work as "assistant drivers" to more experienced motorists for three to five years before being assigned their own vehicle. From that day forth, if they did their job competently and renewed their certificate every year, drivers never had to worry about making a living ever again.

They usually didn't worry about the cars getting stolen, either. There was no way to hide a stolen vehicle and no one to resell it to. Everyone who knew how to operate an automobile was employed by the Party, which knew where they lived. In this case, the Mercedes was parked inside of a walled, guarded compound. What was there to fear?

Shin stared at the key dangling in the ignition. Clouds of vapor formed in the cold nighttime air as he breathed in and out, the possibilities rushing through his mind. This had to be his chance. Surely, this had to be his chance.

"Why do you want a map?" the Deputy Director asked, eyeing Shin suspiciously.

Shin cleared his throat. "Well, I'm having a hard time memorizing the names of the battlefields where the anti-Japanese war led by Kim Il-Sung took place, especially in Manchuria."

"You *must* add 'the Great Leader' when speaking about our Fatherly Leader."

"Sorry. Yes, the war led by the Great Leader Kim Il-Sung."

"I'll bring you a map. You must concentrate hard on your studies."

"Yes, sir."

There were Japanese consulates in Vladivostok and Nakhodka in the USSR, and, as of January 1, 1979—as Shin learned from picking up the South Korean frequency, at night, on his bedside radio—there would be an American embassy in Beijing. China seemed the most accessible option. If he could drive the one hundred miles to Chongju, a city in the northwest corner of North Korea, and then get past the last few remaining towns between there and the Yalu River—Korea's natural border with China—then somehow get across the river . . . He remembered the Su'pung Dam, which the Japanese had built in the late thirties, when he was just a child, and thought he might be able to cross there. After that, all he would have to do was jump on a train, or follow the railroad tracks west, and find Beijing. If he were to escape, Shin speculated, the North Koreans would probably assume he would try the shortest way to South Korea and so look to the south for him, rather than to the north. That might give him a couple of days' head start before the search parties even looked to the Chinese border. By then, hopefully, he would be gone.

All he had to do now was be patient and wait until the lake on the grounds froze over. Then, he thought, the Yalu would be frozen solid too and he could walk across. Every day, he went over and over the plan in his head. When his attendants offered him warmer winter clothes, he picked out as many gray and green shades as possible so that he would be able to hide more easily.

On December 19, a sheet of ice covered the lake.

Ten days later, confident that the ice was there to stay, Shin decided to make his escape.

The wind was so strong it rattled the windows. One of the young female attendants pushed open the door to Shin's bedroom and checked that he was in bed, asleep. Satisfied, she pulled the door half shut and retreated down the hallway.

Shin waited a few seconds before getting out of bed. He grabbed the makeshift sack he'd crafted out of old clothes and hidden behind a sofa and stepped quietly into the hallway. In the kitchen, the card game was well under way; the rest of the house was silent and empty. The house staff had retreated to their own bedrooms. Shin tried the front door and found it unlocked. His guards, he thought, must have felt confident he couldn't make it past the guardhouse and off the grounds, so why lock the front door?

Shin was about to open the door but quickly hid as one of the card players went outside briefly to urinate on the side of the path. "Damn, it's cold," the attendant muttered as he came back inside. Shin slipped out of the house and crept over to the car. It was a loud, unsettling night, the trees bumping and wailing in the gale. He popped the car door open as silently as he could. They key was where he expected it to be. He quietly turned it halfway and the dashboard gauges lit up. Just under half a tank of gas. Maybe enough to make it to Chongju, maybe not.

Too late. It was now or never. He dropped his sack on the passenger seat and, climbing in, put the gear in neutral and released the hand brake. Slowly, the car rolled downhill. The next few minutes, Shin knew, would be crucial. If another of the guards came out to urinate, or if anyone looked out the window and saw the car moving, he was done for.

No one did. Once the car had rolled far enough, he flicked on the ignition, turned on the lights, and hit the gas, steadying his foot, driving casually. He reached the guardhouse and took a deep breath. Seeing him coming, the guard saluted sharply and let the car through. Shin drove normally until the next turn, took it—and then hammered his foot down on the gas.

If I ever make another movie, this experience will come in handy, he thought as he floored it toward Pyongyang. When he got to the city, the streets were empty, no one paying any attention to the routine sight of a recklessly driven Party Mercedes tearing down the streets. He located the right road out of the city and followed it. The speedometer on the dashboard was bobbing just over eighty miles per hour.

He had formulated his plan carefully, but he couldn't account for everything: not knowing his way around unfamiliar roads in the dark, for instance, or how much effort the authorities would put into finding him. He hadn't considered just how easy it would be to track down such a conspicuous car in a nation where cars were vanishingly rare. Most important, he did not know that almost one in three North Korean citizens were government informers, and that informing was such a pervasive part of the culture that there was no such thing as darkness to hide within. Nor did he know that the Party so tightly controlled its citizens' movements that even traveling from one town to another required applying for a detailed permit weeks in advance.

Looking out at the road illuminated by his headlights, ignorant of all of this, Shin felt hardy and optimistic.

He was halfway to China when he came to a fork in the road that he didn't remember from the map. He picked an option and kept going. It was the wrong one. He found himself driving along on a minor, gravel road. Suddenly someone, perhaps a farmer, appeared in the glare of his headlights and Shin instinctively jerked the wheel. The car skidded noisily and crashed into a ditch. By the time he had extricated himself from his seat the farmer had disappeared. Jumping back in, Shin put the car in reverse and hit the gas. The rear tires spun wildly, the car unmoving.

It took half an hour to get the car out of the trench. Every panicked second, Shin wondered whether the guards at the Chestnut Valley house had noticed yet that he or the car was missing. The back of the car was badly caved in, almost touching the back wheel. Shin pulled the jack from the trunk and fixed it the best he could. As he threw the jack back into the trunk he checked his watch: 10 p.m. already. He got in the car, switched on the engine, and sped back to the crossroads, tires screeching sharply as he took the road he should have taken almost an hour before.

The accident had frayed his nerves. At Sukchon, just a few miles farther—and only halfway to Chongju—Shin ran into his first military guard post, controlling vehicles crossing the Chongchon River. He had thought that perhaps he would bluff his way through, or that the guards, recognizing the Party car, would just wave him along. He couldn't manage the former and the latter wasn't happening. The bridge was a narrow single-lane construction. Instead of stopping, Shin ignored the guard's signal and blew right past him. It started to snow. The road, if one could call it that, was little more than patches of gravel and rocks, the Mercedes bouncing and clanging along the surface as Shin insisted on driving as fast as his steering could handle. One of the rear tires popped loudly. The country roads three hours outside of Pyongyang clearly weren't made for town cars.

Unwilling to quit, Shin ground along with a flat tire until the Chongju train station came into view, a big, beaming portrait of Kim Il-Sung adorning its brightly lit façade. Shin took a right, and the Su'pung Dam rose ahead. Railroad tracks were running alongside the road now. This was where Shin had planned on dumping the car. He pulled up off the trail, turned off the ignition, and hopped out.

It was freezing. On foot he followed the train tracks. A soldier spotted him, briefly, and called out to him, "Comrade! Comrade!" Shin pretended he didn't hear and kept going. The soldier was too cold to bother chasing him. "I started to run," Shin said. "I could barely breathe, but I knew if I stopped it would mean the end for me." After what felt like ages he arrived at a small train station. Large freight crates sat by the platform, labeled "explosives." He huddled behind them, out of sight. It was eleven o'clock now, the night still young. I wonder when someone will find the car, Shin thought. Is the driver back at the house still playing cards? Or has he already discovered my escape?

It wasn't long before he heard the sound of an approaching freight train. An old steam locomotive, the only kind of train North Korea could afford, was slowly trundling toward him. Crouching down by the track, Shin waited for the train to ease by and then jumped aboard an empty freight car full of stones, probably some kind of ore. Shin sat down and stretched his aching legs. His whole body was rigid with tension.

"Thank you, God," he said out loud.

He leaned his head back and dozed off.

Just a couple of stops later three men dressed as railroad workers exited the station, walked straight over to the car in which Shin was hiding, and dragged him out. A man from the state police was waiting on the platform, rubbing his eyes, looking as if he'd just been woken up. "Are you the one who ditched the Mercedes?" he asked in a half yawn.

Shin didn't know that the North Korean railroad posted guards at half-mile intervals to catch illegal travelers and prevent accidents. He had been spotted as soon as he boarded the train.

Shinonchon station, where he was caught, was less than ten miles from the Chinese border.

16

Shin Sang-Ok Died Here

They marched him inside the station, Shin dragging his makeshift rucksack behind him on the ground. All the energy had drained out of him. His face was smeared black from the coal dust blowing through the train. He felt wretched, pathetic, but he was also filled with an odd kind of relief. I don't care, he thought. I'd rather die than be stuck here. They can do anything they want to me.

"Give me some water to clean up," Shin said to the man from the state police.

"Give it to him," the man drowsily ordered someone.

"Where's the bathroom?"

They let Shin relieve himself and wash his hands and face. When he came outside, a jeep was pulling up near the tracks, the Deputy Director in the passenger seat, a furious look on his face. Shin could hear a helicopter thrumming up above. He closed his eyes and tried to empty his mind.

They handcuffed him, and led him outside.

It was like a scene from a movie, Shin thought when it was all over.

The helicopter hovered down to the ground at a small, deserted airfield. They pushed Shin out of the aircraft and bundled him into another jeep, a hood over his head, only taking it off once he was out of the car and inside a large building. He was led down a long corridor with stretches of identical doors on either side. His guards stopped at one of them, opened the door, and sat him on one of the three chairs that were the room's only furnishings. On the other two, facing him, sat the Deputy Director and a fat man Shin didn't know, so pudgy he sunk into his seat as if he had no spine. They both had pencils and paper in their hands.

The fat man spoke first, in a voice that shook from deep inside the blubber. "You were headed north, past Chongju, in North Pyongan Province. That's pretty far north." He seemed to reflect on that for a moment. "You were headed that way by mistake, yes?"

Shin didn't know how to answer. "Did you take the wrong road or not?" the Deputy Director snapped. "Don't you understand the question?"

"I meant to go in that direction," Shin said.

"Why?" The Deputy Director's voice was so angry and threatening that Shin felt it would pierce through his body.

"Because I couldn't bear living here anymore," Shin replied.

The fat one was scratching Shin's answers down on his pad. The Deputy Director stood up and the fat man followed. As they left the room four guards stepped in, their cold eyes locked on Shin.

In a few minutes, the two interrogators returned and sat back down across from Shin.

"Then does this mean you lied in your New Year's congratulatory letters?" the Deputy Director asked. Like Choi, Shin had been required to handwrite holiday letters of gratitude and admiration to both Kims.

"Answer the question!" the fat man bellowed.

"I wrote what I was told to write. I was writing letters to men I've never met. I thought I did quite well."

The two stared at him, astounded. After what seemed like a long time the fat man blinked and wrote the answer down, and they left the room again. The four guards returned. As he sat there Shin realized his interviewers were relaying his answers to someone and then returning with that person's next line of inquiry. It wasn't hard to figure out who that person was likely to be. Kim Jong-Il probably can't believe I wanted to escape after being treated so nicely, Shin thought.

The pair returned. "Where did you want to go?" the Deputy Director asked.

"I was headed for China."

The two stepped out again, the four guards stepped in. A moment later, the interrogators returned with a new question.

"How did you plan to get there?"

"By riding the rails."

" 'Riding the rails'?" the fat one echoed, as if he had never heard the expression.

"Yes. By riding the rails."

They left the room again. The routine continued, back and forth, more times than Shin could count. When it was over he had told them everything. He felt nothing but exhaustion, fatigue like a heavy blank sheet blotting out every other emotion. They walked him outside and, blinking in the afternoon light, he realized he was in Pyongyang. A statue of the Great Leader, the omnipresent smile on his face, stood in the front yard.

Shin got back in the jeep. As the army vehicle drove through the city, Shin looked out the window. "It was a bleak, dismal scene. There were no signs of people. The streets were dead."

It was December 30, 1978. They drove him to prison.

The North Korean prison system has existed for as long as the People's Republic has. There are an unknown number of prison camps throughout the country. Though the DPRK regime officially denies their existence, many are clearly visible on Google Maps. They hold an estimated 220,000 prisoners. Every North Korean knows of someone—a family member, a friend, a work acquaintance—who was taken away in the middle of the night and sent to the prison camps, never to be seen again. Though no one speaks of them, everyone—*everyone*—knows about them.

The largest known prison camp, complete with mines and factories, covers a surface area greater than that of the entire city of Los Angeles. Citizens can be sent there for any offense—real, perceived, or trumped up—and, as North Korean law attributes collective guilt, a criminal's act taints the rest of his or her bloodline, so that entire families, across three generations, are routinely condemned to hard labor or death. (Spouses, not being blood, are sometimes spared; but they are forced to divorce, their *songbun* is downgraded, their assets confiscated, and, if they have any relatives in the army or university, they are immediately expelled and "sent down to production," which means being sent to work in the mines or iron-smelting furnaces.) The treatment in these prisons is so harsh and life threatening that a sentence longer than a few years is as good as the death penalty. Prisoners work long hours doing hard labor and are brutally punished if they fail to fulfill quotas. They are fed gruel and sadistically abused.

Because of the way North Korean society is subdivided, from the hostile class to the core class, only "trusted" citizens are allowed to work in the prison camps as guards. "Trusted," in practice, means the wealthy elite. These guards are trained to dehumanize their prisoners, to see them as "dogs" or "animals" rather than people. They are also rewarded for preventing escapes, so stories abound of guards pretending to help a prisoner escape only to shoot or watch as he or she is electrocuted to death on electric wire, before dragging the body back to collect a bonus.

The worst internment camps, the *kwanliso* (literally "custody management center"), are for traitors, political prisoners, and anyone found guilty of committing an "anti-state" crime, such as plotting to take over, collaborating with the imperialists, or, more innocuously, reading a foreign newspaper or cracking jokes about either Kim's appearance or intelligence. Modeled on the Soviet gulag, the *kwanliso* were set up by Kim Il-Sung shortly after he took power as places to send anyone who threatened his regime. Sentences to the *kwanliso* are never for anything less than life, and public executions are commonplace. It's hard to know what, exactly, goes on in the *kwanliso,* as few ever escape to tell. According to a few witnesses, prisoners are not allowed to have sex, so in mixed-gender prisons abortions and the killing of newborns are sanctioned by the state. These forced abortions are carried out by injecting poison into the fetus, simply cutting the mother's womb open or, if all else fails, strangling the child the second it has taken its first breath. Informing is rewarded, so prisoners routinely turn on each other, behavior strongly encouraged by the prison administration. One former prisoner described witnessing a failed escape attempt. As the would-be escapee lay beaten on the ground, the prison's other inmates were ordered to walk across him, pounding and crushing his bones and organs until he died. When an inmate was killed by hanging, his fellow prisoners were ordered to throw stones at him while he kicked and thrashed. Bodies were then left out overnight, sometimes even for days, as a reminder and an example.

In some camps prisoners are assigned to each other, two by two, to watch each other as they sleep, reporting anything suspicious that might be said. Medieval torture—beating with sticks and rocks, hanging over bonfires, the sinking of hooks into the flesh, the breaking and ripping and chopping off of fingers and limbs—is used in interrogations. In something called the Clock Torture, the prisoner is made to stand on a table in front of the other prisoners; the warden or a guard then calls a time and the prisoner has to re-create the hands on a clock face with his body and hold the position until the next time is shouted out. This is done until the prisoner collapses, and is done to children and pregnant women just as often as to able-bodied men. Guards are authorized to rape. Children are executed in front of their mothers, wives in front of their husbands. If they don't die of violence or torture, the inmates will often die in work accidents in the mines or in the blazing factories; and if they survive even that they will die of starvation or of one of the many untreated illnesses that abound in a place where people are not allowed to wash or to change their clothes, where they are made to eat filthy food and sleep huddled against one another on cold, mattressless floors. If an inmate dies, family outside will not be informed; and if a prisoner is eventually released, he or she will be made to sign a confidentiality agreement, undertaking never to disclose what happened behind bars. Most prisoners are never told what crime they were found guilty of committing in the first place.

Just one level down from the labor camps for political prisoners are the "reeducation camps," or *kyohwaso* (literally "enlightenment centers"), with much the same conditions but smaller than the sprawling internment camps. There are about twenty such prisons all over North Korea, the inmates of which are termed "bad" or "subversive elements" guilty of political crimes, common crimes (murder, traveling without a permit), or economic crimes (Pyongyang's euphemism for theft, illegal border crossings, smuggling, or illegal market trading and private enterprise). Unlike the internment camps, where prisoners are considered "irredeemable," prisoners in these reeducation facilities undergo ideological instruction every day and can entertain a slight hope of returning to "normal" society. Some prisoners are kept in their cells, but the majority work every day from 7 a.m. to sunset, stopping only for dinner and for ideology sessions. Officially, the reeducation camps are not prisons but rehab facilities, and the government claims that the inmates, "unable to live with their guilty conscience(s)," turned themselves in and volunteered to stay there.

Here torture was still the norm. One woman, Lee Soon-Ok, says her interrogation for a petty offense began with being thrown on the floor and covered in a blanket while twenty or thirty men kicked and punched her repeatedly until she passed out. She was then questioned for three days straight and hit whenever she closed her eyes or drifted to sleep. She was abused for several months after that—shoved into a brick pottery kiln until she lost consciousness from the heat, flogged while strapped naked to a chair, strapped to a bench and had water forced down her throat, had her teeth punched out and sticks placed between her fingers and twisted. After passing out from one punishment she woke up to find two men standing on a plank laid across her stomach, and was unable to stand up for two weeks. Her crime was to have refused to give a senior security official extra fabric (beyond his allocated ration) to make himself a jacket in the style of one he had seen on Kim Jong-Il. The punishment for giving the official more than his allocated portion would have been equally bad or worse.

Another North Korean, a school principal, testified to having found the bodies of two teachers at his school; when he reported the crime he was arrested for the murders without any form of investigation. To extract a confession the state police tortured him with electricity until his ears and fingers literally melted. Later, when thieves confessed to the murders, he was released, lame and deformed, under the condition that he sign a form pledging he would never reveal his experience under pain of being imprisoned and tortured again.

There was, literally, no escape. If you killed yourself, and many did, your surviving family members were brought to the camp or, if they were there already, executed or sent to solitary confinement, locked in a cell so small there was only room to sit, with spikes sticking out of the walls to prevent prisoners from leaning against them for rest.

The detention center was loud and crowded. They made Shin strip, took his clothes, and handed him prison dress, which Shin felt sure was an old Chinese uniform from the Korean War. When he was done changing, they threw him in a solitary cell barely big enough to lie down in. There was one tiny slit of a barred window high up on the wall, a steel door on the other wall. The wooden floor was filthy with old bodily fluids. It felt like a dungeon chamber.

They brought him a stone bowl filled "with a mixture of corn and beans sprinkled with rice," and an aluminum spoon with no handle. Two guards stood by the door.

"You must obey the rules I am about to tell you," one of them barked. "First, until I give you instructions to sleep, you must sit up at attention with your back straight and your hands on your knees. You are to look straight ahead with your eyes wide open. You are not to move your head or your hands at all. Do you understand?" Shin nodded weakly. He took a mouthful of gruel and spat it out. It was full of stones. "Second: to use the toilet, you will raise your hand and ask for permission. Third: at lights out a bell will ring. When the bell rings you are allowed to move. After the bell rings we will check your cell and give you permission to lie down. Only then can you lie down. Do you understand?"

"Yes."

Shin forced himself to finish the food. The guards took the empty bowl and locked the steel door. The sun sank lower than the window, and Shin Sang-Ok was left in darkness.

In prison, Shin suffered from hunger, sickness, and loneliness. One of his toes, frostbitten during his escape attempt, became infected. He shivered with anxiety constantly and grew to crave food "like an animal." As he sat in his cell, back straight and hands on his knees, he could hear other prisoners being beaten for disobeying orders or for breaking position without permission. One day he heard a woman cry and realized the prison was unisex. Fights broke out regularly among the guards, usually sparked by one of them calling another a "liberal" or a "democrat," the two worst insults in the prison.

Shin was bewildered by his treatment. The guards cursed and barked at him as they did everyone else. He had neither soap nor toothpaste, instead using salt to brush his teeth, and he ate the same pebble-filled saltwater slop, always meatless but occasionally fortified with chunks of radish or cabbage, given to every other prisoner. But when he fell ill a doctor was called, and when the nights were cold the guards brought him several extra blankets, both luxuries other inmates were not afforded. When a certain woman was on kitchen duty, in addition to his gruel Shin received a bowl of rice pot tea, a staple Korean drink also known as burnt-rice tea, made by swirling some water around the pot used to cook rice, scraping the burnt rice off the bottom of the pot, and pouring the warm mixture into a cup. The tea tasted delicious, like his mother's when he was a child.

His cell also seemed to have become the place where guards stopped on their patrols up and down the hall. Inevitably they would lean on the door and wait for him to notice their unmoving presence. Then, in a low voice, they would ask him questions about life in South Korea.

"In South Korea, there are places with women for entertainment, aren't there?"

"Of course there are," Shin replied.

"And if one goes there . . . can you fondle and fool around with the women?"

"Well . . ."

"If you pay them," the sentry continued, "you can do anything, right? Right?"

Shin nodded. "Sure," he said.

The man nodded, a grin on his face, and stepped away from the door.

The next day, a different guard asked Shin, "Can anyone buy chocolate in the South?"

"If one has money, one can go to any store and buy it," Shin answered.

"You mean only the high-ranking officials, right?"

"No, everyone can."

"Oh, sure!" The guard walked away, shaking his head.

"A wind this strong blows the roofs off all the huts in South Korea, doesn't it?" another guard asked sarcastically, on a day when a gale was blowing around the detention center.

"I have a hard time with your capitalist smell," yet another guard whispered. "How can you reek of it so much?"

"I smell like a capitalist?"

"That strong smell of cosmetics." Shin realized the guard could still smell the Japanese soap he had used at the guesthouse. I can't believe he can still smell it, let alone find it too strong, he thought.

The silent, snatched conversations gave Shin an opportunity to ask his own questions.

"Comrade—" he started with one guard.

"We are not your comrades. Call us 'sir.' "

"Sir, where is this place?"

"What use is it for you to know?" the guard asked. "You want to know where you are? This is a detention center."

"Is it the place for . . . ?" Shin asked, drawing his hand across his throat. The guard shook his head.

"This isn't that kind of place. Those people are put somewhere else."

As the sun rose and set, Shin used stones picked from his rice to count the days, reaching up to place one on the windowsill every night before he went to sleep. Mice ran in and out of holes in the wall, climbing into the dry toilet and trying to feed on the feces within. When the guards weren't looking Shin picked up his handleless spoon, the only object he was allowed inside his cell, and carved his name in the wall, then a full sentence. "The concrete wall was hard and my carving barely left a mark," Shin said, "but slowly it started to become visible." The sentence read *Shin Sang-Ok died here one day in 1979.* He didn't expect to see the outside of the prison again. From now on his life was wasted. Maybe someone from the next generation would one day stand here and read the faded pronouncement.

Maybe, one day, "my family and the world would know: I had no other way out."

There were fifteen pebbles on the windowsill when Shin was called out of his cell by the center's warden. The warden's office was in a separate building about a hundred yards away; the guards drove Shin there in a jeep. He held his face out in the fresh air, relishing every second. Inside the warden's office were his old instructor the Deputy Director, the warden, and a man Shin did not know, sent from the Ministry for Social Safety. The deputy director asked Shin if he regretted his actions and saw the error of his ways. Shin hung his head.

"I have given a lot of thought to my actions," Shin said. "I realize how wrong I was. I didn't know Comrade Kim Jong-Il's true intention for me, so I made a foolish mistake."

"Not just 'Comrade' Kim Jong-Il," the man from the ministry cautioned, "but *our beloved Leader* Comrade Kim Jong-Il."

"Yes, sir, I didn't realize our beloved Leader Comrade Kim Jong-Il's intent and I made a mistake. I have thought about my foolishness and repented."

"Is there anything else?" the Deputy Director asked coldly. Shin's escape must have gotten him in serious trouble. Shin couldn't think of anything to say.

"Give me at least one egg a day, please," he finally blurted out. The Deputy Director wrote down his answer and then he and the man from the ministry stood up and left. The guards took Shin back to his cell.

This procedure was repeated several times over the next three months. Every time Shin groveled. "If Choi Eun-Hee is alive, let me see her," he told the Deputy Director once, "and we will work together for the Great Leader and the Dear Leader. We will work diligently." "I tried to escape for my family," he pleaded on another occasion, "but now I will sacrifice what is insignificant for the greater good. Give me a chance." The lies came easier every time. He would have done anything to get out of that prison.

One day, after another of those absurd ersatz parole hearings, the doctor visited Shin and gave him Russian multivitamins. After that the vitamins came every day. They were another excuse for his jailers to linger around his cell.

"I heard that if you take these every day, you don't get hungry," one of the guards said one morning, holding one of the pills up to the light and studying it curiously.

"No, it's just a dietary supplement," Shin answered. "You still need to eat."

"I heard someone say it, though . . ."

"People take a lot of vitamins in the South," Shin said, steering the conversation where he knew it would head anyway.

"What?" The guard looked at him. "The officials, right?"

"No, no. They're sold in pharmacies."

"Anyone can buy them?"

"Of course," Shin said.

The guard shook his head at the wonders of the South. Suddenly he punched the door to the cell next door and shouted at the prisoner inside. "Answer so I can understand you, you dog! You slime!" He laughed out loud.

"What's that fellow in for?" Shin asked.

"An economic offense," the jailer asked.

"There's such a thing as an economic offense?"

The guard spat. "He's a thief, understand?"

On April 9, five days after his youngest child's third birthday and shortly after they started giving Shin vitamin pills, the warden came to fetch Shin and took him to an office, where a guard cut his hair into a military crew cut with a shaving razor. Then Shin was led to the employees' bathroom and told to take a shower. The clothes he wore the day of his failed escape were returned to him. When he was washed and dressed the warden walked him to his office, where the Deputy Director and the fat man from his original interrogation sat waiting.

The Deputy Director nodded and the fat man stood. "Comrade," he began, his guttural voice shaking, "you have destroyed state property and planned to escape from our country. You should be given the death penalty." Shin stopped breathing. "*However,* we have decided to overlook your offenses this time, so you must work hard for the People and the state. Do you understand?"

"Yes," Shin answered, "yes!"

"Don't forget the warmhearted generosity of the state," the fat man warned.

"Thank you," Shin agreed.

Another anonymous Mercedes waited outside. The Deputy Director walked alongside Shin as he stepped up to it. He hadn't said a word to Shin since that first interrogation, three months ago. He looked thinner, Shin thought, as if he were undernourished; perhaps even like a man who had gone through some suffering. Maybe he had been punished for allowing Shin to escape. As Shin opened the car door the Deputy Director stared at him bitterly.

"You look like hell," he snarled. "Just look at yourself."

The Mercedes drove Shin back to the Chestnut Valley, this time to a house farther down the road, over the Taedong River and past a huge painted billboard showing a smiling, hardworking Kim Il-Sung instructing the local farmers. The new house was smaller and less luxurious than the last one. There were bars on every window, guard posts out front and in the back, and searchlights on every side.

As they entered, the Deputy Director chastised Shin for "causing so much pain" and told him he hoped he would stay out of trouble from now on. He sat Shin down and ordered him to write a letter of apology to Kim Jong-Il.

It took Shin three days to finish the letter to the Deputy Director's satisfaction. Within a month, he had started to save food for another escape.

17
The Torture Position

"I've decided to live in North Korea for good," Shin told the Deputy Director. "Maybe I could tell you about my life, and you could give me some advice."

He settled into his ideological studies with all the fervor he could muster. He read the three volumes of *The History of Kim Il-Sung's Anti-Japanese Struggle,* wrote the most ingratiating book report the screenwriter in him could write, and even memorized long passages to impress his instructor. They watched two North Korean movies a day, one in the morning and one in the afternoon. When Kim Il-Sung's birthday came around on April 16, Shin joined in the champagne toasts, even though he usually didn't drink. "I quaffed [my first drink] in a single gulp and asked for another glass," he recalled. "Then I made a toast, too. 'I wish our beloved Great Leader Kim Il-Sung long life and prosperity!' "

Vigilance at the house had been stepped up. Shin's bedroom was located on the upper floor, with the other rooms on the same level arranged so that his room was visible from each, allowing them to monitor his comings and goings. Downstairs had the usual living room–cum–projection room, a dining room, and a third bedroom for another live-in attendant. Two guards lived with Shin. He was told they were his "cook and receptionist." The Deputy Director, who had slept in the same house as him in the Chestnut Valley, now stayed elsewhere and only came by to give Shin his lessons. Shin wasn't allowed out of the house, not even in the backyard, unless the

Deputy Director was with him. All windows except one in the dining room were literally nailed shut. At night when everyone was asleep a ferocious dog was let loose on the grounds.

April turned into May, May into June, and suddenly it was July. It was hot and muggy, the flowers and plants outside the house a dazzling array of colors. All day the air throbbed with the thick hum of locusts. Locked away indoors, Shin collected everything he came across—scraps of food, salt, matches—in an improvisational frenzy, without taking time to think what purpose they might serve. "I knew this would be my last chance," he said. "If I was caught, I would be killed."

The hours crawled by, the days filled with "anxiety, planning, and waiting for my chance," Shin recalled. Almost every night thunderstorms broke the sweltering heat. The bellows of the thunder and the sound of the heavy rain smothered the other noises in the house, and the guards gave up their patrols and huddled under shelter. Even then Shin couldn't get past the guard dog, but he didn't plan to. His scheme was both simpler and more daring than his last.

On one such stormy July night, he crept into the upstairs guest room, where he had noticed that the three radiators were on wheels, and that if one was moved, a panel in the wall behind could also be moved, revealing a small empty space in the wall itself, just big enough for a man to hide in. He pushed aside the radiator in question, removed the panel, and slipped into the space, carefully replacing the panel behind him. From its position behind a desk, the radiator made it difficult to notice any alteration to the panel.

Shin crouched within the wall, his pockets stuffed with food and supplies he had amassed over the previous weeks. He expected he might have to stay in hiding for three or four days—without stretching his legs or relieving himself in any way—while his captors, thinking he had escaped, set out on a massive manhunt. "Later, when the furor died down," Shin wrote, "I would leave the house and head toward one of the ports, or the border, and eventually make my way to the Soviet Union."

When dinner was served that night and Shin Sang-Ok could not be found, pandemonium broke out. Within a couple of hours officers had arrived to search every corner of the house—but instead of then deserting the property entirely, as Shin had expected, they set up their search headquarters in the study, right across the hall from the room in which he was hiding. Shin was stunned. He had assumed his captors would behave the way he planned—according to the script he had written in his mind—when they found his room empty. Even from his hopeless position Shin still believed he could plan a scene and direct it to his intention.

Lying scrunched up inside the wall, his back already aching and his throat tight with thirst, Shin listened anxiously as cars screeched to a halt outside the house and men stomped in and out of every room. Walkie-talkies crackled loudly. He heard some of the men knocking on the ceilings and walls to determine if they were hollow. "I could hear men on the roof," Shin wrote later. "My bedroom and the study became the search headquarters. People were coming and going; orders were given and reports delivered in these rooms. There were drivers in the room I was hiding in. They came by to listen to the radio." At three in the morning, bursting to pee, Shin crept to the bathroom and relieved himself, waiting for the dogs to bark or the thunder to crack before flushing the toilet.

On the third day of Shin's concealment an attendant entered the guest room to clean it. As he approached the desk he saw that the radiator had been moved and that the panel behind it was slightly open; in fact, he could see part of Shin's body. He shouted immediately. "He's here! He's here! The gentleman is hiding in the aide's room!"

Moments later, policemen rushed in. A man in his thirties, wearing a gray Mao tunic rather than a police uniform, seemed to be in charge. Once Shin had been dragged out of his hole the man in the Mao tunic sat him down and began inquiring, politely:

"Why try to escape again?" he asked. "Why cause so much trouble again?"

"Because I can't live here," Shin replied. "I don't have my wife, my kids, and my family. My friends. They are all in the South. How can I live here all by myself?"

"But you never requested for your family to be brought to you," the man said, shrugging. "If you had just asked, it would have been arranged."

"How could you bring my family from the South? The government is probably watching them very carefully."

"Why can't you ever believe in the power of the People? You just don't understand the power of the People . . ." The man sighed. "You've committed an offense and betrayed the state by trying to escape from this country. These are serious offenses. You deserve to be executed."

"I'm a South Korean. What crime is it for me to try to go back?"

"You are a citizen here. Citizens here must obey the law of the land."

"I'm not a citizen here," Shin protested, "I'm still a South Korean—"

"Ha—nonsense. The Democratic People's Republic of Korea is the true government of the Korean peninsula and therefore, you are a citizen of North Korea."

That was the end of the conversation. Other senior officials came by to take a look at Shin, later discussing his case in one of the downstairs rooms. The Deputy Director appeared as well, "looking at me with the eyes of a viper," Shin observed, before being asked to leave. When, eventually, Shin was taken down for dinner, he was served a prisoner's meal consisting of salt soup, a tiny handful of rice, and no meat. More guards and dogs were brought in, and by the next morning barbed wire had been installed outside every window.

With his spirit destroyed, Shin now slipped into limbo, waiting to be taken away any minute to be executed. Both times he had tried to escape he had genuinely believed he would succeed. "My escapes were like those in a movie," he reflected years later. "Perhaps I had confused fantasy with reality. . . . But without at least attempting to escape, I could never have endured the anxiety, the loneliness, and the fear. In such a stark reality, with so much free time, it was only natural that my fantasies and dreams started to merge into reality." Twenty days after Shin's hiding place was found, two security officers came to the house and said they were there to take the prisoner "to a place where you will pay for your crime." They are finally going to kill me, Shin thought as he climbed, handcuffed, in the back of yet another Mercedes, his belongings thrown in the trunk.

They didn't kill him. The Mercedes drove for three hours, in the dark, into the heart of nowhere, and deposited him in front of a fortified building.

Shin had arrived at Prison Number 6.

The detention center had been one thing. Prison Number Six, the "enlightenment center," was another.

The Venezuelan poet Ali Lameda, who traveled to Pyongyang to translate the collected works of Kim Il-Sung into Spanish, was arrested and convicted in 1968—on no explicit charges and with no evidence—and then spent six years in Prison Number 6, which he knew as Suriwon Prison, after the nearest town. He wrote, "The conditions of the prison were appalling. No change of clothes in years, nor of food plates. . . . There are no rights for the prisoner, no visits, parcels or cigarettes or food or opportunity to read a book or newspaper, or write. . . . Hunger was used as a control. . . . In my opinion, it is preferable to be beaten, as it is possible to grit one's teeth and withstand physical beating. To be continuously starving is worse." A guard told him six thousand or more men and women were held in the prison, "a huge circular place with an enormous courtyard," at any one time. Lameda could hear some of them wailing in other cells, and added grimly, "You can soon learn to distinguish whether a man is crying from fear, or pain or from madness, in such a place."

It was here that Shin Sang-Ok was banished after his second escape attempt. Formally indicted and convicted, he was made to change into prison garb—cotton, secondhand, and unwashed from the previous "renter"—and taken to the small, damp, filthy cell that would be his new home. He had to crawl into it through a flap on his hands and knees. Cockroaches swarmed the toilet bowl.

As he quickly learned, prison policy forbade him from meeting or exchanging words with other inmates. Chatter, laughter, and singing were forbidden. Prisoners were allowed to wash their clothes but not themselves. The weekly bodily and cavity search was administered more like a ritual humiliation. Even when the prisoners sunned themselves in the yard they were kept in individual wire cages, like in a zoo, with cement sides so they couldn't speak to or look at one another. The food was little more than "grass and salt" in water, with the odd ball of rice.

Along with his fellow inmates, Shin was instructed to sit in his cell in a cross-legged position, head down—and not to move again. The slightest flicker of a muscle was met with a beating, the prisoner most commonly being asked to put his hands through the bars on the door and having his fingers smashed violently with a guard's baton. Defector Hyok Kang, whose father underwent the same treatment, wrote of it, "The prisoners took up their cross-legged position . . . and had to remain silent and motionless. This was real torture, because while the lice ate you up, all you could do was watch them go about it, since the slightest movement was punished. . . . My father still bears the marks. Only once a day, the prisoners enjoyed a break during which they were allowed to move. It lasted ten minutes. The prisoners, whose legs were often swollen and puffy, because their blood circulation stopped almost completely in that cross-legged position, could barely get to their feet." ("The prisoner[s] sat for sixteen hours a day looking at the wardens and the prison bars," Lameda added. "Prisoners must stay awake throughout the day, the official explanation went, since how could a prisoner continually ponder his guilt if he slept?")

This was called the torture position. It was to be Shin's daily regime for over two and a half years.

18
Division 39

On the outside, in another kind of prison, Choi Eun-Hee had somehow gotten back in Kim Jong-Il's favor. She didn't know why, but one day Kim invited her down the newly opened Wonsan Expressway to his beachside resort. "It was a four-lane highway," Choi remembers, but "there were no guardrails and the people just walked haphazardly in the middle of the road. The tunnels [along the way] were all given names such as 'Juche,' 'Loyalty,' or 'Triumphal Return.' The longest one, they said, was four kilometers long." Ordinary villages could be seen from the motorway, but there were no exit ramps leading to them. When they arrived at the five-story villa on the beach, Kim Jong-Il was waiting outside beaming, as ever.

"Mrs. Choi! Welcome. Long time no see. How is your health? Is this your first visit to Wonsan?"

Jong-Il had other friends over, and the evening was taken up by a long dinner, after which the guests formed groups to drink, shoot some pool, or play mah-jongg or cards. "It was just the same as in any capitalist society," Choi thought. The next morning Jong-Il had Kang take her to nearby Mount Kumgang, also known as the Diamond Mountain. Choi had never seen it, but it had been celebrated in songs and in art by her people for many centuries, immortalized as one of the most beautiful mountains in the world, its dark rock weathered and carved by nature into dramatic peaks, cliffs, and ravines.

The visit, however, was a crushing disappointment, unerringly representative of North Korea. There were antiaircraft guns installed on every mountain peak, "so that the bastard American aircraft cannot penetrate our country," Choi's guide told her. Tunnels had been blown into the rock face and filled with emergency war supplies and provisions, then closed off with ugly wooden planks. Barbed wire sealed off the beach in case of a water landing. The mountain, frighteningly, looked like it was *bleeding*. When she approached the wound Choi saw that the "blood" was the word JUCHE, carved in the stone face of the mountain then painted red. "Mottos and slogans had been carved into the base of nearly every boulder and large rock there," Choi remembered, "all honoring Kim Il-Sung and his father and mother and other family members and the Korean Workers' Party." The bright words defaced the mountain wherever she looked.

"Look at that!" Mr. Kang was shouting. "You have to go up close and stand by it and then you will see the true size of the word. One letter is the length of the car!" Choi had never seen him looking so proud.

Worst of all, for Choi, was the realization that from the top of one plateau, she could see South Korea. While she fought back tears, her guide obliviously droned on. "When our sworn enemy the Yankee bastards invaded this place, they cruelly beat to death the village chief. . . . But over there is Height 351, where we fought fiercely against the Yankee bastards and their South Korean puppets for our nation's liberation. And over here . . ."

After the beachside resort visit came an unexpected invitation to vote in the rubber-stamp Party Assembly elections, shortly followed by a 5 a.m. call from Kim Jong-Il requesting her to come join a party at the Fish House—a debauched mess of drunken men stumbling around with women she'd never seen before, Kim Jong-Il standing in the middle of it, eyes bloodshot from alcohol and his speech slurred—and then after that, an invitation to visit another of Kim Jong-Il's resorts, this one by an enormous artificial lake, where Jong-Il terrified his guests by driving his speedboat recklessly around the water "at a very high speed, turning it this way and that, laughing and obviously enjoying himself." If that weren't enough to confirm that Choi was back in the Dear Leader's good graces, she soon found herself once more packed into a Mercedes in the middle of the night and moved to a spectacular new residence, farther north.

She couldn't help but gape in wonder. Painted bright white and three times as large as the guesthouse in Tongbuk-Ri, this house had carpets in every room, luxurious furnishings, and every amenity imaginable—including, naturally, a film-screening room. It possessed none of the tackiness of the other houses. "It was beautiful," Choi remembers. This was the Mount Paekdu Guest House, located at the foot of the mountain of Jong-Il's official birth, and the most sumptuous of his twenty-four personal villas.

Kim Jong-Il had spent much of the late 1970s securing his lavish lifestyle. It was almost certain now that he was going to take over when his father died. Kim Il-Sung was nearing his seventies and had no clear plan for North Korea's future. His military attempts at reuniting Korea had so far failed, and the *juche* economy, strong for a few years, was slowing down. The people adored him. The Supreme Leader, ready to enjoy his old age in leisure, had put his son in charge of most of the day-to-day running of the People's Republic. It was only fitting, Jong-Il may have reasoned, that his manner of living be upgraded to match his new position.

Most of Jong-Il's two dozen resorts were finished between 1979 and 1981, either built new or freshly refurbished at a total estimated cost of $2.5 billion. They were built purely for Kim Jong-Il's enjoyment and hobbies, of which he had many. According to defector Han Young-Jin, the retreats included a house in East Pyongyang where "deer are fostered as pets"; three in central Pyongyang, including one in which an entire floor was decked out with arcade games, slot machines, and "machines for entertainment"; the beach house in Wonsan, which boasted a full-size cinema, basketball court, and massive swimming pool with two waterslides; a country manor with a bowling alley, roller skating rink, and shooting ranges; and mountain chalets near lakes for Jet Skiing and fishing and game reserves for pheasant hunting. A house in Changsong, near the Chinese border, was where Jong-Il kept his horses; and another home, on a lake in Hamkyong

Province, allegedly boasted three stories built below water level, with thick glass walls providing a panoramic view of underwater life. One house near Pyongyang was attached to a mammoth exterior waterslide full of loopy twists and turns worthy of a water park. One smaller house, on a stream in Yonghung, was built solely so that Jong-Il could stop by for the local rainbow trout, which he liked baked in aluminum foil. He even had a luxury villa built near the brand-new Youngbyan nuclear research facility so he could inspect the facilities in comfort.

Kim's sushi chef, Kenji Fujimoto, saw many of his guesthouses and recalled that the clocks inside were all Swiss made, the furniture mostly imported from France and Switzerland, and the room temperature, in every room of every villa, kept at 22 degrees Celsius (71.6 degrees Fahrenheit) at all times, whether Jong-Il was on the premises or not. Before his arrival his favorite perfume was to be sprayed throughout the building. All of the homes were near water—a lake, a river, a reservoir, or the sea—because Jong-Il found being near water made him feel peaceful.

Jong-Il liked to live in a style commensurate with his oversize surroundings. He traveled by car only if necessary, preferring to take his personal bulletproof train, which in parts of the country ran on its own exclusive tracks. He loved the companionship of dogs and for most of his life kept four shih tzus, who traveled everywhere with him. He gambled and played golf (one of his Pyongyang homes had a three-hole course in the backyard). He kept a stable of racehorses (Orlovs, a Russian breed, were his favorite), a fleet of speedboats, a collection of racing cars, a whole cornucopia of motorcycles, Jet Skis, and golf carts, but, crippled by a lifelong fear of flying, no planes and only one helicopter. He liked to ride them all as fast as he could make them go. He hunted deer in the mountains and seagulls off his yacht. He had his own cruise ship and, from the 1990s, his own ostrich farm. In addition to Fujimoto he employed a multinational team of personal chefs working with ingredients specially flown in from around the world. His cellars were full of the finest, most expensive wines and liquors. He was fussy about his food, discussing menus with his chefs every day and noticing if even one ingredient had changed in a recipe. He loved shark-fin soup, *boshintang* (dog soup), lobster, fresh pastries, and *toro* (fatty tuna), always asking

Fujimoto, in broken English, for "one more." He smoked Rothman Royal cigarettes, which he had chosen in 1977 after ordering his overseas embassies to gather samples of every single foreign cigarette brand and fly them to Pyongyang for him to try personally. Once he had chosen the Rothmans he built a factory tasked with creating a local brand for his people with the same taste and called it Paektusan Glory; for himself he spurned the cheap knockoff and kept importing the Rothmans. He spent, according to Hennessy, almost $700,000 on Paradis cognac every year.

Naturally, a question arises: How could the Leader's son afford all of this? The DPRK had no private economy, and the state was barely generating enough money for the people to survive, so where was the Dear Leader finding the resources to bankroll his extravagant lifestyle?

The truth was simple, and almost unbelievable: Kim Jong-Il was the head of an international criminal syndicate, one of the most powerful in the world, whose activities served to support him—and only him. In the mid-1970s North Korea had defaulted on its foreign loans, and Moscow and Beijing were beginning to ask questions about how the billions of dollars they were sending the Supreme Leader were being spent. With limited resources and having fallen so far behind industrially that it couldn't make competitive goods to export, North Korea was quickly becoming so poor it received aid even from countries like Bulgaria and Cuba. Kim Il-Sung, who saw that his people were still housed and fed, did not anticipate the impending crisis. His son, however, saw what was on the horizon; and he understood that soon a time would come when North Korea would have only enough money to support either the people or the regime, but not both. So Jong-Il split the North Korean economy into two columns: one that fed back into the national economy, and one that served to fund only him.

"His" economy reserved for itself the exclusive use of the most high-performing industries. According to Hwang Jang-Yop, Kim Jong-Il "established a separate economic unit . . . in the name of managing Party business. [He] selected well-equipped business entities, especially those with significant earning records in foreign currency, and grouped them together. In other words, he took the cream of the crop and set up an independent economic unit [for himself]." Gold mines were first on the list, since gold could so easily be turned into hard, foreign cash; the Mansudae Art group followed, alongside the film studios, for which Kim had big moneymaking ambitions. Then came the export of ginseng, shiitake mushrooms, seafood, silver, and magnesium. Every business or factory with any potential for profit was added to the list and given priority access to electricity, to fuel, and to all first-rate goods. Kim Jong-Il had no interest in sustainability. He sucked every penny of immediate profit out of gold mines, coal mines, and the soil, setting impossible production targets and depleting reserves. When he had asserted his control over all the national economy and found it was still not enough for his appetite, Jong-Il ventured forth into an ingenious new territory: state-sponsored organized crime.

"Counterfeit cigarettes and medicine (including fake Viagra), drugs, insurance fraud, fake money, trafficking people and endangered species," *The New York Times* wrote, ". . . the Kim regime has done it all." *Time* magazine once compared Kim Jong-Il to Tony Soprano, while *The New York Times* chose Vito Corleone and called the Kims "one of the world's most sophisticated crime families."

In the Pyongyang government, Kim Jong-Il's office was known as the Third Floor, after the floor which housed the Dear Leader's offices in the Central Committee office in downtown Pyongyang. The Third Floor was staffed entirely by graduates of the new Kim Jong-Il School of Military Politics, who were so devoted to the young Kim they were known colloquially as the Combatants. Among the departments on the Third Floor, three were most influential: Division 35, Division 38, and Division 39, all of which reported directly to Kim Jong-Il. Division 35 managed and coordinated intelligence collection, producing intelligence briefings for the Dear Leader, and coordinated and planned covert and terrorist operations, such as Shin and Choi's abductions, at Kim's behest. Division 38 managed and invested the Kim family funds, taking ownership stakes in legitimate businesses such as hotels and eateries, including a chain of "Pyongyang" North Korean restaurants built in foreign cities throughout Asia and Europe. Division 38, a little like the olive oil business of the Corleone family in the *Godfather* films, served mostly as a front for Division 39, the largest of the three offices, whose purpose was simple: earn foreign currency for Kim Jong-Il, by any means necessary.

Discreetly created by Kim as a subunit of the Central Committee of the Workers' Party's Finance and Accounting Department (one thing dense, bureaucratic Communist governments are good for is hiding sinister activities), Division 39 eventually grew to include some 120 trading companies, employing over fifty thousand North Koreans and accounting for anywhere between 25 percent (according to researchers at the Samsung Economic Research Institute) and 50 percent (according to Hwang Jang-Yop) of North Korea's total trade and money circulation. Those 120 companies changed names regularly to keep themselves hidden from UN sanctions. A 2010 report by the U.S. Army's Strategic Studies Institute traced Division 39's origins to 1974, and estimated its yearly income as between $500 million and $1 billion a year, stashed away in banks in Macao, Switzerland, Austria, and Luxembourg.

Through Division 39 Jong-Il ran a crime syndicate, but with the tools and resources of a sovereign government: soldiers, merchant and military vessels, diplomats, embassy posts, collective farms, and factories. Division 39's existence was an open secret among the Pyongyang elite, who called it "the keeper of Kim's cashbox."

The drug trade—mostly opium, cocaine, and methamphetamine—was estimated to net Kim revenues of $60 to $70 million per one thousand kilograms of drugs (the South Korean newspaper *The Chosun Ilbo* estimated that North Korea has sent as much as three thousand kilograms of drugs per year to Eastern Europe alone). In certain North Korean villages, one-third of the available soil was set aside for poppy growing (limiting, crucially, the amount of farmable land for food in a country already low on agricultural resources). Schoolchildren and members of the Party's youth brigade farmed the poppies, which were then sent to factories run by chemists whose education had been paid for by the state and who turned the raw poppies into opium and heroin. Diplomats were used as drug mules, but certain operations were also outsourced to Chinese triad gangs, whose ships met North Korean army ships for drug drops in the West Sea, as well as the Japanese yakuza and Russian mafia, even the Official Irish Republican Army. The *Chosun Ilbo* once reported that it was not uncommon for the Third Floor to send "up to 20kg of drugs" to each of their diplomats in selected embassies around the world, ordering "each diplomat to raise US$300,000 to prove their loyalty." As early as 1977, Venezuela expelled all North Korean diplomats for trafficking drugs, and by the late 1990s North Korean attachés had been arrested in Russia (one with fifty pounds of heroin, two others with thirty-five kilograms of cocaine), Germany and Austria (heroin), Taiwan (also heroin), China (cocaine), Japan (methamphetamine), and Egypt (half a million tabs of the date-rape drug Rohypnol).

It wasn't just drugs, though, that made Kim Jong-Il money. North Korean counterfeiters made such good copies of the U.S. $100 bill that the U.S. Secret Service nicknamed them "Supernotes" and even Las Vegas casinos couldn't recognize the fakes. The American Treasury reportedly redesigned the bill to thwart Kim's con men, only for Pyongyang to start making near-perfect copies of the new design, too. Division 39 also dabbled in documents and insurance fraud. "For Kim Jong-Il's birthday, North Korean insurance managers prepared a special gift," Blaine Harden wrote for *The Washington Post* in 2009. "They stuffed $20 million in cash into two heavy-duty bags and sent them, via Beijing, to their leader in Pyongyang," a fortune paid out by some of the world's largest insurance companies, including Allianz Global and Lloyd's of London, on spurious claims of factory fires, flood damage, "and other natural disasters." And of course, in the twenty-first century, trading in nuclear secrets was added to the list of goods and services in Division 39's inventory, permitting it not only to make even more money but also, in a time of crisis, to threaten to hold the whole world hostage.

Because it had the might of a state behind it, Division 39's control, adaptability, and profit margins were high. It made plenty of money, more than enough to finance Jong-Il's lifestyle and to keep the army generals and Pyongyang elite, whose support the Dear Leader needed, loyal and in line. David Asher, a former head of the U.S. State Department's Illicit Activities Initiative, said of Division 39 that it "is like an investment bank. It provides the money for the stuff Kim needs. Like any organized-crime syndicate, you've got a don, and you've got accountants, and it's a very complicated business, keeping track of all this money and making sure the boss gets paid. But when members of the organization don't deliver, they get killed."

Jong-Il's villa at the foot of Mount Paekdu was accordingly sumptuous, and his inviting Choi there, whether she realized it, was a sign of his acceptance and trust.

Ho Hak-Sun went with Choi, to serve as her attendant and cook. She had earned her Party cook's license just a few days before the move and was as proud of it as anything she had ever earned. The house was brand-new. Choi could still smell the paint and wallpaper paste in some of the rooms.

While there Choi was assigned an additional attendant, a young woman in her twenties named Kim Myong-Ok. Miss Kim was slim and pretty and freshly indoctrinated. She was also rude and temperamental and acted like a watchdog. She barked out orders and often spied on Choi through keyholes and the cracks of open doors.

Miss Kim was in charge of Choi's continuing reeducation. Mr. Kang had come along, but as her schooling intensified, it had been decided Choi would receive supplementary lessons from Miss Kim and from the local section chief. As she came to learn more about the young woman, Choi realized that Miss Kim knew no history before 1945, no geography beyond North Korea's borders. "Nothing is important except the revolutionary history of Kim Il-Sung," Miss Kim told her pupil. "If I say that [other] crap doesn't matter, you accept what I say. My duty is to reeducate you—don't you forget it."

Choi did her best to remain positive. If she was stuck here she might as well learn about the Marxist view of history, she thought. "But much to my surprise, this was not what I would learn. The topic of the lectures was Kim Il-Sung's ideology on sovereignty and his so-called *Juche* thought." Her instructors lectured her from 9 a.m. to 1 p.m., then again from 3 p.m. to 5 p.m., every day. They made her write down everything they dictated. Choi felt as if her arm was going to fall off from all the writing they made her do. During her lunch break and again before supper she was required to review what she had just learned. In her free time they asked her to read more biographies of the Kims: *The Immortal History* and *At the Foot of Mount Paekdu*.

Miss Kim, like the other teachers, insisted that the South Korean people were starving and revolting against the Yankee imperialists; indeed that the whole world was engulfed in famine, conflict, and injustice, save for the Democratic People's Republic of Korea, whose people were the luckiest on the planet—thanks, of course, to the beloved Great Leader Comrade Kim Il-Sung. Sometimes Choi protested and told Miss Kim that "South Korean industry has developed very rapidly, I've seen it with my own eyes. . . . The true state of these industries is very different from what you believe to be true here in North Korea." Miss Kim and the others inevitably rebuked her. Allowing any doubt or debate, they explained, was the same as encouraging impure, subversive thoughts. True belief in the People could only be total.

The education had the opposite of its desired effect, of course. "Far from being indoctrinated," Choi later wrote, "I had many more doubts about the system."

Early one morning in late October 1979, Choi was helping Ho Hak-Sun put food away in the kitchen when they heard a scream outside, followed by Miss Kim running into the kitchen.

"They're saying Park Chung-Hee is dead! He's dead!" Miss Kim panted to Hak-Sun.

Choi froze, frightened. Hak-Sun wiped her hands on her apron. "Where did you hear this?" she asked.

"I just now heard it on the radio. They say he was shot." Choi turned on her heel and raced upstairs to her bedroom, jumping on the bed and tuning in to the South Korean station. It was the middle of the day, so the signal was weak and filled with static, but she could make out, at intervals, the announcer repeating, "President Park has been assassinated." How in the world can this have happened? Choi thought.

The last year of Park's dictatorial rule had been turbulent. In spite of Park's viselike control on government and media, he had almost lost the

1978 election to the opposition. Jimmy Carter had withdrawn his ambassador to Seoul in protest at Park's oppression of political opponents, and now there were sit-ins and demonstrations in the streets of the capital. On October 16, antigovernment activists had set fire to thirty police stations in Pusan. Three days later students marched through the streets of nearby Masan, quickly joined, in popular uprising, by regular citizens of all ages and backgrounds. Park was about to order the army to fire upon demonstrators when, on October 26, after a day of ribbon-cutting ceremonies and PR work, he sat down for dinner in a Korean Central Intelligence Agency safe house inside the presidential compound. At the table with him was Park's chief bodyguard and Kim Jae-Kyu, the director of the KCIA. As they dined they argued over how to handle the protests and restore order to the country. Demonstrators, Park said, should be "mowed down with tanks." At some point Kim Jae-Kyu left the room. When he returned he was holding a Walther PPK semiautomatic pistol. He shot the chief bodyguard in the arm and stomach and Park in the chest and head. Kim's motive was never certainly established. He had come from the same hometown as Park; they had been classmates at the military academy. He was one of Park's closest friends. But during his trial, he stood simply and testified, "I shot the heart of Yushin [the name of Park's 1972 constitution, which made him president for life] like a beast. I did that for democracy in this country. Nothing more, nothing less."

Choi knew none of this, only that a man she had known had been killed and the home country she hadn't seen in nearly two years was reduced to chaos. She felt more keenly how brief and unpredictable life was.

Nobody ever knows their own destiny, she thought.

19
The Hunger Strike

In Prison Number 6, Shin passed the time in remaking all his films.

"In the torture position, which I had to assume immediately after breakfast," Shin wrote, "I had to look straight ahead with my hands on my knees. . . . I calculated that every day, out of the seventeen hours from the time I got up until the time I went to bed, I spent about sixteen hours in this position. In this position, all I did was think." He reflected on his past and found the usual mistakes: "I had the opportunity to think endlessly about my life, my mistakes, how I could have spent more time with my children." But mostly, "I still lived with films," Shin said simply. He found that the only way he could endure was to disappear into the world of film, into creation—to let his mind roam back to a place and time when he was still a film director. In his mind's eye he rewrote, reshot, and reedited all of his old films, "over and over again," listing their flaws and picturing how he would fix them if he could. In South Korea he had constantly been hustling, constantly keeping up with costs, bills, and the 250 employees who needed to be kept busy and on salary. Here, for the first time, this most ambitious, restless of men was forced to stop. In the unbearable conditions of the prison, when he sometimes thought he was losing his sanity, this imaginary career was his only comfort. He found an unexpected satisfaction in it. Before being kidnapped he had struggled with the plot for his *Sleeping*

Beauty project, but now "I was able to figure it out so easily," he said. "I was delighted."

In Seoul, wealthy, famous, and free, he had been proud of his films, almost arrogantly so. In the desolation of the prison he found them shallow and insubstantial. "I thought about my movies and decided they had to contain more social responsibility," he reflected. "The greatest weakness in my films, as I [saw] it, is that they lack the thick scent of life and a vivid reality. This is my frank confession. I became famous unexpectedly at a young age, and since then I've been so deeply into film that I haven't had a moment to look anywhere else. As a result I haven't had the luxury of having a diverse range of experience and sensing and thinking about the depth of life." Silently he reclassified all his films into three groups: the satisfactory films, "the ones that needed to be partly remade, and another group of films that should be trashed entirely." When he was done going through them there wasn't a single film that satisfied him. He was disappointed by the results—"I had thought my movies depicted real life. Now I knew otherwise"—and embarrassed by how he had dismissed peers with a social consciousness and how glib he'd been, in interviews, about the social outlook of his own work. "I had been very proud of myself," he said. "I now realized that I completely misunderstood the true meaning of life and pain."

Remaking his films in his head also stoked his desire to leave prison and remake them in real life. As soon as he'd arrived, Shin had requested permission to send a letter of appeal to Kim Jong-Il, "to tell him about my mistakes and my thoughts about the North Korean movie industry." He had expected to be executed for his repeated escape attempts, and he was smart enough to recognize that Kim wouldn't have kept him alive if he didn't, still, have some hope for his usefulness.

No explicit update on Shin's request for contact was forthcoming, but every now and then he was pulled out of his cell and taken to another chamber, this one with a writing desk and a chair, and asked to write a letter of "self-criticism" about his crime. "I purposely wrote slowly to pass the time,"

Shin explained. "It took me a week to write the fifteen pages, which I submitted. In the letter, I thanked Kim Jong-Il for his benevolence and apologized for my escape attempts." The letter was soon returned to him and he was told to write a second, better draft; this one took him a month. ("The longer the piece of self-criticism, the better," wrote Hyok Kang of his own experience. "Ten pages are better than five. So you have to season your contrition with commentaries, digressions, expressions filled with political jargon, useless words, synonyms, and all kinds of repetitions. Emphasis is the most important ingredient in this bitter dish, in which adverbs (basically . . . resolutely . . . truly . . . firmly) act as a kind of sweetener. . . . And as the icing on the cake you need a grandiloquent, solemn oath in which you declare that you will never again bound into such monumental errors unworthy of a good socialist member of society. Then you add the date and sign.")

A short while after Shin submitted his second self-criticism, the warden informed him that he had permission to write Kim Jong-Il another letter, this one addressing the problems of the North Korean film industry and possible solutions. "I suggested methods for movie production and means for reducing the cost and improving the quality of North Korean films. I [also] suggested breaking away from old-fashioned production methods and instead producing films based on historical events" and on the exploits of real North Korean "champions." Whenever they allowed him to go to that room he wrote letter after letter, handing them to the guards despite never hearing back. "Though Kim Jong-Il had kidnapped me," he reasoned, putting himself in his kidnapper's shoes, "he had treated me with hospitality and concern. In spite of it, I had tried to flee twice. He may have considered it a betrayal." He didn't know if Kim ever read his letters but later assumed that since Kim liked to know everything, he probably did. In any case, Shin, like Choi, diligently pursued his ideological studies and endless letter writing to pass the time.

The days turned into weeks, the weeks into months, 1979 into 1980. Sometime in January Shin was moved to a different cell, at the other end of the prison, with heated floors and a functioning toilet. The room was still too small for him to lie down in, but he was allowed bedding, soap, a toothbrush and toothpaste, and a washbasin. He was ordered to make them all last—the bar of soap for six months, the toothpaste for seven—and warned he would be given no replacements if he went through them too fast. At mealtimes he could expect rice and soup, sometimes even a thick chunk of glistening pork fat. The torture position remained his daily routine. On the wall someone had written, in flawless calligraphy, seven lines of text, under the heading "Warnings."

1. *Obey the orders of the guards without question.*
2. *Don't try to find out about the other prisoners.*
3. *Don't eavesdrop on conversations between guards and other prisoners.*
4. *Never talk with other prisoners.*
5. *If you catch another prisoner violating regulations, you must report him immediately.*
6. *Patients must absolutely obey the doctor's orders.*
7. *Never damage any of the daily necessities including the bedding, for they are the property of the State.*

The next day Shin was taken to the bathroom for his biweekly ablutions by a trusty—a prisoner given preferential treatment by the guards in exchange for being trusted with specific tasks, such as cleaning or running messages. "Although [this trusty] treated the other prisoners roughly, he was kind to me," Shin wrote. He allowed Shin longer than the five minutes allotted by the rules and showed him how to adjust the water temperature. As Shin splashed water on himself, the trusty eyed him carefully. "I know who you are," he said. "You're Choi Eun-Hee's husband, aren't you?"

Shin was stunned. After the years of solitude and removal from the world, to be speaking to someone who knew who he was, in Shin's words, was "like meeting Buddha in hell."

The trusty handed Shin a mirror and a razor, luxuries by the standard of Prison Number 6. As he wiped his pale, emaciated face—it was the first time he had seen his own features in a long time—Shin asked, "How do you know of me?"

"Fellow, how could I not know you? I was a South Korean spy. I was captured and sentenced to twenty years. I still have five to go before I get out."

"I was kidnapped in Hong Kong," Shin replied, overjoyed to have someone to openly talk to. "I tried to escape, but they caught me. If I have six hours by myself I can escape. The six hours are the problem."

"Choi Eun-Hee was here for three months," the trusty said abruptly. "After she got here she refused to eat. Even when they gave her cookies she wouldn't eat. She barely ate anything. Three months later they released her. It was the first time anyone ever got out of here in only three months."

"Choi Eun-Hee was here?" Shin said. Why was she imprisoned? he wondered.

The trusty nodded. Their conversation was cut short by the next prisoners in line for the bathroom, and Shin went back to his room plagued by fearful thoughts. As the evening wore on, sitting in his cell staring at the door, he found the trusty's story sat with him awkwardly. Surely a captured South Korean spy would be executed, not just condemned to twenty years, when ordinary North Korean citizens were shot or hanged for much less? How did the trusty know so many details about Choi's stay at Prison Number 6, such as its exact duration?

The next day Shin asked the trusty to describe the woman he claimed to have seen. It quickly became clear the man had mistaken someone else for Choi Eun-Hee, even though he knew Shin well enough to recognize *him* on sight, when he was the one of the pair who worked *behind* the camera. Was the trusty mistaken, or lying? Was it a test?

"I wanted to speak with the trusty, but it was difficult," Shin recalled. "I could exchange only a few words a day with him. On bathing day I could manage to talk with him for one or two minutes. That was only once every two weeks." Over time, Shin managed to piece together the prisoner's full history: he had been in show business himself since 1945, and claimed he had been the first director of the Korean Army Show, the South Korean troop-entertainment organization Choi Eun-Hee had forcefully been made a part of during the Korean War. After the retreat of UN forces from Pyongyang in 1951, the trusty said he had been convinced to stay in the North as an undercover intelligence agent, that when the war had ended he had found himself stuck in North Korea, and that he had reluctantly settled down outside Pyongyang, married, and fathered three children. Fifteen years later state security had come to arrest him, charge him with espionage, and throw him in prison for life.

The more he spoke, the less Shin believed the man's narrative. Originally the trusty's sentence had been twenty years, now it was life; he said he recognized Shin from his time in the South, but Shin wasn't famous yet during the war. When pressed on how he had recognized him in spite of living in the North, the trusty answered that he knew him from listening to South Korean radio broadcasts (how he could recognize a man on sight from hearing about him on the radio, Shin didn't bother to ask). The man also had the habit of complaining about the North Korean system to see if Shin agreed. "This is the epitome of the socialist state," he told Shin once while patching up cracks in the hallway, one of his duties. "They use only five sacks of cement where ten are needed. Then when the work is done, they shout hurray for us because we exceeded our norms and saved materials. And they get the title of Labor Hero. What a goddamn sight this is. They're all asses." Shin always made sure to reply with fulsome praise for the Great Leader and the *juche* way. By now he felt sure the trusty must be working for the warden, maybe even for state security. "He lied to me," Shin realized, "to sound me out."

The man's last name was Choi—he never told Shin his given name—and Shin wondered if the name had also been chosen deliberately, to keep the thought of Eun-Hee fresh in his mind. The trusty kept talking about her, too. He claimed she hadn't been kidnapped at all but had come to North Korea voluntarily after eloping with a famous North Korean actor named Chun. "You were at the height of playing around with your love affairs and she was very depressed, wasn't she? Well, she fell in love with Chun and promised to run away with him to North Korea. And later she did it. She fell in love with him and eloped with him." Another time he poked Shin in the ribs, grinning, and said, "If you get out of here and make movies, you can have your pick of any People's Actress or Meritorious Actress that you like, you know. Even the best actress will be yours. The Party will arrange it." He was obviously gauging how Shin felt about his ex-wife, but it was unsettling nonetheless. Doubt kept niggling at Shin's mind. Sitting in the torture position, he had a lot of time to obsessively run through every aspect of the trusty's tales for possible truth.

As time passed, Shin realized he must have been passing all the tests, for his treatment steadily improved. He started receiving some cookies or candies once every month, sometimes even a boiled pollack or a chunk of some other kind of fish with his rice ball and soup. He gained weight. On some days they gave him so much food he actually left some on his plate.

One day in the fall of 1980, a guard took Shin out of his sunning cage and took his photograph, Shin assumed so that it could be sent to Kim Jong-Il as proof that he was looking healthier. The next spring the trusty Choi came by Shin's cell and whispered, "Got some good news for you. They say you'll be getting out soon. You'd better straighten out your clothes and things—someone might even come to get you late tonight." Shin was jubilant. He was so excited he skipped his dinner and couldn't go to sleep.

But the call never came.

"You're driving me nuts," Shin seethed at the trusty when he came around with the breakfast cart the next morning.

"You are to be released soon," the trusty said. "Just wait a little longer."

Time passed. By August Shin had fallen into despair. Tomorrow would be the same, and so would the next day. So he decided to take matters in his own hands: he went on a hunger strike, determined to attract Kim Jong-Il's attention or die in the process.

Once again he planned it badly. For the first few days he didn't touch his meals, but snacked away on candies hidden inside the toilet cistern. "Why don't you eat?" asked a confused guard after Shin hadn't touched his lunch or dinner on the first day. "Are you sick?"

"No, sir. I'm on a hunger strike and I'm prepared to die if necessary. I'd rather die than go on like this."

"A hunger strike, you say?" The guard guffawed. "Just wait. Soon you'll be begging for food."

The next morning Shin ate none of his breakfast. "I want to see the investigator, sir," Shin told the guard who came to take the plate away.

"Sure. If you don't eat for a month, we'll let you meet him. A hell of a lot of good that'll do, anyway."

Shin thought that after three days the guards would respond to his strike and be forced to take action. He was wrong. The candies were making him hungrier and lethargic, and the sugar, the only thing in his stomach, gave him diarrhea. Sitting in the torture position with no fuel exhausted him. Refusing water as well as food, Shin quickly grew dehydrated. He was so thirsty he considered drinking the dirty water from the toilet.

Seventy-two hours after his first skipped meal, as usually happens, the pain really kicked in. Starved of nutrients, Shin's body started using up his own muscle protein to make the glucose it needed to keep functioning. He quickly lost weight. Even sitting down he felt nauseatingly dizzy. His blood pressure fell so low he could barely feel his pulse.

On the fifth day Shin collapsed and lost consciousness. Had the strike been another failure? Didn't Kim Jong-Il care?

When he woke up in the infirmary wing, with an investigator and a military officer standing by his bed, Shin was relieved to find that, unlike with his escape attempts, this time he had been successful.

He had finally drawn Kim Jong-Il's attention.

20
Director Shin Is Coming

After two and a half years at the guesthouse in Mount Paekdu, Choi Eun-Hee was moved back to Tongbuk-Ri, where she spent another year, resuming her endless rounds of sightseeing and ideological lessons. She went walking around the woods every day, along the same path she had followed nearly three years earlier, hoping to run into Catherine Hong, the beauty from Macao, wondering if she was still in the compound and what had happened to her. Three days after she moved back in they bumped into each other. They were both elated.

"How have you been getting along?" Choi asked.

"I cried so much after you left," Ms. Hong said, hugging her. "I used to see you in my dreams. Let's never be separated again."

They walked together, talking for a long time. Catherine's Korean had drastically improved and their conversations became more layered and far ranging. For the next several weeks they met every other day at prearranged locations and times, sometimes sharing a bottle of ginseng liquor as they talked.

"Sister, do you have a religion?" Catherine asked Choi one afternoon.

"Well, sometimes I pray, but you can't really say I have a religion," Choi said.

"I'm Roman Catholic," Catherine said. "My baptismal name is Maria. What do you think about Catholicism?"

"I've always found something attractive in it," Choi answered, vaguely.

"Well then, why don't we pray together to God?"

"All right," Choi said.

She followed Catherine deeper into the forest and, as there was no body of water deep enough within the compound walls, Catherine baptized Choi by dunking her in the fallen leaves, red, golden, and soft. She wasn't really qualified to baptize, Maria told her, but under such circumstances she felt she could. "Now you are Catholic too, and we can pray together. I'll give you a baptismal name. I think it would be nice if it started with an M, like Maria. I think Madeline would be good?" Choi nodded. "Good. From now on, you are Madeline."

Choi and Catherine prayed together and gave each other courage; it reassured Choi to have something private, even if it was just a name—Maria, Madeline, like a secret code—with the only person she knew who understood how she felt. In her memoir Choi puts it simply: her only friend was a Catholic, "so I became one too."

In early March they relocated Choi again. The day before she was to be moved, Choi had one last meeting with Catherine, who gave Choi a necklace as a gift. Choi, who didn't have anything she felt suitable to give, tried to give her friend two $100 bills she'd had since her last day in Hong Kong. But Maria gently shook her head. "That's all right," she said. "I receive a salary, you know. I think you'll need it more than I." Choi couldn't bear leaving the only person with whom she could share her true feelings and thoughts. She pressed the money into her hand, turned around and started to walk away. She had only taken a few steps when she heard: "Madeline!" She spun to face her friend.

"Sister," Catherine said, "we'll meet again someday." She hurried to Choi and hugged her, resting her head against her chest. Choi and Catherine both cried until they were exhausted, then said good-bye. In later years Choi learned that Catherine had been relocated here and there within the country and finally had been assigned to teach Cantonese to North Korean espionage agents. They never saw each other again.

One person Choi continued to see plenty of was Kim Jong-Il. They met regularly through 1981 and 1982, usually at his Fish House parties. He looked "very thin" to her. "It's because I'm exercising every day to lose weight,"

Jong-Il told her. He was still smoking but drinking less, and now spent most of his parties sipping bottled water—although he still egged on the guests to drink more. Their relationship had settled into an almost mother-son routine; she was, after all, sixteen years older than him. She teased him about improving his diet and did her best "to win [his] trust." The only way she could preserve some kind of freedom and sanity was to appear content, even charmed, and she resigned herself to performing as pleasantly, but never sycophantically, as possible.

It's likely Jong-Il was also getting himself into shape in preparation for the higher public profile he was taking. In October 1980 Kim Il-Sung had officially announced to the Sixth Congress of the Workers' Party that Kim Jong-Il would be his successor, a move met with international condemnation for its nepotism and authoritarianism, not just in the West but in many socialist states of Eastern Europe and Asia. At the same congress, Jong-Il announced that North Korea would move away from traditional communism toward self-reliance and the renewed promotion of the *juche* idea. The Party members who had attended the congress returned home with a gift of the most exciting new cutting-edge technology: a family-size modern refrigerator, made in Japan. The front of the fridge was emblazoned with the word PAEKTUSAN ("Mount Paekdu") in large letters. The fridge, each party member was told, was a personal gift from the Dear Leader. In February 1982 Jong-Il was "elected" to the Supreme People's Assembly and the title of Dear Leader was made official to the wider public. The young man was also busy overseeing the preparations for his father's seventieth birthday on April 15, 1982; along with the many lavish celebrations, Jong-Il was completely redesigning the layout of Pyongyang to accommodate a 170-meter high *juche* tower, an arch of triumph, and a Kim Il-Sung Square plaza, all of which he insisted be built in a perfect line crossing the city. He was, finally, in production on a multipart epic movie biography of Kim Il-Sung, *The Star of Korea,* in which the Great Leader finally appeared as an on-screen character.

Following the official announcement that Jong-Il would be the successor to the Party leadership—the general public would not be informed until Kim Il-Sung's death fourteen years later—the regime began to deify

Jong-Il as it had his father. In practice this meant Jong-Il was turning himself into the son of God. Until then, Choi's sightseeing excursions had mostly been to sites dedicated to Kim Il-Sung, but now she was taken to a "Kim Jong-Il Revolutionary Site," glorifying the son rather than the father. The site consisted of a "history" museum, a mountain park they told her had been Jong-Il's military training ground, and a lecture hall dedicated to filmmaking and Kim Jong-Il's exceptional creative talents. The buildings were all brand-new, the tour guides all female members of the military. On the walls of the lecture hall were articles from foreign newspapers—*The New York Times*, for instance—praising the Kims. When Choi looked closer she saw they were paid ads, mocked up to look like features.

During their most recent meetings, Kim had claimed repeatedly that "Director Shin is coming," implying that Shin was about to defect. Once he was so specific as to say, in the middle of a conversation about movies, "Oh, by the way, I've heard from Director Shin. He'll arrive here on April 15, the Great Leader's birthday." Choi was dubious. The man she knew would never have defected to North Korea.

Even so, Jong-Il's assurances that Shin would be coming to join them, made so often and so confidently, distressed Choi. If he does come, she thought, then what will happen to our children? Has he been taking care of them during my absence? Anyhow, how could he be coming here? He wouldn't be able to stand it here for even a day. But if he did come here, it might give me the will to go on living . . . She spent hours arguing with herself.

Director Shin *absolutely* should not come here.

It *would* be wonderful if he were coming just for my sake . . .

He should not come. He *must* not come.

"The more I thought about it," Choi wrote later, "the more confused I became. Wherever I went, thoughts of Director Shin went with me. He often appeared even in my dreams." In one of them, she says, she was filming on location but couldn't find Director Shin; she wandered around and finally found him facedown in a ditch alongside a field, curled up in the fetal position. She did her best to get him to stand but failed. When she woke, she was convinced that something terrible had happened to her ex-husband.

April 14, 1982, the day before Kim Il-Sung's birthday, came without further news of Shin. Before supper Mr. Kang and another of Choi's tutors sat her downstairs to listen to a tape recording listing Kim Il-Sung's achievements. Then they listened to another listing those of his late wife Kim Jong-Suk, then yet another praising his entire family—father, mother, brothers, uncles. No one was permitted to speak or close their eyes while the tapes played. It was state-imposed tradition on the eve of the Leader's Day, Choi learned later, and every single person in the country was spending their evening in silence, listening to these stories, produced by the central news agency. "While the recorder ran for an hour and forty minutes," Choi said, "I was lost in my thoughts of Director Shin."

The next day—the Leader's Day—Kang returned to the house with a bouquet of azaleas from the Dear Leader. The official North Korean story is that in 1945, when Kim Il-Sung and his guerrillas finally pushed the Japanese oppressor over the Sino-Korean border and set foot, after a long exile, back on their homeland, they found azaleas blossoming in the first village they entered and were overwhelmed with joy at being home. Since then the azalea had been the national flower of North Korea.

In keeping with Kim Il-Sung's smiling, rosy-cheeked, Santa Claus–like representation in North Korean iconography, his birthday had been turned into a sort of Christmas feast for all citizens: it was a rare holiday for the workers and students, everyone got meat in their rations, and children received presents from the state, usually candy or fresh school uniforms, for which they had to thank the Great Leader by bowing to the official, legally required portrait of him that every household hung in the center of the main wall of the main room. The portraits were distributed to all citizens free of charge, along with a special white cloth to be used to clean them, and only them. Once a month inspectors from the Public Standards Department dropped in to check on the cleanliness of the portraits. A few specks of dust

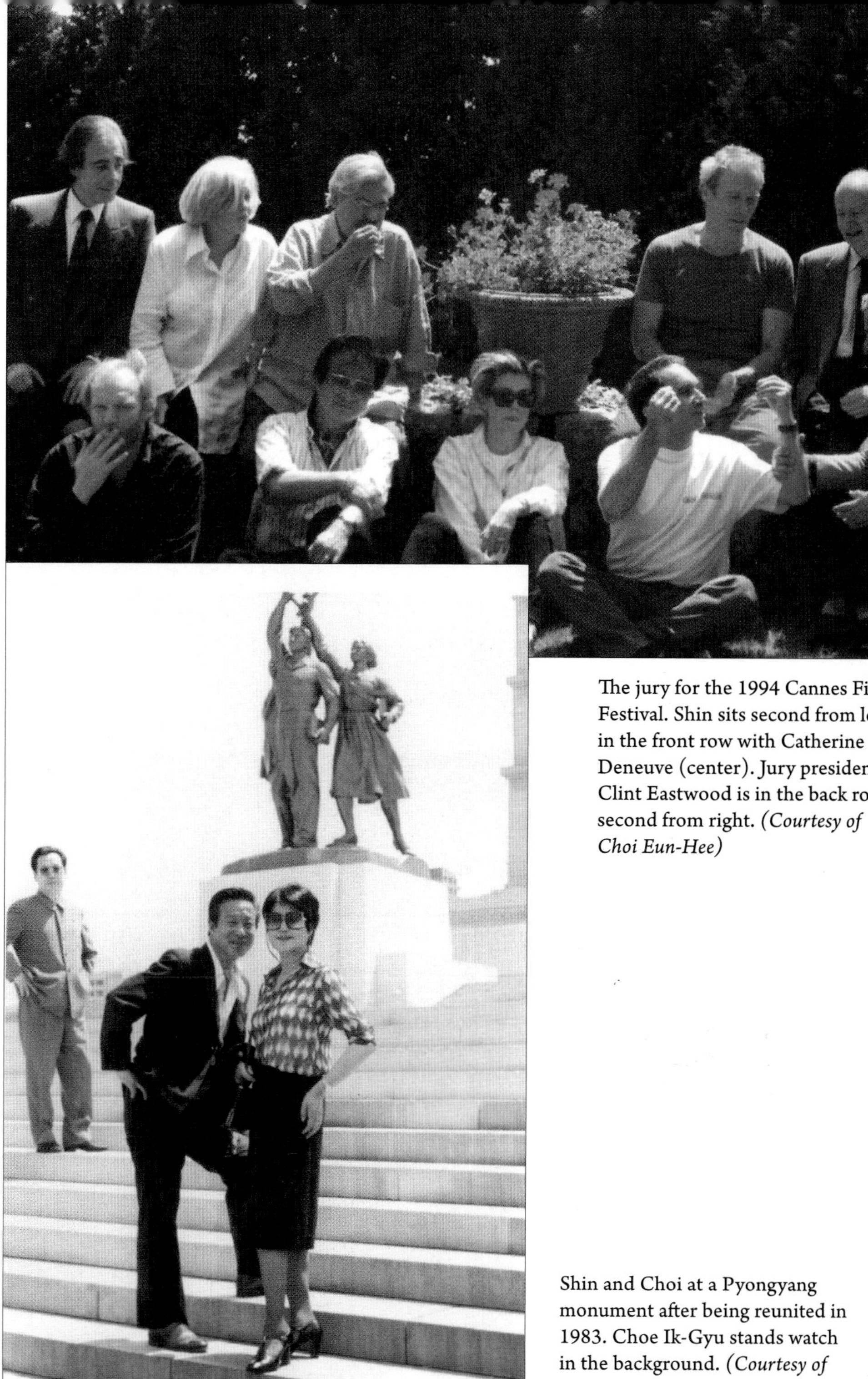

The jury for the 1994 Cannes Film Festival. Shin sits second from left in the front row with Catherine Deneuve (center). Jury president Clint Eastwood is in the back row, second from right. *(Courtesy of Choi Eun-Hee)*

Shin and Choi at a Pyongyang monument after being reunited in 1983. Choe Ik-Gyu stands watch in the background. *(Courtesy of Choi Eun-Hee)*

Choi Eun-Hee stars in *Salt,* the fourth film she and Shin made in North Korea. Choi won the Best Actress award at the Moscow Film Festival for her performance as a struggling mother during the Japanese occupation. *(Courtesy of Choi Eun-Hee)*

Shin filming a scene from *Salt* in the North Korean countryside. His work ethic and physical endurance became legendary among North Korean crews. *(Courtesy of Choi Eun-Hee)*

Shin Sang-Ok sets up a shot during the filming of *Emissary of No Return* in 1984 at Barrandov Studios in Prague, Czech Republic. *(Courtesy of Choi Eun-Hee)*

The poster for *The Flower Girl* (1972), North Korea's single most iconic movie and the defining motion picture of Kim Jong-Il's film career. He produced and oversaw the writing of the film, which became a hit throughout communist Asia. *(Korea Film Export & Import Corporation)*

Official state portrait of Kim Il-Sung, the Sun of Korea, first Supreme Leader of the Democratic People's Republic of Korea. *(Author's photo)*

Official state portrait of Kim Jong-Il, the Dear Leader and Beloved General, second ruler of the Democratic People's Republic of Korea. *(Author's photo)*

Kim Jong-Il's official state biography begins with a messianic birth on the snowy slopes of Mount Paekdu, considered by traditional Koreans as the source of their people's ancestral origins. In this "historical" Party portrait the child Kim Jong-Il is shown sitting on his mother's shoulder and holding his father's hand. The cabin of his birth can be seen in the background, and all three wear the revolutionary uniforms of the Korean Liberation Army. *(Author's photo)*

Kim Jong-Il's state funeral, on December 28, 2011, stunned the world with its televised images of the thousands of hysterical, sobbing North Koreans lining the procession route in subzero temperatures. Military vehicles and goose-stepping soldiers escorted the Dear Leader's body to its final resting place in the luxurious Kumsusan Memorial Palace. *(AFP/Getty Images)*

Kim Jong-Il welcomes Choi Eun-Hee to North Korea at Nampo harbor, January 1978, in a photograph taken by a press officer he brought with him to the dockside to record the moment. *(Courtesy of Choi Eun-Hee)*

Choi Eun-Hee accepting the Best Actress award for *Salt* at the Moscow Film Festival, July 1985. *(Courtesy of Choi Eun-Hee)*

Shin and Choi's official Party portrait, taken at Kim Jong-Il's offices on October 19, 1983. Earlier that evening the couple had secretly tape-recorded their first production meeting with Kim. *(Courtesy of Choi Eun-Hee)*

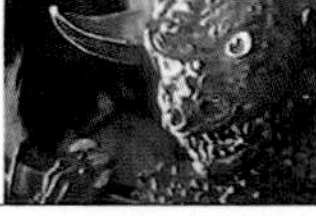

Shin's most famous North Korean film, *Pulgasari,* was a monster flick inspired by Godzilla. Years after it was made it became a cult classic on the U.S. home video and midnight-movie screening circuit. *(Twin Co.)*

Choi Eun-Hee, Kim Jong-Il, and Shin Sang-Ok at the party thrown by Kim to reunite the South Korean couple in March 1983. Shin had been released from brutal Prison Number Six only two weeks earlier, and the evening was the first time Shin and Choi had seen each other in more than five years. *(Courtesy of Choi Eun-Hee)*

Shin and Choi on Shin's thirty-fourth birthday in 1960, during the happiest years of their first marriage. Choi is in period costume, Shin in the suit-and-skinny-tie uniform he wore as a young director, and the moment was the extent of their celebrations, a few minutes stolen on set. "We were always so busy," Choi said. *(Courtesy of Choi Eun-Hee)*

were enough to be reported, a couple of failed inspections enough to be imprisoned. The portraits, made to be hung high on the wall, had a wider edge at the top of the frame to cut out reflections and also to draw the eye and intensify the Great Leader's gaze on the house's inhabitants.

Along with the flowers Kang carried another box. A proud smile was pasted on his face. "The Dear Leader sends you this gift," he told Choi. "Now I am going to perform the required ceremony." He ordered Ho Hak-Sun and Miss Kim to follow him upstairs, cleared the first-floor living room, in which was suspended the house's compulsory Kim Il-Sung portrait, and placed something that resembled an apple crate in front of it. He asked Choi to stand on the crate and stare up at the picture.

"In a formal ceremony, we should sing 'The Song of General Kim Il-Sung,' but let's skip it today," Kang said. "Just take the oath of loyalty."

Choi had been asked to learn and rehearse the oath several times, but being told to do it for real caught her off guard. She hesitated. "Come on, quickly," Kang pressed. She knew there was no avoiding it. She decided to get it over with.

"I thank you, Great Leader, for your most kind treatment accorded to me and for allowing me to participate in the glorious revolution. I swear I will work hard to repay your kindness. I wish long life to our Great Leader." She then bowed to the picture. "Though I acted in many films," she said later, "this performance was by far the most embarrassing." Kang, however, looked pleased. He untied the package he held in his hands. Inside it were Japanese fruit, a box of canned fish, several banana bunches, and a "name watch," engraved with Kim Il-Sung's name—the very type of watch that Ho Hak-Sun had longed for her whole life. Choi felt overcome with guilt to be the one to receive it, having done nothing to merit it and having no desire for it. Abruptly her thoughts were broken by a high-pitched, girlish voice.

"Wow! What's this?" exclaimed Miss Kim. She grabbed one of the fruit bunches. She had never seen bananas before.

Just under a year later, in 1983, Choi stood under the same smiling portrait, in the same room, surrounded by the same people. After an identical ceremony, she was handed another gift box. Inside this box was a second name watch, a solid-gold Omega—Choi could feel Hak-Sun's envious stare—and alongside it a ribbon in the colors of the national flag, a golden stripe running vertically down its center. Kang pinned the ribbon on Choi's chest. "The Great Leader Kim Il-Sung and the Dear Leader Comrade Kim Jong-Il have awarded you the Order of the National Flag, First Class." It was the second-highest civilian order in the People's Republic, after the Order of (who else) Kim Il-Sung. Choi didn't know what she possibly could have done to merit the award, but she knew one thing: it came with a duty to serve the state. Kim Jong-Il, she felt sure, was about to finally put her to a purpose.

What purpose exactly she didn't know—until one day, at a party, Kim turned to her and said, simply: "Director Shin is here."

After his hunger strike, Shin languished in Prison Number 6 for another agonizing year and a half. Slowly his circumstances changed. The warden began summoning him regularly to ask about his films—questions so specific that Shin was reminded of that interrogation, years earlier after his arrest at the train station, in which the men from state security had kept running in and out of the room reporting his answers to Kim Jong-Il and returning with more questions. Only one person in North Korea could know officially banned South Korean films well enough to pose the questions he was being asked now.

A short time after the movie inquiries had begun, Shin was interviewed by the Minister of People's Security. "If you could live with Choi Eun-Hee, would you stay in North Korea and stop trying to escape?" the Minister had asked.

"Of course," Shin said. He laid it on thick—a little too thick, he worried later. "A common man like me would be happy to accept a situation with a pleasant home life. I will take part in the revolution. From now on I will solely rely upon the Party and act according to its wishes. I have finally understood the truth of our Korean Workers' Party slogan: *Absoluteness and Unconditionality*. Before I couldn't understand it because I had been coming at it from a capitalistic point of view." Inside, Shin was cringing. This was some really bad dialogue the state wanted its people to read.

"Yes," the Minister nodded. "Absoluteness and unconditionality can have no limits. You finally understand it."

A few months later, in December 1982, another envoy was sent from Pyongyang to meet with Shin. The man asked Shin to write down everything he knew about every South Korean film director he could think of, after which he interviewed Shin about how he saw his own future filmmaking career. Shin told him that in prison he had repented "a thousand times a day" for his past life, and that he had changed his beliefs and point of view. "I realize now that all my films made in South Korea clouded the people's class consciousness, much as religion has served the capitalists. If I have a chance to make films, I will direct them with class consciousness." This man, too, seemed pleased with Shin's answers.

And then, right after breakfast on February 23, 1983, a guard opened Shin's cell door and let him out. He was taken to have a bath, then handed the wrinkled brown suit he had been arrested in and told to change, after which the guards walked him to the building's visiting room. Three men waited for him: an inspector Shin had met before, an official in a Mao tunic, and, as always, the trusty, Choi, in a corner. The inspector made small talk for a while, asking Shin about his health, and then the man in the Mao tunic cracked open his briefcase and took out a single sheet of paper. "Please stand at attention and listen to this carefully while I read it," he asked. Holding it before him he read out, loudly and with authority: "Comrade, despite the fact that you have committed a serious crime, we will forgive you. Therefore you shall now devote yourself to the Great Leader and to contributing to the completion of the revolutionary task of the *juche* fatherland. Signed, Kim Jong-Il, February twenty-third, nineteen-eighty-three."

No sooner had the briefcase snapped shut than Shin found himself outside, faced with the ubiquitous Mercedes, this one blue and brand-new. Shin got in. As the car pulled away, he kept his eyes on the prison building, the car's back window framing it like a wide-screen moving picture, until it disappeared from sight.

Taken to a People's Security safe house, Shin was made to take the oath of loyalty and then gradually restored to health by large meals and material comfort. He was given new clothes, a medical checkup, and a haircut. On March 6, a mere ten days after arriving at the safe house, he was told to prepare to meet the Dear Leader.

He was going to his first Kim Jong-Il party.

Choi had already arrived at the Fish House. The gala was like every other that she had attended in her five years in Pyongyang, only bigger, filling the whole of the large banquet hall, with twice the usual number of guests in attendance. There was trepidation in the air, too. Kim Jong-Il looked especially pleased with himself. Earlier in the evening someone had come up to Choi, taken her elbow, and said, "Today will be the happiest day of your life!" Choi shrugged it off. By now she was used to the North Korean propensity for elation and exaggeration.

Shin was tense and anxious as the car drove up to the concrete building, outside of which were parked a long row of identical Mercedes-Benzes. He stepped out of the car and walked up to the entrance. Two attendants bowed their heads and opened the door for him. As soon as he entered, the packed banquet hall broke into applause.

He looked around in bewilderment. Ten days before he had been sitting in the torture position inside a prison camp, starved of food, the screams of prisoners being tortured and executed waking him up at night; now he was in a room that felt like "a luxurious nightclub in Seoul," filled with men in uniforms or in identical Western suits with identical red flag pins bolted to their chests, drunk on the most expensive liquors in the world, gorging on the most luxurious variety of dishes. Teenage girls danced, flirted, and giggled their way from table to table.

Standing at the center of it all was Kim Jong-Il, the man who had imprisoned him for years and who had now, inexplicably, brought him here. "I had seen pictures and paintings of Kim Jong-Il numerous times," Shin later wrote, "but this was the first time I had ever seen him in person. He was small and had big, bright eyes. His skin was flushed, as if he was beginning to show the effects of alcohol." He wore a tunic consisting of comfortable trousers and a loose button-up shirt, an ensemble almost resembling pajamas. He smiled in greeting.

Shin began to make his way toward him.

Choi missed the arrival of the evening's special guest. When the music stopped abruptly and the crowd erupted into applause, she didn't think to take notice until a woman approached her and pointed toward the door. "Look who's here!" she said. Choi turned to the entrance. A very gaunt man stood there. She didn't recognize Shin at first, then she froze. It felt like her heart had stopped. "Why are you just standing there?" the woman asked, dragging her forward.

Shin was approaching Kim Jong-Il, his pulse racing, when he suddenly caught sight of Choi. She was wearing a traditional white *hanbok* dress and huge smokily tinted sunglasses. Until tonight, he hadn't seen her in over five years, and he had never been sure that she was actually in the country or even still alive. He stared in blank disbelief as she was pulled toward him. They both just stood there, not knowing what to say or do, agonizingly aware of the dozens of eyes glued to them. Silence, and a stifling stillness, had replaced the applause.

"What happened to you?" Choi finally managed. Shin smiled weakly.

Jong-Il lingered nearby, an enormous grin on his face, looking like a kid who had just pulled off the most improbable prank. "Well, go ahead and hug each other!" he said. "Why are you just standing there?" Shin and Choi hugged, awkwardly at first, and then sank into the comfort of each other's arms. Cheers and applause broke out again. Flashbulbs popped.

"All right, all right—stop hugging and come over here," Jong-Il ordered. Shin and Choi did as they were told, keenly aware of being on show. Shin gave a polite bow to Kim and shook the younger man's hand. Jong-Il heartily squeezed Shin's. Placing Shin on his left and Choi on his right, Jong-Il made them pose for a picture—"Relax," he joked, "this won't end up in the South Korean papers"—and then turned to the crowd. "Comrades," he announced, "from now on Mr. Shin is my film adviser." Deafening applause. "And Madame Choi is now a representative for our Korean women!" More applause. Jong-Il looked from Shin to Choi. "Let's have a wedding ceremony for you—on April 15, the Great Leader's birthday."

Shin stared, stupefied, as the riotous applause continued. It was March 6, 1983. Had he and Choi never divorced, today would have been the eve of their twenty-ninth wedding anniversary.

The Dear Leader had directed his little scene to perfection.

INTERMISSION

The People's Actress Woo In-Hee

Woo In-Hee was said to be the most beautiful woman in North Korea. Like the ideal women on propaganda posters and postcards, she had the soft, oval-shaped face so traditionally prized, and a delicate but curvy figure. Audiences had thronged to see her in *The Story of a Detachment Commander* and *The Town Where We Live,* and had formed lines around the block to watch her play a woman's entire life, from youth to old age, in *The Girl from Diamond Mountain*.

Even her life story warmed people's hearts with pride and affection. She had been born in Kaesong, right on the border between North and South, in an area that became a permanent battleground during the war—taken by the North in the summer of 1950, lost again that October, and finally regained, with the help of the Chinese army, in December 1950. The young Woo In-Hee kept working throughout the fighting, an example to every child in the Workers' Paradise. The very pretty little girl became a skilled dancer, and soon she was discovered by a famous actor of the time, who brought her to Pyongyang to study acting. Within a year she had been selected as the lead in *Tale of Chunhyang,* playing a chaste and noble girl of low rank who braves the disdain of the aristocracy to marry the district magistrate she loves. She stays loyal to him when corrupt rivals try to blackmail her into being their concubine—even when she is condemned to death on false charges. In the end she is rescued by her husband, and their devotion conquers all. The role made Woo In-Hee an immediate star. She starred in dozens more films after that, each more successful than the last. She won countless government awards and was ranked a People's Actress, the highest honor in her field. She was favored by Kim Jong-Il and treated like royalty. She was even allowed to go to Czechoslovakia to study Western acting techniques. Upon her return, she married Yoo Hosun, North Korea's most gifted director, and they had three children. Her life seemed charmed. The people who had met her in person confided that she did not disappoint: the People's Actress was a gentle, kindhearted young woman.

But beautiful, desirable Woo had a flaw. She was a romantic and always falling in love. Her heart was always yearning for something that her marriage, fame, and success were not giving her.

The first man had been a member of a film crew. The others, too, were involved in the world of film—creatives, officials in the film department, other crew members. There were probably not that many men, but reputations grow fast and out of proportion to the truth. Quickly Pyongyang's film sets throbbed with rumors that Woo In-Hee, the People's Actress, was at best a party girl who didn't hesitate to enjoy the men her looks and status made available to her, and at worst a loose woman, a hussy who happily and easily let herself be seduced by any and all. There was something vulgar, malicious, and misogynistic to the stories, a silent snigger and a raised eyebrow in the way they were told.

Woo In-Hee was no temptress. Maybe she was lonely, maybe she simply longed for something she was still missing, or maybe, like most romantics, she was always falling in love with the next person. Whatever the reason, it made her easy to seduce, her hopes and cravings like a question only needing a man to volunteer himself as their answer. Every time she was seduced she would fall in love, and every time—after the man's conquest had been accomplished, and the sexual novelty exhausted—she was the one discarded. But this was North Korea in the 1970s, a country where a husband kept all property and rights over children in every divorce, even if his physical abuse or faithlessness was the cause of it—where indeed it was socially accepted, and not uncommon, for some men to have several wives. As for women, their behavior was scrutinized and judged. It was illegal to wear short sleeves or skirts cut higher than the knee. Marriages were arranged by families or by the Party. Premarital sex was forbidden, and even something as innocent as holding hands in public was sternly frowned upon. Perversely, these very rules made women like Woo In-Hee—who longed for a true connection, to be valued—more vulnerable. They starved and suffocated her longings so much that she was desperate to make them come true, no matter the risk.

There was one other thing to keep in mind about North Korea, especially for a People's Actress: society did not allow for anything resembling a private life. Everything was public, from your haircut and the age you got married to your innermost thoughts and loyalties. Spying, informing, and gossiping were virtues that kept the people on their toes and the system working. The Workers' Party made blank cogs of workers. Your heart and sex life were no different, whether you were ripping wheat from chaff on a collective farm or crying hot, melodramatic tears in front of a film camera on the back lot of the Korea Film Studio. There were lines not to cross, and as invisible or murky as those lines were, once you crossed them there was no coming back.

Especially when Kim Jong-Il was involved.

By the late 1970s, the stories about Woo In-Hee had become so commonplace that one day she was confronted with them directly. In a self-criticism session—compulsory meetings in which each worker was expected, in front of colleagues, both to list the ways she had failed the Party that week, and also to denounce someone else—a man in the group denounced Woo for her affairs and loose morals. Instead of hanging her head in shame, verbally flagellating herself, and expressing her fervent wish that Kim Il-Sung would give her one more chance to redeem herself (the expected response to any charge, big or small), Woo In-Hee fought back. The accuser was one to talk, she barked. Hadn't he been one of the men who seduced her? In fact, she went on, pointing at one man here, another there, "You've all seduced me, haven't you?"

Woo's career went into free fall. The men would not let her get away with that. She was downgraded from her rank as People's Actress, first to a simple stock player, then demoted off the screen entirely and assigned to work in the boiler room of the film studio. For a year she worked as a stoker, manually feeding coal into the blazing furnace of the boiler, hard, exhausting, and dangerous work. In 1979 she was allowed to return to filming, straight back into leading roles, such a quick and positive reversal of fortune that it shocked those who had taken pleasure in her punishment. Woo In-Hee was an extremely popular actress, and it was certainly a waste to keep her off the screen for very long, but there was something else to it: another man. A man who understood passionate souls trapped by public expectations, who was used to flaunting his power and taking advantage of beautiful women in precarious positions, a man with a famous soft spot for actresses, who was, arguably, the only person capable of overturning the severe punishment that might befall a People's Actress.

We'll never know exactly when Woo In-Hee's affair with Kim Jong-Il began, whether there had been dalliances years before or whether the younger Kim saw an opportunity when the gorgeous woman had lost everything—that she would worship a man with the power to restore it all to her. By this point Kim already had not one but two consorts, and his personal life was a highly classified secret; once you stepped inside that circle, your life was all but his. Revealing any of it, privately or publicly, meant a prison camp. Even if Kim merely suspected that you might reveal any of it, your life was in danger. Woo In-Hee never should have gotten involved with Kim Jong-Il. But she was shoveling coal twelve hours a day, and besides, saying no to the Dear Leader, heir to the Sun of Korea, is easier said than done.

If getting involved with Kim Jong-Il was dangerous, starting an affair with someone else at the same time was suicidal. But Woo In-Hee could not resist. She fell in love, again, this time with a young Korean from Japan, whose wealthy businessman father had generously supported the Kim regime over the years. He had now sent his only son, who had grown soft in the comfort of Japan, to North Korea to work and become a man. This young man was assigned to work at a radio station. While there, he met Woo In-Hee and immediately, desperately pursued her. She liked the romantic, different boy, but Woo In-Hee stayed away. He didn't give up. He showered her with gifts and attention and finally she gave in.

Neither of them could go home—Woo had a family, and the young man's circle surely would gossip if the People's Actress turned up in their midst—nor could they spend time at the studio, where Woo's reputation still clung to her like a sweat-soaked shirt. Kim Jong-Il had assigned another actress to shadow Woo during work hours and report back her every move. Hotels were out, as owners were obliged by law to check overnight permits, refuse any couples, and report all guests to the police. By virtue of his father's standing, the boy had a car, a luxury Mercedes, and since he had driven his whole life in Japan he had no need for a chauffeur. So the Mercedes became their meeting place. They would drive around for hours or park in dark, out-of-the-way spots.

One freezing winter night in the winter of 1980, they parked the car out of sight and made love. Maybe it was the first time, maybe the hundredth. With the engine still running and the windows shut tight to keep them warm, they fell asleep in each other's arms. When the car was found in the morning the boy was dead of carbon monoxide poisoning. Woo In-Hee was unconscious and barely breathing.

It took two weeks of hospital treatment for Woo In-Hee to grow strong enough to blink her eyes open. Once her health had returned, the soldiers came. The son of a high-profile donor to the Party was dead because of an affair with a married woman whose history of scandalous behavior was well known. People up high had questions, and they wanted them answered. There is no record of the interrogations, but at some point Woo In-Hee brought up the name of Kim Jong-Il. Maybe he could save her one last time. The soldiers left the room. When they returned they told Woo In-Hee to stand up. She was being released and taken home.

Dozens and dozens of buses were parked in a line outside the film studio, their engines idling, the drivers smoking and gossiping. There was still a chill in the air from the dying winter.

That morning, every single worker in the movie industry, from the directors down to the typists, had received orders to assemble and board the buses for an emergency collective activity ordered by the Party. They were not told where they were being taken, even after the bus doors closed and the vehicles pulled onto the road. Among the passengers was the director Yoo Hosun, Woo In-Hee's husband and the father of her children. He had not seen her in weeks, since she had been taken to the hospital after being found with the young Korean-Japanese. She had not returned home or to work. Woo imagined she was serving some kind of temporary punishment, as when she had been assigned to boiler duty, or in prison.

Today must have taken his mind off his worries. Nothing like today's mysterious trip had happened during his career at the film studio, and everyone was intrigued. Were they being ferried to a pleasant day of historical sightseeing, perhaps to the Great Leader's birthplace in Mansudae or to some revolutionary monument? Was there a big policy announcement coming regarding film's future in the country? Perhaps they were just being taken to a drab, mass self-criticism session—though it seemed like a lot of trouble for a meeting, especially when the film studio had plenty of auditoriums big enough to gather everyone in.

The several dozen buses drove in a convoy out of the city and into the suburbs, a ride of at least forty-five minutes. Finally they stopped outside a rifle range. There were dozens of these facilities near Pyongyang and hundreds around the country, many adorned with illustrations of wolves in U.S. Army uniforms to serve as targets. Older children would regularly be taken there to practice their marksmanship, especially as July 8, Anti-American Day, approached. Today the range itself was deserted, but bleachers had been set up opposite the targets, and ordinary civilians, about five thousand of them, were already occupying the back rows or standing along the sides. The movie people—two thousand strong, by industry estimates—were told to disembark and fill the available remaining bleacher seats.

A white curtain had been stretched up in front of the targets, and a tall wooden stake had been set in the ground in front of the curtain. For a few minutes the spectators waited in hushed, anxious expectation. Then an army jeep pulled up and parked between the white sheet and the targets. Presently a woman's desperate scream ripped the air from behind the curtain. A tingle of electricity rippled through the crowd. Whatever they had been brought here to see, this was it.

Just that morning Woo In-Hee had been told she was free to go home. Only when they loaded her into the jeep and blindfolded her did she know that she had been lied to.

The soldiers dragged her out in the front of the curtain, blindfolded, her hands tied. In the audience it now was her husband's turn to scream.

Executions, like so much else in North Korea, are designed as a theatrical show, with the condemned as the unwitting lead performer. Woo In-Hee would have been dressed in a prisoner's outfit, which it was rumored had been specially designed by North Korean army scientists for public executions: a thick, grayish suit of fleece and cotton designed to soak up blood, turning a dramatic deep, dark red as it does. Woo In-Hee was tied to the wooden post by two ropes, one at her chest and the other around her legs. Throughout it all she never stopped screaming. She screamed for Kim Jong-Il and others in the Party leadership—some witnesses remember that she was cursing their names; some that she was still pleading to speak to Kim, to explain, to beg his forgiveness. One of the soldiers then stepped up to a microphone, and his voice boomed and echoed from the loudspeakers, barely drowning out her cries. "For committing immoral and licentious acts, the People's Actress Woo In-Hee has been condemned to death. She will be executed by firing squad, in the name of the People." Within a second of his speaking the last words, "in the name of the People," the sound of gunfire tore through the air.

The firing squad, three soldiers strong, did it the usual way. The first burst of bullets broke the chest-height rope, causing Woo's body to tip forward as if in a final bow to the audience. The next volley aimed for the head, exploding it in a soggy, spectacular mess of flesh and bone and brain. ("In the winter," wrote the North Korean defector Hyok Kang of executions he had witnessed as a child, "at temperatures of minus twenty or minus thirty

[Celsius], there's a lot of steam when that happens, because of the difference in temperature between the body and the atmosphere.") Finally, one last salvo shredded the rope holding Woo In-Hee up at the legs, her body dropping with a thud into the bag laid out at her feet.

In the audience Yoo Hosun went limp and collapsed. He was not conscious to witness the soldiers kicking and shoving his wife's body into the bag, and throwing it back into the jeep. After an execution, Hyok Kang writes, the norm was for the body to be "abandoned somewhere in the mountains without being buried, for the [wild] dogs to eat." The car doors closed on the People's Actress Woo In-Hee, and the jeep drove away. Behind them there was a brief silence, broken by the children in the front row dashing forward with excited screams to fight over the spent rifle cartridges littering the bloodstained earth.

After that, Woo In-Hee's films were banned, her magazine photographs were cut or blacked out, and the pages mentioning her in film history books and pamphlets were glued together. If her classic films were rerun on television, every scene featuring her was edited out, turning narratives into incomprehensible messes, but also sending a clear message to the audience, who lived in a world ritualized enough to understand such messages. Her husband, Yoo Hosun, was exiled to the countryside and sent down to production. A suppression decree was issued to the thousands who had witnessed the execution, threatening them with death if they ever spoke about it. But why build bleachers around an execution ground and bus in six thousand witnesses unless you want them to talk?

And talk about it they did, in whispers and with furtive looks over their shoulders. Three years later, in the luxury villa in which she was held, Choi Eun-Hee overheard her North Korean staff telling each other the story loudly enough, by accident or by design, for her to hear. The message was not lost on her.

The one man who had the power to order the summary execution of a famous, honored actress who had disappointed him—and to do so with such a ruthless sense of drama and showmanship—was Kim Jong-Il.

REEL THREE

PRODUCED BY KIM JONG-IL

All the world's a stage,
And all the men and women merely players.
They have their exits and their entrances . . .
—Jaques, *As You Like It* (Act II, Scene vii),
by William Shakespeare

Truman (Jim Carrey): Was nothing real?
Christof (Ed Harris): You were real. That's what made you so good to watch.
—*The Truman Show,* screenplay by Andrew Niccol,
directed by Peter Weir

21
Together

The tragic story of the People's Actress returned to Choi as she observed the drunken guests around her at the reunion banquet. This was the film world she and Shin were now entering.

Nearby, on Kim Jong-Il's right-hand side, sat Shin. Jong-Il was pleasant and courteous, almost contrite, toward the older man. The Dear Leader had been spoiled his whole life and given everything he wanted, so that by now only a select few experiences must have felt thrilling and new. Surely this was one of them. Shin Sang-Ok was the first filmmaker of international renown he had ever met, a director whose every film he had seen—and whose work he had liked and admired enough to think him worthy of bringing to North Korea to be his star director.

"Mr. Shin, please forgive the dramatics," Jong-Il said, turning his big, bright eyes on his guest. "I'm sorry to have caused you so much suffering." He took Shin's right hand, put it on his own knee, and squeezed it. Before Shin could answer, Jong-Il went on, "No one ever laid a hand on Madame Choi," then, raising his voice, to the rest of the table: "I send her back to you exactly as she was! Mr. Shin, we Communists are pure. Aren't we, comrades?"

"Yes, sir!" came the reply in unison, punctuated with a burst of applause.

"Let us all be devoted to the Dear Leader!" shouted a man who Shin later learned was the head of the Party newspaper *Rodong Sinmun*. Everyone at the table echoed the toast and knocked back their drink.

"Let's all work together to accomplish the task!" cheered someone else once the glasses had been refilled.

Toast followed toast, and soon Jong-Il had declared a "liquor offensive," one of his favorite party games, in which the assembled guests had to chug round after round, shouting loyalist slogans after every drink. Shin usually didn't drink, but he thought it unwise not to join in. It was a shrewd decision, for Kim valued men who could drink, seeing it as a sign of strength and self-control. Being unable to hold your cognac was a mark against your manhood. Everyone seemed to want to pour Shin a drink and pat him on the shoulder. At one point Kim Jong-Il's younger sister, Kyong-Hui, whom Jong-Il had been fiercely protective of since his younger brother Shura's death in the garden pond all those years ago, refilled Shin's glass and said quietly to him, "From now on, please help my brother." Her own glass needed frequent replenishing as well: she was in the early stages of severe alcohol dependency, an addiction that would later risk her position in the Party and find her seeking rehab treatment in China.

Endless toasts led to hours of drinking. The band played a series of (officially banned) South Korean pop songs, surprising Shin, who in his years in North Korea had only heard war songs and hymns to the Great Leader. The guests sang along to some of the songs, a triumphalism in their voice, Shin observing that "they sang South Korean popular songs not because they liked these songs, but because they thought the South belonged to them," and its music with it.

The cognac was making Shin's head swim. He looked over at Choi, who was smiling and chatting to the people on either side of her. She seemed at ease with everyone, almost as if she were one of them. She is playing up to Kim Jong-Il and his cronies, Shin thought. Or has she been completely brainwashed? Was this why they had kept them separate for all these years only to reunite them now? Has she been indoctrinated and is under instruction to find out what I'm really thinking? Shin felt woozy and paranoid. He wished he could lie down.

Luckily the evening seemed to be drawing to a close. Then suddenly the Dear Leader turned to Shin and asked, "What do you say to watching a movie?"

Kim, Shin, Choi, and a few others left the ballroom and filed into a small screening room to watch a couple of short propaganda films. It took about twenty minutes, and then they all returned to the party, which had found a second wind. The "eating, drinking, singing, and dancing went on until 3 a.m.," Shin remembered, at which point Jong-Il suddenly noticed Shin's exhaustion. He called a man over, who Shin would later learn was Choe Ik-Gyu, Jong-Il's filmmaking mentor and the man Shin would be working with from now on. "We'll send the couple home first," Jong-Il said. "Take them in my car."

Jong-Il walked them to the Mercedes. Shin and Choi were quiet. What was expected of them next? Choe Ik-Gyu got in the driver's seat. Shin opened the car's back door. Laughing out loud, and with obvious innuendo, Kim shouted, "Since it's a special day, you two go to your bridal chamber, and *rest*!"

So it was that Shin and Choi were driven back to the very first villa Choi had been kept in, the tacky house with all the chandeliers. They said good night to Choe Ik-Gyu and went upstairs to the luxurious bedroom, which had been made ready for them, cognac and a fruit basket freshly placed on the coffee table. As soon as they had closed the door, Choi said, "Dear, if you don't love me, let's sleep in separate rooms from this moment on. Tell me right now."

Shin looked at the woman he had adored most of his life. He had loved her from the moment he met her, had lived, slept, and worked with her almost his entire adult life. But as he admitted later, he was too proud "to just say *Yes, I love you*." So he just smiled. Choi understood. He stepped forward and embraced her. For some time they stood that way, in silence.

Finally, Choi stepped back and looked at him. "Wherever you've been, your face is not the same . . ." she said.

"I'll tell you about it, little by little," Shin said. "How have you been getting along?"

"I'll tell you about it, little by little," she echoed. "But I don't know where to begin."

"Dear, you seem a little strange . . ." Shin ventured, looking in her eyes. "Have you been . . . brainwashed?"

The word, out loud, sounded idiotic. Choi burst out laughing. She gave Shin a gratified, coquettish little look. "Why, the movie director can't even recognize acting when he sees it," she teased.

"I underestimated her," Shin later said. "She was a great actress in the South, on-screen, and in the North offscreen."

It felt marvelous to be in the same room with one another. "We had so much to tell each other," Shin recalled. Scared that the room was bugged and that their conversations would be recorded, they went to the bathroom, turned the faucets in the tub on full blast, and whispered. They told each other about the last few years and exchanged their stories of suffering. They discovered they had been abducted on the same freighter, from almost the same beach. Choi learned that Shin had stayed in one of the villas she had stayed in just weeks before she had. She recounted the execution of the People's Actress Woo In-Hee. Both were carefully deciphering what had changed in the other, whether they had been subtly indoctrinated, and the extent of their trauma.

One thing Choi said, as they sat by the bathtub talking, made an impression on Shin that stayed with him until the moment he drifted to sleep. "Darling," she said, "we have acted and directed the lives of others in films. From now on, let's act and direct our lives ingeniously."

They had to make the most of their plight. And every day, carefully, they would plan for the one thing that truly mattered: their escape.

22
The Tape Recorder

Imagine, for a moment, that by the grace of God, or the luck of the draw—whatever you choose to call it—you were born and raised in North Korea. Most likely you would be born to a family of the neutral or hostile *songbun* class, not one of the elite, and live outside Pyongyang, in the harsh, mountainous countryside. At the age of two you were taken to revolutionary day care and preschool, where you spent most of your time, rather than at home, and whose teachers became your primary influences and authority. Toy pistols and rifles lined the shelves of the playroom, alongside a framed poster depicting bright-eyed children attacking a bloody U.S. soldier.

Day care and preschool consisted of fourteen-hour days, usually six days a week. At a young age you were taught endless slogans—"What the Party decides, we will put in practice" or "Let us become human bullets to defend the Great Leader!"—and to always call the elder Kim "Great Leader Grandfather Kim Il-Sung" or later "Comrade Great Leader Kim Il-Sung." His son was "Comrade Dear Leader Kim Jong-Il." After preschool came nursery school, then four years of primary school and six of secondary school. The uniform at every establishment was cut in a military style. During those years you learned Kim Il-Sung's biography, by rote, down to the smallest detail. (After the late 1980s, you would also learn about the life of Kim Jong-Il, your teachers telling you he grew up such an idealist he climbed trees to catch rainbows—and was such a virtuous genius he succeeded in grabbing them.) You learned that the food you received was a gift from the Great Leader, and that you must be grateful to him for receiving it. You learned math by adding, subtracting, and multiplying numbers of dead American soldiers or the number of apples stolen from the local farm by a dastardly Japanese; you learned conjugation by repeating, "We fight against Yankees. We fought against Yankees. We will fight against Yankees"; you learned history by reciting the state-sponsored biographies of Kim Il-Sung. Reading was taught through stories about revolutionary heroes fighting the Japanese or dark tales of Yankees—you were told to never call them Americans, always "Yankees," "Yankee dogs," "Yankee imperialists," or simply "the long-noses"—and you would sing popular kids' tunes like "Shoot the Yankee Bastards" ("Our enemies are the American bastards / Who are trying to take over our beautiful fatherland / With guns that I make with my own hands / I will shoot them BANG! BANG! BANG!").

At recess you and the other children were allowed to play with the teacher's blond, beak-nosed dummy of a Yankee imperialist. You all took turns hitting it with sticks and pelting it with stones as the teacher looked on approvingly. Occasionally for fun you might have been taken to a shooting range. You were never told, in so many words, that the Leaders were gods, but, in the words of researcher Lee Su-Won, "the process in which people start to see God and Jesus as absolute entities is very similar to the way Kim Il-Sung and Kim Jong-Il are revered [in North Korea]." All children learn that it is heresy to doodle or draw the Leaders, and that no picture of them may be folded or thrown in the trash (which is also why the *Rodong Sinmun* newspaper is posted under glass in public places rather than distributed). It is blasphemy to insult the Leaders or make jokes at their expense. At the age of ten you joined the Young Pioneers—the DPRK's version of the Boy Scouts or, more fittingly, the Hitler Youth—and at twelve you received your own Kim Il-Sung badge, to wear on your chest whenever—*absolutely whenever*—you left home. At the same age you began performing your patriotic duties on Sundays, working in rice paddies or elsewhere in the countryside to assist the republic's progress.

Outside of school the world was even odder. From the beginning of your life you'd noticed everyone was suspicious of everyone else, all the time.

There was no way of telling who, no matter how close a friend or family member, might be an informant or an undercover security agent. Everyone knew the stories of the families sent to the camps because a careless child or grandparent let something delicate slip to the wrong person. So life even at home was guarded, performed. Everyone, in the words of Hyok Kang, "always looked as though they were wearing a mask." You never celebrated your own birthday, only those of Kim Il-Sung and Kim Jong-Il. On those days you received a gigantic two pounds of chocolates, gummies, chewing gum, and cookies, and when you did you lined up in front of the home's portraits of Kim Il-Sung and Kim Jong-Il, bowing deeply and saying, "Thank you, dear father Kim Il-Sung," several times.

When you turned seventeen you received your "citizen's certificate," modeled on the old Soviet ID document, a twelve-page booklet about the bearer containing your name, photograph, place of residence, date of birth, marital status, police and behavior record, and permission (or absence thereof) to live in Pyongyang. The citizen's certificate was to be carried with you at all times and renewed every ten years. Being arrested meant the confiscation of your citizen's certificate: during time spent in prison, you would no longer be a citizen, and you would no longer have any (notional) rights.

After school there was military duty to be served, ten full years of it, most of it spent not in maneuvers but as a cheap workforce for the state, putting up buildings and laying down roads. After that you were assigned a job in a factory, office, or agricultural collective, most likely; the good jobs were reserved for party members, and your *songbun* would never permit you the clearance necessary for one of those plum positions. From now on you received your rations every two weeks, measured by weight and doled out in a volume relative to your type of work. The usual daily ration was a bowl of rice with kimchi and a smaller bowl of soup, no meat—meat was added only to mark special occasions, like the Leader's birthday or Liberation Day. By the early 1980s your rations were often delayed, or tampered with; your family would receive a frozen pig rather than one preserved in salt, so that when the animal was cooked it turned out that half its weight was water, evaporating into the air; more commonly, rice bags were simply loaded with stones to deceive the scales of the rationing office. By the

1990s, for months at a time, the rations stopped coming altogether. You couldn't complain, of course: no one complained.

You worked long hours every day, six days a week. After work you went to compulsory self-criticism sessions. If a new movie was released by the state studio overseen by the creative genius Comrade Dear Leader Kim Jong-Il, you were required to immediately go to the cinema (or to the projection room in the factory or Party office if your village was so small as to have no cinema) and watch it. The movies all had titles like *Fate of a Self-Defense Corps Member, The Song of Camaraderie, Five Guerrilla Brothers,* and *Again to the Front,* and the screening was followed by an education session in which you and the others were asked about the film's seed and which characters in it should be emulated. The seventh day of the week was reserved for "volunteer" work—cleaning the streets, helping out on state farms or construction sites, preparing for big events such as the Mass Games. There was no such thing as free time. Body and mind were made to serve the regime.

One day you found a person to marry, so you asked the state's obligatory permission; when it was received you were married by a local Party worker under your town's statue of Kim Il-Sung. Your husband or wife likely had the same *songbun* as you, and that *songbun* would be passed on to your children. You probably didn't know much about the opposite sex. Since 1971 a "special instruction" by Kim Il-Sung had decreed men should be thirty when they married and women twenty-eight, and any contact between unmarried adults, even hand-holding, was severely frowned upon. The exact knowledge of what happened in a bed between a man and a woman might still have been vague and confusing as you walked back to your state-assigned home after your wedding.

You and your spouse stayed in the same area you were both born in. Relocating was rare, and traveling from one village to another, even for a day, required an official permit. Every overnight guest in your own home required advance permission from the village police. You lived in the same block of flats or houses as the work colleagues from your unit, and a local auntie kept an eye on all of you for the *inminban,* the people's group, which reported back to the Public Safety Department. And that was your lot, really, for the rest of your life. The loudspeakers went on telling you war and reunification were imminent, the Yankee threat ever present. Every year the Mass Games rolled around. North Korea was a cashless, taxless, salaryless society, so nothing could be privately sold; all the necessities, including housing, food, education, and health care, were free and provided by the state. Private enterprise was banned, promotion unlikely, changing career paths unheard of. You might receive a commendation for consistently fulfilling work quotas, but probably nothing more exciting than that. Maybe one day Kim Il-Sung would visit the town for an on-the-spot guidance visit, and you and the other villagers would be mobilized to scrub the streets and houses from top to bottom; after the Great Leader left, whatever room he had stayed in, whatever furniture he had sat on, anything he had touched, was roped off, given a plaque, and turned into a historical site or a local relic. (In this way thousands of rooms throughout North Korea were used by Kim Il-Sung or Kim Jong-Il for one night and then never used again, pockets of sacred emptiness in every town and village.)

As you grew old you were reminded, endlessly, how lucky you were to live in the Workers' Paradise: that you were one of the single luckiest people on Earth, a chosen people with "nothing to envy" anyone anywhere. South Korea, you were told on the evening news, was "a living hell, with its traffic accidents and collapsing buildings. . . . Do you know how many cars are stolen every year? The place is full of thieves. One hundred twenty people disappear every day; everywhere there are assaults, violent gangs; the subway is a hell-way. . . . It's five, ten times the level of [crime] of other countries . . . the whole country consists of snitches and police detectives." South Korean children were said to rummage for food in trash heaps while American soldiers shot at them for target practice or ran them over for fun. American soldiers, in fact, were said to be everywhere in South Korea, in their riot helmets and dark sunglasses, raping women in alleyways and publicly beating men, subjugating boys as sexual slaves. Even after the economic miracle of the mid-1970s to the mid-1980s, the media told you the South's growing prosperity was just another sign of its moral depravity and dependence on the Yankee teat. South Korea, the propaganda said, was "the flashiest of American colonies . . . a foul whore of America . . . covered in bruises from where it has been kicked black and blue by the American soldiers' boots, decaying from where the American sewage has seeped in. . . . It turns the stomach just to think of it."

The television news was full of footage of student riots in South Korea, bloody miners' strikes in the United Kingdom, endless murders and crimes in the United States, half-naked savages in Africa who behaved, you were told, essentially like animals. There were environmental disasters everywhere, great tragedies all of them, except for the earthquakes that befell Japan, which you were told were divine payback for their decades of oppression of the Korean people. The Chinese people were starving after giving up strict socialism and opening up to world markets. In the 1980s a new disease, AIDS, was ravaging the Western world, the abominable consequence of the Yankees' same-sex, interracial, and promiscuous premarital fornication; and covert operatives were reporting that the U.S. military was building a base in South Korea to which were assigned only servicemen suffering from the disease. "The bloodsuckers and butchers are trying to force the AIDS disaster, as well as a nuclear holocaust, upon mankind!" shouted the histrionic news anchor. Every day, luckily, there were also cheering "human interest stories" in the paper or on the television: of heroic citizens who had lost their lives trying to rescue their Kim portraits from a fire or flood, or of children dutifully snitching on their own parents and having them sent to jail, bravely combating unpatriotic behavior in their own homes. On the best days miracles were part of the program: fog had descended to protect Kim Il-Sung from snipers, or snow had melted and flowers grown under Kim Jong-Il's foot as he walked in Hwanghae Province.

There was a statue of Kim Il-Sung in every single town in the country. Every citizen, like you, wore a badge bearing his likeness, always, every second they were outside the home. On every floor in every workplace and office building, in the main hallway, was a little book of the Great Leader or Dear Leader's thoughts, handwritten and updated each month. The museums glorified the Kims. The bookstores were exclusively full of books by them or about them. A radio station known as the Third Broadcast played in every household and office building during daylight hours, sharing news about the Kims, maxims attributed to them, and songs of devotion and celebration about them. It could be turned down but not off. Every night the news closed with a maxim attributed to Kim Il-Sung or Kim Jong-Il. The same portraits kept in your living room were in every factory, every courtyard, every schoolroom, every coal mine, and every prison.

When you died—in 1980 your life expectancy was sixty-eight years, six years less than the average Yankee imperialist and eight years less than a neighboring Japanese—your body stayed in your home for three days, watched and mourned over by your children and grandchildren, who would then go to the local Party automobile factory and beg for a truck or cart to carry your body to the cemetery. A bribe, big enough to take a year or two to pay off, usually did the trick. At the end of the third day the family sat down to eat a plain, freshly cooked bowl of rice, then took you to the plot assigned by the local authority outside of town and buried you, themselves, with no help, in the same clothes you had worn your whole life—with the exception of your Kim Il-Sung pin. It would not do, of course, to cover the Great Leader's likeness in soil and leave it in the cold ground. In life the Leaders were everywhere. In death, however, you were on your own.

It was folly for anyone to question any aspect of this way of life, however small. Speaking or acting against the system would see you and your entire family condemned to labor camps or death—and why question it? For your whole life, every newspaper article, television broadcast, book, film, song, conversation, and billboard had drilled the Truth into you and everyone around you. The country was hermetically sealed to any communication from the outside world that might break the illusion: you likely never felt the urge to question any of it. For the most part, you might have lived a happy, contented life within its carefully drawn limits, as long as you never tried to go beyond those limits, never tried to think for yourself, never tried to question reality.

The *songbuns,* the prison camps, and the myths that Kim Il-Sung had single-handedly liberated Korea had foundations as far back as the 1940s, but the ritualization of daily life, the eradication of every discordant note and opinion, the raising of thousands of statues and monuments, the imposition of

Kim Il-Sung pins on every chest and Kim Il-Sung portraits in every household—all this was orchestrated by Kim Jong-Il. The elder Kim had been raised in a Presbyterian family, with a Protestant minister grandfather and a father who had gone to missionary school, and had fought a Japanese enemy who believed their emperor was a god. Once in power he banned the Bible and tore down the churches, appropriating religious imagery and worship for his own purposes. He *knew* religion. His son, on the other hand, had grown up in a world devoid of it, but he understood how to harness the power of culture and entertainment.

As the DPRK defaulted on its foreign loans and its economy slowly foundered, as the world outside moved toward the future while North Korea dug deeper into the past, Jong-Il understood that he would not be able to improve his country's fortunes without jeopardizing his own hold on power—and the nation's very existence as a state separate from South Korea. Since he couldn't change his people's reality, Jong-Il elected to change their *perception* of it. Between the late 1960s and the end of his life he created one vast stage production. He was the writer, director, and producer of the nation. He conceived his people's roles, their devotion, their values; he wrote their dialogue and forced it upon them; he mapped out their entire character arcs, from birth to death, splicing them out of the picture if they broke type. And with the informers, patrols, and *inminbans* he had inherited from his father constantly watching everyone, it was like always being on film. The camera was always rolling. The director never shouted "cut." And the extras, day and night, kept playing their parts.

For extras—bit players, background actors, walk-ons—were exactly what the North Korean people were. The word *extra* itself ideally describes the citizens in Kim Jong-Il's gigantic masterpiece production. They were secondary, peripheral, nonessential. Disposable. There were millions more like them, and more created every day.

Shin Sang-Ok and Choi Eun-Hee woke up in this North Korea on March 7, 1983. Miraculously together, and freer than either had been in five years, they were also now the new leaders of the nation's filmmaking industry.

The sun was high and bright in the sky as they headed down for breakfast. Five people—two female attendants, a male attendant, and two cooks—had been assigned to live with them in this house. Shin and Choi ate and made small talk. They had decided they would not speak freely inside the house in case it was bugged, saving all private conversation for unaccompanied walks around the grounds. Choi was horrified by the state of her ex-husband: he had lost weight, his ankles were swollen and misshapen, his face covered in psoriasis from months spent sitting in a dark cell, and his skin riddled with sores and ringworm scars. His eyes were ravaged, too; images on the television or on the cinema screen appeared blurry and soft to him. Reeducation had taken its toll.

Over the ensuing weeks they attended more of Jong-Il's parties, sometimes several nights in a row. Shin quickly grew tired of these events, but unexpectedly, he found himself enjoying his conversations about cinema with the Dear Leader. Jong-Il promised not to impose political messages onto Shin's choice of films, but admitted he would have to approve all proposed stories to make sure they were conceived "for the sake of national reunification." His favorite stars were Sean Connery and Elizabeth Taylor, Jong-Il said, his favorite movies the James Bond pictures, *Friday the Thirteenth,* and, ironically, *First Blood,* the wildly successful adaptation of the very novel Shin had hoped to make before being kidnapped. The picture had finally been made in Hollywood in 1982, while Shin held the torture position in a dank, dark cell.

Jong-Il told Shin about his vast movie collection, confiding that he owned every film the South Korean had ever made, including, according to Shin, some for which Shin himself had no master copies.

The filmmaker found the young Leader a fascinating, contradictory figure. Shin had bled and suffered in prison next to men sent to do hard labor merely for reading a foreign newspaper; he had heard the tales of men volunteering to shoot their own wives to please the Dear Leader. Jong-Il seemed to take this level of devotion for granted. But then, at one party, ten pretty teenagers of the Joy Brigade took to the stage and jumped up and down squealing "Long live the Comrade Dear Leader!" with bright eyes full of tears, and Jong-Il waved his hand to make them stop. When they didn't, galvanized by what they thought was false modesty, Jong-Il chuckled awkwardly, took Shin's hand, and swung it back and forth as if to distract him from the chants of devotion. "Mr. Shin, don't believe any of it," he muttered. "It's all bogus. It's just pretense."

Kim Jong-Il gave Shin and Choi six months' "vacation" to go sightseeing before they began work. Now that they were allowed out, Shin and Choi were also able to observe more than the life of the elite. They were able, finally, to get their first, albeit controlled, glimpses of "real" North Korean society, the society the Kims built.

The country looked to both of them like the set of a dystopian Hollywood sci-fi film: devoid of color, with identical, utilitarian, and monochromatic houses of faded cement and limestone. The roads were empty, the buildings broken down and uncared for. Only the cult of personality was well maintained; Kim Il-Sung's godlike face, painted in golds, yellows, and reds, smiling down from billboards, steles, statues, and mosaics on the drab green, brown, and gray of the fatherland.

The state had a relentless, dehumanizing interference into even the most mundane aspects of its people's daily lives. North Korean adults were visibly weary. Women wore knee-length skirts and their shirts buttoned all the way up, with no makeup or jewelry. The men wore identical, slightly ill-fitting shirts and trousers made of shiny, synthetic vinalon, locally produced in Hamhung and cheaper than regular fabric. Everyone wore the ubiquitous red pin on their chest and, perpetually fearful of reprisals, no one asked too many questions or looked too long at your face. Perhaps most wearying of all, as the Black Panther activist Eldridge Cleaver, who spent several months in Pyongyang in 1970, recalled, the people "were fanatical in their promotion of their premier, Comrade Kim Il-Sung. . . . You could not say 'Good morning' or 'Hello' to them without their responding: 'Yes, it is a beautiful day, thanks to the inspired teaching of our beloved revolutionary leader, Comrade Kim Il-Sung, who has filled our hearts with the truths of Marxist-Leninist analysis and daily supports in our borders and obligations'—that was good morning, and after six months it began to lose its novelty but not the power to bore."

One place Shin was eager to visit was the Dear Leader's film vault. His wish was quickly granted, and within weeks of their reunion, Shin and Choi were invited for a tour of the Film Archive, as it was now known.

A three-story building in the center of Pyongyang, the archive was as fortified as Fort Knox. Several security checks and a set of heavy metal doors had to be cleared to gain access to the building's reception. "We were told that fifteen thousand copies of films were stored here," Shin said, systematically compiled and filed over many years. Shin thought it likely that this was the largest personal film collection in the world. (According to one Russian diplomat, by 2001 the number of titles had swelled to well over twenty thousand.) "The width of the building was about one hundred meters, and all three floors stretching one hundred meters were filled with films," Shin described. "The room with the best equipment was the one holding North Korean films. In that room every single North Korean film ever made was stored according to chronological order. The room boasted of a perfect temperature and humidity control system" so as to preserve the celluloid.

South Korean films and soap operas, considered especially politically sensitive, were kept in a separate section of the library, most of them acquired through business connections in Hong Kong; Shin and Choi couldn't help wonder if these "business connections" were the same people who had helped abduct them or other people they had worked with over the years. True to Jong-Il's word, every one of Shin's fifty-plus films was there on the shelves.

Kim Jong-Il was so ever-present in his nation's filmmaking history that many North Korean defectors today still speak of the films they saw as children as "a film by Kim Jong-Il" or "Kim Jong-Il's film," rather than by their writers, directors, or stars. *On the Art of the Cinema* was commonly considered a masterpiece and Jong-Il a genius artist and theorist of film. Here, inside all these film cans, was the source of all Kim Jong-Il's knowledge about narrative and performance. And it was no surprise he was an unparalleled genius: only he was allowed to screen them.

Until now. As the archive manager led Shin and Choi back to the reception, he told Shin that, by invitation of the Dear Leader, he was welcome to visit the archive again whenever he chose and to watch as many of the films as he wished. Shin was acutely aware that no other filmmaker in the country had ever, or would ever, be allowed inside the archive, as many of the films in it depicted worlds in direct contradiction with the DPRK's stringent ideological policies. Those policies had been created by Kim Il-Sung and were now enforced by Kim Jong-Il, who dearly loved the movies stored within it. The North Korean people were completely severed from the outside world, but the man who was isolating them most certainly and actively was not.

Now that they had seen the archive, Shin and Choi's day trips switched back and forth from ideological education to professional research. Mr. Kang and Choe Ik-Gyu—"Director Choe," as they came to know him—gave them a tour of the Korea Film Studio and of the offices of Kim's creative staff at the Mansudae Creative Group. Regularly Jong-Il assigned Shin or Choi to critique a premiere or a rehearsal at the Mansudae Art Theater or the Pyongyang Theater. In their spare time Shin and Choi watched as many of the films in Kim's library as they could stomach, "in preparation for [our] meeting with Kim Jong-Il," Shin said. "I intended to surprise and impress him."

One day, on the drive back from inspecting a film-processing plant, Mr. Kang and Director Choe stopped at the Taedong River department store, better known as the Foreigners' Store, where, using U.S. dollars, Japanese yen, British pounds sterling, or West German deutsche marks, Pyongyang's few foreigners could purchase anything from groceries to electronics to cosmetics, all at shockingly inflated state-set prices. The store was another surreal experience, stocked with large numbers of uniform models of every product: a single shoe style in two or three colors, a single type of television, one type of dress in six colors, a limited range of symmetrically organized fruit and vegetables. The Canadian cartoonist Guy Delisle, who visited Pyongyang several years later, found the experience of the Foreigners' Store "like looking at an installation in a contemporary art museum."

A few Korean-born Japanese were milling around the store, picking out items as gifts for their North Korean relatives. Choi chose a sewing machine and an electric iron, somehow also finding a necklace with a black heart-shaped pendant, a bronze figure of the Virgin Mary holding the baby Jesus at its center. The words AVE MARIA were inscribed in small letters on the figure. Christianity was outlawed in the DPRK, but the staff of the store seemed completely ignorant of what the woman and baby represented (the vast majority of North Koreans had never heard of Jesus Christ, or, for that matter, Santa Claus, Elvis Presley, or almost any other iconic Western figure). The necklace reminded Choi of her new faith and of her lost friend, Catherine Hong. She picked it up and added it to her purchase pile.

Shin browsed in the electronics department for a while, picking up a solar-powered transistor radio. When he came across a microcassette recorder, an idea formed in his mind. He walked over to the counter and casually put down both items, the radio and the recorder. Kang asked Shin and Choi if they were done shopping and they replied that they were, so he nodded to the clerk and ordered her to pack their things and take them to the car.

Shin sat in the back of the Mercedes, the wheels in his head whirring at full speed. He and Choi needed a way to let the world know where they were, how they had gotten there and why; they also needed proof that their fantastic story was true. There were strict rules against recording or filming the Leaders of the Party, their violation punishable by death.

Shin Sang-Ok, however, had decided to do just that.

23

Lights, Camera . . .

The opportunity to record Kim proved remarkably elusive.

After a spate of parties, Shin and Choi now found themselves seeing less of Kim. For three months he was only intermittently in contact; he would call to ask their opinion on a play that was in development, or a Mercedes would turn up to take them to a film event. Now and again gifts would arrive from the Dear Leader: Estée Lauder cosmetics for Choi, a Rolex for Shin. Unbeknownst to them, Kim Jong-Il, paranoid about American spy satellites, had recently started spending just sixty-five to seventy days of the year in Pyongyang, dividing the rest of his time between his new countryside villas and resorts.

While they waited for Jong-Il to feel safe enough to return to the capital, Shin and Choi watched North Korean films—120 or so films in three months, Shin calculated—acquainting themselves with the country's idiosyncratic filmmaking. He found *My Home Village* a very good film, though the quality had steadily gone downhill after that, with *Sea of Blood* and *The Flower Girl* the two possible exceptions. North Korean movies, Shin later wrote, "were not made for entertainment or for artistic purposes but were used as a political tool. Political power and moviemaking were inseparable." And while the Soviets had employed much the same approach, in the process they had created timeless masterpieces and had innovated, unlike the North Koreans. This, Shin now understood, was the problem which he had been "hired" to resolve, and he set his mind to doing so, partly because he loved a filmmaking challenge, but principally because appeasing Kim Jong-Il was his and Choi's only hope of ever escaping North Korea. Shin needed a slacker leash, more freedom of movement, and Choi had told him the only way to achieve that was to play along, by impressing their captor and pretending to aspire to the same goals.

Shin and Choi's routine became the same day in and day out as, confined to the house, they watched an average of four films a day. The movies were chosen for them with no consultation and included films from the Soviet Union and Eastern Europe as well as two American films, *Dr. Zhivago* and, oddly, *Papillon,* about a Frenchman unjustly sent to a brutal penal colony in French Guiana, where he endures solitary confinement and eventually escapes after a first failed attempt. Shin never learned why those two particular films were chosen for them. Perhaps the answer was that both had been adapted from books, a popular trend in both Koreas at the time, especially the North, where original scripts were a rarity. But both films were fiercely individualistic in content. North Korean movies didn't favor the love-against-all-odds theme of *Zhivago* or the one-man-versus-the-system message of *Papillon*. They couldn't, surely, have been intended as examples?

The days ticked by. Shin requested meetings with Kim several times, in vain, and worried that he was being toyed with and ignored. In fact, Kim was touring China with his father. It was the first time the leader-in-the-making had shadowed his father on a state visit. When he returned in May 1983, a propaganda documentary covering the visit was brought to the villa for Shin and Choi, not to critique but, Shin thought, to make them aware Jong-Il was now more than just a Leader in name: he was openly involved in policy making. For two more months Shin's pleas for a meeting went unanswered. Then, on August 19, the phone finally rang. As always, Kim opened with a question about Shin and Choi's health, then he told Shin that he had set up their offices and work was ready to commence. He was sending a car to get them right away.

The car took them to the center of Pyongyang, to a two-building complex, one building five stories high and the other three. Jong-Il had moved into what had been his father's offices seven years before, in 1976, when Kim Il-Sung had moved his own quarters to the opulent new Kumsusan Palace that Jong-Il had built for him. The building Jong-Il personally used was the smaller one, purposefully placed so that the taller one could block unwanted eyes from seeing what happened on the inside. Though luxuriously ornamented, with high ceilings, and what looked like marble floors, and elaborate granite reliefs, both buildings were in fact all iron and concrete. Their outside walls were almost a meter thick, designed to withstand bombs. The complex had seven entrances, an automatic gate at each of them, remote-controlled from a guard post on the inside. There were allegedly underground tunnels, wide as roads, leading from the building to one of Jong-Il's villas in case he needed to escape at short notice.

Shin and Choi exited the Mercedes and were welcomed by several members of staff. The five-story building had been the home of the Paekdu Creative Group (Kim's previous top filmmaking staff), but they had been moved out to make room for the new talent. The entirety of one wall in the ground-floor lobby was a mural of Mount Paekdu. Off the lobby was a large and comfortable three-room office for Shin and Choi's personal use, with its own bathroom. The whole second floor was a state-of-the-art conference room, to be used only by Kim Jong-Il and his associates (at that point, Shin was told, Kim had yet to ever make use of it). The wall in that room boasted a mural of Kim overseeing the filming of *Sea of Blood,* his most famous "Immortal Classic." The mural for the largest wall on the third floor was a medley of scenes from *Sea of Blood, The Flower Girl,* and *Destiny of a Self-Defense Force Member.* The rest of the floor was occupied by a huge screening room.

Shin and Choi spent the next few months getting settled in their offices and, as always, waiting for Kim. There was still no meeting planned. And then finally, on October 18, Shin's fifty-seventh birthday, Jong-Il, who had a penchant for celebrating birthdays and anniversaries, called Shin in to wish him a happy birthday and ask him and Choi to supper. It would be their first formal meeting.

Shin made sure he had the tape recorder at hand.

Shin was prepared to talk cinema with Kim, but he also intended, for the first time, to ask directly why he and Choi had been kidnapped. He wanted reasons, but he also wanted evidence, in case he and Choi made it out of North Korea, that they hadn't defected. Otherwise his and Choi's accounts might not be enough to exonerate them. He needed proof direct from Kim Jong-Il's mouth.

Secretly recording either of the Kims was an extremely serious crime. Shin had already spent time in a reeducation camp, and being caught now, after months of feigning cooperation and commitment, would eliminate all hope for the future. Without a doubt, he would be executed.

The plan called for the tape recorder to be hidden inside Choi's handbag, with Choi starting and stopping the recording as needed. Before the meeting the couple experimented with how she could do this discreetly, what position the recorder needed to be in to get a recording of the highest quality, and whether Choi could get away with keeping her handbag partially open for minimal audio interference.

At roughly 5 p.m. on October 19, Kim Jong-Il's personal limousine took Shin and Choi to Kim's office at the Central Committee Headquarters. In the back of the car Shin silently rehearsed his questions over and over. The Mercedes drove to a side entrance and through two heavy iron gates decorated with the symbol of the hammer, sickle, and writing brush, then pulled up to a stop. Kim's office took up the whole of a small building, separate from the main building and heavily protected. Inside, an armed security guard sat at the reception desk; he sprang to his feet, saluted the distinguished guests, and ushered them through, without searching them. Shin and Choi were shown to the elevators and sent to the third floor.

Kim Jong-Il was waiting for them when the elevator doors slid open. He greeted them with a big smile. "It's been a long time!" he exclaimed. "I've been so busy I haven't even had the time to get together with you. I really must apologize." Photographers were with him to commemorate the meeting. After a few pictures, the Dear Leader waved away the photographers, told Shin and Choi's minder to wait outside, and went into a reception room alone with them.

Choi reached into her handbag and switched on the tape recorder.

The reception room was huge. On one side there was a large desk, on the other a few easy chairs and a round glass table. To the right of the desk, positioned to be viewed by the person seated behind it, were six television monitors. As soon as he entered, Kim turned on one of the televisions, bringing up the news on KBS, the South Korean Broadcasting Service. Immediately he switched it off, explaining that MBC, the other major South Korean network, "has a drama on at this hour" and flicking on another monitor. "Sa Mi-Ja is a good actress," he added, instantly recognizing the relatively unknown actress in the scene. Having demonstrated his knowledge of foreign television, Kim then switched it off, turned back to his guests, and asked them to sit down as a young waiter brought in soft drinks and laid them on the table. "Let's talk for about an hour," he said, "then we'll have dinner together."

Kim spoke for two hours with barely a pause, of which Choi was only able to record forty-five minutes—a full side of the cassette, which she could not flip over. (Much later, when the tape eventually hit the media, it was a sensation, the first time the general public had ever heard Kim Jong-Il in candid private conversation.)

Kim Il-Sung's adviser Hwang Jang-Yop once recalled that Jong-Il spoke extremely fast, to the point that many of his elders found him hard to understand "unless you completely focus," Hwang said. Shin and Choi's experience of him was the same. "[Kim's] words poured out in rapid fire," Shin remembered, "like a machine gun. . . . His voice was high and he spoke rapidly. He rambled on, often speaking in partial, ungrammatical sentences, moving to a new thought without ever finishing the previous one." This was not the polished Dear Leader whom Shin had met on more public occasions. "He was completely different from when we met at the party. Perhaps because he was excited, his voice was like that of a man having an argument. . . . [He] launched into a long discussion that ran the gamut from his reasons for kidnapping us and the preparations for the kidnapping to the status of the North Korean film industry and the reasons for its backwardness. He never stopped to rest and the words just kept cascading forth in a stream. Once Kim started speaking, it was almost impossible for us to get a word in."

The tape recording is simply extraordinary—so much so that, while it has been authenticated both by the CIA and KCIA, conspiracy theorists would later question its validity. It took no encouragement for Kim to explain, almost boastfully, their kidnappings. He had been informed, he told Shin, calling him *sunsaeng* (teacher), and addressing him throughout in formal pronouns rather than the familiar (much like *vous* and *tu* in French), "that you were the best director in South Korea. We were talking about film directors, and Choe Ik-Gyu said you're the best. And knowing that you were born in North Korea"—another propaganda bonus—"it helped us to decide." On the tape the Dear Leader can be heard laughing, with Shin and Choi joining in. "We learned your situation wasn't very good in the South. You were having problems with Park Chung-Hee and we figured that Park was going to try to hang on to power for a long time and that it would be difficult for you to work in the South and you would try to work abroad. . . . We heard you wanted to go abroad to make films."

"That was when my business license was canceled," Shin helpfully offered.

"Yes, that's right," answered Kim. "So I thought, I've got to bring him here. But it's going to be impossible to bring him here because he's a man. Impossible, so we try to find a way to lure you, to entice you to come here. We needed something. So we brought Teacher Choi here to tempt you." Again Jong-Il laughed and the couple joined in. "Frankly speaking . . . I absolutely needed you. So I began to covet you but there was nothing I could do. I told my comrades, if we want to get Director Shin here, we have to plan a covert operation to bring you here." Just ten days before this conversation, on October 9, 1983, Kim Jong-Il had ordered an assassination bombing operation in Rangoon targeting South Korea's president, Chun Doo-Hwan, while he was on a state visit to Burma. Chun, delayed in traffic, had survived, but twenty-one others died. "[But] even after bringing him here," Kim continued without pause, "how do we make him feel at ease and happy? Then there was the unavoidable situation—I'm going to be very candid with you, so please don't think badly of me—the fact that we kept the two of you separated from each other. It wasn't my original intention. My comrades thought that if Madame Choi comes here, Teacher Shin will naturally come. But as you know, our working-level officials are too subjective and bureaucratic, so in dealing with the matter they did not handle it properly. . . ." This was Kim's attempt at an apology, blaming his underlings. Jong-Il assured them both that the people responsible had been punished. "There have been a lot of problems. . . . Our comrades on the inside, and especially the comrades who carried out the operation, have fallen into subjectivism. They have gone through a great deal of self-criticism as a result. I've also conducted my own self-criticism. Because I never told my subordinates in detail what my plans were, I never told them just how we would use you. . . . I just said I need those two people; bring them here, so my comrades just carried out the operation. So in handling you, they put you in different guesthouses and treated you like prisoners, criminals. As a result, there have been a lot of misunderstandings."

Kim had wanted them as guests, he explained, and he saw them as equals; the disrespect with which they had been treated was not his fault. He had faced reluctance from comrades, he continued, who did not believe that Shin and Choi truly wanted to "assist in upgrading the North's film industry" but were here solely to please him. "My belief is that South Korean people—filmmakers—come to this side and feel real freedom, well—in making films, without trouble . . . my thoughts—well—for me—" On the tape Kim seems to get lost in his own speech and hesitates. There is a pause. "Take our country," he finally continued. "North and South are facing off. . . . For a Communist country people can only travel to places that share our ideology. It's impossible to go anywhere else. We are trading with Japan, but in practice, if we want to send our technicians there to learn and adopt new skills, Japan won't accept them, because they have to make a show of a hostile attitude toward us. So I was thinking—yes, only in my head—my intention was, well, I hadn't talked to anyone about this . . . I thought, what people have mastered Western skills that we don't have here . . . who could come here to produce something with my support? Then we could flip the situation so we could culturally penetrate the West. . . . As you've seen in this country, people here only see inside this country. They are happy with what they are able to see. They're not able to compare it with what others have on the outside.

"We're on a lower level," he added. "To speak honestly, South Koreans try hard to get things done—here people are different. Things are given to them. North Korean actors aren't improving. They have no acting skills at all. In the South when you introduce a new actor, you make sure they'll be better from film to film. When new faces are shown here, we cannot expect they'll be any better in the next film. Here are two things I've analyzed. It's needed that we invest in directors and in our actors and actresses. And, those people should work hard or else they can't survive in the industry. Hard work is key to success."

"I have felt that as well," Shin answered. "I could use the resources here. I could teach technical skills—not just copying South Korean films but also being creative. I think it's possible, so I've been longing for a meeting with you, Dear Leader," he finished.

Kim seemed satisfied. "I told people: Shin and Choi came here because we have a superior system. You came here voluntarily. I didn't say my real intentions. Some people have their doubts. . . . What my intentions were, well—it's complicated. The fact is I am a politician who has wishes and desires. You were demanded by these wishes and desires. So you are here.

"It's been difficult to talk about this. . . . We have to admit that we're falling behind. We have to acknowledge that we are behind. I'm in the position to say it. If others said the same thing, they would be in trouble for criticizing the system. I am the only one who can say this. And I can only tell you two. There is nothing challenging when a film is made here. They [the crews] don't try a single new thing, so they can't improve. They repeat scenes we've already made before. We should make films that stay with you and give you something to think about later, an ideology. . . . Why do we only make rubbish?"

Kim promised he would protect Shin and give him whatever he needed. "I will be your shield," he promised. "My intention is for you to show how you make films, and people here will naturally follow your path. You are pioneers." He was getting excited now. "Why don't you do this? You can say, when you meet outsiders, that there is no freedom in the South, no democracy. And that there is too much interference in the creative industries. There is only anticommunism. That's what Yun I-Sang [a respected South Korean composer who was then in exile from his country] used to say, you know."

"Well, I was kicked out from the United States when I was there," Shin contributed.

"Right. You came here to find real freedom—that should be what's said. Freedom of expression. We want to lead our film industry to become even more advanced than that of advanced countries. I think that would sound natural. Well," he chuckled, "better than saying you were forcefully dragged here." He interrupted himself to tell Shin and Choi a story about how, years ago, he had had a North Korean film shown to the Cambodian Film Festival, only for the country's ruler, Norodom Sihanouk, to become offended because he thought the film was a metaphor supporting leftist Cambodian guerrilla groups. "We had to apologize several times because we hadn't thought of that," Kim said. "You see how small-minded we are. We don't have any films we can show an international audience."

The tape is inaudible for a moment, then resumes with Kim apologizing. "I am sorry that we haven't pleased you so far," he told Shin and Choi. "People here . . . they are stubborn. I'm worried we will become the world's worst film industry. It will happen if we don't do something *now*."

"Dear Leader, how lucky these people are to work under a film fan like you," Shin said.

"They must be pleased," Choi added.

"They should try harder," Kim answered. "They can even use me as an excuse if they try but fail to make our film industry better."

"I'm impressed," Shin said. They started talking about specific films, and the subject of *The Star of Korea* came up. Kim had thrown all his resources at the epic eight-part film series, going so far as casting an unknown in the lead and giving him extensive plastic surgery to make him closely resemble the young Supreme Leader (and then sending him down to work in production once the film had wrapped, never to appear in another picture again); but the movies were limp and lifeless. "It's embarrassing to talk about openly," Jong-Il admitted. "*The Star of Korea* is history. It is suitable for those who have a difficult time reading history, but it is not art. It could have been better, in a more artistic, more subtle way." Shin agreed and Kim continued, "The state pays for everything for its people. They don't need to fight for food. So, screenwriting has become just a hobby for the screenwriters in this system, because they don't need to worry about making money to be fed. I told our propaganda workers once that there is a real problem in socialism: no incentive for success."

"Maybe there should be a film award that filmmakers can get excited about," Shin suggested.

"With the creative departments we can give that a go. But what about the crews? They don't even have a sense of saving film rolls. They can waste as much of it as they feel like, because they don't have to pay for it. . . . The North's filmmakers are just doing perfunctory work. They don't have any new ideas. Their works have the same expressions, redundancies, the same old plots. All our movies are filled with crying and sobbing. I didn't order them to portray that kind of thing," Kim insisted, again shirking responsibility. "I don't know why they make movies that way . . ."

There was a brief silence and he went on more confidently. "This is only a transitional phenomenon and we'll solve our film dilemma. I'm determined to overcome all the barriers to make people open their eyes to the creative mind. I [can] confess the truth only to you two people. I would appreciate it if you keep this a secret just between us." It was unusual for the confident, authoritative, insolent young Leader to address his elders formally and call them Teacher, let alone ask for someone's advice and follow their guidance; yet this was the surreal situation Shin and Choi suddenly found themselves in. Having spent most of the meeting pacifying his two guests, Jong-Il was now working toward the main point of his lecture.

"For the purpose of developing [the] industry," he told Shin, "you must serve as a model so that our film directors will follow naturally. You will play the role of a pioneer. That was my intent when I brought you here, but your role goes further. It goes without saying," Jong-Il added, "that you must say your defection to the North was of your own free will, and that the South's democracy is bogus. It is a sham camouflaged with anticommunism. There is no genuine democracy. There is only anticommunism and interference in the creative work. You must say that because of the restrictions on art, you defected to the North where you could enjoy genuine freedom, the guaranteed freedom of creation."

So Kim didn't just want Shin and Choi to make movies for him. He wanted them to be a publicity tool for North Korea, personifications of the North's superiority. They would be director and actress in their work but also the leading couple of North Korea's deluded self-narrative.

Kim knew the story might be met with skepticism, especially since the outside world had heard nothing of Shin or Choi for five years. He had a solution to this problem, however. People would not jump to the conclusion that they were imprisoned in North Korea for the simple reason that they wouldn't be.

He was sending them abroad.

24
Out of the North

Kim Jong-Il talked and talked, chain-smoking nonstop as the waiter patrolled in and out of the room, emptying ashtrays, refilling drinks, and keeping a watchful eye on the Dear Leader's safety. As they overran the allocated hour for the meeting, Choe Ik-Gyu knocked on the door and poked his head in the office once, then twice. "Just wait outside for us," Jong-Il said, waving him away. The older man could not have been happy at his exclusion from the talks.

"Deputy Director Choe is the right person to help bring about change in our film industry," Jong-Il was saying, as the room filled with bluish cigarette smoke and the ashtray overflowed with crushed Rothmans. "He is well versed in motion pictures. He is the best man for this work. . . . But as you can see, Deputy Director Choe can't do it all by himself." North Korean cinema then consisted of two production companies, both under the leadership of the Paekdu Group, which Jong-Il himself oversaw. "I am asking you to set up one more production company," he told Shin.

"Thank you very much," Shin answered. "That's exactly what I would like. If you do so, I would like to name the company Shin Film." Five years later, and after everything he had gone through, the closing of his studio in Seoul still rankled. He wanted his name back at the front of a film's credits. Shin didn't expect Jong-Il to consent, since North Korean films didn't have on-screen credits and no creative endeavor in the People's Republic had ever been named after an individual other than the Supreme Leader.

But Jong-Il shrugged. "Fine," he said, "whatever you like. You will be the president and Teacher Choi the company's vice president." They discussed what films the new Shin Film would produce, and their end goal of participating in foreign film festivals, winning international awards, and maybe even securing commercial distribution abroad. Jong-Il stunned the two South Koreans by promising them funding of U.S. $2 million a year to be used "whenever you want"; the amount would rise each year, exponentially if they exceeded expectations. Shin and Choi would have the whole of the national industry at their disposal: they would be able to select cast and crew as they saw fit, to instruct other directors and producers according to their own principles, and to request any equipment they needed. Jong-Il would approve every film's subject, or better yet conceive it in tandem with Shin; Choi would star in as many of them as possible and, following her role as academy head at the Anyang school of performing arts, would train the current generation of actors and actresses of the Korea Film Studio. And, crucially, Shin and Choi would be traveling abroad, both to shoot films and to attend film festivals, as the new faces of North Korean cinema.

This was a miraculous stroke of luck. Their current life in North Korea was one of imprisonment at the heart of a set of prisons of increasing size, one inside the other, like Russian dolls: the guarded villa inside the fenced compound inside the Pyongyang perimeter inside the heavily patrolled North Korean borders. Going abroad, even if they remained heavily guarded by around-the-clock "attendants," as they were in Pyongyang, unscrewed the heads of the outer matryoshkas and removed their layers. Surely somehow an opportunity for escape would present itself.

Jong-Il called Director Choe back into the room. "Have them photographed for passport pictures," he instructed. "Have their passports issued tomorrow." Choe nodded and led the couple to a photography studio in another part of the building. A photographer took pictures of them separately and together. In the joint shot, Shin is in a dark suit and striped tie, his hand resting on the back of an expensive-looking occasional chair made of wood and flowered embroidery, on which sits Choi, in a white jacket and skirt and darker blouse, her hands clasped in her lap. In the photos she is clearly still better at faking a happy smile than Shin is.

When the photo session was over Shin and Choi were walked to the central Party building's dining room, where Kim Jong-Il and a handful of film industry cadres were waiting to start dinner. Shin, Choi, and Director Choe took their seats.

"You're an extremely strong man to be able to work until late at night," Shin told Kim Jong-Il, who, as always, was seated next to him.

"The doctors say I look ten years younger than I actually am," the Dear Leader answered proudly.

The dinner lasted until midnight and was an extension of their production meeting, Jong-Il instructing all present to follow Shin and Choi's instructions and to start presenting them with personnel and equipment the very next day for their review. After being driven home the couple went up to their bedroom, closed the door, walked to the bathroom, and turned on the taps. They were both febrile with anticipation as Choi took the tape recorder out of her bag, rewound it, and pressed play. They hadn't had an opportunity to flip or replace the tape, so they'd only recorded forty-five minutes of Jong-Il's production-meeting monologue, but the sound quality was good. They carefully hid the tape along with the pictures Kim Jong-Il had been sending Choi since her kidnapping, including the one of their first meeting at Nampo Harbor.

"I was too excited to sleep that night," Shin recalled. They had managed to record the Dear Leader without getting caught, and their show of loyalty and obedience seemed to be convincing their captors. Most exciting of all, however, was one fact: "I could start making movies again."

Shin and Choi got to work in the morning. Shin, eager to please the Kims and, he hoped, cause them to ease their watchfulness, was determined to have their first film ready to release on the Leader's next birthday. That was on April 15, and it was already October 20. There was no time to waste.

The very notion of no time to waste, however, was different in North Korea than it had been in Seoul. "I later realized that the concept of time was quite different in North Korea," Shin said. "They had no sense of urgency there." He and Choi went through the head shots of every North

Korean actor and actress on the books and, with ambitions to make forty films a year, requested a staff of 230: a relatively modest number compared to the two thousand staff with which the national Korea Film Company struggled to make ten films a year. Shin would later experience why the socialist system was so inefficient when Shin Film ended up swelling to seven hundred employees. In his words, "I had to enlarge the staff because of the inefficiencies endemic to the socialist system. . . . To get materials necessary for sets and so on, you couldn't just pick up the phone and ask for them. You had to first formulate a plan a year in advance, listing your future requirements [so that] the state could set up its annual plan. If you needed wood or lumber, you would . . . put in a request a year ahead of time and the state would allocate the logs, [but] you had to have a person to estimate the requirements, a person to request allocation, another person to expedite the delivery, another one to deliver it, and so forth." Shin ordered cameras, cranes, and editing machines, all to be shipped in from Germany, the finest equipment in the Eastern Bloc. For each of his productions he would also select his own actors, but without meeting them in person: he would be handed binders of head shots and choose on that basis (the collective filmmaking apparatus of North Korea kept no official credits or résumés). This system resulted in Shin, on at least one occasion, casting a lead actor far shorter than the rest of the cast, and having to manipulate camera angles to make him look taller.

The conference and dinner with Kim Jong-Il on October 19 was the last time they saw the Dear Leader for several months, but their new executive producer was as good as his word. Less than a week after their meeting, Choe Ik-Gyu met with Shin and Choi to give them their brand-new DPRK diplomatic passports. The next day the three of them, plus Choi's ideological instructor and attendant Mr. Kang, drove to Sunan Airport, the small, single-terminal airport outside Pyongyang, and boarded a Russian-made Aeroflot airliner. They sat in first class—the DPRK may have claimed to be an egalitarian socialist paradise, but its national airline had three classes, like all others. In their carry-on bags Shin and Choi had $20,000 of spending money, given to them by Kim. The plane taxied over to the end of one of Sunan's two runways, took off, and headed west.

They were traveling, via Moscow, to East Germany, Hungary, Czechoslovakia, and Yugoslavia, filming location scenes for *Emissary of No Return,* their first North Korean picture. *Emissary of No Return* told the story of the Hague "secret emissary affair," as it was known in Korea and Japan. At the 1907 Hague peace conference, a precursor to the Geneva Protocol meetings in 1925, three secret emissaries sent by the Korean emperor had tried to disrupt the talks held between the world powers, in an attempt to build international pressure on Japan, which was in the process of colonizing Korea. The foreign delegations, led by the United States and the United Kingdom, turned the emissaries away on the basis that Korea was no longer a sovereign nation and that Japan had already assumed responsibility for its international relations. Their rejection was quick and quiet. In Korea, however, the event had taken on mythical proportions, and Shin's film followed the official North Korean history, in which one of the emissaries forced his way into the hall, delivered an impassioned speech for independence and the right to self-determination, and then, unable to sway the imperialist powers, committed hara-kiri (ritual suicide) on the convention floor, shocking one and all with his devotion.

Shin had chosen the subject matter after a discussion with Kim Jong-Il. Like many of the younger Kim's movies, *Emissary of No Return* was based on a play Kim Il-Sung had allegedly written as a young guerrilla. Shin had thought it safest, for his first film, not to veer too far into new territory, and he was the one who had asked to adapt one of the Supreme Leader's works. He had intentionally chosen a story set in The Hague in the hope that he would be allowed to film there, but Jong-Il had then clarified that when he said they could film "anywhere," he'd meant anywhere *this side of the Iron Curtain.*

In East Berlin, where they spent three days, Shin and Choi scoured the city for suitable locations, shadowed every step of the way by their North Korean minders. These men were with Shin and Choi twenty-four hours a days, seven days a week. Kang would only give Shin and Choi their passports to walk through border control; at all other times the two booklets sat in his pocket, out of their reach.

Walking down one Berlin street, Shin spotted the American flag floating over a building behind heavily armed gates; it was the first time he had seen a U.S. embassy since Hong Kong in the summer of 1978. Choi, eyes locked on the flag, tugged on his sleeve and looked at him, hard, wanting to make a run for it. But Shin "had tasted the punishment that was meted out when [he] had tried to escape and failed," he said, and he had no desire to put his wife through it. "What's the matter with you?" he hissed to Choi under his breath. "I will not make an attempt unless it's one hundred percent certain. If they caught us, we'd be dead." This time, they would plan properly, take no avoidable risks, and do it right.

In every city, Kang and Director Choe booked the rooms next door to Shin and Choi's, often with connecting doors allowing them access. Kang ordered the South Koreans to call and notify him if they ever left the room, but he also kept a close eye on their room door in case they ignored the order. Any other phone calls, Kang insisted, must be made from his own room. The first evening they were in Prague, after dinner in the hotel restaurant, Shin asked Kang to use his phone and called an old friend, Japanese film critic Kyushiro Kusakabe, under the pretext of wanting to discuss starting a film festival in Pyongyang. Kusakabe was a close friend and Shin trusted him, but he and Choi had chosen him somewhat by default: Kang would have never authorized a call to South Korea, or to someone he suspected to be a personal, rather than professional, acquaintance. Kusakabe was the person who best fit the bill.

To appease his watchdogs' suspicions Shin made the call from Kang's room, acting relaxed and keeping the conversation about film, hoping his friend would be able to read between the lines. Kusakabe was stunned to hear Shin's voice after all these years. He had thought, he said, that Shin was dead; that was what the South Korean media had been reporting. Kusakabe also suggested that he meet Shin in Budapest, if Shin could somehow get there. Shin responded that he would try, as cheerfully as possible, so that Kang and Choe "would not suspect anything."

A few days later, filming began on *Emissary of No Return* at the Barrandov Studios lot, in Prague, Czechoslovakia. Barrandov was Roman Polanski's favorite studio; Miloš Forman's *Amadeus* would film on the same soundstages the following year. The complex had nine fully serviced stages and a 160,000-square-meter outdoor lot in the hills outside Prague, as well as top technical crews. One of the cavernous soundstages was being turned by Shin's crews into a replica of the Ridderzaal, or Hall of Knights of The Hague, in the Netherlands.

Shin leaned into the Arriflex camera and, one hand gently steadying the tripod, pressed his right eye against the viewfinder. A wide-angle lens was fixed on the front of the camera body, capturing the actors in full body shots, everything in sharp focus. With his thumb he nudged the tripod's panhandle, adjusting the frame slightly. Two North Korean assistants crouched by the camera, following his gaze, expectantly hanging on his every instruction.

Satisfied with the shot, he stepped back and looked around, mopping the sweat off his brow. The room was large but crowded. The set, including movable walls and fake ceilings, made the soundstage feel considerably smaller, and there were people everywhere: actors, crew members, assistants. Czech technicians and production designers spoke to Shin and the other Koreans through interpreters, broken English the language of choice since the Koreans understood no Czech and the Czechs no Korean. For every two people talking and pointing, there were another half-dozen standing behind them, frantically flipping through scripts and shot lists covered in notes in different alphabets, trying to keep up. The bright set lights baked the room in steaming heat.

One hand on his hip and the other clutching his stapled script, Shin did his best, too, to keep up with the conversation between his assistant and the head of the Czech crew. He'd put on weight in the ten months since his release from prison. The Richard Burton hairstyle was back, his black hair splashed over his temples. A silk Hermès scarf was tucked into the collar of his dark shirt and a director's viewfinder, like a short telescope allowing him to visualize what a scene might look like in different focal lengths and aspect ratios, hung on a lanyard around his neck. His shirtsleeves were rolled up, revealing the gold Rolex, a gift from Kim Jong-Il, sitting snugly on his left wrist. Choi Eun-Hee stood nearby, in a newsboy cap and large sunglasses, her pen hovering over her own copy of the script. There was no role in this film for her, so she was acting as Shin's second-in-command and codirector, focusing on the actors and their performances.

Although they were still in captivity, this, Shin later wrote, "was a historic thing for me." He was so excited, he had taken the camera away from its operator and shot as many of the day's scenes as possible himself. He was directing a motion picture, which he had felt convinced for several years would never happen again. Making films had been his calling, his passion, his life, and it had been taken away from him.

In November 1983 in Prague, Kim Jong-Il gave it back.

25
Like a European Movie

Making films over the next three years, Shin and Choi fell back in love—if they had ever truly fallen out of it.

In an environment where separately they had nothing, each found that the other person became their everything. They depended on each other for their sanity and focus, and they were each other's last remaining link with their former lives. But there was more to it than mere circumstantial need. Prison had changed Shin and given him perspective. He realized, perhaps for the first time in his life, that he was not the most important person in the world. As his new situation cut Shin's ego down to size, he grew less rebellious, headstrong, and selfish; and as time passed Choi felt a newfound devotion to a man who represented her ideal of commitment, talent, humor, and strength. After five years missing and fearing for each other every single day, and then being thrown together in a situation where they were both bereft of anything else, Shin and Choi's love was rekindled with a new depth.

One person who was much less keen on Shin Sang-Ok than his ex-wife was Choe Ik-Gyu. The forty-nine-year-old was a director in his own right; he had run the North Korean film studios and proven his worth by overseeing Kim Jong-Il's two biggest films, only to now find himself demoted to babysitting a pampered capitalist from the South. On set Choe often questioned Shin's decisions, for instance telling him, loud enough for the crew to hear, "This other angle is better than the one you're choosing. Why are you shooting from this angle?" He scoffed and sniggered when Shin walked around the set with his viewfinder to test various shots.

One evening, after the day's filming on the streets of Prague had wrapped, the Koreans were sitting at dinner when Director Choe, slightly tipsy from the compulsory toasts to Kim Jong-Il and Kim Il-Sung, "stood up and started walking back and forth in front of the dining table," Shin remembered. Choe held his hands up in front of his face, thumbs touching and palms open outward, as if framing a shot. In this position he hopped from one side of the table to the other, crouching down and spinning around. Shin realized Choe was mocking him. "Why are you always moving around here and there?" the North Korean sneered. "With all those foreigners out there watching you are making us lose face, walking back and forth like that, forever changing camera positions."

"I was trying to avoid getting all the modern buildings and automobiles in the picture," Shin shot back. "The film is set in 1907. I had to move around to find the right angle." Besides, he added, North Korean film might have often used only one shot for an entire scene, but in the rest of the world, films were made more dynamic by cutting from one angle or shot size to another.

Shin's answer frustrated the North Korean. "Oh, come on!" the North Korean barked. "Just do as I tell you!"

Shin had been waiting for an opportunity to test a theory of his, and this was his chance. Matching Choe's volume, he slammed his fist on the table and sprang to his feet. "Fine, then: from this moment on I give up responsibility for this film! You take charge. And I'll report what just happened to the Dear Leader Comrade Kim Jong-Il." He and Choe stared each other off. After a few moments Mr. Kang, who had been quietly sitting at the table with a bitter expression on his face, most likely hoping the situation would just blow over, cleared his throat and said to Choe, his voice filled with exasperation: "Comrade Deputy Director, you have gone too far. What's the matter with you? Control yourself!"

Choe looked from Shin to Kang and back again. It seemed he might say something, but then suddenly he looked deflated. Putting his hands down, he walked back to his seat. "I made a mistake," he mumbled, sitting down.

Shin was satisfied. In a moment of tension he had pulled rank and called upon Kim Jong-Il's name, and their watchdog had backed off. Choi Eun-Hee had noticed it, too. She and Shin both filed the prerogative away.

Shin and Choi finished up in Prague and returned to Pyongyang, where they were to film the movie's Korean scenes and begin editing as quickly as possible, Shin still set on April 15 of the following year as his premiere date. Within days of their return, Kim Jong-Il invited them to his office and showered them anew with luxury gifts: two brand-new, dusty brown Mercedes-Benz 280 sedans, the most expensive Mercedes cars in the world, flown in straight from the assembly line in Stuttgart. The license plates on both cars started with the number 2-16, for Jong-Il's birthday, February 16.

Kim Jong-Il thanked Shin and Choi for their "hard work" while abroad, as well as for their cooperation in spending time in Eastern Europe to "lessen complaints and criticism and give people the impression you are working freely and doing as you please." Whatever the watchdogs had reported back had pleased him, and he was already enthusing about the possibility of opening a Shin Film studio in Eastern Europe—in Yugoslavia, maybe, or Hungary. "In the future, if we want to expand," Jong-Il told Shin, "you will need a base of operations." He ordered Shin to travel back to Eastern Europe and scout a suitable location for the venture.

Armed with this vision, Shin and Choi planned their next trip west, this time to Budapest, where they intended to meet Kusakabe. They stopped in Prague on the way to hold talks at Barrandov about working there again in the future and in Yugoslavia to inspect sites for the planned Shin Film studio, before proceeding to Hungary. Shin found Budapest beautiful, and he couldn't help notice that the Hungarians seemed happier, better off, and better fed than people living in the other non-free-market countries he had seen.

Hungary was intriguing for another reason: Hungarian immigration law allowed people holding diplomatic passports—people like Shin and Choi—to enter neighboring Austria without a visa. Austria was on the other side of the Iron Curtain, and its capital, Vienna, had become the crossroads between East and West, a hotbed of spies, defectors, and visa seekers of all kinds. Shin had never set foot in Austria, but he imagined the city as pictured in the classic film *The Third Man,* full of refugees desperate to get out. He wasn't far off. Maybe, he started dreaming, if he and Choi could find a way to get there, they too could find a way to get out . . .

On the morning of December 10, 1983, Shin and Choi sat in their hotel room in the Budapest Hilton, anxiously waiting. Every now and then Director Choe called on the phone from next door to make sure they had not slipped out. Finally there was a knock at the door. Shin sprang up to open the door, and Kusakabe quickly slipped in.

A few days earlier, while working on reshoots at Barrandov, Shin had managed to elude Choe and Kang for a second, find a phone, and arrange the meeting with his Japanese friend. Kusakabe could not help them escape, but he was a lifeline, a link to the outside world. Shin and Choi led Kusakabe to a far corner of the room, away from the wall adjoining Choe's room, and told their old friend everything about their kidnapping and their current work—but not about their plan to escape. "I was uncertain about our situation," Shin later said. Even with such a "very faithful friend" as Kusakabe, the filmmaker was wary. He didn't know whom he could trust. They gave Kusakabe their prized tape recording of the Dear Leader, as well as the photograph of Choi's first meeting with Jong-Il and letters they asked Kusakabe to secretly deliver to their family in Seoul. The tape and photo, they warned Kusakabe, were to be kept a secret for now. "This is *absolutely* a secret between you and me and Eun-Hee only," Shin said. "Please keep them for six months—but if you don't hear from us again after that time, give everything to the Japanese and Korean news media." If tragedy befell him and Choi, Shin felt, he wouldn't need the insurance the tape provided—but he still wanted the world to know what had happened to them.

They hugged Kusakabe good-bye. He walked to the door, made sure the hallway was clear, and slipped out. Shin and Choi worked in Eastern Europe for another week, shooting with their five main actors, who had been sent from Pyongyang and were surveilled as closely as they were. There was a brief delay in the filming when it transpired that the actors, who had never traveled outside of Pyongyang, had flown with no suitcases, the concept of luggage being utterly foreign to them; but by December 16 filming was wrapped and the entire cast and crew flew back to snow-covered North Korea. Sitting in their villa, guarded by their attendants, Shin and Choi filled the last days of 1983 writing, out of habit, their sycophantic New Year's greetings to the Kims.

As Shin and Choi worked on their film throughout January and February, they continued having meetings with Jong-Il, who was growing ever more eager to expand filmmaking operations. "He was very concerned about improving North Korea's image in Southeast Asia," Shin later wrote. The Rangoon bombing three months before had backfired and badly damaged the country's standing internationally, and "Kim Jong-Il wanted desperately to redeem the image of North Korea." Film and culture, he hoped, would be one way to do so. Shin and Choi had once again expressed to Kim their concerns about the well-being of their children back in Seoul, and the Dear Leader had agreed to let Shin and Choi communicate with their family via the Chosen Soren, the organization for ethnic Koreans living in Japan, which, since the division of Korea, had functioned as North Korea's unofficial agent in Japan. In January Shin and Choi received from the Chosen Soren letters and a package from Shin's niece, who promised to write more. Their friend Fumiko Inoue wrote to them telling them their daughter, Myung-Im, had married, and that their son, Jung-Kyun, was living with Choi's family. Oh Su-Mi had married a photographer named Kim. A few weeks later, again through the North Korean mission in Japan, Shin was able to correspond with a family friend in New Jersey in the United States to ask him whether he would legally adopt Jung-Kyun. His friend, a man his age by the name of Kim In-Sook, "was stunned to hear my voice. He thought I had been killed."

Shin didn't want his son in Pyongyang, but he didn't want him in South Korea, either. He didn't trust his own government—and he had heard of the stigma associated with having defectors, as the world would brand him and Choi the second their first film was released, as family members. No, Jung-Kyun was better off abroad.

In the meantime Shin and Choi managed to complete their movie on March 13, over a month ahead of their self-imposed deadline. Shin informed Kim Jong-Il, who was so delighted he announced a special preview to be held three days later at Party headquarters.

The screening was a "historic" event in North Korean cinema, Shin said. When the lights dimmed in the Party Central Committee building's screening room that evening, the party cadres, including those who until recently had run Kim's studio, were treated to a film unlike anything they had ever seen before. Light faded up on the screen to reveal the streets of The Hague, selected from documentary stock footage, which soon cut to shots taken at Barrandov studios and on the streets of Prague, standing in for the Dutch city. It was the first foreign footage ever used in a North Korean film, and the scenes were full of European characters played by actual Western actors. They were dubbed into Korean—Jong-Il had drawn the line at actual foreign languages being spoken—but the impression was still astonishing. At the end of the movie, instead of immediately fading to black, the action transitioned to a credit roll, the first time a North Korean film had individually credited the cast and crew. The most prominent credit read, in big bold letters: "Director Choi Eun-Hee, under the general direction of Shin Sang-Ok."

When the lights came up, Jong-Il was ecstatic. "It's fantastic!" he enthused. "It's just like a European movie!" The rest of the audience, none of whom had ever seen a European movie, loudly agreed. Jong-Il stood up and congratulated Shin and Choi, to applause from the crowd. As the guests filed out of the screening room and headed upstairs for dinner, Kim took Shin's arm. The Dear Leader was beaming. His dream of establishing a world-class film industry seemed to be within his grasp.

"When this movie comes out," he told Shin, "there are going to be a lot of jealous people."

26

The Press Conference

"I was so astonished by the video that my heart was pounding and I could hardly watch," Shin later recalled. Mr. Kang stood in the living room of the Pyongyang villa, angrily pressing the volume button on the Japanese-made television. The screen in front of Shin was showing photographs of himself and Choi in North Korea, the very photographs they had given Kusakabe five months before. ". . . and her ex-husband, the director Shin Sang-Ok," the newscaster was saying, "both missing from Hong Kong since 1978, were kidnapped by the North . . ." The camera panned over images of Shin and Choi's letters to their children, of the hard copies of the photographs, and even of the cassette tape containing their recording of Kim Jong-Il. Shin recognized his own handwriting on the orange label and the decoy case, originally for a record of pop songs, that they had hidden the tape in. Shin felt his heart drop into his stomach. ". . . supported by sound tapes and letters the couple sent clandestinely to relatives in Seoul," the news anchor droned on. "It is reported that under North Korean coercion Shin and Choi are making a movie to be presented to Kim Il-Sung as a birthday gift. The film slanders the Republic of Korea and several top officials . . ."

Shin looked at Kang, who was fuming. He was terrified. His last two attempts to dupe his kidnapper had ended with him being thrown in prison and tortured. Surely Jong-Il would have no mercy now.

After the triumphant preview of *Emissary of No Return* for Kim Jong-Il, Shin and Choi had braced themselves for the world's inevitable shock when, five years after disappearing from the face of the Earth, they both resurfaced, together, working for one of the world's most notorious dictators, and with a new film, made for him, to promote.

Their return to filmmaking was exhilarating, and having work to focus on had made the last several months fly by. But Shin and Choi were still obsessed with escaping from captivity and returning home. The only way to do so, they knew, was if they were allowed close enough to the Iron Curtain that they could skip over to the West. There were only two places where that was realistically possible: Berlin or Vienna. The paradox confronting the couple was that their only chance of escape lay in convincing their jailer, Kim Jong-Il, that they wanted to stay in North Korea. But Kim Jong-Il, it seemed, would only be convinced if they managed to convince the rest of the world first. If they wanted the freedom of movement to travel to either of those cities, Shin and Choi would have to start singing the praises of the North Korean regime to the Western world.

Jong-Il had arranged a second preview of *Emissary of No Return,* this one for his father on the Supreme Leader's birthday, to be attended by four of the European cast and crew, whom Jong-Il promised to fly to Pyongyang; he would also throw a special Friday night party in their honor. Eager to impress Kim Il-Sung, Shin asked Jong-Il for permission to travel to Leningrad to capture a handful of additional shots that would enhance the film's production values even further. Jong-Il agreed, and in late March Shin and Choi spent three closely supervised days in Russia with a skeleton crew, filming in Leningrad's baroque quarter and at the old Korean legation in the city center. The days were short, the sun rising after nine and setting long before five, and relentlessly wet and cold, temperatures dropping to minus ten degrees Celsius. Indoors, following Russian tradition, rooms were kept extremely warm, and Choi, who was unprepared to constantly go from one climate to the other, fell ill. Their flights to Pyongyang were booked for

March 29, and Choe Ik-Gyu refused to change the schedule. So he, Shin, and Kang returned to North Korea, leaving Choi Eun-Hee with the other minders to wait in Russia until she was healthy enough to fly.

Back in Pyongyang, Shin spent several uneasy days worried about his wife. He filled the time cutting the new scenes into the existing version of *Emissary of No Return* and watching films in Jong-Il's film library. On April 2, with the screening day drawing near, Shin returned to the villa late in the evening and found the maid waiting at the door for him, flushed and anxious. Kim Jong-Il had called several times while Shin was out, she said, and had ordered them to put him on the phone, but no one could find him. Shin must stay in for the rest of the evening, she said: the Dear Leader would be calling again.

Shortly after that, the hotline phone rang. Shin nervously picked it up.

"The South Korean Agency for National Security has issued a communiqué. They are saying you were kidnapped." Jong-Il's voice was tense on the other end of the line. "I'm sending Kang to brief you. Call me right after."

The news report was accurate and exhaustive, and led the news on both KBS and NBC, South Korea's two biggest television channels. It named not just Shin and Choi but Kusakabe, Fumiko Inoue, and Kim In-Sook. Kusakabe, it seemed, had gotten cold feet as the six-month deadline Shin had set grew near, so he had gone to the authorities early. The South Korean government's report of the evidence was lengthy and divided into chapters, with titles like "The Abduction of Choi Eun-Hee," "The Abduction of Shin Sang-Ok," and "The North's Operations Using Shin Sang-Ok and Choi Eun-Hee Against the South." Within hours the story was picked up by the international newswires and caused a sensation, not just in Asia but everywhere. It was 10 p.m. in Pyongyang, 9 a.m. on America's East Coast. Commuters in New York, Boston, and Washington, D.C., were able to read about it in that same day's evening newspapers. BIZARRE KIDNAPPING CASE REPORTED, bellowed one headline; ACTRESS, HUSBAND SEIZED BY NORTH KOREANS, declared another. Among Korean communities, in South Korea and abroad, the story sparked intense debate. Could it be believed? Was it a publicity stunt to jump-start the stalled engine of Shin's failing career? Or was the news being manipulated by the South Korean government to slander the Kims?

For Shin, the day's events were likely to have immediate, possibly extremely unpleasant, consequences. As soon as Kang stopped the VHS tape, Shin walked over to the hotline telephone and called Kim Jong-Il. He knew Jong-Il was a night owl and was expecting his call, but part of him still hoped the Dear Leader had gone home for the night. On the other hand, Shin would have to face the music sooner or later, and if so, he'd rather get it over with now and be done with it. He would apologize wretchedly and hope for the best.

Jong-Il picked up almost immediately. "You need to deal with this," he said before Shin could speak up. "I think maybe your elder brother reported this to the NSP [National Security Planning, South Korea's intelligence service]. We need to deal with it."

Shin, who was sure Jong-Il must have known he had betrayed him, was stunned. He didn't know yet that Kim Jong-Il recorded every one of his own meetings himself, including the same one he and Choi had secretly taped, so that his every instruction could be transcribed and put into immediate practice, even if he'd forgotten he had said it in the first place. Neither did he know that Jong-Il was suspicious of the Chosen Soren, whose first loyalty was sometimes to its members rather than to him. Clearly Kim suspected that the Chosen Soren, who handled Shin's approved communications with his brother back in Seoul, had either been infiltrated by the South Koreans or had itself leaked the letters and, somehow, the tape recording.

That could have been it—or, Shin speculated later, maybe Kim knew what was going on, but punishing the South Korean couple would mean publicly admitting he had failed to convert them. So perhaps he was ignoring the truth.

In any case, Jong-Il, a man famous for his explosive temper, sounded fidgety but otherwise calm. "What do you intend to do?" Shin asked. Jong-Il's focus was already on countering the South Korean claims, and the only way to do so was to try and disprove them. "You and Madame Choi had better pretend to be working in Eastern Europe, not in Pyongyang," Kim said. "She is still in Moscow?"

"Yes," Shin said, "she's in Moscow. She has a cold."

"Okay. That's good. An NHK correspondent is in Pyongyang now." The NHK was the public Japanese Broadcasting Corporation, Japan's equivalent of the BBC. "I will ask him to call Madame Choi and arrange for her to make the correspondent believe that you are both right now working in Eastern Europe."

"I see," Shin answered. "I'll telephone her and tell her the cover story."

"Yes, that'll be good. As for you, you must immediately go to Budapest or Belgrade and hold a press conference to explain that you were not kidnapped, but voluntarily came to Eastern Europe to work there. Take the videotape and show it to Madame Choi later."

"I will do as you instruct," Shin said.

"Good."

The line clicked off. As Shin put the receiver down he exhaled deeply. A moment he had desperately hoped to avoid was now upon him.

It was time for him and Choi to lie to the world. And to lie *convincingly*. Their lives depended on it.

Shin flew to Belgrade the next morning and booked a press conference in the conference room of the Intercontinental Hotel, where he was staying. Three days later, twenty or so reporters turned up at the set time, neither a great crowd nor an empty room. Most of them were from the Communist bloc, but there were also representatives of Reuters and the Associated Press.

When the journalists arrived at the hotel, so did the Yugoslavian police.

There was confusion as the policemen blocked entry to the conference hall and, through interpreters, explained to Shin and the North Koreans that as far as they were concerned, the event was an announcement of propaganda, not news, and that as such it was an unapproved public political gathering and could not be held out in the open. If the Koreans wanted the interview to go ahead, they would have to continue in the privacy of their room. After discussing the situation with Mr. Kang, Shin went to the front desk and upgraded his room to a suite, so that it would be big enough to fit everyone, then headed back into the lobby to tell the waiting journalists about the change of plans. For many of them the novelty of the occasion had already worn off, so that when Shin got into the elevator to go to the new room, only five reporters followed—one of whom was the North Korean Central News Agency correspondent. The rest had gone home.

Upstairs Shin opened the gathering with prepared remarks. "My wife and I were absolutely not kidnapped," he said. "We voluntarily fled from South Korea to Europe." In the back of the room, as he remembered, the Associated Press man "listened to a few of our remarks, then snickered as if it were all a big joke, and left."

After suffering censorship and rough handling by Park Chung-Hee's government, Shin told the remaining journalists, his production company had been shut down and he and Choi had temporarily gone to stay in West Germany, where, he now claimed, one of Kim Jong-Il's envoys had approached them with a proposal of funding from the Dear Leader. "Kim Jong-Il offered to sponsor us without political oppression," Shin said, "to make movies for the purpose of national reunification." Shin had accepted and opened an office in Budapest. "We are now working in Eastern Europe."

"Why have you been silent for so long?" one of the reporters asked.

"We had to hide in West Germany because of intimidation from the South," Shin mumbled.

"Choi Eun-Hee disappeared before you, and you declared publicly you thought she was kidnapped. Where was she before you disappeared?"

"I had her hide in the house of a friend in West Germany," Shin lied, embarrassed. It made no sense and he knew it. With every question the story unraveled a tiny bit more. Neither Shin nor Choi could explain why they had not been seen publicly in five years if they really had been working freely in Eastern Europe since 1978, or why Shin had kicked up such a fuss about Choi's disappearance before his own if, as they were saying now, Shin knew where she had been the whole time. It also struck many in the room as unusual that Kim Il-Sung, a man usually so hungry for good publicity, would have kept such high-profile defectors—a real propaganda coup—a secret for so long.

Shin did his best to field several more questions about why it had taken so long for them to go public and what their plans for the future were. Then, hoping it would lend him credibility, he told the journalists that he could be reached at the Shin Film head office in Hungary, street address Roosevelt Ter 2, Budapest, on the banks of the Danube. What he didn't say was that that was the address of the Hyatt Hotel in Budapest, where Mr. Kang had only just booked room 602 and had it hastily disguised into a believable temporary production office to deceive any particularly nosy newsmen. The "office" telephone number Shin read out to the journalists was for the Hyatt's front desk.

Before returning to Pyongyang, Shin called the Dear Leader to make sure he was happy with his public performance. Kim Jong-Il sounded satisfied. He instructed Shin to move forward with plans to find a more permanent office in Eastern Europe. So Shin Sang-Ok, who was a gambler and shrewd enough to know that sometimes the moment of greatest risk is the perfect time to act, launched into action.

"The world will be watching our next move with even more interest than usual," Shin told his young captor. "Now is the time to really drive the point home if we want to convince them. What if, instead of Budapest, we opened our Shin Film office in neutral Vienna?"

Kim Jong-Il agreed.

27

Same Bed, Different Dreams

When *Emissary of No Return* was released to the general North Korean public, it was a gigantic hit. The North Korean people had never seen anything like it, and for everyone aged thirty-nine or under, who had been born after the 1945 division, the opening shots of The Hague were literally their very first glimpse of the world outside. Shin's film, like all previous North Korean films, was used as propaganda, with screenings compulsory and followed by group talks in which audiences were encouraged to reflect on what the main characters' climactic suicide taught them about the level of devotion expected of them, the ordinary North Korean people. But it marked a turning point in North Korean culture: the very first time that even the citizens with the lowest *songbun* were able to see, however subtly, that the world outside the Workers' Paradise was not the hell Kim Il-Sung told them it was.

Emboldened by its reception, Kim Jong-Il submitted the movie to the Karlovy Vary Film Festival in Czechoslovakia, a leading festival in the Communist bloc, where *The Flower Girl* had also played twelve years earlier, the last time a North Korean film had been accepted to any international festival. Shin and Choi were sent to the July 1984 screening, where at first attendance was underwhelming. "While other countries advertised their films enthusiastically, we didn't have any publicity posters," Shin said. "When our film was screened only a handful of people turned out to see it." With a captive domestic audience of fifteen million people, who could be sent to a prison camp for missing the opening day of a new film, it seemed it hadn't crossed the Dear Leader's mind that he would have to market his new work abroad to gain an audience. Looking on as audiences queued for the Western movies—that year Peter Fonda and Italian actress Monica Vitti were the star guests of the festival—Shin felt "alone and without much support."

And then, to everyone's surprise, the festival's jury awarded *Emissary of No Return* a special Best Director award, which, due to the wording of the film's end credits, they gave to Choi. As she stepped up to the stage to accept the crystal trophy she was overcome with joy. After years of isolation and loneliness, locked away in a villa with round-the-clock guards, the world had acknowledged her, even if in this small way. In the audience Shin stood up and held up his camera, like a proud father at a school play, photographing Choi as she shook hands with the head of the jury. He felt enormous pride that he had, on the first try, achieved one of Kim Jong-Il's goals. He pictured the Dear Leader's face. This has to win us Kim Jong-Il's complete confidence and trust, he thought.

Sure enough, shortly after they returned to their room, with their North Korean minders just on the other side of the wall, the phone rang. "Our country has never won an honor like this, Teacher Choi," Jong-Il told Choi when she answered. He sounded ecstatic. He repeated his approval for them to open an office in Vienna and his promises to let them spend more and more time in Europe: in Budapest, Prague, Vienna—and the United Kingdom. *Emissary of No Return* would be playing at the London Film Festival in November.

There is an old expression in Asia, "same bed, different dreams," representing the relationship of a married couple whose lives are intertwined but who do not communicate and who, in spite of sleeping side by side every night, are each living completely different lives. Those were the words Shin had in mind as he and Choi traveled to London that fall. "While Kim Jong-Il intended to use me as a means of propaganda," he wrote, "I intended to use the opportunity to escape.

"There was no doubt that London was the best place to attempt an escape to freedom," he added. But if he had hoped to have some freedom of movement, Shin was wrong. Choe Ik-Gyu left for London first, with a group of fourteen bodyguards and "delegates," who would be making arrangements and preparations for Shin and Choi's arrival.

The South Koreans left a week later, via Budapest and Vienna, with a larger entourage than they had ever had—one supervised by Im Ho-Gun, the Deputy Director of the secret police, and that included one of the long-haired young men who had kidnapped Shin in Repulse Bay. When he met Shin again, Shin said, "the young man just looked at me and smiled."

Shin and Choi landed in London at 7 p.m. on Wednesday, November 28, 1984. Prime Minister Margaret Thatcher had just survived the Brighton hotel bombing, briefly knocking out of the headlines a controversial national miners' strike—two events which, back in North Korea, the Korean Central News Agency had made much of to portray Britain as a land of inequality and turmoil. The film festival's highlights were Joe Dante's *Gremlins,* the Coen brothers' *Blood Simple,* and Roland Joffe's *The Killing Fields.* Shin and Choi's film would be showing out of competition.

The North Korean delegation caused a minor sensation. The Home Office had long refused their visas, only finally granting them a day before the scheduled screening. Helen Loveridge, the hospitality manager and assistant to the program director at the festival, was told to expect twenty-nine North Korean guests, but in the end forty turned up, which may have partly explained the delay with visas. Choe Ik-Gyu had given the festival a list of names, "but it was fairly useless," Loveridge said, since most of the names were fake. Once in London the entire delegation stayed at the same hotel and traveled to screenings on a private hired coach, initially causing havoc by being unable to understand the seat rows and numbers on the tickets they had requested for screenings, thereby holding up the start of the showings, to much displeasure from the other guests and critics. On one occasion Choe Ik-Gyu was caught by news crews hectoring Asian students queuing for a film outside the National Film Theatre, shouting loudly: "In North Korea you can study for free! In North Korea there are no starving people! People eat well and live well, thanks be to the Great Leader!"

For Shin and Choi, the forty-six-hour trip was agonizing. They were in the free world but surrounded, around the clock, by armed "bodyguards," employed by Kim Jong-Il not to protect them but to confine them. The National Film Theatre, on the South Bank, was bordered by bright cultural landmarks: the National Theatre and the Royal Festival Hall. There were cabarets and clubs just over the Thames in the West End, and punks in leather jackets and brightly colored mohawks in next-door Brixton, a melting pot of races and nationalities that, a year after Shin and Choi's visit, would see its second major riot in five years, both sparked by police attacks on black Britons. There were strikes and protests and, by the time Shin and Choi arrived, twinkling Christmas decorations hung across Regent Street and the hordes of shoppers rushing in and out of Selfridges, Liberty, and Hamleys. The daily newspapers printed what they wanted, each disagreeing with the others, beholden only to the law and their circulation figures. For all the mess, noise, and violence—maybe even because of it—Shin and Choi longed more than ever to be part of this world where such chaos was allowed. It seemed to them the polar opposite of Kim Il-Sung's sterile, inhuman theater-state. Freedom was all around them, but they could not partake in it.

A small group of South Koreans picketed the screening of *The Emissary of No Return,* shouting "Good-bye!" at Shin and Choi as they entered and left, their Communist minders pushing them into the waiting bus as quickly as possible. The following morning at 5 a.m. one of the bodyguards woke Shin and Choi and insisted they pack and leave immediately, since "the North Koreans had intercepted a message sent from the South Korean embassy in London to Seoul and the situation had taken a bad turn." In truth the Home Office had issued them visas valid for the day only. In the dark, damp early morning Shin and Choi were hustled to Heathrow, loaded onto a plane, and flown back to Budapest. Before arriving in London both had been given new gold watches by Choe in order to impress their Western hosts. Now that they were on the plane back to North Korea, Choe ordered them to hand the watches back.

28
A Full Shooting Schedule

"My dear Eun-Hee," the August 1984 letter began, "You must be well and healthy no matter what. Let's have a wonderful ending to our lives together. . . ." Shin's characters were scribbled and rushed, in black ink on coarse brown paper. The letter had been sent from Pyongyang to Choi Eun-Hee's hospital room in Budapest. Lying in bed, recovering from surgery, Choi smiled.

She and Shin had become full partners in the North Korean incarnation of Shin Film, so that now, for instance, three months before the London fiasco, Shin was finishing a film in Pyongyang while she had already begun preparations on their next picture. Suddenly, however, Choi was struck by a painful attack of gallstones. *Juche* was well and good, but Kim Jong-Il did not trust his star actress to Pyongyang hospitals, so he had arranged to have Choi flown to Hungary for an operation. Shin rarely wrote letters, and this one, even though it was short and quickly moved on from inquiries about Choi's health to discuss the films currently being produced, made Choi's heart warm with joy.

The next day Choi left the hospital and was moved to her hotel room, to rest a few days before being brought back to North Korea. It was here that Shin found her. Missing her terribly, he had jumped on a plane from Pyongyang at the first opportunity. She looked "very pale," Shin remembered, and "upon seeing me she rejoiced as if she were seeing Christ himself." Shortly after he arrived, Choi looked at him and said, shyly, "Darling, why don't we celebrate our wedding here? We've been husband and wife for thirty years, but we have only ever registered our marriage—we never did have a proper wedding ceremony."

She was right, they hadn't. Kim Jong-Il's announcement that they were remarrying had not been followed up: in North Korea, the Dear Leader's announcement was law, no ceremony needed.

Shin looked at his wife and smiled. "Darling, let's do it. That sounds good." He kissed her.

In Eastern Europe their North Korean guards occasionally relaxed their watch, so that Shin and Choi were even allowed to go out by themselves from time to time. After all, where could they escape to? Their passports were withheld and they were still on Communist ground. So the couple told their watchers that they were going out to shop for a couple of hours and went into town, past the old Turkish baths and the Magyar palaces, and bought two simple wedding bands. The next morning, August 26, they slipped out of their room before their minders had woken up, jumped in a taxi, and asked to be taken to church. The streets were dark and quiet, the air cool before dawn, the summer heat still at bay. The taxi driver took them up a hill of old crooked streets to the Matyas Templom, one of Budapest's large, gothic Roman Catholic churches, in the Castle District by the river. The sun was just rising over the Danube, pink light twinkling on the water and spouting in shafts between the medieval houses. The last of the Hapsburg kings, Charles IV of Hungary, had been crowned here in 1916.

As Shin and Choi got out of the taxi, the bells at the top of the cathedral's stone tower struck six. They passed through the huge arched doorway and found a small gathering already lined up at the pews and the morning service just beginning. They stood in the back during the mass, the first Choi had ever attended, the first chance she had had since Catherine Hong had baptized her in fallen leaves two years before. They listened to the priest, to the prayers and sermons in the beautiful, unusual language. Finally, many minutes later during communion, they joined the line and walked up to the old father and asked him, in broken English, to pray for them. He nodded and offered them a prayer in a soft voice before moving his hand over them in blessing. Without saying anything more Shin took out the rings.

He put a ring on his wife's finger and she one on his, their eyes locked. With that done, their wedding ceremony, thirty years after the fact, was accomplished. They walked back down the nave, out into the early-morning sunlight, and down the cathedral's front steps, their hands together. Later, packing in the hotel room, Choi's eyes lingered on her husband's letter.

"Let's have a wonderful ending to our lives together . . ."

They returned to Pyongyang, and to thoughts of escape.

Their interactions with the Dear Leader now took place mostly over the phone, in purposeful, irregular conversations always initiated by Jong-Il, who called the hotline reserved for him at either the villa or their office. One of them, which Shin tape-recorded in the summer of 1984, went as follows:

"Hello," Shin said as he picked up.

"I'm so sorry," Jong-Il said, without explanation.

"It's me," Shin answered. "Thank you for calling me."

"That's all right. Visiting socialist countries is obviously easy for us. But capitalist or neutral countries . . . those are the countries we have to think of going to visit. If you only visit socialist countries it will look like your travel is being controlled. We don't want to give that impression. You should be ready to introduce your name to Europe. There is a South Korean security police presence in those countries, but we'll be fine if we move you around in a group. You can go anywhere you want—if the South Korean guys see that, it'll hurt them, to see you enjoying true freedom."

"Yes, that's a good idea," Shin said hopefully.

"Yes, it is," Kim said. "Interviews with Western journalists aren't enough, also. We can be more aggressive. You and Choi are setting up your film studio and you've settled down. Even if you have a different plan for life than mine, you might still enjoy the life here. Oh, by the way, Yun I-Sang [the expatriate South Korean pianist, whom Kim had tried, unsuccessfully, to kidnap] is here again," Kim lied. "Would you be interested in meeting him?"

"Yes, please."

"You two can meet then. You might have to tell him the same thing, that you are very happy in North Korea and so on."

"Yes, I know. I'm aware that a lot of people are as naïve as I used to be," Shin said, playing the transformed man.

Kim laughed. "So, you might say to Yun that you belong in the country, and that we might go to West Germany, say, to work on films if needed—of course, this is something we'll need to sort legally on this end."

"Yes, you're right. It will make sense because my nationality is here," Shin said. "I'm so impressed with you, and I adore you."

"Good, good," Kim said, and hung up.

In 1984, acknowledging that the North Korean economy could no longer drive itself forward, Kim Jong-Il relaxed investment rules slightly and passed a new Joint Venture Law that encouraged select companies to seek financing and coproduction from abroad. The law had failed to attract any investors other than ethnic Koreans living in Japan, who were lobbied by the Chosen Soren, but Jong-Il was convinced films, especially those made by Shin, would become a commodity he could export and profit from. Such commodities were rare in the DPRK, which could offer for export only some minerals, mainly zinc and coal, and in later years nuclear weapons. Shin Sang-Ok and Choi Eun-Hee's first trip to set up a European base in Vienna was approved by Kim in July 1984.

To Kim Jong-Il, the trip to Vienna was the next step in gaining prestige for North Korea. To Shin and Choi, Vienna was the perfect escape route—if only they could both make it there. In the case of that first journey, Choi would not be allowed to travel farther than Budapest, leaving Shin to go on to Vienna alone. If he did escape, he would be leaving her behind. (The same rule had long applied to North Koreans who traveled abroad on government business: they were required to have a family, so that if they defected, they left behind a wife and kids as hostages.)

In Vienna, "three or four" North Korean staff were with Shin every waking hour. They took the room next to his at the Intercontinental Hotel and confiscated his passport, as always, once he had cleared immigration. His first day in Vienna, Shin set up a bank account—ironically, at the Bank of America—for Kim Jong-Il to deposit funds into; they had agreed that once Shin managed to open the office, his $3 million yearly budget would be kept in Vienna. Shin opened the account in the name of Shin Film, using the registered address of one of the employees of the North Korean embassy, with a first deposit of $10,000 in cash. When the teller asked him whether more than one signature would be requested on the account, Shin shook his head and dashed off only his name on the application. He would be the sole person authorized to make payments and withdrawals without any outside countersignature.

That done, Shin went looking for an office to rent, the bodyguards with him every step of the way. After ten days he returned to Budapest, and from there he and Choi traveled to Pyongyang. They continued to do everything they could to gain Kim's trust. When an interview with Shin denying any abduction and confirming his free life in Eastern Europe was published in a Japanese magazine, Shin immediately sent Kim a copy and received a happy phone call in return, authorizing even more trips to Western countries.

Shin and Choi's relationship with their jailer was a peculiar one. Over the years Jong-Il had developed a reputation as a warm, caring studio head, at least to those workers who were loyal to him. The stories of his time at the studio, from official sources and defectors, paint a man who treated his workers kindly and generously, although he could also be unpredictable, moody, and impatient. Jong-Il often turned up on set, sitting with the production units "without ceremony" and asking them about their personal and professional lives, sometimes promising to clear away a problem they might have, like a mafia don in a Francis Ford Coppola movie. Sometimes he stayed on set the whole day. This happened less frequently on Shin's sets, perhaps because Kim didn't want his new protégé to chafe under an ever-watchful eye.

When it came to the filmmaking process, Shin said, there were "fewer restrictions than is commonly believed" in terms of what he was or wasn't allowed to film. But every film was developed in story conferences with Jong-Il, who insisted the film's "seed" had to be suitable "from the point of view of ideological education." They met in person only for these conferences and at parties, which Shin disliked and which he and his wife now avoided if they could. For the day-to-day running of affairs, Choe Ik-Gyu, whom both Shin and Choi deeply disliked, was their liaison to the Dear Leader, passing on any messages and requests.

Unexpectedly, while Choi had spent more time with Jong-Il, it was Shin who had the better rapport with the Dear Leader. Shin found himself having "mixed feelings," he admitted, for the man who had taken away his freedom and sent him to prison, only to gift him with more filmmaking and creative freedom than he had ever had. Shin had come to respect Kim's taste in and keen understanding of movies even if, he realized, the Dear Leader had trouble differentiating fact from fiction, and often talked of James Bond or Rambo films as if they were "social realist docudramas." Shin tried to dispel this notion while remaining careful not to make the young man feel disrespected or talked down to. On the whole, at least when it came to cinema, "he was like any ordinary young man. He liked action movies, sex movies, horror movies. He liked all the women that most men like."

The Dear Leader had a sense of humor and was the funniest North Korean they met; "half the time our phone conversations with Kim were taken up with jokes," Shin said. He was, overall, honest: "when [Jong-Il] made promises, he kept them," Shin said, and claimed Kim spoke to him openly on many topics, including the manufactured aspect of the "idolatry of the leaders" he was imposing on his people. "Many times Kim expressed his concerns about his country to me" with a candor he could not permit himself publicly, Shin said. He was nothing like the "madman" he would soon be portrayed as in the press, Shin insisted, even though he was clearly sociopathic—rather, he was "a meticulous planner who executes his projects with iron determination." And in the end, Shin concluded, "the revolution justifies everything. The end justifies the means."

Even Choi reluctantly found the young man charismatic and decisive. "He pays attention to everything, he keeps track of everything. . . . He is simply amazing," she said at the time. But "he thought he could do anything he wanted." He had a habit of trying to keep the people around him on their toes, alternately praising them and putting them down so that they never knew what would come next. Sometimes he treated Choi like a respected elder, like a mother or grandmother; other times he was scathing and disdainful. Some days he flattered and praised her, while on other occasions he would criticize her clothes in front of associates. At some of the parties, he would start gossiping about South Korean film and television stars, including loudly talking about Shin's alleged affairs, while Choi sat right next to him.

Whenever Jong-Il tried hardest to seem powerful and effortless was when he came off looking like a child. So many of his emotions seemed fake and calculated—the way he took your hand at just the right time, or cried at old Soviet folk songs—but then there were the all-too-frequent bursts of wild jealousy or anger, which could cost you your job or your life. Shin and Choi had both met men like Kim Jong-Il, on a smaller scale: talented but not quite talented enough, powerful, jealous, insecure, and boastful; with an overinflated sense of their own importance in the world, a short temper, and an obsessive need to micromanage. Kim was, they thought, the archetypal film producer.

After being released from prison, Choi said, Shin "worked like a madman." Among the North Korean elite, where laziness and inefficiency were condoned by a collective system that encouraged shifting blame and everyone received his minimum rations regardless of the quality of his work, the only person who was working harder seemed to be Kim Jong-Il, who was up at all hours, whether working on a film or planning a terrorist attack.

Shin's work ethic was famous among North Korean crews. In behind-the-scenes stills the fifty-eight-year-old man can be seen lying flat in the mud, operating a handheld camera himself, or standing in the center of large crews, ordering them around like a general. In the span of three short years, Shin and Choi directed seven movies and produced countless others, all of them bolder and better than every North Korean film that had come before them. The couple took real pride in their films. They were pushing boundaries not just for the sake of artistic experiment, but to give real pleasure and enlightenment to their audiences. They both later spoke, repeatedly, of their hope that the films were bringing some joy to the dark lives they saw around them. "In North Korea the social impact of movies was huge," Shin said. "I don't think I could have made films [just] for Kim's family . . . [so] when I made films, what I was thinking of the most was the North Korean people who would enjoy my films." It hadn't taken long for him to "hate" communism, which he felt made "dead values" of love and family. "It was wretched lunacy," he said of the ideology he saw at work every day.

Of the seven films they ultimately made, only the first two—*Emissary of No Return* and its follow-up, *Runaway*—were nationalistic dramas in the usual propagandistic mold. In 1985 and 1986 they made a lighthearted romantic melodrama, *Love, Love, My Love;* a social-realist tragedy, *Salt;* an extravagant musical reminiscent of Busby Berkeley, with fantasy creatures, expensive costumes, and underwater scenes, *The Tale of Shim Chong;* and North Korea's first martial arts action film, *Hong Kil-Dong*. Every one of the pictures broke with tradition. *Love, Love, My Love* was the first time romance had been portrayed on a North Korean screen, the regime having previously allowed for the concept of "love" only insofar as it related to the Party; indeed, the movie featured the first use of the word *love* in a North Korean film title as well as the first on-screen kiss in the country's history. And *Salt* was full of sex and eroticism, including a shot of Choi breastfeeding, her bosom in full view, but also a violent and harrowing rape scene more graphic than anything Kim Il-Sung had ever allowed a filmmaker to get away with (in this case, the Supreme Leader personally sent word to praise Shin for his "commitment to realism").

Isolation and the state's focus on film had already turned North Korea into a nation of cinephiles. Admission prices were deliberately kept low—the same price as a soda or candy bar—so that the average North Korean visited the cinema roughly twenty times a year, ten times more often than the average South Korean. The crowds were highly engaged and active, loud and rowdy. They oohed and aahed at the screen, cheered good guys and heckled the baddies. But Shin's North Korean films changed everything. Now the audiences saw every movie not because film was a novelty, or because it was part of their ideological education, but because they *loved* them.

Hyok Kang, who grew up in North Korea in the 1980s, remembered that in his hometown of Onsong, near the Chinese border, "when a new film came out . . . the whole city flocked to see them. An unbelievable crowd . . . People fought to sit down on the wooden seats." *Love, Love, My Love,* in which Shin marshaled the precision and choreography of the Mass Games for the purpose of gigantic song-and-dance musical numbers, was so popular that for the first time ticket scalpers appeared on Pyongyang's sidewalks, reselling admission stubs taken from the local Party office. Several defectors remember seeing the movie seven, eight, in one case twenty times. The end-credits song is one of the most famous tunes in North Korean history. Students put pictures of the film's leading man up in their rooms—the first time the picture of an ordinary North Korean other than Kim Il-Sung or Kim Jong-Il appeared on residence walls, albeit unframed and on a separate wall, hidden away—and went home to fantasize not about the revolution but about him, the first North Korean leading man to be allowed sex appeal and tenderness. Citizens with neutral or hostile *songbuns* lobbied for jobs in the movie theaters, where they would be able to watch Shin Film works over and over again.

Choi Eun-Hee, who starred in *Salt* and took supporting roles in *Runaway* and *Shim Chong,* was a household name again, known throughout North Korea. She and Shin were the most famous people in the Workers' Paradise—excepting Kim Il-Sung and Kim Jong-Il, of course. (They finally met with the Supreme Leader at one of his New Year's Day lunches, exchanging handshakes and small talk with him for several minutes, the pinnacle of achievement for a North Korean.) Every outdoor shoot was mobbed by hundreds of people eager to see the famous filmmaker and his actress wife at work. Laborers stood by as scenes were shot near construction sites. "Almost everyone knew our names," Shin remembered. "When we were out shooting our films, children often followed us, shouting *Shin Sang-Ok! Choi Eun-Hee!*"

Shin's films, in the words of one North Korean defector, clearly hinted at "different things" than Kim Jong-Il had so far allowed: sex, sensuality, action, *fun*. Shin's fantasies suggested to ordinary North Koreans the possibility of life, of encountering something unexpected, in contrast to their real lives, which were so bland, codified, and controlled. "The most attractive thing for audiences," one woman said, "was that [Shin Sang-Ok's films were] a bit erotic." Another woman agreed, adding that the most popular films were those with "kiss scenes." Shin and Choi had been famous in the South for their strong female characters and their stories of women fighting the limitations of a patriarchal society; now they would break women free from their typecasting in North Korean cinema as mothers, wives, and fighting comrades, and allow them, finally, to be *in love.*

Some of the changes were subtle. *Love, Love*'s leading lady, Jang Son-Hui, had sharp, almost Western features that went directly against Kim Jong-Il's ideals of beauty, which usually determined the choice of star; and in *Salt* Choi spoke in a northern regional dialect, rather than the "national" accent the Workers' Party insisted upon. Other changes were much bigger, such as the beginning of *Runaway,* which opens with a quote from *Les Miserables* ("So long as ignorance and misery remain on Earth, books like this cannot be useless . . ."), by Victor Hugo (a foreigner, no less), rather than the usual epigraph by the Supreme Leader; or the ending of *Hong Kil-Dong,* in which the hero turns his back on his native land and chooses exile over struggling for the collective dream.

Kim Jong-Il admired Shin's work and could not deny him things that he knew were necessary to make better films, even if this required bending his own all-important rules. Above all the Dear Leader wanted success, and he had it—but it backfired. One woman who later defected said that until 1984, "we just watched our films and documentaries and accepted them the way they were. We thought that's how movies are. But after the Shin Sang-Ok era, we had new eyes. We could judge which movies are interesting and which are not." A former student agreed: "Before the Shin Sang-Ok era, the movie plots were really transparent and simple. Even if we only saw the first half of a movie, we already knew the whole story. The plots were always the same. The main character went through many hardships and was always saved at the end through Kim Il-Sung's love. Shin Sang-Ok brought a more realistic approach to cinema. . . . The traditional films were so boring—we wanted to see Shin's films." This was more than mere filmgoing excitement. Up until then, the student said, "we had been taught that the whole world consisted of our regime and our country. We couldn't think outside of that." But then *Runaway* was released and it showcased not only footage of Paris and Tokyo, but also a soundtrack of ABBA covers. Suddenly young North Koreans were humming ABBA tunes on their way to work or school and standing in the fields to re-create the dance moves they had seen on-screen. Among the elite the youth threw private (officially illegal) parties to play ABBA records imported through the Chosen Soren. And quietly everyone whispered about the foreign cities they had just seen: their bars, restaurants, and nightlife; the cars; and the white people with their variety of clothes and hairstyles. Compared to that, they thought, Pyongyang was most certainly not "the perfect, the best, the ideal city."

There is an old Asian saying that "drop by drop, the water perforates the stone." Kim Jong-Il had kidnapped Shin Sang-Ok and Choi Eun-Hee to help promote his regime and tighten his control on his people's thoughts. Instead, Shin and Choi's movies were drops of water, each one slowly but surely wearing away the Kims' supremacy.

Working for Kim, Choi Eun-Hee later said, was "luxury filmmaking." Nothing was refused them. When they needed a fan to simulate wind, Jong-Il sent them a helicopter. When they requested fake snow in the middle of spring, Jong-Il flew the entire crew to the top of Mount Paekdu, the only place in the country where snow still lingered. When they planned a scene with thousands of extras, Jong-Il put at their service the entire military. And, in what he later called the high point of his directing career, when Shin needed special-effects scale models to achieve a shot of an exploding train for the climax of *Runaway,* he asked, tongue-in-cheek, whether Kim wouldn't just give him instead a real train to blow up. To his surprise, an actual, functioning train was delivered to the set, loaded to the brim with explosives. Shin had only one take to get it right, but that was a lovely problem to have. *Runaway*'s final train explosion became one of North Korean cinema's iconic images.

Salt received rave reviews internationally—another first, as critics tended to disparage North Korean films, even Shin's—and Choi won the Best

Actress award at the Moscow Film Festival, the most prestigious prize ever received for a North Korean film and the second international award of the Shin era. Choi's performance was unprecedented in North Korean cinema history for its naturalism and nuance. (Choi was permitted to go to Moscow to accept the award, and after the ceremony she and Shin sat in their hotel room taking pictures with the small trophy: they knew they might never win another, and that this one, as soon as they touched the tarmac back in Pyongyang, would be taken to Kim Jong-Il and forever remain his.) *Hong Kil-Dong* was a huge box-office hit in the Eastern Bloc, becoming one of 1986's top-grossing films in Bulgaria and the Soviet Union. These were relatively humble achievements, but still unprecedented in the history of North Korean film, as well as heights it would never scale again.

With every success, Shin and Choi's travel restrictions were eased slightly. They were frequently in Budapest and Moscow, giving interviews and taking meetings, in the hope that these short trips would convince the world they resided in Eastern Europe of their free will; and now Kim Jong-Il allowed them to travel as far as West Germany, where they filmed the underwater scenes of *The Tale of Shim Chong* at the Bavaria Film Studios in Munich. Alfred Hitchcock had shot his first film there, and in recent years the soundstages had played host to *The Great Escape, Cabaret,* and *Willy Wonka and the Chocolate Factory*. Now Shin and Choi walked this hallowed ground, albeit shadowed nonstop by seven bodyguards, who hovered over them on every set, at every production meeting, at every lunch. Unlike the previous minders—usually film workers—these guards had been taken from Kim Jong-Il's own bodyguard corps.

Jong-Il's elite team of bodyguards was one of the most sinister, intriguing aspects of his way of life. He kept 120 of them and preferred them to be orphans; once hired they were not permitted to visit home or to ever leave the Leader's side. If they wanted to marry, they were only allowed to marry a typist or secretary from a specific unit of the Party, and the matchmaking procedure itself was bizarre. A bodyguard had to apply to his supervisor for marriage, and if the application was approved—likely this decision was Jong-Il's—the bodyguard would be called to his supervisor's office on the Third Floor. Twenty photographs were placed on the supervisor's desk, facedown. Blindly the bodyguard would pick a picture, which the supervisor would then flip over. The woman in the photograph would be the man's wife. If the bodyguard refused to marry the stranger, he would have to wait another two years before being able to reapply—and this time he would have to marry the girl whose photograph he had blindly drawn, whether he liked the look of her or not, at risk of being dismissed. Once married, the guard and his bride were provided with a house, paid for by the Party; the wife would be installed there, and the guard would be permitted to visit her once a week.

The bodyguards were trained at a special college outside Pyongyang where the curriculum taught them how to blindly put their lives on the line for Kim Jong-Il, and how to most ruthlessly eliminate any potential threat. Jong-Il preferred them polite and quiet. In later years he took to showing new recruits the Clint Eastwood action picture *In the Line of Fire,* about a Secret Service agent who is haunted by his failure to save President Kennedy and determined to save a new president from the threats of a maniac, as a how-to video of what he expected of them.

Once selected, the guards were erased from the files the Party kept on every citizen. "The security personnel do not show up on any record, have no identification number or card," wrote former member Lee Young-Kuk. "It is as if they do not exist."

These were the men who, from 1985 on, guarded the couple on their every trip to Europe. They stood outside bathroom doors when Shin or Choi went to relieve themselves and took turns sitting at a desk in their hotel suite when they slept at night. They were highly trained and blindly devoted.

Still, the couple felt increasingly certain that filmmaking would be their way out. They worked so hard that they barely paid attention to their failing health. Between 1983 and 1986 Choi was in and out of hospital with gallstones, infections, and an influenza she could not shake off. Shin was also often exhausted and found himself dropping cameras during takes, unable to support their weight. They were both entering their sixties now and had been through far too much. They had not seen their children, families, or friends since 1978. They lived in opulent captivity, in a large villa compound with staff and chauffeur-driven cars, all the while shamefully aware of the poverty and suffering of the ordinary people around them. And they were worn down by absurd rules and regulations. In 1984, for instance, there had been, in quick succession, a "necktie instruction" and a "hat instruction" from Kim Il-Sung, mandating that all Party officials now had to wear ties and hats at all times; Mr. Kang turned up to work one day suddenly sporting a ridiculous bow tie and a porkpie hat.

Unable to forget his two failed escape attempts, Shin was adamant that he would only try again when he felt certain of their chances. But would that moment ever arrive? More to the point, would it happen while Choi and he were together, with enough strength to follow through?

The six movies he had made so far had been great successes. But he needed something more—he needed a film Jong-Il would deem good enough to pitch to Western Europeans, the Japanese, even Americans. He needed something *sensational.*

29
The Rubber Monster

That something sensational was *Pulgasari.*

By far the most famous film that Shin Sang-Ok made in North Korea, *Pulgasari: The Iron-Eater* was so representative of the absurdities and contradictions of North Korean cinema, of Shin himself, and of Kim Jong-Il, that it has become one of those so-bad-it's-good cult movies, alongside Ed Wood's *Plan 9 from Outer Space,* Nicholas Webster's *Santa Claus Conquers the Martians,* and Tommy Wiseau's *The Room.* The most ambitious blockbuster a national film industry had ever attempted, it's the sort of terrible classic that is given midnight retrospectives in underground and art-house cinemas around the world.

Until *Pulgasari,* Shin had been a good, sometimes great, filmmaker. He had made his share of drivel in South Korea, but those had been exploitation pictures shot in a couple of weeks with very little effort and released off-the-cuff to make a quick buck. *Pulgasari* marked a turn in Shin's career: the first time he had put all his energy into a picture and created a stinker. It was a sudden, inexplicable transformation, after which Shin never recovered his magic touch.

A glorious failure was never how Kim Jong-Il and Shin Sang-Ok saw it. *Pulgasari* was, upon first release, their greatest success. Shin never said exactly whose idea the film was, but it isn't hard to guess. Shin's cinematic heroes were Chaplin, Renoir, and Rossellini. His producer's touchstones were Bond, Rambo, and Jason Voorhees. And it was Kim Jong-Il who had made a habit not of leading, but of following: of copying foreign successes he had just seen and enjoyed. *Nation and Destiny* was an answer to a long-running film series in Japan, *Unknown Heroes* a rip-off of German and Czech spy thrillers, *The Flower Girl* an extension of classic Chinese melodrama. Now he was ready to copy another one of his favorite franchises, this one also from Japan.

Godzilla had first appeared in the 1954 monster film of the same name and had quickly become an international phenomenon, in Japan because it touched a nerve about the nation's World War II defeat and the destructive heritage of the atom bomb, and in the rest of the world as one of the great cheesy bad movies. Between 1954 and 1975 the franchise spawned fifteen installments, in which Godzilla went from radioactive monster to playful, family-friendly hero; his popularity declined as the films grew more light-hearted. After a nine-year absence from screens, the monster came back in 1984's *The Return of Godzilla,* an appalling picture that failed at the box office and drew guffaws from critics (Roger Ebert wrote of the film, "My favorite moment occurs when the hero and heroine are clutching each other on a top floor of a skyscraper being torn apart by Godzilla and [a] professor leaps into the shot, says 'What has happened here?' and leaps out again without waiting for an answer"). But *The Return of Godzilla* was the first Godzilla film to be dubbed in Korean, so Jong-Il certainly saw it; and its release was accompanied by a hugely popular Godzilla festival which drew thousands of devoted followers to Tokyo to discover the film and buy truckloads of merchandise. This Jong-Il had also watched with great interest. The monster film, he decided, would be North Korean cinema's entry into the international marketplace.

Pulgasari was to be North Korea's *Godzilla*. Only instead of Godzilla's nuclear fallout paranoia, a topic close to home for the Japanese in the wake of Hiroshima and Nagasaki, *Pulgasari*'s subtext concerned class warfare, communism, and the collective good.

Pulgasari is set in a Korean province in medieval times. The farmers, oppressed by a despotic governor and his soldiers, are starving. An old blacksmith who refuses to obey the governor's orders is arrested and imprisoned in a wooden hut. Out of boredom, he carves out of mashed-up rice a small dragonlike figure with horns. Following his death in captivity, his daughter inherits the figurine. In a surreal twist, the daughter pricks her finger while sewing and a drop of blood falls onto the small dragon. The dragon, Pulgasari, is magically brought to life by the little girl's blood. Feeding on metal, as befits the creation of a blacksmith, he eats all the iron he can find, and quickly grows from a cute pet who sleeps in the little girl's bed with her to a gigantic, fearsome, invincible monster with devil's horns, a muscular chest and stomach, and big, sharp fangs—a monster, yes, but one with a social conscience. Instead of leveling everything in his path like Godzilla, Pulgasari sides with the farmers against the governor and attacks his palace. The governor's soldiers do everything they can to stop him (including firing rockets at him—thirteenth-century rockets, no less) and eventually manage to set off a rock avalanche that buries the beast. But they fail to account for the blacksmith's daughter, who cuts her arm and spills her blood all over the pile of rocks, miraculously (and inexplicably, since none of the blood actually touches Pulgasari) bringing the monster back to life. Pulgasari kills the remaining soldiers, splatters the governor underfoot, and smashes the palace to pieces. The farmers are free and virtue prevails.

But it's not over. Pulgasari's appetite is endless. He has consumed the soldiers' swords, armor, and weapons. Next he goes for the farmers' tools, their domestic pots and pans—everything made out of metal. The peasants' economy cannot sustain the creature's life. It is implied that, if the village cannot find a way to sustain him, the monster's appetite will devastate the entire world. Finally the little girl who created him hides inside a big bell and lures the monster to eat it. Pulgasari swallows the bell, with the little girl inside, but he cannot digest her and explodes into pieces, leaving behind only a tiny Pulgasari of the original size. Before this small dragon can wreak any havoc of its own, a beam of divine light shines down and destroys it. The film ends with a shot of the little girl among the rubble, a single tear trickling down her face.

The film is long, leaden, and dreadful. Pulgasari stumbles forward clumsily, like a toddler learning to walk, his face frozen in papier-mâché anger, his size changing arbitrarily based on the action portrayed at any given moment. He rips apart buildings that are clearly hollow behind their cardboard façades.

The film was shot in just under a year in 1985, the last film Shin Sang-Ok made in North Korea. Knowing, like all good film executives, that the best way to re-create a film's success is to hire the people behind it, Kim Jong-Il put aside his anti-Japanese sentiment and flew in the best Japanese technicians to work under Shin, including the special-effects crew behind the Godzilla films and Kenpachiro Satsuma, the man who had worn the Godzilla suit in *The Return of Godzilla*. According to Satsuma, he was originally told he was being hired for a big-budget Hollywood film being shot in China; but after a few days' filming on a soundstage in Beijing he and the rest of the Japanese crew, numbering seven in all, were flown to North Korea and told that was where the majority of the film would be shot. As soon as they landed in Pyongyang, Satsuma said, their passports were taken away, allegedly "for our own safety."

Satsuma was housed in a vacation villa in the same compound as Shin and Choi's; his room had a vast bathroom and ornate dangling chandeliers. When the Japanese were allowed into Pyongyang, Satsuma was shocked by its cleanliness and quiet. It felt like Tokyo Disneyland to him. Three interpreters followed them wherever they went and often stopped them from taking pictures, especially of any soldiers or military vehicles, even though the military were everywhere in the city. The film seemed to be behind schedule and everyone acted frantic and rushed. The North Koreans didn't have adequate special-effects equipment, and anytime Satsuma or Teruyoshi Nakano, the special-effects director, requested a new piece of equipment or gear, the shoot had to stop while the Party read over the request and then gave its approval. This had to be done often, because at the end of almost every day the North Korean technicians walked away with the tools, down to the nails, they had been given to work with, and returned at the start of the next day claiming they hadn't stolen them and asking for new ones. Then there were the delays caused by the endless power cuts. Satsuma remembered Kim Jong-Il visiting the set on several occasions but only speaking to the Korean crew. With the Japanese he kept an absolute distance. The

Japanese crew worked mostly in isolation anyway, rarely interacting with the Koreans themselves, which may partly explain the film's lack of coherence.

As a result, in spite of playing the film's eponymous monster, Satsuma only met his director, Shin Sang-Ok, once, and only because he bumped into him at the production office. Shin was overworked: he was working on *Hong Kil-Dong* at the same time as *Pulgasari,* his health was declining, and the stress of life in Pyongyang was weighing heavily on him. They had a short conversation in Japanese, Shin bringing up projects he hoped to make in Japan one day. Satsuma was intrigued. He had heard that Shin had been kidnapped, in which case Kim Il-Sung would surely never let him go to Japan. But he'd also heard rumors that Shin had defected to the North willingly, and he'd seen footage of him saying so in a press conference. Which was true?

"Are you planning on going back to South Korea?" Satsuma asked the Korean.

There was a pause. "It would be too complicated, politically, to go back," Shin answered, and left it at that.

Filming on *Pulgasari* wrapped on December 28, 1985, and when the film was released several months later it became Shin's greatest hit in North Korea. Crowds stampeded to the cinemas in such numbers that two separate defectors, one who had lived in Pyongyang and the other in the provinces, vividly recalled people being crushed to death in the fray. Theaters were so full that many North Koreans never managed to see the film despite several attempts.

Jong-Il, too, was thrilled with the film, which he saw as expressing the people's struggle against greed, private wealth, and oppression. The monster symbolized the Party, their collective representative, or, better still, Kim Il-Sung himself, the man who had freed a nation from oppression. But was it the correct reading? When the film, many years later, was finally shown outside North Korea, there were many who argued that Shin's intended interpretation was that the honest people were starving themselves for the benefit of Pulgasari, until finally the innocent spirit of the masses itself, in the person of the little girl, who had created the monster out of her own blood, sacrifices herself to restore freedom. To them Pulgasari still represented Kim Il-Sung: once the people's hero, now a selfish beast of destructive and unquenchable appetites, who could only be gotten rid of by spilling blood.

So was Pulgasari the most outrageous, obvious Workers' Party propaganda, as Jong-Il saw it? Or was it Shin's allegorical mutiny, cleverly disguised? Shin himself never gave a satisfactory answer. "It's a pure monster film," he said when asked. "I didn't put any ideology in it." Some observers pointed to the long history of Korean protest films, first made under the Japanese occupation, which disguised anti-Japanese propaganda behind an obvious plot. These people—scholars and academics among them—were convinced Shin's film was a sophisticated masterpiece, its imagery and subtext a serious critique of Kim Il-Sung's regime.

Whatever Shin's true intentions, *Pulgasari* defined his career and changed his life. It was the worst film he had ever made, and became without doubt the most widely famous—even better known than his 1960s South Korean masterpieces.

And, once Kim Jong-Il saw it, *Pulgasari* saved Shin Sang-Ok and Choi Eun-Hee's lives.

After Shin finished *Pulgasari,* he sent Kim Jong-Il an advance copy, along with the newly finished *Hong Kil-Dong.* Less than a week later, on New Year's Eve 1985, Choe Ik-Gyu burst into the Shin Film office. The Comrade Dear Leader, he announced with excitement, had watched the latest films and was so delighted with Shin and his staff that he wanted to reward them for their efforts. Shin followed Director Choe through the building's auditorium, outside of which three trucks loaded to the brim were pulling up. The seven hundred employees of Shin Film were summoned. Loudly, Director Choe announced, "The Comrade Dear Leader is delighted with *Pulgasari* and *Hong Kil-Dong.* He has sent these gifts in recognition of your efforts, which is a great honor." Then, as the trucks started unloading, he read off a list of the contents.

"Gift list: fifty deer, four hundred pheasants, two hundred wild geese, two hundred boxes of oranges . . ." Out of the trucks came fifty deer, freshly killed; four hundred pheasants, yet to be plucked; two hundred smoked geese; crates and crates of oranges fresh from Japan. Many of the workers cried as Choe Ik-Gyu read out his message. "The Dear Leader was very pleased that all the workers under President Shin and Vice President Choi of Shin Film have worked so hard to create such excellent movies," he said. "He instructs you to work even harder in the new year to make even more good films . . ." In true North Korean custom, the letter went on and on.

When Choe was done reading, the heads of each Shin Film division stepped forward, each in turn, to swear their loyalty to Kim Il-Sung and Kim Jong-Il, and then the whole staff sang "The Song of General Kim Il-Sung" ("So dear to all our hearts is our General's glorious name / Our own beloved Kim Il-Sung of undying fame . . .") and "The Song of General Kim Jong-Il" ("He's the artist of great joy / Glorifying the garden of *juche* / Long live, long live General Kim Jong-Il!"). Shin Film's administrator spent the entire night dividing the gifts among the staff, with top cadres taking home whole deer and boxes of oranges and those below contenting themselves with a few oranges and a bit of pheasant. The next day, January 1, Shin and Choi threw their own party for their executive staff, about forty people in all. Everyone was still reeling with happiness from the unexpected gifts. Jong-Il frequently gave gifts to his inner circle, but rarely did regular staff receive presents, since official Workers' Party rules forbade gift giving between members, claiming that it went against socialist principles. The night was filled with eating, drinking, singing, and dancing; even Shin and Choi joined in with traditional Korean songs.

The couple had reason to be happy, but they also felt a powerful melancholy. The songs they sang—"A Song of Hope," "Arirang"—were farewell songs, and this, they hoped, would be their good-bye party.

Pulgasari had convinced Kim Jong-Il that Shin Film and North Korean cinema were ready to be formally presented to polite society. It had always been his artistic dream to make internationally recognized movies, but now there was an added financial urgency: North Korea was bankrupt. It could not draw any more loans from foreign countries, including its longtime allies China and the Soviet Union. Kim's counterfeiters were struggling to keep up with his appetites. And despite the glowing reports Jong-Il sent up to his father, productivity in the country's mines, fields, and factories was tumbling. Kang Myong-Do, a member of the ruling elite who later defected, said, "The government had no bank reserves and was nearly broke. So from the mid-1980s most foreign trade had to be done on credit. Anyone who could borrow $1 million from another country was considered a North Korean hero."

The top-grossing film of 1985, *Back to the Future,* had made *$210 million* in cinemas in the United States alone. Clearly the Dear Leader didn't expect Shin Sang-Ok and Choi Eun-Hee to rival Robert Zemeckis and Michael J. Fox, but *Pulgasari* had cost only a couple of million dollars to make—the return was almost guaranteed. And Kim, who was an intuitive capitalist himself, looked to *Godzilla:* there was money to be made from the merchandise, the toys, the sequels . . .

So it was that in the weeks before New Year's Eve 1985, after talking about it and dithering for over eighteen months, Kim Jong-Il finally formally greenlit Shin's plan to establish a full-time office in Vienna, which would produce North Korean films and export them around the world. The first stage of Shin's mission, Kim told him, was to find an Austrian coproducer interested in a 50 percent stake in the company, as well as funding for Shin Film Vienna's first motion picture: *Genghis Khan.*

Shin had always dreamed of making a film about the great Mongol conqueror, who in the thirteenth century had built the largest contiguous empire in history. He was surprised to find out that Kim Jong-Il had had the same ambition, and for almost as long as he had. The two of them bonded over their frustration at Khan's cinematic portrayals. The Mongol's life had been depicted on cinema screens five different times by then, but Khan had never been played by an East Asian actor. His most famous portrayals had been by Omar Sharif, an Egyptian, in 1965; and a decade before that by John Wayne, in billionaire producer Howard Hughes's CinemaScope Hollywood epic *The Conqueror* (tagline: "I fight! I love! I conquer! . . .

like a barbarian!"). The Hughes film used Navajo Indians for its Mongols, was a humiliating flop, and contributed to the bankruptcy of its studio, the legendary RKO. Shot in Utah in high summer, just a year after extensive aboveground nuclear weapons testing had been carried out at a site 130 miles upwind, *The Conqueror* also quite possibly contributed to the deaths by cancer of 50 of its 220 cast and crew members, including director Dick Powell (blood cancer, died 1963) and all three of its stars: Agnes Moorehead (uterine cancer, 1974), Susan Hayward (brain cancer, 1975), and John Wayne (stomach cancer, 1979). Howard Hughes never produced another picture.

Shin Sang-Ok and Kim Jong-Il had both seen the John Wayne film, even if they might not have heard of the controversy that surrounded it, and they agreed that the Mongol emperor, one of the most iconic figures in Asian history, deserved better treatment. And of course, Jong-Il said, Khan's life story lent itself particularly well to ideological treatment: Was he not, after all, the founder of a great empire, who had united the Asian people behind him?

The *Genghis Khan* envisioned by director Shin and producer Kim would be expensive. Shin estimated the budget at $16 million, by far the costliest North Korean film ever made. (By way of comparison, the first *Star Wars* picture, in 1977, had cost $11 million.) A plan was agreed upon: under Shin Film Vienna's Austrian license, Shin would seek coproduction funds to make the blockbuster, which would be a landmark in North Korean film history. It would require a PR offensive. *Pulgasari,* the studio's upcoming monster epic, would certainly help to impress Westerners, but Shin Sang-Ok and Choi Eun-Hee would be required to do the rest. For the first time, Shin and Choi were approved to travel together to the other side of the Iron Curtain, to Vienna via Germany. Kim Jong-Il, it seemed, fully believed Shin and Madame Choi had been successfully indoctrinated, and also showed how little he understood capitalism. "He trusted us one hundred percent," Shin said, because he thought the price of their loyalty had been met. "He thought with the house, the money, and the studio, that there would be no reason to escape. That is the weak point of growing up in a socialist country: it is easy to fool oneself."

This was the moment they had been waiting for and working toward for eight years: an opportunity to escape. Failure would mean either prison, with no chance of release, or death.

30
Vienna

Shin and Choi spent the first months of 1986 preparing for their escape attempt. As they thought about finally leaving North Korea, they realized how much of a life they had unwittingly built in Pyongyang and how much they cared about some of the people they had come to know. They gave their staff final instructions—"things we wanted them to know as movie people"—finished their films, and, so as not to invite suspicion, continued to oversee the construction of the new house and studio that Kim Jong-Il had given them. As the days passed Choi found herself tearing up and choking on her words at unexpected times, often when, in the middle of speaking to an actor or wardrobe mistress, it dawned on her that it might be the last time she would ever exchange words with that person. In particular, she was saddened at the thought of parting from Ho Hak-Sun, the kind woman who had shared her home for over eight years. Ho had done everything she could to console Choi in the early years, and had celebrated Shin's return into Choi's life. Choi thought of her as a sister, the only person in North Korea other than Catherine Hong with whom she had felt such a bond. And yet she could not show the gratitude she felt or her sorrow at leaving her behind.

On January 29, 1986, at exactly 9:10 a.m., Choi and Shin left their villa in Pyongyang. They had packed only what they needed for a six-week journey abroad. They would, officially, be attending the Berlin Film Festival and from there going directly to Vienna to set up the Shin Film Europe branch. They made sure to leave their rooms looking as if they would return.

They walked out of the villa, the driver carrying their bags to the car trunk. As they got in the Mercedes, Ho Hak-Sun waved good-bye.

"Have a nice trip," she said.

"Stay healthy," Choi replied, hoping this was good-bye but unable to say so. She felt especially conflicted because she knew that if their escape was successful, Hak-Sun, along with everyone else who had been put in charge of their supervision, would be punished: demoted, sent to the countryside or to a prison camp, maybe even tortured or put to death. Choi had never met a person so devoted to Kim Il-Sung's cause as Hak-Sun, but her devotion would mean nothing to the men she worshipped. The kindhearted, hardworking woman had come so close to her humble dreams—a Kim Il-Sung watch, full retirement rations—but she would now lose them because of her, Choi Eun-Hee, who had lived in luxury and sported a Kim Il-Sung watch on her wrist. Choi could scarcely bear the guilt. Shin, who knew Choe Ik-Gyu would also suffer if they managed to escape, had a calmer conscience. He had never liked the arrogant, narrow-minded bulldog. "If we were gone, Choe would be in trouble," Shin wrote several years later. "It could not be helped." The ink almost shrugs on the page.

Their plane took off at ten. "The Song of General Kim Il-Sung" drifted from the cabin loudspeakers as the aircraft gained altitude.

Bright traces of blood on the crags of Jangbaek still gleam,
Still the Amnok carries along signs of blood in its stream.
Still do those hallowed traces shine resplendently
Over Korea, ever flourishing and free.
So dear to all our hearts is our General's glorious name!
Our own beloved Kim Il-Sung of undying fame!

Shin looked out the window as the plane banked stiffly on its side, groaning, and pointed northwest. Down below, the North Korean plains were dry and dark brown, the color of burned bread. Somewhere down there were the villas in which they'd been held captive, the prisons where Shin had suffered and gone cold and hungry. Off the shore in the distance, the Korea Bay sparkled blue in the spring sunshine.

Who is the partisan whose deeds are unsurpassed?
Who is the patriot whose fame shall ever last?
He severed the chains of the masses, brought them to liberty,
The Sun of Korea, democratic and free.
So dear to all our hearts is our General's glorious name!
Our own beloved Kim Il-Sung of undying fame!

Shin took a deep breath and squeezed Choi's hand.

For the next two months every passing day took its toll on their nerves. In Budapest Shin met with the Hungarian National Film Studios, where the film would be partly shot, to finalize the budget for *Genghis Khan,* and he met with an Austrian producer, Helmut Pandler, interested in investing in Shin Film's Viennese arm. When February 16 rolled around, he and Choi made sure to write and send "home" a letter wishing Kim Jong-Il a very happy birthday. The same day, they flew to Berlin for the film festival, where Shin took meetings to try and license *Pulgasari* to Western distributors.

West Berlin was where everything changed. Their dozen bodyguards became "very tense, from the time we crossed the checkpoint from East to West Berlin," and instead of having their own hotel room, Shin and Choi were assigned a room in a suite shared with their watchdogs, who, as on their previous visit to Berlin, shadowed them at every turn and watched them sleep. They had no privacy. What if they never had a second alone in Vienna either?

Anxiously they returned to Budapest, for more work on a film they never planned to make, and finally, on March 12, Shin and Choi were driven to Vienna. They had to go by car, inefficiently, because their minders had no visas to Austria, and visas were not required at the land border for passage from Hungary. It was Shin and Choi's first stroke of good luck. Along the way it had been decided that a group of fourteen would draw unwelcome attention at the road check, so only three of the North Korean bodyguards would accompany them.

Shin and Choi's second break came at the hotel check-in.

Opened in 1964, the Intercontinental Hotel Wien was one of Europe's largest and most prestigious hotels. Overlooking the Stadtpark, the city's major public park—home to the Kursalon, where Johann Strauss gave his first concert, in 1868—it was Vienna's first, and for eleven years only, international hotel.

On Wednesday, March 12, 1986, Shin Sang-Ok, Choi Eun-Hee, and three North Korean bodyguards walked into the Intercontinental's grandiose, old-world lobby. Husband and wife were anxious as they filled out the registry form and handed over their passports to reception to be copied and held overnight, as required by Austrian law, but they tried hard not to show it. When they learned that the North Koreans hadn't booked a suite in advance, and that there were no connecting rooms available, the couple fought back expressions of excitement. Unlike in Berlin, Shin and Choi would not be sharing with their guards.

It was a promising and particularly fitting development, considering their surroundings. The Intercontinental, the most luxurious hotel in a city that had become a crossroads between East and West, was well known for housing defectors. As the hotel of choice for diplomats and foreign dignitaries from both sides of the Iron Curtain, it witnessed defections regularly. "To say it was routine would be an exaggeration," said former general manager John Edmaier, "but at least once, twice a month." Someone would run into the hotel, often through the back doors, and tell an employee that they needed help; hotel staff would put them in a room; and then, Edmaier said, "we would call the [American] embassy, and embassy men would come and take them away." Sometimes a defection was more dramatic. A few months before Shin and Choi's visit, a group of Czech "tourists" had stayed at the hotel, and on the day of departure one of them had dashed off the bus, crisscrossed through the Stadtpark to lose pursuers, then cut back and burst through the hotel's kitchen doors, screaming for help.

Shin and Choi signed in, thanked the receptionist for their key, and, shadowed by their guards, walked to the elevators, determined to carry out their own desperate, unpredictable plan.

Vienna had been carpet-bombed in the last few months of World War II. During peace talks, the ruined city was divided, like Berlin to the north, into four occupation zones ruled over by the various Allied forces: the USA, the Soviet Union, France, and the United Kingdom, with the city center jointly patrolled by all four. In 1955 Austria, accepted by all not as a guilty party in the world war but as Hitler's "first victim," was given its independence, under one condition, insisted upon by Moscow: that Austria commit to remaining permanently neutral, a buffer between East and West.

And so it did. But as a result, the country—and its capital, Vienna, in particular—became a hotbed of spy craft, secret trading, and double-dealing. There were more intelligence agents in Vienna during the Cold War than in any other capital in the world. The CIA and the KGB competed fiercely for knowledge from informers. The pockets of the great powers were so full in the 1950s, and those of the Austrian people so empty, that within a few months every cook, dishwasher, valet, taxi driver, cabaret dancer, and room service waiter in the city was eligible to be recruited by one of the espionage agencies. Then came the Eastern European refugees, desperate for passage to the West. They filled every hotel room and occupied every small private room to rent. And they, too, sold everything they knew: if possible for a visa, but more often than not for little more than a bite of food or a bottle of cheap alcohol. The great city was crawling with sleeper agents and turncoats. By the fountains of the Maria-Theresien Platz, in the shadows by the Staatsoperhaus, and in the quiet of the Karlskirche, hundreds of people blackmailed, betrayed, and sabotaged one another daily.

Shin and Choi were about to join the ranks of those vying for their freedom. Over the previous three years Shin and Choi had laid the groundwork for their eventual escape attempt: gaining Kim Jong-Il's trust, lulling their watchdogs' attention, and occasionally pulling rank to ascertain exactly how much slack they would have under Kim's patronage. It was uncommon for North Koreans to challenge authority, and they tended to recoil when someone confidently exercised it. Shin and Choi were, after all, Kim Jong-Il's prized filmmaking advisers, to be given everything they asked and obeyed without question.

The Viennese part of the plan was, superficially at least, simple. Among their film meetings, Shin and Choi had scheduled a meeting with Akira Enoki, a Japanese journalist friend from the old days. An independent thinker, Enoki had risen through the ranks of Kyodo News, Japan's biggest newswire agency. He had been in tight situations before and would be quick on his feet. The lunch, Shin and Choi boasted to their bodyguards, would be another PR coup for Kim Jong-Il, an interview that would convince the capitalist world that they were living and working for Kim of their own free will. But the Japanese press was harder to convince, they said, and arriving with three North Korean guards might reinforce the theory that they had been kidnapped and were constantly surveilled. With this explanation, Shin and Choi convinced their three minders, for the first time, not to ride in the same car with them or even to sit in the same room when they were conducting the interview. The North Koreans agreed to follow in a separate car, wait for them outside the restaurant—watching every exit—and then follow them back to the hotel.

When checking in to the Intercontinental, Choi had noticed that the young receptionist was Japanese. The night preceding their decisive lunch, Shin called down to the front desk and asked for the Japanese employee to come upstairs. When the young man knocked on the door Shin quickly pulled him inside, whispered to him that he was seeking asylum in the United States, slipped a note into his hand, and pushed him back out. The note said, in English: "We are Shin Sang-Ok and Choi Eun-Hee, husband and wife. We want to take refuge in the U.S. Embassy." And below that, in Japanese:

"We are not diplomats, but we have diplomatic passports. Please report to the Austrian police that we illegally possess these diplomatic passports and have us arrested and escorted to the police station. We are staying at the Intercontinental Hotel in room 911." The English was Plan A—a forewarning to the American embassy to be expecting them. The Japanese was Plan B. Shin then called Enoki, the journalist, and, trying his best not to raise the suspicion of the minders listening in, asked him to meet them outside the hotel tomorrow at half past noon exactly, with a taxi waiting.

The next morning Shin invited their bodyguards over to their room for a friendly breakfast. The Intercontinental's rooms were small—mercifully, too small for a bodyguard to drag a desk inside and sit all night keeping watch over the sleeping couple—and they chatted and ate in cramped, artificial geniality. Then Shin had himself driven to the Bank of America, which held the Shin Film account, its current balance approximately $2.2 million, and picked up some blank international checks that could be used to make withdrawals later.

At twelve thirty Shin and Choi, their minders at a respectable distance, stepped out of the Intercontinental and found Enoki-san standing by an idling taxi. As Enoki tried to introduce himself to Choi, whom he had never met before, Shin shoved them both into the taxi, talking rapidly, his anxiety taking over. The Austrian taxi driver asked for a destination. Shin, with Enoki translating, told him to drive around the city center for a while. Their North Korean minders, suddenly realizing what was happening, dashed to the sidewalk and tried to wave down a taxi.

As quickly as he could, Shin explained the situation to Enoki, to whom he had not been able to say a thing beforehand for fear of being overheard: he told the Japanese journalist that they had been kidnapped, that they were trying to escape, that they wanted to go to the U.S. embassy and were using meeting him as an excuse. The press conferences about voluntarily defecting had been lies; they could not bear to live in North Korea a day longer. As he spoke, Choi, sitting in the front seat, looked in the rearview mirror and spotted a white taxi following them. She made out, besides the Austrian driver, three Asian faces staring and pointing behind the windshield.

"Don't look back," she said tersely. "Something isn't right."

Shin and Enoki did just that, turning and looking over their shoulders. For a while Shin was quiet. "Go around the park," he finally told the driver. Slowly they went around the quiet road lining the park. As other cars overtook them the white taxi, moving equally slowly, stayed behind them.

As Shin and Choi were racking their brains for a next move, their car pulled back onto the main road and a couple of cars slipped behind them, creating a buffer between them and the white taxi used by the North Koreans. Then, by pure luck, they were the last car to pass through the next intersection before the light turned red, leaving the white taxi behind. This was their chance. "We have to do it now," Shin pleaded. "Please help us."

Before Enoki could say anything the taxi's radio crackled and the dispatcher's voice asked the driver which way they were headed, so he could tell the other taxi in their "convoy." Enoki-san was no stranger to drama; eight years earlier, while serving as Kyodo News's bureau chief in war-torn Beirut, he had been one of two people accidentally shot in the head by the first secretary of the Japanese embassy; the other had died, but Enoki had survived. Now, without answering Shin, or indeed without translating the dispatcher's question for him, Enoki pulled a fistful of money out of his pocket and leaned over the front seat to shove it in the driver's hand. "Tell him we went the opposite direction," he told the Austrian. The driver took the money and did just that. Shin and Choi, tingling with anticipation, excitedly shouted out, "U.S. Embassy!" The driver made a sharp turn.

"[Choi]'s face was white as a sheet of paper. My heart was racing like a motor," Shin wrote a year later, "fearing we might run into the white taxi on our way to the embassy. . . . The U.S. Embassy was five minutes away. It felt like five hours."

Boltzmanngasse, the embassy's quiet side street, is one-way and often congested with cars trying to drive by or get clearance through the main gate. Parking restrictions on both sides meant traffic often ground to a standstill entering the street. Shin and Choi's taxi found itself stuck at the bottom of the hill, unable to go any farther, about fifty yards from American soil. Breathlessly Shin asked Enoki to stay and watch them until they were safe. Without saying good-bye, he pushed his door open. From the front seat Choi did the same. They ran as fast as they could, reached the embassy door at the same time, and tried to shove each other out of the way in their rush to reach safety. They burst through the doors, sprinted to the receptionist, and told him their names. Shin handed him a Shin Film card—address, Pyongyang—and tried to explain their situation in broken English. The receptionist took them to another embassy worker. Shin asked to see the consul. The young man recognized their names and escorted the two South Koreans through a metal detector where a security guard gave them a pat-down, then walked them into a small room and asked them to wait. They were served a cup of tea, the young official stepped outside, and the door closed behind him. Choi was trembling. Shin still expected to see the North Koreans come blazing into the embassy. It was 1:15 p.m.

As the clock ticked steadily from one minute to the next they sank into their seats, relief washing over them. A smile floated on Choi's face as she turned to her husband. "You tried to get through the embassy doors before me, didn't you?" she asked. Shin laughed. "I don't remember," he said, blushing. For years thereafter, she would tease him about it, saying that Shin had chivalrously pushed his way ahead of her to save his own skin.

After about fifteen minutes another American, a man in his thirties, entered the room. He had been expecting them, he joked, but not this soon. It turned out that the Japanese hotel employee had dutifully passed Shin's message along, and that the American put in charge of the case had spent the morning looking up Shin and Choi. The reason it had taken fifteen minutes for him to get here was that, as they were bursting through the embassy doors, he was at the nearby police station, trying to establish whether the Austrian police had already busted the South Koreans with falsified papers. The American quickly debriefed Shin and Choi, then asked them to follow him outside. With two other U.S. officials sticking close by, they climbed into two unmarked cars, which drove them to a house on a quiet residential street. They rushed inside. The American in charge of their case left the room for a minute and returned with a pink rose. With a big smile he handed it to Choi.

"Welcome," he said, "to the West." Choi Eun-Hee took the rose and burst into tears.

31
From Kim to Kim

"People of the world, if you are looking for miracles, come to Korea! Christians, do not go to Jerusalem. Come rather to Korea. Do not believe in God. Believe in the great man."

—Official *Rodong Sinmun* editorial about Kim Il-Sung, December 1980

Foreigners who look at pictures of Pyongyang often inquire about the unusual white dots, crosses, and numbers painted on the asphalt of Kim Il-Sung Square and all the main streets running to and through it. The marks form a complex grid used to orchestrate mass political events and gatherings, indicating to citizens where to stand and where to move, like tape on a theater stage indicating where furniture and scenery is to be placed or an actor's "mark" on a film set, a taped cross on the ground indicating where the performer must stand to be in frame and in focus. Pyongyang's grid is the clearest sign that the DPRK's capital is not a city but a stage on a monumental scale.

Losing Shin Sang-Ok and Madame Choi was the beginning of the end for Kim Jong-Il's career as a movie mogul. It would take another twenty years for the North Korean film industry to collapse, but that day in March 1986 was its start.

No one really knows how Kim Jong-Il reacted to the news of his beloved filmmakers' defection. He was undoubtedly surprised, and would have felt betrayed; the North Koreans in charge of making sure that something like this didn't happen would have been severely punished. Choe Ik-Gyu was suspended from the Propaganda and Agitation Department and sent down to production, his exact whereabouts unknown for several years. Ho Hak-Sun was almost certainly removed from the Tongbuk-Ri guesthouse and expelled from the Party, but her punishment is unclear.

Shin and Choi's escape created a minor diplomatic stir. Kyodo News, Enoki's employers, were the first to break the news, based on the testimony of "a trusted source," Enoki himself. Over the days that followed, the U.S. and North Korean embassies exchanged recriminations in the newspapers and over the newswires. The North Korean government first accused the United States government of "tricking and kidnapping [Shin and Choi] in agreement with the South Korean puppets." It repeated its claim that Shin had been persecuted by the South Korean government and voluntarily sought domicile in the North, and that "we helped him, because he asked for our help." The North Korean ambassador in Vienna put out a mournful appeal, like a parent seeking a missing child. He told the news that Shin and Choi had been taken from the Intercontinental against their will, "and they have not returned. Since then we have been looking for them."

This all changed when Shin and Choi gave their first press conference, announcing to the world that they had been kidnapped but now were free. Kim Jong-Il's diplomat became indignant. Yes, Shin and Choi had escaped, he now told the media, not because they had been prisoners but because—corrupt, untrustworthy South Koreans that they had been from the start—they had stolen the $2 million with which Kim had generously and kindheartedly entrusted them to restart their failed careers. (Shin later disclosed, "When I thought about the eight years of personal and public loss we had suffered, I thought it only fair for us to keep the money," but it was a decision he would regret.) The American wolves, predictably, had helped them in their deception and betrayal.

Shin's name was immediately removed from the credits of *Pulgasari,* with credit passing to his assistant. When the film was released on North Korean screens just weeks after Shin and Choi escaped, it was an unprecedented success. Kim personally ordered a nationwide campaign of lectures and ideology sessions to discredit Shin, demanding that "every single North Korean" accept Shin no longer as a cultural hero, but as a traitor. Shin's name became unmentionable without punishment, and the films he had directed were removed from circulation.

North Korea would soon have bigger problems than the loss of its only good filmmaker. Five decades of political isolation, technological stagnation, and economic mismanagement were taking their toll, impacting every single part of the economy starting with the country's very soil. Kim Il-Sung had so abused his country's resources and infrastructure that growing and harvesting food now became well-nigh impossible. Whole swathes of the countryside had been ruined by reckless deforestation, and the DPRK's dam and irrigation systems had fallen into disrepair, devastating the surrounding farms and plots. North Korea's problems were compounded by the changing face of the world at the end of the Cold War. In the late 1980s the DPRK's two biggest (and arguably only) allies, China and the USSR, opened diplomatic and trade relations with South Korea, a slap in the face for the Kims. Around the same time, the Chinese and Soviets, themselves facing economic difficulty, started asking for cash up-front from North Korea for any new deliveries of food and fuel. The North owed its allies roughly $10 billion in loans by this point, none of which it could pay back. Two-thirds of North Korea's food imports, and three-quarters of its fuel, came from its Chinese neighbors. The rest was imported from the Soviet Union, which collapsed in 1991, ceasing trade with the DPRK entirely.

The North Korean economy ground to a halt, and "soon the country was sucked into a vicious death spiral," the journalist Barbara Demick wrote a few years later. "Without cheap fuel oil and raw material, it couldn't keep the factories running, which meant it had nothing to export. With no exports, there was no hard currency, and without hard currency, fuel imports fell even further and electricity stopped. The coal mines couldn't operate without electricity [and] the shortage of coal worsened the electricity shortage. The electricity shortage further lowered agricultural output." Soon North Korea ran out of food. And as people began to starve and die, the ambulances ran out of petrol, the hospitals went dark, and all communication broke down.

By 1998, depending on whose numbers you go by, between sixty thousand and two million North Koreans—as much as 10 percent of the entire population—had died from famine. Those who survived resembled what Westerners were more used to seeing in Somalia or Ethiopia: people with sunken eyes, distended bellies, and dry skin stretched over bone. People laid traps to catch birds, rats, even mice. The country's entire frog population was eaten to extinction within a year. People scraped and chewed the bark off trees, and dug through cowpats for undigested corn and wheat. There were reports of parents arrested for eating their children and of black-market stalls selling human flesh. Corpses lay unclaimed and unattended in the streets and on the steps of train stations. The only thing that kept North Korea going was aid, over $2 billion of it, most coming from the "murderous Yankee wolves" of the United States.

Kim Il-Sung, whose health had long been declining, finally died in 1994, at the age of eighty-two. He had spent his final two decades sleeping with the teenage girls of the Joy Brigade and surrounded by doctors and nurses at the Kim Il-Sung Longevity Institute, created by his son to try and keep the Supreme Leader alive. The old guerrilla's mind and body had weakened considerably. His eyesight and hearing were failing. The doctors recommended laughter and health foods, as well as transfusions from the blood of younger men, to rejuvenate the Sun of Korea. But there was nothing to be done. One scorchingly hot July day Kim Il-Sung's heart gave out. He had been the leader of his country for forty-six years. He had outlived Mao by nearly twenty years and Stalin by forty; his reign had seen off nine U.S. presidents, twenty-one Japanese prime ministers, and six South Korean presidents. And he had succeeded in passing the reins of power to his son.

When the Korean Central News Agency anchor, in a black suit and black tie, announced the news of Kim Il-Sung's death, a howl rose from the streets. Entire families ran out of their homes and banged their heads against walls and pavements. Many started to scream and wail. People killed themselves by jumping off rooftops or, in the longer term, slowly starving themselves. (Even suicide is difficult in North Korea, where nobody has sleeping pills to overdose on and only soldiers have bullets with which to blow their brains out.)

Over the next few days, mass hysteria swept over the country. People gathered around statues of Kim Il-Sung to pour out their grief. Things became warped and absurd. First people turned out because they were genuinely distraught, then they returned because they were hungry and the authorities had started handing out rice cakes to everyone who paid their respects. And then they returned again and again because it was expected, and later demanded, of them. What had begun spontaneously became a duty. An order was put out that each group of mourners must bring flowers to leave at the Leader's foot, and the *inminban* were watching to spot people whose grieving wasn't clear or convincing enough, in case they were traitors, or wavering. Jong-Il released a propaganda film claiming that the Great Leader might come back to life if people grieved hard enough for him. Conspiracy theories spread that the Great Leader had been assassinated by the Americans or South Koreans: How else could he have died?

According to Communist tradition begun following the death of Lenin in 1924, Kim Il-Sung's body was embalmed and put on display for his people to see. The process involved removing all of the Supreme Leader's organs before bathing his hollow corpse in a formaldehyde bath and injecting liters of chemical balsam, a cocktail of glycerine and potassium acetate, in his veins to keep his flesh lifelike and elastic. Finally makeup and lipstick were applied to Kim's face to restore the illusion of youth. A team of Soviet biochemists, who called themselves the Mausoleum Laboratory and had carried out the mummifications of Lenin, Stalin, and Ho Chi Minh, were flown in to Pyongyang to do the job.

An elaborate funeral was arranged over two days, July 19 and 20. Two million people lined the capital's streets as the coffin, on the roof of a Cadillac, cruised down to its final destination: Kumsusan Palace, which Kim Jong-Il turned into a memorial and mausoleum. Mourners and visitors were sanitized as they walked in: expensive X-ray equipment peeked into their pockets, revolving brushes cleaned the soles of their shoes, and air cannons blasted the dust and dirt off their clothes as they were moved along a half-mile-long conveyor belt. The belt led to the end of a marble corridor and into a chamber featuring a white marble statue of the deceased Leader, illuminated from behind by pink lights. Through that anteroom was a vast, dark hall filled with somber music. There on a black bier lay Kim Il-Sung, expensively preserved, in a black suit under clear glass. The whole thing cost, by most estimates, over $100 million. North Korea's entire annual trade was estimated at only $2 billion. The day of the funeral, Jong-Il announced that Kim Il-Sung would remain "Eternal President," still walking side by side with his people, ruling and guiding the republic from the beyond.

Though Kim Jong-Il assumed power in the early 1980s, his father remaining the country's head in name only, the younger Kim officially took over just in time to be seen as the one responsible for his country's devastation. Ever the propagandist, the Dear Leader put his publicity machine into overdrive in a desperate bid to save face and explain away the famine. The government first claimed it was stockpiling food to feed the starving people of South Korea on the impending day of reunification. When that story failed to connect, the government alleged that the United States had unilaterally imposed a blockade against North Korea and was keeping food out of the DPRK in a bid to starve the people and destroy the regime. This worked a little better, but was undercut when citizens reported sightings of the North Korean army building fences along the seashores to stop people fishing, because fish were "state property" needed by the Party to feed themselves and the elite. The North Korean news followed up with a documentary about a greedy man whose stomach burst from eating too much food, suggesting that starving was actually good for you. There is no record of how that tactic was received.

In the midst of this human tragedy, Kim Jong-Il decided that the country needed cinema more than ever. North Korean film during the famine dutifully returned to propaganda about the DPRK being the happiest and luckiest country on Earth, a message which had little resonance given the people's daily struggle to survive. At almost the exact same time, international films began to be smuggled into North Korea and reveal to its citizens all they had been missing. Black markets were becoming endemic, run by Chinese smugglers who snuck VHS players and tapes (along with food and other foreign goods) across the Yalu and Tumen Rivers. For the very first time in the country's history movies weren't the exclusive domain of the state. Films and television shows from China, Hong Kong, South Korea, and even the United States appeared on market stalls. Soon Chinese dealers upgraded to DVDs, the thin discs being easier to pack in huge quantities than VHS tapes. Smuggling was easy: all they had to do was fill a duffel bag with hundreds of discs, a carton of Marlboros on top to bribe any inquisitive soldier.

North Korean propaganda could not compete with this. It wasn't just that the films were so much better made, or more entertaining, or that they made North Korean audiences more discriminating and more sharply receptive to the subtexts and rhythms of a motion picture, though all of that was true. The real game changer was that millions of ordinary North Koreans now saw extensive images of the outside world for the first time. They saw cities packed with cars and skyscrapers, homes with dishwashers and laundry machines and televisions—not just wealthy people's homes, but everyone's homes. Romantic comedies ended with people freely chasing each other in airports, surrounded by hundreds of people who could afford (and were allowed) to travel the world for leisure. The South Koreans, once believed to be living under a more severe and brutal government, also appeared to benefit at will from the free world's perks. And the evil Americans they saw in these films seemed too happy and healthy, too busy buying things and falling in love, to be believably related to the hook-nosed, crooked-fingered child killers of North Korean legend.

In 1989, Charles Jenkins and the other U.S. defectors got their own smuggled VHS player, acquired through an Ethiopian student living in Pyongyang. Over the next decade they watched a stack of black-market tapes—*Titanic, Cliffhanger, Coming to America, Die Hard,* the James Bond films—"with all the curtains drawn and the volume turned down as low as possible." Jenkins now had two daughters, born and raised in North Korea, and they found these glimpses of the never-before-seen outside world overwhelming and hard to relate to. "They could hardly make sense of them. In *Coming to America,* for example, Eddie Murphy stars as an African prince who finds a wife in New York City, but [Jenkins's daughters] Brinda and Mika had always been taught that black people in America were still basically slaves, so to see shots of all the races walking around freely and basically getting along with each other on the streets of New York was too much for them."

As electricity to residential areas now became rationed to specific time slots, people—especially younger people—would take advantage of the few hours of power they had every day or every few days to gather at the house of a friend with a VCR or a DVD player, lock the door, draw the curtains, and, in groups of up to thirty, as many as the house could fit, watch as many films as time allowed: South Korean soaps, old American films, Chinese classics, Hong Kong action flicks. Sometimes the police would shut down the electricity early, knowing that tapes and DVDs couldn't be ejected without power, then raid every home in the neighborhood, arresting anyone found with a foreign movie still in their player. DVD smugglers and salespeople were arrested and executed. Jong-Il announced that the influx of foreign culture was a CIA plot to destabilize the People's Republic. "Through all manner of falsehoods and trickery," he declared in a lecture to Party members, "the imperialists and reactionaries are paralyzing the healthy thinking of the masses while spreading among them bourgeois-reactionary ideas and rotten bourgeois customs. . . . What will happen if we succumb and fail to block these customs of living that the bastards are disseminating? . . . We become unable to defend to our death the leadership of the revolution and adhere to socialism." Any North Korean found selling, buying, or watching foreign films or television, Jong-Il decreed, was collaborating with "the puppets under the control of the CIA, who are wickedly conniving to use these specially made materials to beautify the world of imperialism."

But the illegal and dangerous private screenings continued. The North Korean people had a new perspective not just on what cinema had to offer, but on what their lives could and should have been. North Korean cinema, by way of comparison, stayed stuck in the mid-1980s, bereft of an audience. Kim Jong-Il's most vital propaganda tool was rendered, within the space of just a couple of years, completely obsolete.

Meanwhile the North Korean film studios continued to churn out films, or claimed to. In 1988 Deputy Director Choe Ik-Gyu was returned from his exile in the countryside and reinstated as vice director of the Propaganda and Agitation Department. Throughout the 1990s his office claimed the Korea Film Studio made thirty films a year, but by 2000 it was clear the studio had not been used in years. When asked, North Korean citizens were hard-pressed to name any homegrown film they had enjoyed more recently than a film called *A Broad Bellflower,* which was made back in 1987. There was an attempt at a *Titanic* rip-off in the early twenty-first century, but it was, fittingly, a disaster. Instead, today's North Korean filmmakers are encouraged to "Make More Cartoons!" Animation is cheaper, more controllable, and a good way to make use of all the highly trained graduates of the Pyongyang Institute of Art.

And besides, now the performance has moved off the screen and into real life. Diplomats and tourists who visit North Korea today watch as subways are run solely for display for foreign visitors. Fruit, snack, and flower stands are erected to give the illusion of free trade. For visitors concerned by Pyongyang's alleged religious intolerance, showcase churches have been built in which fake Christian services are performed. And every year, the Arirang Mass Games, overseen by newly appointed minister of culture Choe Ik-Gyu, make headlines on television broadcasts around the world as a demonstration of the North Korean people's devotion, single-mindedness, endurance, and military precision. The people are still required, under pain of imprisonment, to thank Kim Il-Sung and Kim Jong-Il every morning for their food, even though Kim Il-Sung is dead and they have no food.

It is all absurd. It is all fake. But it doesn't matter. North Korea itself, as a Kim Jong-Il production, had become a theater state: a ritualized experience, a system of symbols, spectacles, and theatrics designed to maintain the authority and legitimacy of a regime that, in reality, has neither.

There is a revolution going on. The performance cannot be allowed to stop. The screens cannot be allowed to go blank.

32
The Stars and Stripes

Choi slept for four days after their daring escape in Vienna. While she rested, her husband looked after her. It was the first time in their three decades together that *he* was the one cooking for *her*. Over the next week the CIA agents moved them from safe house to safe house, to make sure they had ditched any North Korean surveillance. Suspicious-looking Asian men had been spotted lurking around the American embassy; when Austrian police had stopped them they had found them armed with handguns. The Americans told Shin and Choi of rumors that Jong-Il had put a price of half a million dollars on their heads. Finally, one morning the agents handed the couple traditional Middle Eastern attire, covering their heads and, in Choi's case, part of her face. The agents drove them in these disguises to the airport and, with an armed marshal as their escort, put them on a plane to Washington, D.C.

Like many filmmakers, Shin Sang-Ok and Choi Eun-Hee had dreamed of Hollywood. They had not dreamed of Reston, Virginia.

Asylum had come in exchange for a promise to provide the CIA with all the information they could on Kim Il-Sung, Kim Jong-Il, and North Korea. They were the first reliable witnesses of the Kims' habits and behavior to make their way into the hands of the American national security agencies. So when they flew to America it was to a three-story rented house in Reston, just outside D.C., paid for with taxpayers' money, and with live-in CIA bodyguards.

It was not quite the freedom they had imagined, but it did feel safe. Reston had been built as a planned community in the 1960s by a real estate mogul, Robert E. Simon, funded entirely with the proceeds of the sale of Carnegie Hall, a family heirloom. It had attractive homes, bike paths, tennis courts, golf courses, swimming pools, a zoo, two art galleries, a history museum, and boat rentals on Lake Fairfax. It was here, too, that Shin and Choi were finally reunited with their children. Their daughter was happily married in Seoul, but Jung-Kyun, now twenty-three, came to live with them. The last time Choi had seen him he had been a teenager with braces on his teeth. His face was long and thin, and he was cooler, more aloof. While Shin and Choi were in North Korea he had learned, through the press, that he was adopted; his parents had never had the chance to tell him themselves when he reached a certain age, as they had planned.

They learned that Oh Su-Mi had divorced her photographer husband, dropped out of the film industry, and was struggling with drug addiction. So her two children with Shin—Shin Sang-Kyun, now thirteen, and Shin Seung-Lee, just ten—came to live with them in America, as well. Choi had eight years of pent-up motherly energy to relieve, and somehow she pulled them all together into a coherent family. It was a strange and at times absurd domestic atmosphere, with the CIA agents barbecuing steaks for everyone or taking the family on the ferry around Jamestown and Colonial Williamsburg to celebrate Shin's sixtieth birthday.

Shin and Choi kept busy giving a series of interviews to *The Washington Post* and writing their Korean-language memoir, which filled nine hundred pages and was published in Korea in 1988. At first it sold astonishingly well, but after the initial media interest faded, the memoir fell out of attention and out of print, and was never translated into English. They were disappointed when the $2.2 million in the Austrian bank account, which Shin hoped to use as seed funding for a new film career in Hollywood—the least, he figured, Kim Jong-Il could do to repay them—was seized by the Austrian government, to whom the Kims owed money.

They became U.S. citizens and, at Choi's request, finally got married properly, in the Italian embassy, which the CIA considered the safest location. Shin wore a tuxedo, Choi a white lace dress and head scarf. He was sixty, she was fifty-six. They had been famous together and poor together, adopted children and made films, rubbed shoulders with presidents and dictators, married, divorced, remarried, survived kidnapping and imprisonment.

"Thank you for being stubborn about me when we first started dating," Madame Choi told her husband. "You were brave to choose me, considering the situation."

"No, I wasn't brave," Shin answered. "You were just so beautiful that I had no choice."

Choi would have been happy living out her life as a mother and wife again, safe in the knowledge that her children slept under her roof, and that she was free to come, go, and do as she pleased. But her husband wanted to be in California. He wanted to work. "We didn't escape to live like the dead," he would grumble restlessly.

"What about your age?" Choi would ask him.

"What age?" he would answer.

Deep dissatisfaction defined the last chapter of Shin's life. "I wish I was ten years younger than I am now," he would growl to his wife. "I wish I spoke better English." More than one person who interviewed him in his later years noted that life in Virginia was the only topic he could not comfortably discuss. Prison he could talk about; Kim Jong-Il he could talk about; but sitting in a big house in Virginia at someone else's expense, not making films . . . about that Shin was speechless.

So after three years of living under the protection of the CIA, Shin and Choi left Reston and headed west, for California, to start their careers fresh. Shin had dreams of making it big in Hollywood. Through mutual connections they found a Korean-Japanese businessman who had made a fortune in real estate in Hawaii, remembered their films, and was willing to fund their efforts. He had a house in Beverly Hills and offered to let them stay there. Shin and Choi ended up living there for nearly four years, as Shin went to work on a third start to his career. He now went by the name of Simon Sheen, the Christian name he took when Choi convinced him to convert to Catholicism prior to their wedding ceremony in Washington.

Choi quickly realized that, at sixty-three, she was too old and too little known in the West to print out head shots, get an agent, and fight for bit parts in a town swimming with young, fresh starlets. Besides, she struggled to pick up English, and even after years in the United States couldn't string more than a few words together. Shin fared little better. *Genghis Khan,* which he now reimagined as an epic musical, fell through, and door after door was closed in his face when he proposed a film about his and Choi's North Korean experience, the rejections casually stressing the grim commercial prospects, in America at least, of a project with three Korean lead roles.

In 1990 Shin briefly returned to Asia to direct *Mayumi: Virgin Terrorist,* based on the real story of a female North Korean agent who had bombed a Korean Air flight in 1987; he made the film, he later said, to "confirm his identity" and prove he wasn't a Communist. The effort backfired dramatically. Despite having the largest budget of any Korean film to date, being shot in seventeen countries, and having been preselected as an entry to the Venice Film Festival (as well as South Korea's official Best Foreign Language Picture submission for the Academy Awards), the film was met with largely mocking reviews upon its release. To make things worse, he was slapped with a defamation suit by the families of the victims of the bombing, who claimed Shin had won the right to tell their loved ones' stories by promising he would make a film that would honor the victims but instead had made a "blood-soaked" and tactless spectacle. They especially criticized *Mayumi*'s largest set piece, the bombing sequence, which was shot in a grotesquely violent manner, intercut with documentary footage of the real families mourning their lost ones. The two-and-a-half-minute sequence had cost nearly half of the film's total $2 million budget, and Shin, after settling the suit out of court for an undisclosed sum, later sheepishly admitted that shooting it had been the main draw of the film for him. Some viewed *Mayumi* as little more than thinly veiled South Korean propaganda, an anti-North film the government required of Shin to publicly establish his antagonism for the North. Most just thought it was a bad film: rushed, cheap, and poorly acted.

Shin scuttled back to Los Angeles and directed a film portraying the 1980s South Korean military dictatorship in an unfavorable light, maybe to redress the balance. That also tanked. After those experiences Shin decided to stay away from politics for a while. The success of *Home Alone* and America's intense Asian martial arts fetishism—born with Bruce Lee, but feeding off the *Karate Kid* franchise of 1984–1994 and the Teenage Mutant Ninja Turtles craze—inspired Shin to create *3 Ninjas*, a Disney movie franchise about three all-American kids who use martial arts to fight crime. Shin had a script written and entered talks with Disney to finance and distribute the film. He might have been the biggest filmmaker in both Koreas, but he found himself awed by actual direct talks with a Hollywood studio. Disney lawyers were famous for their heartless intransigence, and it didn't matter that Shin was in his sixties or had survived kidnapping and the gulag. In May 1992, while the Rodney King riots tore Los Angeles apart outside their hotel window, Shin, his lawyers, and Disney's lawyers locked themselves in a suite for a whole night, arguing an arcanely detailed licensing agreement. Shin, who was used to doing everything on a handshake, a wink, and a prayer, with some forged papers to back it all up if necessary, was completely lost. "Everything was different," he said. "I did my best to accept everything they suggested."

The series had three films in all, Shin directing one and producing and writing all three. He had hoped they would rival *Home Alone* in popularity. In fact, they were all box-office and critical failures, box-office receipts for each installment diminishing dramatically following the first film's respectable return on investment; but they later found something of a kids' following on television and home video, riding the zeitgeist (and, incidentally, launching the career of director Jon Turteltaub, who later directed *Cool Runnings* and the *National Treasure* blockbusters). Shin also sold the Disney Channel television network a kids' movie remake of *Pulgasari* entitled *The Legend of Galgameth,* a film so bad that it makes *Pulgasari* look good; and a year later produced *The Gardener,* a forgettable thriller starring Malcolm McDowell.

Turteltaub remained a friend for the rest of Shin's life, and Angie Everhart, who costarred in *The Gardener* and suffered a miscarriage during the film's shoot, remembered that Shin made sure the production halted for as long as she needed and that she received the best care. "Sheen was very kind to me," she said. He was on set every day, "serious and quiet," embarrassed by his poor English. Everyone on the crew remembered his assistant, a young Korean woman whose face was covered in scars: a former gang member in L.A., she had been disfigured when a rival had spat razor blades in her face and pushed them into her skin. It's unknown how Shin had found her, but he gave her her break in the film industry. Even in America, it seemed, tragedy could strike anyone at any time—women especially; it was always worse for women, Shin despaired.

Something had clearly changed in Shin Sang-Ok the artist. Here was a filmmaker who had spent the 1960s and 1970s pushing boundaries, who was most famous for his films' eroticism and sensuality. Now, he could only manage Disney Channel drivel. What had been shrewd populism earlier in his career had become trite and manipulatively labored. Perhaps he was desperate for a hit and thought that copying mainstream trends was a way to translate his talents. He certainly found it hard fitting into the Hollywood way of doing things, and it is telling that in six years in California he produced five films but only directed one (he would later shrug off even that, and say that he had never directed in Hollywood, in spite of the credit). He said later, "I suddenly, and I must say brutally, realized the cultural differences between our two civilizations. I felt very far away."

Beverly Hills was hard on Madame Choi, too. While her husband struggled to make his way professionally she spent her days with the children or taking walks around the neighborhood. She was the only Asian woman in the community, as far as she could tell, and she was keenly aware of the gazes of the other wives, who mostly seemed to fall into two categories: power wives, the skin on their foreheads and cheekbones tight, their whole bodies seemingly on the verge of snapping, always rushing to some meeting or lunch; and trophy wives, youthful and firm and perky, either in jeans or bright leggings, eating health food and always returning from the beach or an exercise class. Each had her own brand of power and independence. Madame Choi, who had no meetings or classes to go to and who always wore black, with black sunglasses and a large black hat shading her pale skin from the sun, felt old and witchy and out of place.

Now that she was divorced, Oh Su-Mi had started flying to California to "see her children," she claimed; but Choi felt sure it was the Hollywood glamour that was drawing the former starlet like a moth to a flame. She had, after all, never sought to visit Reston. Oh would take both children on outings, leaving Choi behind feeling lonely and dejected. She never could forget that Oh was the children's biological mother, and that she had never been able to bear her own children. Oh seemed not to care if her flying visits made life difficult for the kids. She had a drug and alcohol problem, and when she and Choi would argue, sometimes in public, it wasn't uncommon for Oh to throw wine in Choi's face or pull her hair in the middle of a restaurant. She would bring up wanting to take her kids back to South Korea with her, and then relent and agree they were better off with Shin and Choi. One day Oh called Choi to tell her she was getting married, to a Frenchman she had met. Shortly after that she was in a horrific car accident in Hawaii and died. She was only forty-two years old. Shin was on a film set working, so Choi flew to her cremation in Hawaii with Sang-Kyun, Oh's son. There was no one else there, and after the service Choi was left in the crematorium on the very foreign island, holding a box full of ashes. Her feelings were, she said, "complicated." She thought of how there was no one else there for Oh, and wondered how she would have felt if she had known Shin's wife would be the only person at her funeral. Sitting alone with the ashes, Choi cried, as desperately as she had when Su-Mi had first come into her life. She didn't know what to make of any of it.

After eight years out of the world, Shin and Choi were strangers everywhere, at home nowhere. The United States had welcomed them with open arms, and they were grateful. But home—the home they had been taken away from in 1978—remained South Korea.

They were wary of returning. The South's National Security Law was still in full force, and it wasn't uncommon for Koreans who had been taken by force to the North to be thrown into prison as traitors when they returned. And they had been away so long that they feared they wouldn't feel at home any more. But they couldn't stay away. So, in 1999, twenty-one years after their abductions, Director Shin and Madame Choi finally returned permanently to Seoul.

The South Korea from which they had been taken in 1978 was a military dictatorship, the streets of Seoul frequently thick with tear gas and riot police, the arts and media tightly censored. The country they found in the final years of the twentieth century was wealthy, democratic, peaceful, and urbanized. It had successfully hosted the 1988 Summer Olympics, and in 1990 the people had chosen their first truly democratically elected president, Roh Tae-Woo. South Korea seemed to have become what Shin, Choi, and millions of South Koreans had been hoping it would become for decades.

As soon as they stepped off the plane, Shin and Choi were met by the Korean CIA and taken to interrogation rooms, where they were hooked up to lie detectors and questioned for hours. Stupidly, they were still wearing the watches given to them by Kim Jong-Il: Shin his gold Rolex, Choi her first Kim Il-Sung name watch. Both were confiscated. At the end of a long day of questioning—during which, Shin claimed, his interrogators accused him of being a North Korean spy—they were released, on condition that they give several press conferences and public interviews denying any allegiance to the North. They did so in their usual attire: Choi perfectly coiffed and made-up, in large sunglasses and tailored clothes, Shin in his French-cut black suit and silk patterned necktie. Witnessing the elegant couple, the South Korean people refused to believe that Shin Sang-Ok and Choi Eun-Hee had been kidnapped. *This,* they said, did not look like two people who had gone through such a terrible ordeal. They looked wealthy and old. Hadn't Shin just made that terrible *Mayumi* film, the one that took advantage of the grief of the families of hijack victims? And the book they wrote, wasn't that just another way to make money?

The whole thing, Choi said, was "brutal" and "emotionally harrowing." Everywhere else in the world they were treated with respect, but their own countrymen refused to believe and accept them. "Everyone was against us," she said. "When we actually asked some of these people if they had read the book, we found most people hadn't. They just heard things from someone and then went on talking about it, about how unrealistic the whole story was." Worst of all, they were immediately turned into pawns in a political game. Anyone with right-wing sympathies took them up as examples of the ruthlessness of the criminal North Korean government. Those on the left saw them instead as tools of the South Korean conservative establishment and refused to believe in their story, claiming their abduction and escape were invented, their book ghostwritten by government staff, and the tapes of Kim Jong-Il fakes manufactured by the KCIA using voice actors. Shin couldn't work in the South, so he had gone north, they said, and then he either had a change of heart or was stolen back by the KCIA. They shrugged off evidence to the contrary, and these doubts, over time, stuck. While to the world at large there was no doubt that Shin and Choi were victims, kidnapped by the North, in South Korea rumors still abound attacking the credibility of their story.

After everything they had endured, they asked themselves, this was their welcome home?

They rented a small house in Seoul and tried to get back to work. But times were hard. They were both exhausted and in debt. It was always unlikely that Shin, a relic from a filmmaking era over thirty years prior, would easily find a place in South Korea's new edgy, youth-oriented film industry. A Japanese film buff and sometime distributor of wacky and cultish movies, who wrote for Japanese *Playboy* under the pen name Edoki Jun (a Japanese version of "Ed Wood Jr."), had just bought Japanese rights to *Pulgasari* and released it in his home country to stupendous success. Shin sued to have his name put back on the film, but lost, since the film was governed by North

Korean law, and North Korean law was Kim Jong-Il's will. A couple of years later *Pulgasari* was released on VHS and DVD in the United States, where it was widely derided but became an instant cult classic. Shin never saw a penny.

At least he still had his sense of humor. Reporters visiting his office on the outskirts of Seoul never failed to notice that, alongside the pictures of him and his wife in the 1960s, or him, Catherine Deneuve, and Clint Eastwood in Cannes in 1994, he also proudly displayed the surreal pictures of him and Choi alongside Kim Jong-Il and Kim Il-Sung. Speaking to a journalist in 2003, Shin admitted, "When I think of having money, I think of North Korea." Later in the interview, when asked about Kim Jong-Il's impact on his life, he playfully nudged his wife. "He played a positive role for us," he smiled. "Perhaps *she* told Kim to kidnap us, she was so keen to get back together."

He made light of it, but for such an ambitious man, who had always craved to be at the center of things, the world's casual indifference to him was even worse than its disbelief and suspicion. He directed one more film in South Korea, *A Story of Winter,* a small, serious-minded drama about senile dementia and the fragilities of old age.

It went unreleased. It would be his last time behind a film camera.

Epilogue: 2013

Sitting in front of the old lady is a lemon tea and hot water. It's over one hundred degrees Fahrenheit outside, suffocatingly humid and sticky, but she can no longer drink cold drinks, she explains, because of problems with her throat and esophagus. Her eyes are bright and focused. When she moves, which she rarely does, she is slow and deliberate.

Madame Choi is eighty-eight years old and can only get around in a wheelchair. She looks as good as anyone could expect to at eighty-eight. She wears very big prescription glasses under a gray cap, from which short white hair slips out in wisps, and subtle but full makeup on a pale face. She has on trousers and a blue jacket blouse over a burgundy top, expensive-looking silver shoes with a small heel, and a big, square silver medallion hung low around her neck. There are rings on three of her fingers, one of them her (second) wedding band. You hear people talk of a movie star or a rock god entering a room and the air pressure changing with their presence. Choi Eun-Hee, in her eighties, in a wheelchair, has that quality.

In an eatery called Pop Street, one of those South Korean establishments that is part restaurant (serving everything from traditional Korean fare to spaghetti Bolognese, hamburgers, and chicken Caesar salads) and part Starbucks-style coffeehouse, Madame Choi recounts her story over a period of four hours, fielding the questions with quiet charm and grace. When asked, in summary, if there is only one thing that she hopes readers will take from her and Shin's story, she doesn't even think before replying.

"The most important thing to me," she says, "is for people to finally accept that the truth is the truth."

Shin Sang-Ok died on April 11, 2006. Even today, years later, when she is unable to sleep in the small hours, Madame Choi imagines walking into his study, expecting him to be there, working, the way he used to do right up until his final days.

He had stopped talking a couple of years before his death. When spoken to he would just smile, sad and dog tired, instead of answering. If he did answer, he would whisper, "I don't have much to say." A liver transplant in 2005 took poorly, and a second operation followed a few months later; he was old, weak, and struggled to recover. Choi couldn't afford a car, so she made long bus journeys, alone, to visit Shin in the hospital every day. She now blames one of Shin's nurses for exercising him too much, for rushing his recovery. She also blames Kim Jong-Il, more fairly, for the years that Shin spent weakening in a gulag. While still in hospital Shin contracted hepatitis, and his health deteriorated so rapidly he seemed to be getting worse every hour. The night of April 11, at the end of her visit, Choi kissed him and prepared to leave.

As always, she asked him if he needed anything. Shin, smiling, replied, "Hold my hand. So I can see how strong you are." She gave her husband her hand and he held it for a while. His hands, she remembers, were warm and comforting. After a long time he let go and, in a low, quiet, loving voice, said, "You can go now, Madame Choi." Choi smiled and told him she would return early the next morning. Later that night, Shin's body gave out. His last words were spoken to his nurse, as he watched his blood drip from an open sore, off the bed and onto the floor. "Please," he said, "clean this mess I made."

Madame Choi's mobile phone rang as she was just getting off the bus that took her back home. She couldn't process the news. When she and Shin were divorced, she says, "I could still hate him, and miss him," because she knew he was out there, living in the world somewhere. Now he was gone, and there was nothing left. "Death," she says, "is a cold thing."

The funeral took place at the Seoul National University Hospital. Movie stars from the 1960s and 1970s, most of whom hadn't seen each other since the golden days, filed into the old building to pay their respects. The actor Shin Young-Kyun, one of Shin's favorites, who had starred in *Eunuch* and *Red Muffler,* among countless others, spoke at the altar, crediting Shin with making the Korean industry what it became. The South Korean culture and tourism minister, Kim Myung-Gon, himself a former actor and screenwriter, paid his respects and placed the Gold Crown Cultural Medal, the highest honor in South Korea for an artist, onto the casket. Newspapers around the world, from *The New York Times* to *The Guardian,* carried his obituary. Every tribute defined Shin's life first and foremost by his kidnapping, not his films; or, as the *Times* headline summed up: SHIN SANG OK, 80, KOREAN FILM DIRECTOR ABDUCTED BY DICTATOR, IS DEAD.

Kim Jong-Il drew his last breath five years later, on December 17, 2011, at the age of seventy. He died on his private train, which then halted on a siding while the Workers' Party figured out how to announce the Dear Leader's passing and handle his succession. After two long days the official North Korean media finally announced that he had died of a massive heart attack brought on by "overwork." Some reports later insisted the heart attack had struck while Kim was ranting at underlings "in a fit of rage" over the shoddy work at a power plant construction site. His son, Kim Jong-Un, was announced as his successor in the newscast that reported his death. Kim Jong-Nam, the eldest son, had fallen out of favor a decade earlier following his humiliating arrest at the Tokyo airport for attempting to enter the country on a fake Dominican Republic passport in the name of Pang Xiong ("Fat Bear" in Mandarin Chinese). The incident was made even more ridiculous by Jong-Nam's being accompanied by two women, neither of whom was his wife; by his traveling with a suitcase full of cash; and by his claims that he only wanted to visit Tokyo Disneyland (he was actually most likely traveling to Japan on Division 39 business). In the weeks that followed, the Japanese newspapers were full of the unflattering testimony of hostesses at the seedy massage parlors Jong-Nam liked to frequent when in Tokyo. After that Kim Jong-Il had quickly turned his favors to his younger, and much better behaved, son Jong-Un.

The same newscaster who had announced Kim Il-Sung's passing on state television told the people of Kim Jong-Il's death, while wearing the same traditional black mourning outfit. The Central News Agency reported that throughout the country the people were "convulsing with pain and despair" at the loss of their leader. "Our people and army are beating their breasts."

Kim's body lay embalmed in Kumsusan Palace for a week for the people to visit. After his state funeral there was a further twenty-four hour mourning period, the end of which was marked by heavy artillery fire, followed by three minutes of silence, followed by "all official vehicles, locomotives, and vessels [sounding] their horns."

No government officials from South Korea paid their condolences, but restrained sympathies were communicated by the UN Secretary General and a European Union high representative; the most heartfelt condolences came from Azerbaijan ("I was deeply saddened to hear [of] this heavy loss," said President Ilham Aliyev), Bangladesh ("The people of the DPRK have lost a great leader and we have lost a dear friend. . . . We pray that they will be able to bear this irreparable loss with courage and fortitude," said President Zillur Rahman), and Syria (Jong-Il's death was "a great loss not only to the Korean people but to the people of all countries struggling for freedom, justice, and peace," said President Bashar al-Assad). In Cuba, Fidel Castro's Council of State announced a period of official mourning and flew the country's flags at half-mast for two days.

The day of the Dear Leader's funeral saw Pyongyang clothed in crisp, pure white snow, a favorite symbol of the Kim regime, which liked to present North Korea as a victimized child in a world of wolves and predators. In a highly choreographed event, a procession of black cars rolled slowly down streets lined by an estimated two hundred thousand hysterical North Koreans. There were army jeeps and Mercedes limousines, military trucks filled with wreaths and flag-carrying generals, a fleet of gleaming white Mercedes sedans. Goose-stepping infantry marched among the cars, the entire convoy escorted by a military band.

At the center of everything was a black hearse. On its roof, inside a black coffin draped with the red DPRK flag, was Kim Jong-Il's body. The hearse was escorted, on foot, on the left side by uniformed generals and on the right by leading members of the Workers' Party, black clad and grim faced. First among them was the favored son and successor, twenty-eight-year-old Kim Jong-Un.

The Central News Agency broadcast "spontaneous" interviews with spectators along the route. One beautiful female soldier, her breathless tones and choked voice straight out of one of the Dear Leader's movies, said, "As I see the snow fall, I shed more tears, thinking about our General's hard work." Another male soldier laid it on even more thickly: "How can the sky not cry? The people are all crying—crying tears of blood." Each interview was as melodramatic as the scripts that Kim Jong-Il had loved so much. One person in the crowd shouted: "How could you leave us? What are we supposed to do without you?"

The North Korean people were told this broadcast was live, but it wasn't; it was aired several hours later, the government having given itself time to edit and manipulate the event even further, digitally erasing the state film crews littering the whole route and scripting the perfect commentary.

A funeral is a ritual; in North Korea it becomes, like everything else, a show. Kim Jong-Il's funeral had to be the biggest show in memory. Loudspeakers blared carefully selected revolutionary hymns; the "spontaneous" crowd had been arranged with the more attractive female soldiers grouped together in the front. In one clip of the broadcast, a group of generals is looking on as the coffin drives nearer. When one general raises his hand to wipe away his tears, the other three copy him immediately. Farther down the road people repetitively pretend to be collapsing under the weight of their pain. They hold on to one another by the elbows and sway up and down. There are people doubling over suddenly, as if struck by a burst appendix. All of them are freezing, hatless, breathing clouds of vapor in the icy temperatures. In close-ups you can see apparently tearful eyes open and look around, completely dry, before the person resumes "crying" again. The footage is theatrical, dehumanizing, and humiliating to watch.

The funeral convoy drove for forty kilometers (roughly twenty-five miles) through Pyongyang's west side, the city's attractive showpiece district, bypassing the east side of the Taedong River, which still looks like it did in 1955. There isn't enough of Pyongyang's west side for a forty-kilometer route, so the procession had to loop around some of the same streets, and did two circles of Kim Il-Sung Square. After three hours Kim's body ended up back at Kumsusan Palace, where the funeral took place behind closed doors. His body was then put on display next to his father's, where it still lies today, visited by busloads of worshipful pilgrims. And four months later—four months *after* his death—Kim Jong-Il was promoted to Supreme Leader of North Korea, ascending like his father before him to an eternal position of leadership in the Communist afterlife.

In Seoul, about a hundred right-wing protesters gathered to burn North Korean flags and portraits and effigies of the Dear Leader. When night fell, they let off celebratory fireworks.

Choi is very serious, at times almost mournful. She doesn't do much these days. After Shin's death she moved into a much smaller house, in a run-down neighborhood on the south side of Seoul, just three subway stops from trendy Gangnam but a world away from its hip nightclubs and flagship luxury stores.

Her poor health leaves her tired much of the time. She prays a lot. She used to do calligraphy, but because she can't sit or stand straight for any period of time, she had to stop. When people seek her out, it's always about her time in North Korea. The last time she acted was in 2001, at the age of seventy-five, when she "pushed herself" onto the stage for a musical version of Hemingway's *For Whom the Bell Tolls*. "I did okay," she says. But she won't ever act again.

In spite of everything, she lights up when she talks about Shin. She cracks huge smiles and her voice turns admiring. Her devotion to the man is incredible. The pictures taken of them in their seventies seem as happy and romantic as those taken when they were in their thirties. Shin loved her, and after their North Korean experience he was more committed to her. He felt more settled, and didn't have the same need to chase after other women. But he never hid the fact that she was not his greatest love and passion. Movies were. His autobiography is titled *I Am Film*. That book, which Choi edited and completed after Shin's death, talks almost exclusively about films and the experience of making them, not about personal events. In one passage Shin writes that he would happily sell his wife to another man if doing so helped him make a film. Choi relates this comment affectionately. Still she never felt that she came second. "His passion for the movies and his passion for me were the same," she says.

When asked how she would describe the man she loved to someone who never met him, she smiles and her voice grows even softer. She thinks carefully before answering. "A bachelor," she says. "Rebellious. In one word," she adds, before proceeding to use many more, "crazy about movies, a great artist. He had a really good memory. He always talked about film and work." She loved how clumsy he was, that he would throw himself into his films so wholeheartedly that he lost all awareness of the world around him. Asked if she thinks they would have remarried had they not been kidnapped, she replies, firmly, "No. We had no plans. We were moving in different directions."

As for her time in North Korea, there were no happy moments, Choi says, not one in the eight years that she spent there. Even when she experienced joy or relief—at seeing Shin again, for instance—she had simultaneously felt sadness, loss, and despair. Every day of the eight years, "every time I closed my eyes, I had my children in my eyes," she says, using a Korean expression for having something lodged constantly in your mind, absorbing your consciousness.

In older interviews she expresses anger and resentment toward Kim Jong-Il. Now, however, she says she feels compassion for a man whom she sees as "a poor soul in need. . . . I feel sorry for him as a human being. I [sometimes] feel very mad. Because of him we lost money, status, and the school," which she valued so much that she regrets losing it as much as she regrets missing out on her children's teenage years. But she no longer carries ill will toward him or anyone involved in her kidnapping. "God sends people to Earth with his own plans for them," she says, "and mine was one of them. It may sound like Kim Jong-Il took everything from me, but in the end it's God who gives, and God who takes away." She talks of God a lot. Her faith helps her to come to terms with things so far out of her control, things done that can never be undone.

Shin, a man who lived and breathed cinema, would have wanted to be remembered for his films. And, although Kim Jong-Il and North Korea will perhaps always take precedence, he is. In 1994 he was a member of the jury at the Cannes Film Festival. Alongside his fellow jurors, Clint Eastwood and Catherine Deneuve, he bestowed the Palme d'Or on *Pulp Fiction,* by a rising indie director named Quentin Tarantino. In 2002, Shin was the subject of an eleven-film retrospective at the Museum of Modern Art in New York. His films are now studied in film schools, both in Korea and abroad. His work may be little known and hard to find, but when found much of it is unforgettable.

Choi says she has no desire to be remembered or immortalized. More than anything, she wants "the world to accept our story as true and not question it as invented. I can't understand why people want to twist our story to fit their own purposes." After saying this she is quiet for a few more seconds. "I lived a very truthful and honest life. People often invent the story they want to be true. But I want to say: I lived honestly."

So much of this story is about human will, about what we can do when we come up against forces bigger than ourselves. Whatever your beliefs or your lack thereof, we will only live one version of this life, and where and when that life starts determines so much. We all, we are told, have the power and free will to do whatever we like with the hands we are dealt. Thinking of

Choi Eun-Hee, a woman born in a country torn in two by greater powers, and whose life has in so many ways been defined by Director Shin and Dear Leader Kim—two men with large egos and the ambition to determine, control, and direct—calls to mind the twenty-four million other shrimp among whales, north of the DMZ, unwilling players in that large-scale production of a nation.

The force of Choi Eun-Hee's will is undeniable. None of the crowd in the coffee shop around her would recognize her or can imagine what she has lived through. But today her name still invokes recognition, tinged with awe, in many more Koreans than Shin's. She is an icon of the Korean film industry. She refuses to let Kim Jong-Il, North Korea, or her eight years of captivity define who she is or was. She is a star—in 2014, aged eighty-eight, at a time when movie stars barely exist anymore.

There is a picture of Madame Choi and Marilyn Monroe, taken in Seoul in 1954 during a post–Korean War goodwill tour by various Hollywood stars. Choi and Monroe were the exact same age, both born in 1926. They started their careers at roughly the same time; Choi's first on-screen credit is dated 1947, Monroe's 1948. When that photograph was taken, Marilyn was in her prime, fresh off *Gentlemen Prefer Blondes* and *How to Marry a Millionaire*, with *The Seven Year Itch* and that famous billowing white dress just a few months away. Choi was years from her most iconic roles, newly married to Shin Sang-Ok, and just emerging from the trauma—rape, abuse, abduction—that she had endured during the war.

And yet looking at that photograph, even with Monroe's iconic face, her hair, her lips, already burned into your consciousness, you would be hard pressed to tell who is the bigger star, who more draws the eye. Monroe is in a bomber jacket, laughing, eyes half closed; but even she is looking at Choi, who is smiling but whose eyes have a sharp steeliness. Nothing about her accepts that she is the token Korean picked for a photo opportunity alongside the Hollywood goddess. She is the star.

Eight years after that picture was taken, Marilyn Monroe was dead. Today, sixty years later, Choi—having suffered scandal, divorce, kidnapping, exile, and widowhood—is still alive, and in her culture no less iconic.

Shrimp among whales we may be, but some of us refuse to accept the whales as the masters of our own fate. Looking at Choi Eun-Hee, there is a lot to be said for that.

Afterword

The story of Shin Sang-Ok and Choi Eun-Hee, like most eyewitness accounts of North Korea, relies heavily on the participants' telling of their own tale. The Hermit Kingdom is so tightly sealed, and its rulers so adept at blurring and confusing the picture, that it is a constant challenge for all those who write about it to confirm the facts upon which we are building our accounts. When it comes to North Korea, most facts need to be double- and triple-checked in case they turn out to be repetitions of a rumor that has been around so long that it has been accepted as truth. Accordingly, I have done my best to make sure nothing appears in the book that has not been as rigorously corroborated and fact-checked as possible.

While forced to use Shin and Choi's accounts of their time in Pyongyang as my main source, I approached them, from the start, with all the skepticism I could muster. All timelines and dates in this book have been checked and compared with accepted histories. Geographical descriptions were confirmed through photographs and third-party eyewitness accounts. In the case especially of Repulse Bay, Prison Number 6, and the villas Shin and Choi resided in, I analyzed Google Earth images of each location. I traveled to Pyongyang and stood outside the Fish House and inside the film studios. I stayed in their hotel room at the Vienna Intercontinental and looked at floor plans and photographs of the hotel prior to its post-1986 restoration. I spoke to every non–North Korean mentioned by name in Shin and Choi's memoirs, or if that wasn't possible tried to track down family, colleagues, even biographers. (A fuller list of the people who have generously contributed time and knowledge to this book can be found in the acknowledgments.)

Shin and Choi were kidnapped in 1978, right in the middle of not just one of the North's periods of intensive kidnapping, but also the only time period (1977–1983) during which Pyongyang has admitted kidnapping people. The kidnapping methods Shin and Choi described—men disguised in long wigs, secluded beaches, being subdued and put into some sort of bag, the small skiff, then the larger ship—fit exactly with the methods used by North Koreans in other, proven kidnapping cases, methods that were not yet public in 1987, when Shin and Choi wrote and published their first memoir. I submitted their memoir and my own questions both to Robert S. Boynton of New York University, an expert on Southeast Asian kidnapping as a political tool, and to the National Association for the Rescue of Japanese Kidnapped by North Korea, who found no gaps in it and confirmed that the events as described were logical and within the range of known North Korean methods and activities. The Tongbuk-Ri and Chestnut Valley guesthouses were found on satellite images by expert Chris Marker, who analyzed the images for a UN report. (Prison Number 6 is clearly visible on other satellite images, and in the exact area Shin claimed it to be.) Shin's time in Prison Number 6 holds up credibly against other eyewitness accounts, including that of South American poet Ali Lameda, down to the smallest details, such as the soup spoon without a handle, which is mentioned in Hyok Kang's *This is Paradise!*

There are many, especially in South Korea, who do not believe Shin Sang-Ok and Choi Eun-Hee were kidnapped by North Korea, but that they defected to Pyongyang willingly. The case for a defection rather than a kidnapping is built on hypotheses: "It could be imagined that Shin, his career over in the South, was convinced to start over in the North" or "It's possible that Shin defected willingly and then changed his mind later, and made up the kidnapping story so he wouldn't get in trouble in South Korea." The suspicion has been fed by the repetition of inaccuracies: one "historical dictionary" of the DPRK claims that he could have defected to the North because he was originally from the northern city of Chongjin and his parents still lived there, when they in fact were long dead by 1978; another book describes Shin as a "displaced person," who lived in North Korea post-division and as such fit a certain type of profile once he moved to the South (Shin was in Seoul in 1945 and didn't set foot north of the thirty-eighth parallel between then and 1978). These "facts" have been picked up and reprinted, and over the years have muddied the waters and become part of the public perception of Shin Sang-Ok and Choi Eun-Hee's story. Most of the skeptics I have spoken to refer back to one volume, *The Fictional Image,* by Nishida Retsuoh, to explain their doubt of Shin and Choi's trustworthiness. Retsuoh (a pseudonym) was a Japanese journalist who claimed to know Shin, Shin's brother, and the journalist Kyushiro Kusakabe, whom Shin and Choi had entrusted with their letters and audiotape recording of Kim Jong-Il when they met him in Eastern Europe. This book, I was repeatedly told, ruthlessly and methodically debunked Shin and Choi's story.

I read the book and found that it did no such thing. It is full of errors. Retsuoh claimed to have met Shin in Hong Kong and in Japan in the spring of 1978 and that Shin jokingly told him he was planning to defect—conveniently, with no one else around to hear him. He further claims to know Shin started work on *Emissary of No Return* in 1979 with "carte blanche" from Kim Jong-Il to make any film he wanted, but offers no reason for why it then took three and a half years for Shin to complete that film. He repeats North Korean claims that Shin and Choi were free to travel anywhere they chose (France being one of the examples mentioned), when they were only ever permitted west of Berlin once, to attend the London Film Festival. He also ignored that the North Koreans sent abductees abroad all the time: in August 1979 the DPRK sent four Lebanese abductees to Yugoslavia, so that they could speak to their families and claim they were all right. They were closely watched, but two escaped, ran to the Kuwaiti embassy, and were repatriated to Lebanon. Abductee Kim Yong-Kyu was sent to South Korea to do spy work for the government, whom he had convinced of his allegiance; he surrendered to South Korean authorities and regained his freedom. And most famously, in 2002, North

Korea returned five abductees to Japan, under condition that they return to North Korea after a short visit. The North Korean leaders were apparently shocked when they didn't.

The most glaring hole in Retsuoh's "debunking" of Shin and Choi's story is his version of their escape in Vienna in 1986. Retsuoh, who calls the escape "their U-turn to the West," claims Shin and Choi were in touch with U.S. authorities a full six months before arriving in Vienna, and that Shin and Choi enlisted Enoki as an unwitting witness to a fake escape. Retsuoh says Enoki told him this himself, although to my knowledge Akira Enoki, until his death, gave no interviews and made no public statements about Shin and Choi's escape; it seems, again, extremely convenient that the only one he gave would have been to Retsuoh to confirm Retsuoh's suspicions. Retsuoh claimed that Shin and Choi were working with the CIA on a plan of escape, and that they had to stage a car chase to the embassy to do so. Yet the Intercontinental Hotel was owned by Pan Am, the U.S. commercial airline, and enjoyed a particularly close relationship with the U.S. embassy in Austria. U.S. diplomatic couriers, government employees in charge of carrying classified mail from embassy to embassy, stayed at the hotel, and Pan Am crews on eastern and western routes stopped in Vienna and stayed at the Intercontinental on their crew changes. John Edmaier, who was general manager in the 1980s, had the U.S. embassy's duty officer on speed dial. His instructions, in case of any trouble, were to call the Americans directly rather than the Austrian chief of police. If Shin and Choi had been in touch with the United States about escaping North Korea, no dramatic car chase would have been necessary. They would have simply checked into the hotel, and within a few hours American intelligence agents would have knocked on their door and safely walked them out, as they did countless other defectors before them and after.

While there is no evidence supporting Shin and Choi's having defected to the North willingly, there is significant circumstantial evidence against the theory, such as:

If Shin defected willingly, why did he immediately and very publicly announce that he thought Choi Eun-Hee had been kidnapped? Why wouldn't they defect together, rather than have Shin raise a media circus over her disappearance and then himself defect, in what would be the most convoluted defection in Cold War history? Also, Shin's defection would have been a propaganda coup for Pyongyang, so why would the Kims not have instantly put him on display in a pro-North press conference?

And if he had gone of his own volition to make films for Kim Jong-Il, why did it take him until 1983 to start making his first North Korean film? Surely if he had defected willingly, and then later run into trouble, the dates of his filmography in the North would have been reversed; he would have been very active immediately, then his output would have diminished.

Even if Shin had defected of his own will, what were Choi Eun-Hee's motives? Why leave behind her children, whom she valued above all else?

Perhaps the most definitive evidence that Shin and Choi were kidnapped is the corroboration by North Koreans who had nothing to gain by lying, chief among them Hwang Jang-Yop, one of Kim Il-Sung's most trusted advisers and, some say, the architect of *juche* theory. Hwang told author John Cha that "Division 35 [one of Kim Jong-Il's departments] planned and executed the kidnapping of South Korean actress Choi Eun-Hee and her husband, Shin Sang-Ok." Later, after both men had escaped North Korea, Hwang also participated in roundtable talks with Shin about the Hermit Kingdom.

Former North Korean operatives Kim Gwang-Hyeon, Sin Kwang-Su, and Liu Yong-Hua have admitted to the kidnapping of foreigners; several others have told how the kidnapping of Shin Sang-Ok and Choi Eun-Hee was openly discussed at Kim Jong-Il Military Academy, where they were trained.

The U.S. State Department and CIA thought Shin and Choi credible enough to keep them away from the KCIA and pay for three years of round-the-clock protection. (One of Shin's sons now works for the State Department.) Committees of the United Nations have used Shin and Choi's testimony as a source for human rights documentation. Eric Heginbotham, a former senior fellow at the Council on Foreign Relations, says Shin and Choi's story is believable and consistent with what is known about the Kim regime. Don Oberdorfer, formerly of *The Washington Post,* says he is usually skeptical about the many "questionable" defectors he has interviewed over the years, but that Shin and Choi didn't fall into that category. "I made it a practice not to repeat the various yarns about Kim unless I felt confident from reliable sources they were true," Oberdorfer told fellow journalist John Gorenfeld in 2003. "This one I believed." In his book *The Two Koreas,* Oberdorfer writes, "Some in South Korea and elsewhere have raised doubts about the credibility of Choi and Shin, but they returned with photographs and tape recordings of themselves with Kim Il-Sung and Kim Jong-Il that have been accepted by US and ROK intelligence as authentic. I had three meetings with them, the first shortly after their escape through Vienna, and I believe they are credible."

In 2005, U.S. defector Charles Jenkins and his wife Ms. Soga, a Japanese abductee, brought to light the kidnapping of Anocha Panjoy, a Thai national who was abducted to North Korea from Macao in May 1978. By October 2005 the Thai media confirmed the details and method of Ms. Panjoy's abduction, all of which matched the way Choi Eun-Hee, seventeen years earlier, had described her own kidnapping. It was brought to light that Ms. Panjoy had disappeared the same day as Catherine Hong, who had also vanished from Macao. The National Association for the Rescue of Japanese Kidnapped by North Korea interviewed Choi about Ms. Hong. Choi told them that the Ms. Hong she had met had a mother and a brother in Macao, that her father had been a teacher, that she had played volleyball in high school and then given up on university and gotten a job so that her brother could afford to go to university, that she had worked as a clerk in a jewelry shop and also part-time as a tour guide, that she was Catholic and was twenty years old when she was abducted, in the summer of 1978. All the details "completely matched" the profile of a Ms. Hong Leng-Ieng, who had disappeared from Macao on July 2, 1978. Ms. Hong's family did not know her baptismal name, which she had kept private. Choi told her interviewers it was Maria, and this fact, too, was confirmed by the church where Hong had been baptized in Macao. When shown a picture of Ms. Hong, Choi confirmed she was the woman she met in Pyongyang. In March 2006 she met Ms. Hong's family, who further vouched for the accuracy of her statements.

In the last few weeks of reviewing edits on this book, I met a South Korean who told me that he had worked for U.S. intelligence agencies for twenty-six years, and been mostly assigned with debriefing North Korean defectors. (An independent background check confirmed this.) One of his assignments, in 1986, concerned the escape and defection of Shin Sang-Ok and Choi Eun-Hee. The man says he met Shin and Choi professionally then, after which he remained friends with both of them. Although he is now retired, his employment contract with the United States government stipulates he cannot speak on the record about matters still considered "sensitive." But when I asked him if Shin and Choi's version of the tale was true, his answer was categorical: "Yes," he said.

"Every single detail?"

He nodded emphatically. "Yes!"

Until North Korea opens to the world and Kim Jong-Il's own personal papers—if they still exist, if they ever existed in that form—can be pored over and dissected, it's impossible for anyone to know, with 100 percent certainty, what happened. Until then, I am strongly inclined to take what Shin and Choi say as truthful.

Acknowledgments

This book wouldn't exist without the faith and enthusiasm of Patrick Walsh and Carrie Plitt at Conville & Walsh, who took on a writer's ambitious first book with unwavering insight, intelligence, and support. And I am grateful for the guidance of my editors, Colin Dickerman (Flatiron Books), Panio Gianopoulos, and Joel Rickett (Viking Penguin), who worked together tirelessly to turn hundreds and hundreds of pages of excited words into a *book*.

My deepest thanks to Alexandra McNicoll, Henna Silvennoinen, Jake Smith-Bosanquet, Alexander Cochran, and Emma Finn, and all at Conville & Walsh, for sharing the book with the world; to my researchers and translators J-Min Anh, Hiroko Yabuki, and Soyoung Park; to Jung-Hyoun Han for being my interpreter when I finally met Madame Choi in person; to Liz Keenan, Jasmine Faustino, Patricia Cave, and Marlena Bittner at Flatiron Books, Venetia Butterfield at Viking Penguin, Sophie Berlin at Flammarion, and Nick Marston at Curtis Brown for their relentless enthusiasm, encouragement, and support. To Jurgen, Nadia, Markus, and Michael Fischer, thank you for always pushing me to do the best I can—and for celebrating every small success as if it were your own, the way only family can do.

I am indebted to the many writers and researchers, all smarter and better read than I am, who generously shared their knowledge and resources with me. Chief among them are Charles Armstrong, Robert Boynton, Mike Breen, John Cha, Steven Chung, Heinz Fenkl, Mike Morris, Darcy Paquet, Johannes Schonherr, and Suk Young-Kim. Yoichi Shimada and Tsutomu

Nishioka at the National Association for the Rescue of Japanese Kidnapped by North Korea confirmed details and facts related to the DPRK's use of kidnapping.

In Korea I was extremely fortunate to have the help and guidance of Sue and Jackie Yang, who negotiated and interpreted for me and generally made me look and feel competent and at home in a foreign land. Miyoun Ko selflessly took a full day to show me around Seoul and discuss modern Korea with me. In Vienna I had the generous help of John Edmaier, Christine Gull, Jean-Paul Herzog, Nicole Huber, Thomas Legner, and Rico de Schepper. When learning about 1970s Hong Kong I was lucky to be able to rely on Donald Morrison, James Smith, Douglas Schwab, and Nicholas Wu. Christopher Green of the *DailyNK* spoke to me on a range of subjects linked to North Korea and the rise of Kim Jong-Il as well as the highly politicized context in South Korea related to the North. He and the *DailyNK,* a courageous online resource in the releasing and disseminating of information about the Kim regime, were also instrumental in introducing me to North Korean defectors who had worked in the film industry or had some knowledge of the events and people involved in this book. Many of these defectors—the ordinary people, those who did not have a public profile or position of influence in Pyongyang, and who as such cannot write books, catch headlines, or warrant the expense of public protection—are reluctant to be named, but I am forever in their debt for their time, openness, and courage. Helen Loveridge gave me vital information on the 1984 London Film Festival. Brian Bankston, Wes Gehring, and Michele Jaffa shed light on various points, major and minor, of Shin and Choi's personal accounts. For her strength and honesty, I thank Angie Everhart.

My assistant Annie Ross-Edwards figured out what the weather was in Pyongyang in February 1978, tracked down North Korean freighters, and kept my life in order while I locked myself in a room and wrote. Marie-Jeanne Berger, Walter Donohue, Paul French, Andrew Lang, Ruth Little, Wayne and Lindsey Pelechytik, Jodie Taylor, and Joseph Wobij read various drafts of the book, and I am blessed for their unwavering enthusiasm and positivity. Gary Forrester read the first several drafts of the book and encouraged me every step of the way. For always encouraging and believing in me over the years, I thank Mary Kerr, Michael and Jane Lothian, Clare Kerr and Nick Hurd, and the Kerrs of Ferniehirst, as they will always be to me: Marie-Claire, Ralph, Johnnie, Jamie, Frank, Amabel, Hugh, and Minna. Marie Madeleine Veillard, my favorite primary school teacher, told me when I was still a very small child that she knew I would write a book one day, so to her—*voilà!*

I am, of course, indebted to the indomitable Madame Choi Eun-Hee for her willingness to have her life scrutinized by a stranger from halfway across the world, and for her help, her endurance, and her passion. She was always generous with time and with information, and courageous with putting her life on display, yet again, to a world that has not always treated her openness kindly.

And last but very definitely not least, from every bit of me, my thanks to Kelty and Owen Pelechytik. This whole thing started huddled in a pub in winter with you two, was written with you, and wouldn't have happened without you. I love you both.

Selected Bibliography

BOOKS

Anderson, Joseph L., and Donald Richie. *The Japanese Film: Art and Industry*. Expanded edition. Princeton University Press, 1982.

Breen, Michael. *Kim Jong-Il: North Korea's Dear Leader*. John Wiley & Sons, 2004.

Bren, Frank, and Law Kar. *Hong Kong Cinema: A Cross-Cultural View*. Scarecrow Press, 2004.

Bowyer, Justin, and Jinhee Choi. *The Cinema of Japan and Korea*. Wallflower Press, 2004.

Buzo, Adrian. *The Guerilla Dynasty: Politics and Leadership in North Korea*. Westview Press, 1999.

Cha, John H., with K. J. Sohn. *Exit Emperor Kim Jong-Il: Notes from His Former Mentor*. Abbott Press, 2012.

Cha, Victor. *The Impossible State: North Korea, Past and Future*. Vintage, 2013.

Cho Gab-Je. *Transcript of Kim Jong-Il's North Korea*. Jogapje Datkeom, 2010.

Choi Eun-Hee. *Confessions*. Random House Korea, 2007.

———. *Walks and Works of Sheen Sang-Ok, the Mogul of Korean Film*. Lee Jang-Ho, 2009.

Chung Hye Seung. *Hollywood Asian: Philip Ahn and the Politics of Cross-Ethnic Performance*. Temple University Press, 2006.

Chung, Steven. *Split Screen Korea: Shin Sang-Ok and Postwar Cinema*. University of Minnesota Press, 2014.

Cleaver, Eldridge. *Soul on Fire*. Word Books, 1978.

Coatalem, Jean-Luc. *Nouilles froides à Pyongyang*. Editions Grasset, 2013.

Cumings, Bruce. *North Korea: Another Country*. The New Press, 2004.

———. *Korea's Place in the Sun: A Modern History*. W. W. Norton, 2005.

Delisle, Guy. *Pyongyang: A Journey in North Korea*. L'Association, 2003.

Demick, Barbara. *Nothing to Envy: Real Lives in North Korea*. Granta Books, 2010.

Freeman, Kevin. *Secret Weapon: How Economic Terrorism Brought Down the U.S. Stock Market and Why It Can Happen Again*. Regnery Publishing, 2012.

French, Paul. *North Korea: State of Paranoia*. Zed Books, 2014.

Fujimoto, Kenji. *I Was Kim Jong-Il's Chef*. Fusosha Publishing, 2003.

———. *Kim's Chef, Kim's Private Life*. Fusosha Publishing, 2004.

Gehring, Wes. *Robert Wise: Shadowlands*. Indiana Historical Society, 2012.

Harrold, Michael. *Comrades and Strangers: Behind the Closed Doors of North Korea*. John Wiley & Sons, 2004.

Hassig, Ralph. *The Hidden People of North Korea: Everyday Life in the Hermit Kingdom*. Rowman & Littlefield, 2009.

Hastings, Max. *The Korean War*. Revised edition. Pan Macmillan, 2010.

Jager, Sheila Miyoshi. *Brothers At War: The Unending Conflict in Korea*. Profile Books, 2013.

Jang Jin-Sung. *Dear Leader: North Korea's Senior Propagandist Exposes Shocking Truths Behind the Regime*. Rider, 2014.

Jenkins, Charles Robert, with Jim Frederick. *The Reluctant Communist*. University of California Press, 2008.

Kang Hyok. *This Is Paradise! My North Korean Childhood*. Little, Brown, 2005.

Kim Byung-Kook and Ezra F. Vogel, eds. *The Park Chung Hee Era: The Transformation of South Korea*. Harvard University Press, 2011.

Kim Il-Sung. *With the Century*. Korean Friendship Association, 2003 edition.

Kim Jong-Il. *On the Art of the Cinema*. Pyongyang Foreign Languages Publishing House, 1973.

Kim Suk-Young. *Illusive Utopia: Theater, Film, and Everyday Performance in North Korea*. University of Michigan Press, 2010.

Kinnia, Yau Shuk-Ting, ed. *East Asian Cinema and Cultural Heritage*. Palgrave Macmillan, 2011.

Kracht, Christian, with Eva Munz and Lukas Nikol. *The Ministry of Truth: Kim Jong-Il's North Korea*. Feral House, 2007.

Kurosawa, Akira. *Something Like an Autobiography*. Vintage Books, 1982.

Kwon, Heonik, and Byung-Ho Chung. *North Korea: Beyond Charismatic Politics*. Rowman & Littlefield, 2012.

Lankov, Andrei. *The Dawn of Modern Korea*. EunHaeng NaMu, 2007.

Lankov, Andrei. *North of the DMZ*. McFarland & Company, 2007.

Lee Young-Il and Young-Chol Choe. *The History of Korean Cinema*. Jimoondang International, 1998.

Lifton, Robert Jay. *Thought Reform and the Psychology of Totalism*. W. W. Norton, 1961.

Lim Jae-Cheon. *Kim Jong-Il's Leadership of North Korea*. Routledge, 2011.

Martin, Bradley K. *Under the Loving Care of the Fatherly Leader: North Korea and the Kim Dynasty*. Thomas Dunne Books/St. Martin's Press, 2004.

McHugh, Kathleen, and Nancy Abelman, eds. *South Korean Golden Age Melodrama*. Wayne State University Press, 2005.

Myers, B. R. *The Cleanest Race*. Melville House, 2011.

Ning Tie. *How Long Is Forever?* Shanghai Press, 2010.

Oberdorfer, Don. *The Two Koreas: A Contemporary History*. Basic Books, 2001.

Oh Kongdan and Ralph C. Hassig. *North Korea Through the Looking Glass*. Brookings Institution Press, 2000.

Oshima, Nagisa. *Ecrits 1956–1978*. Cahiers du Cinema/Gallimard, 1980.

Pulikovsky, Konstantin. *The Oriental Express: Across Russia with Kim Jong-Il*. Moscow, 2002.

Satsuma, Kenpachiro. *North Korea as Seen by Godzilla*. Nesco-Bungeishunju, 1994.

Schonherr, Johannes. *North Korean Cinema: A History*. McFarland & Company, 2012.

Shin Sang-Ok. *I Was a Film*. Random House Korea, 2007.

Shin Sang-Ok and Choi Eun-Hee. *The Kingdom of Kim Jong-Il*. Tonga Ilbosa, 1988.

———. *My Name is Kim Jong-Il*. Haengnim Chulpan, 1994.

———. *We Haven't Escaped Yet*. Wolgan Chosonsa, 2001.

Steiner-Gashi, Ingrid, and Dardan Gashi. *Im Dienst des Diktators, Leben und Flucht wines nordkoreanischen Agenten*. Verlag Carl Ueberreuter, 2010.

Suh Dae-Sook. *Kim Il-Sung: The North Korean Leader*. Columbia University Press, 1988.

Sung Hye-Rang. *Wisteria House: The Autobiography of Sung Hye-Rang*. Chisiknara, 2000.

Urwand, Ben. *The Collaboration: Hollywood's Pact with Hitler*. Belknap Press/Harvard University Press, 2013.

Wright, Lawrence. *Going Clear: Scientology, Hollywood, and the Prison of Belief*. Alfred A. Knopf, 2013.

Yi Hyo-In. *Korean Film Directors: Shin Sang-Ok*. Korean Film Council/Seoul Selection, 2008.

Yi Sun-Kyung. *Inside the Hermit Kingdom*. Key Porter Books, 1997.

Zbarsky, Ilya, and Samuel Hutchinson. *Lenin's Embalmers*. Harvill Press, 1998.

OFFICIAL NORTH KOREAN PUBLICATIONS

Great Man and Cinema. Korea Film Export & Import Corporation.

The Great Man Kim Jong-Il. Two volumes. Pyongyang Foreign Languages Publishing House.

Kim Jong-Il Biography. Pyongyang Foreign Languages Publishing House.

Kim Jong-Il: A Brief History. Pyongyang Foreign Languages Publishing House.

Kim Jong-Il: Short Biography. Pyongyang Foreign Languages Publishing House.

Kim Jong-Il: The People's Leader. Pyongyang Foreign Languages Publishing House.

Kim Jong-Il. *On the Art of the Cinema*. Pyongyang Foreign Languages Publishing House.

Kim Jong-Suk: The Anti-Japanese Heroine. Pyongyang Foreign Languages Publishing House.

The Leader Kim Jong-Il. Pyongyang Foreign Languages Publishing House.

SELECTED PERIODICALS, BROADCASTS, AND WEB SITES

(By date of publication)

Oberdorfer, Don. "Kidnapped by North Korea's Premier Film Buff." *The Washington Post,* May 15, 1986.

Oberdorfer, Don. "Escapees Describe Top North Korean Leaders." *The Washington Post,* June 14, 1986.

Oberdorfer, Don. "North Korea Accused of Kidnapping Women." *The Washington Post,* January 24, 1988.

Kang, K. Connie. "Kim Is No Madman, Kidnapped Pair Say." *Los Angeles Times,* July 25, 1994.

Gombeaud, Adrien. "A Conversation with Shin Sang-Ok." www.koreanfilm.org/shinsangokk.html December 2000.

Armstrong, Charles. "The Origins of North Korean Cinema: Art and Propaganda in the Democratic People's Republic." *Acta Koreana* 5, No. 1 (2002).

Cho, Ines. "The Reel Story," *Korea Joogang Daily*, January 18, 2002.

Stephens, Chuck. "Pleasure and Pain." *The Village Voice,* February 26, 2002.

Kher, Unmesh. "Accounted For, at Last." *Time,* October 3, 2002.

Thomson, Mike. "Kidnapped by North Korea." BBC Today, BBC Radio 4, March 5, 2003.

Gorenfeld, John. "The Dictator Who Snagged Me." www.salon.com/2003/03/12/shin/, March 12, 2003.

Gorenfeld, John. "The Producer from Hell." *The Guardian,* April 4, 2003.

Spillius, Alex. "The Dictator's Cut." *South China Morning Post Magazine,* April 13, 2003.

Lee, Adriana. "Secret Lives." *Time,* June 23, 2003.

"Correspondent: The Real Dr. Evil." Broadcast on BBC radio 2, July 20, 2003.

"Correspondent: Inside the Mind of Kim Jong-Il." Broadcast on BBC radio 2, July 21, 2003.

"North Korean Cinema Ready for Its Close-Up." *Los Angeles Times,* October 9, 2003.

Becker, Jasper. "North Korea: At Home with the Kims." *Asia Times,* October 11, 2003.

Montefiore, Simon Sebag. "Why Stalin Loved Movies and Wanted John Wayne Shot." *The Daily Telegraph,* June 4, 2004.

Lankov, Andrei. "The Dear Director." *North Korean Economy Watch* (blog), February 8, 2005, www.nkeconwatch.com/2005/08/02/the-dear-director/.

Sohn, Kwang-Jop. "Kim Jong-Il's Birth and Growth." *DailyNK,* February 11, 2005, www.dailynk.com/english/keys/2003/12/04.php.

Choi, Jin-I. "Unrevealed Story of Kim Jong-Suk, Mother of Kim Jong-Il." *DailyNK,* February 25, 2005, www.dailynk.com/english/read.php?catald=nk01300&num=67.

Lankov, Andrei. "Body Snatching, North Korean Style." *Asia Times,* February 26, 2005.

Han, Young-Jin. "Kim Jong-Il, Where He Sleeps and Where He Works." *DailyNK,* March 15, 2005, www.dailynk.com/english/read.php?catald=nk02300&num=83.

Martin, Douglas. "Shin Sang-Ok, 80, Korean Film Director Abducted by Dictator, Is Dead." *The New York Times,* April 13, 2006.

Bergan, Ronald. "Shin Sang-Ok" (obituary). *The Guardian,* April 19, 2006.

Rayns, Tony. "Shin Sang-Ok—Maverick Film-maker" (obituary). *The Independent,* May 3, 2006.

Francis, David. "So That's Why Kim Jong-Il Is So Happy . . ." *Foreign Policy Passport,* October 5, 2007, http://blog.foreignpolicy.com/posts/2007/10/05/so_thats_why_kim_jong_il_is_so_happy.

Kyodo News, "Police Quiz S. Korean Actress over Abductees to the North." March 12, 2008.

"Les captives étrangères de la Corée du Nord." *Le Figaro,* April 21, 2008.

"Kim Jong-Il Has Plenty of Villas to Recuperate In." *The Chosun Ilbo,* November 4, 2008.

Olsen, Kelly. "North Korea's Secret: Room 39." *Salt Lake Tribune*, June 11, 2009.

Harden, Blaine. "Global Insurance Fraud by North Korea Outlined." *The Washington Post,* June 18, 2009.

Rose, David. "North Korea's Dollar Store." *Vanity Fair,* August 5, 2009.

"The Torrid Romantic Life of Kim Jong-Il." *The Chosun Ilbo,* August 8, 2009.

Samuels, Richard J. "Kidnapping Politics in East Asia." *Journal of East Asian Studies* 10, No. 3 (2010).

Herskovitz, Jon, and Christine Kim. "A North Korean Life Shattered by Kim Jong-Il's Secret." Reuters, February 3, 2010, http://in.reuters.com/article/2010/02/03/us-korea-north-secret-idINTRE6120WJ20100203.

The Associated Press, "North Korea Fires Head of Secret Bureau 'Room 39.' " February 4, 2010, www.ctvnews.ca/north-korea-fires-head-of-secret-bureau-room-39-1.480672.

Glionna, John. "Kim Jong Il's Guard Set Himself Free." *Los Angeles Times,* February 20, 2011.

Boynton, Robert. "North Korea's Digital Underground." *The Atlantic,* February 24, 2011.

Ocken, Jessica Royer. "Kim Jong-Il, the Director He Kidnapped, and the Awful Godzilla Film They Made Together." *Mental Floss,* December 18, 2011.

Glionna, John. "North Korean Defector Says Kim Jong-Il Stole Her Life." *Los Angeles Times,* December 22, 2011.

Rank, Michael. "North Korean Secrets Lie Six Feet Under." *Asia Times,* February 18, 2012.

Greitens, Sheena Chestnut. "A North Korean Corleone." *The New York Times,* March 3, 2012.

Ingersoll, Geoffrey, and Adam Taylor. "North Korea Allegedly Forces Diplomats to Deal Drugs for Hard Cash." *Business Insider,* March 22, 2012, www.businessinsider.com/north-korea-allegedly-turns-foreign-diplomats-into-big-time-drug-dealers-2013-3.

Brady, Lisa. "How Wildlife Is Thriving in the Korean Peninsula's Demilitarised Zone." *The Guardian,* April 13, 2012.

"'Comrade Kim Goes Flying' Is a North Korean Rarity." *Los Angeles Times,* October 6, 2012.

Nordine, Michael. "Godzilla and Flowers: The Films of Kim Jong-Il." *The Village Voice,* January 9, 2013.

Sohn, Kwang-Ju. "Focus Analysis: Kim Jong-Il." *DailyNK,* May 11, 2013.

Richardson, Nigel. "North Korea: Inside the Most Amusing Destination on Earth." *The Daily Telegraph,* May 28, 2013, www.dailynk.com/english/keys/2003/12/04.php.

Johnson, Adam. "Dear Leader Dreams of Sushi." *GQ,* June 2013.

MISCELLANEOUS

(By date of publication)

Amnesty International. "Ali Lameda: A Personal Account of the Experience of a Prisoner of Conscience in the Democratic People's Republic of Korea." February 1979.

Paquet, Darcy. "The Golden Age of Korean Cinema: Seven Directors." Date unknown.

———. "Korean Directors in the 1970s." Date unknown.

———. "Shin Sang-Ok in the 1950s." Date unknown.

"Table Talk: Hwang Jang-Yop and Shin Sang-Ok Talk About the Two Homelands They Have Experienced." *Wolgan Chosun,* March 1999, pp. 609–641.

Park JaeYoon. "Seeing Stars: Female Film Stars and Female Audiences in Post-Colonial Korea." University of Kansas dissertation, May 2008.

Morrell, David. "Rambo and Me: The Story Behind the Story." 2008.

National Human Rights Commission of Korea. "Survey Report on Political Prisoners' Camps in North Korea." Report, 2009.

Kan, Paul Rexton, Bruce E. Bechtol Jr., and Robert M. Collins. "Criminal Sovereignty: Understanding North Korea's Illicit International Activities." Repor, Strategic Studies Institute, March 2010.

Lee Sangjoon. "The Transnational Asian Studio System: Cinema, Nation-State, and Globalization in Cold War Asia." New York University dissertation, May 2011.

Amnesty International. "North Korea: Political Prison Camps." Special report, 2011.

Committee for Human Rights in North Korea. "Taken! North Korea's Criminal Abduction of Citizens of Other Countries." Special report, 2011.

Shim Ae-Gyung and Brian Yecies. "Power of the Korean Film Producer: Dictator Park Chung-Hee's Forgotten Film Cartel of the 1960s Golden Decade and Its Legacy." Thesis, University of Wollongong, 2012.

Committee for Human Rights in North Korea. "Coercion, Control, Surveillance, and Punishment: An Examination of the North Korea Police State." Special report, 2013.

AUDIOVISUAL MATERIALS

Finn, Jim. *Great Man and Cinema*. 2009, www.fandor.com/films/great_man_and_cinema.

Smith, Shane. *North Korean Film Madness. Vice* magazine, 2011, www.vice.com/the-vice-guide-to-film/north-korean-film-madness-1.

Kim Jong-Il's Cinema Experience, www.northkoreancinema.com.

Korean Central News Agency (Pyongyang). *Kim Jong-Il As Film and Opera Director,* www.youtube.com/watch?v=hdjj8JQMQY8.

Korean Central News Agency (Pyongyang). *The Brilliant History of Great Leadership,* www.youtube.com/watch?v=lRC86RAvbdc.

Korean Central News Agency (Pyongyang). *Leader Kim Jong-Il in the Time of Creation of Five Revolutionary Operas,* www.youtube.com/watch?v=--MhqE1N_Wo.

Korean Central News Agency (Pyongyang). *Kim Il-Sung and Kim Jong-Il Made Korea into a Paradise,* www.youtube.com/watch?v=6ji3tqZUynY).